MULTICULTURAL DISCOVERY ACTIVITIES

for the Elementary Grades

Elizabeth Crosby Stull

**THE CENTER FOR APPLIED
RESEARCH IN EDUCATION**
West Nyack, New York 10994

D1613493

© 1995 by
The Center for Applied Research in Education
West Nyack, New York

10 9 8 7 6 5 4 3

Library of Congress Cataloging-in-Publication Data

Stull, Elizabeth Crosby.
   Multicultural discovery activities for the elementary grades /
Elizabeth Crosby Stull.
    p.   cm.
   ISBN 0-87628-586-8
   1. Social sciences--Study and teaching (Elementary)--United States. 2.
Multicultural education--United States. 3. Education, Elementary--Activity
programs--United States. I. Title.
LB1584.S78 1994
372.83--dc20

          94-13222
          CIP

ISBN 0-87628-586-8

Cover art from *Ready-to-Use Multicultural Activities for Primary Children*
(The Center, 1993) by Saundrah Clark Grevious. Used with permission of
the author.

The Center for Applied Research in Education
Career & Personal Development Division
West Nyack, New York 10995

Printed in the United States of America

This book is dedicated to the teachers and children around the world who so warmly greeted our delegations and study tours from The Ohio State University.

Also, special thanks to Susan Kolwicz, Education Editor at The Center for Applied Research in Education, for friendship and excellence in her work with this manuscript.

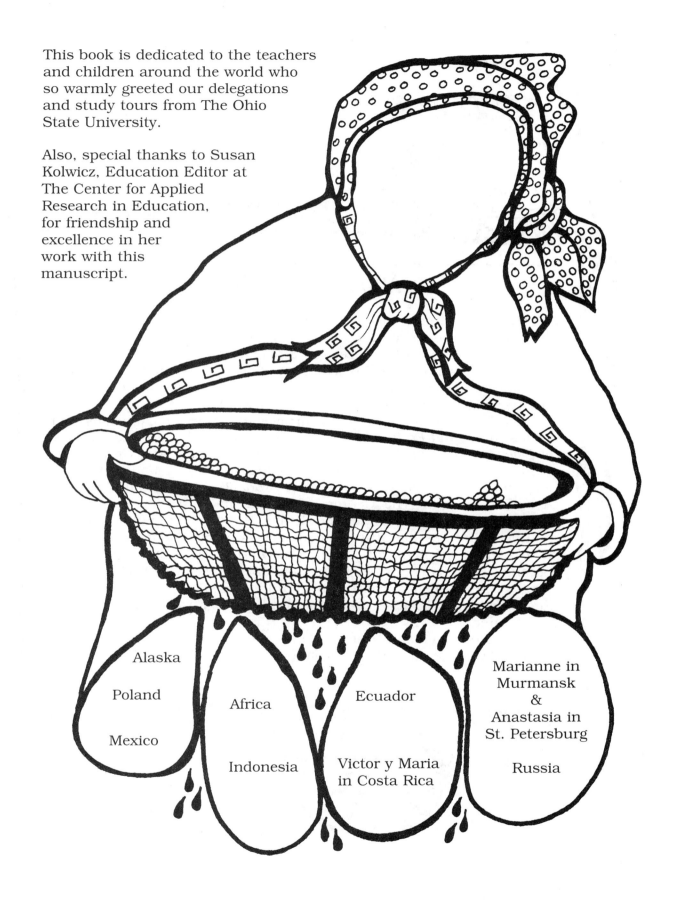

Alaska

Poland

Mexico

Africa

Indonesia

Ecuador

Victor y Maria in Costa Rica

Marianne in Murmansk & Anastasia in St. Petersburg

Russia

ABOUT THE AUTHOR

Elizabeth Crosby Stull, Ph.D. (The Ohio State University), has over 20 years of experience in education as a primary teacher and teacher educator. She began her career as a teacher of grades, 1, 2, and 4 in the publich schools of Greece Central, Camillus, and Pittsford in upstate New York, and is currently an assistant professor of education at Otterbein College in a suburb of Columus, Ohio.

Dr. Stull has published many articles in professional journals such as *Instructor and Early Years* and is coauthor, with Carol Lewis Price, of *Science and Math Enrichment Activities for the Primary Grades* (The Center, 1987) and *Kindergaren Teacher's Month-by-Month Activities Program* (The Center, 1987) and *First Grade Teacher's Month-by-Month Activities Program* (The Center, 1990). In addition, she has written *Children's Book Activities Kit* (The Center, 1988), which pertains to integrating children's literature into the classroom; *Alligators to Zebras, Whole Language Activities for Primary Grades* (The Center, 1991) and *Second Grade Teacher's Month-by-Month Activities Program* (The Center, 1992). She is also a contributing author to *The Primary Teacher's Ready-to-Use Activities Program*, a monthly program also published by The Center.

Dr. Stull is a member of the National Association for the Education of Young Children and the International Reading Association.

ABOUT THIS BOOK

Multicultural Discovery Activities for the Elementary Grades offers a wide variety of information and activities for students in grades K-6. It contains over 400 activities and over 150 full-page reproducible activity sheets.

The book branches out into ten sections with a focus upon cultures around the world. These cultures include Native American, African, Asian, Latin American, European, East European, Caribbean and other islands, Australia/New Zealand, Canadian, and the United States.

Background information is given for each culture. Then common strands include: children's literature; folk tales; celebrations; arts and crafts; games, dances, rhythms; music; food; geography and map study; and author studies for children's literature of today.

FOLK TALES

This is a major section throughout the book. It can be noted that some cultures have a strong tradition in storytelling, and the wisdom of the people has been handed down through the oral tradition. This is especially true of the Native American and African cultures. In many cultures there are common threads or themes, such as kindness that is later repaid, goodness that is rewarded, evil that loses out in the end, the power of love, trickery at all levels, magic objects, wishes that come true after a task, temptations that lead a character astray, and so on. This section shows the commonality of man throughout the world, as these themes are repeated in all cultures.

Most cultures have a trickster figure, and this character can be in the form of a raven, a crocodile, a rabbit, a fox, or a person. But the underlying theme is the same—sometimes the character wins through trickery and at other times the character gets its just due. Many trickster figures appear in tales of the origin of the race of people.

The Cinderella story is a universal one. There are over 400 versions in Europe; however, there is strong evidence that the story originated in China. The tiny shoe suggests that the Cinderella figure was of royal birth, one who was cast out or who left her royal station in life. Cinderella, known by many different names, then seeks to reestablish her rightful ownership. The tale surfaces repeatedly in cultures as far apart as Korea, Egypt, and Native America. This story is a part of the literary heritage of all people.

The United States enjoys the folklore of all cultures and in the past has been especially influenced by the tales from Europe and East Europe. In the southern part of the United States, many African tales came into the Carolinas by way of the Caribbean Islands. The closest that the United

States comes to its own folklore would be the exaggerated tall tales, and tales of building up the country and settling the west.

CELEBRATIONS

All cultures enjoy special celebrations and ceremonies that help bind them together as a race. Many of these celebrations center around religious themes, births, birthdays, deaths, and seasonal celebrations. Throughout the world, almost every culture has a celebration of the fruits of the harvest. Although the celebrations may differ in name, many are carried out at the exact same time of the year. Also, climate influences the nature of celebrations.

ARTS AND CRAFTS

Emerson once wrote, "A thread runs through all things." Taken literally, it would be possible to do a study of cultures through their fabrics and weavings, from beautiful tapestries to story cloths to mats and baskets woven with rough natural plant fibers. In this section, you explore the art that is native to a particular culture.

GAMES/SONGS/DANCE

Each culture has games for young children to play. Variations of the string game are found throughout the world, as well as games played with a ball. Singing and dancing are a major part of each culture's heritage. In these sections you explore the instruments, rhythms, and dance that make each culture unique.

FOOD

What could be more exciting than the various foods that are unique to each culture. Learning about them, creating them from simple recipes, and tasting a variety of foods helps us to gain an understanding of people from around the world.

GEOGRAPHY AND MAP STUDY

These opportunities are presented through folk tale ogres and make-believe animals who find themselves in predicaments. For example, a polar bear on his way to Canada winds up in Mexico, a mouse who is a deep-sea diver is thrown off course, and a series of ogres threaten to eat the ducks, tunas, and birds that they have in their grasp unless we can help them with their geography lessons.

AUTHOR STUDY/CHILDREN'S LITERATURE

One strand throughout each of the ten sections is that of children's literature. Each section contains an annotated bibliography with a minimum of ten books. Multicultural literature is growing at a fast pace. In each section there is an opportunity to do an author study for that culture. Throughout the book, many opportunities are given for story comparisons, creative writing, book making, journal writing, spinning yarns, and storytelling.

Multicultural Discovery Activities for the Elementary Grades can be used as a supplement to the curriculum or as a point of departure for an in-depth study of the many cultures within the United States. It can be used across the ten cultures for a folk tale study, an arts/crafts study, a study of celebrations, and so on. It gives you the opportunity to set up a visually rich classroom environment that resembles a given cultural influence when all of the elements of arts, artifacts, music, dance, games, food, children's stories, folk tales, geography, and storytelling are brought together. It's the next best thing to actually taking a long voyage. Get ready to enjoy the diversity of this learning adventure!

Elizabeth C. Stull

CONTENTS

Games   20

Goose Feather Throwing Game (20) • Jamolibanna (21)• The Jumping Game (21) • Bojuboju (Hide Oh!) (21) • Kini O Ni Iye? (Who Wears Feathers?) (21) • Mawira Maitu Ni Ogwo (This Is the Way Our Work Is Done) (22) • Hand Clapping Game (22) • *Resource* (22)

Songs, Dances, Rhythms   22

The Voice of the Drum (22) • Horn-Type Instruments (23) • We Can Make a Thumb Piano (23) • Playin' the Bones, Playin' the Spoons (23) • Ceremonial Dances (23) • Featuring the Dance Specialists (24) • Imitation of Animals in Nature (24) • *Resource* (24)

Food   24

Suggested Recipes for the Classroom

Peanut Sauce Dish (25) • Sweet Doughnut Balls (25) • Fufu (Dough for Soups and Stews) (25) • Fufu (New World Version) (26) • Fried Plantains (26) • Dovi (26) • Coconut (27) • *Resources* (27)

Reproducible Activity Pages   28

African Storyteller Mask (*storytelling*)
Join the Folk Tale Adventure (*record keeping*)
"Anansi the Spider" Trickster Award (*reading selection*)
Anansi and the Frog Beauty (*creative writing*)
The Role of the Snake in Folk Tales (*research/writing*)
The Lion's Dilemma—An Original Tale (*story starter*)
Shaking the Baby with the Grain (*celebration of birth*)
Endangered Species Department. May I Help You? (*issues*)
In the Spirit of Harambe (*emphasis on cooperation*)
To Market, to Market in Africa (*research/writing*)
Baskets That Can Hold Water (*art design*)
Cronedag Is Hungry for Information (*geography: oceans and seas*)
Do an Author Study—Africa (*Verna Aardema; Robert San Souci; Brian Pinkney*)

ASIA   43

Recommended Children's Books   44

Folk Tales   47

Meet the Four Animals in Asian Legends (48) • Dragons of the East (48) • Introducing Tanuki and Kappa of Japan (48) • Introducing the Asian Unicorn (49) • The Phoenix Rises in Many Cultures (49) • Meet

Food   70

Suggested Recipes for the Classroom

Reproducible Activity Pages   75

AUSTRALIA AND NEW ZEALAND   91

Recommended Children's Books   92

Folk Tales   94

Suggested Activities for the Classroom

CANADA 125

Recommended Children's Books 126

Folk Tales 127

Suggested Activities for the Classroom

Celebrations 132

Suggested Activities for the Classroom

Arts and Crafts 136

Suggested Activities for the Classroom

EAST EUROPE   195

Arts and Crafts   209

Suggested Activities for the Classroom

Creating with Mosaics (209) • We Can Press Flowers (210) • Coloring Eggs for Easter (211) • Nesting Dolls (211) • Bring on the Circus Clowns (211) • The Noodlehead Character in Folk Tales (211) • Dog-Headed People (212) • Bear's Tales (212)

Games   212

Flapping Birds (212) • Nut Relay (213) • Build a "Szopka" (213) • The Bear Is "It" (213) • The Wild Goat Chase (213)

Songs, Dances, Rhythms   214

Whistling to Music (214) • Circle Dancing 214) • The Bulgarian Wedding Dance (214) • Russian Doll Dance (215) • Street Musicians (215) • Fancy Leg Work (215) • Work Songs (215) • Play the Classical Music of Great Composers (216)

Food   216

Suggested Recipes for the Classroom

Salata (216) • Haloopkie (216) • Polish-Style Cauliflower (217) • Chai (Russian Tea) (218) • Pappilan Hatavara (Bread Pudding) (218) • Zupa z Dynia (Pumpkin Soup) (218) • Zupa Jablkowa (Apple Soup) (218) • Mazurkas (219) • Borscht (Ukraine) (219) • Potato Latkes (219) • Wassail (220) • *Resources* (220)

Reproducible Activity Pages   221

Cinderella's Fairy Godmother Compares Versions (*story comparisons*)
The Christmas Angel (*creative storytelling*)
Folk Tale Cottage Shoppe (*identifying folk tale elements*)
Piskies, Knackers, and Spriggins (*finger puppets*)
Matroshka Dolls (*bookmarks*)
You've Got the Beauty, Let's Make the Beast (*four beast versions*)
Beauty and the Beast (*art design*)
The Ugly Ogre Cover-Up Mask for Storytelling (*language development*)
The Giant Venn Diagram Comparison (*analyzing two giants*)
The Dragon Storyteller (*puppet making; language development*)
Kasha the Dancing Bear (*researching information about dance*)
Greetings from the Nutcracker (two pages) (*paper figure; music*)
Hanukkah—Focus Upon Lights (*modern-day lights*)
Do an Author Study—East Europe (*Jewish folk tales*)

EUROPE   237

Songs, Dances, Rhythms   260

Food

Suggested Recipes for the Classroom

Reproducible Activity Pages   269

LATIN AMERICA   289

Recommended Children's Books   290

Folk Tales   293

Suggested Activities for the Classroom

The Very Elegant Rooster Story (297) • R-r-r-r-roll It! (298) • What Superstitions Do We Know? (298) • El Nubera (298) • Getting Started with El Trasgu (299) • Making Spanish Comparisons (299) • The Romans of "Dad" and "Ty" (299) • Spanish Names in Your Community (299) • A Special Book (299) • Another Special Book (300) • Writing Enrichment (300) • If I Lived in Costa Rica (300)

Celebrations   300

Carnival (301) • Carnival in Rio de Janiero (301) • Happy New Year in Ecuador (301) • Pan American Day (301) • National Day in Spain (301) • Days of Independence—September 15 (301) • El Cinco de Mayo (The Fifth of May) (302) • A Village Posada (302) • El Dia de los Muertos (The Day of the Dead) (302) • Orchid Festival in Costa Rica (303)

Suggested Activities for the Classroom

Holiday Booklets (303) • Map and Globe Skills (303) • Celebrate with a Piñata (303) • Folk Tale Maps (303) • People Like to Celebrate (304)• Share Your Celebration (304) • Celebrate Orchids (304)

Arts and Crafts   304

Suggested Activities for the Classroom

It's a Bright, Bright World of Nature (301) • Let's Explore Blue with Pablo Picasso (305) • Set Up a Blue Table (306) • "Found Art" (306) • Time for Textiles (306) • Line Embroidery (307) • Slab Clay Tiles (307) • Make Clay Jewelry (307) • Make a Metal Mexican Lantern (308) • Copper Relief Design or Mask (308)

Games   308

Ring on a String (309) • Pahlito Verde (309) • Musical Chairs (309) • A Piñata (309) • Lobo, Ya Estas? (310)

Songs, Dances, Rhythms   310

Song of the Cockroach (310) • A Chocolate Chanting Rhyme (310) • Little Frog Tail (312) • Cha-Cha (312)

Food   312

Suggested Menu Activities for the Classroom

Learn to Order from a Menu (313) • Calculating Costs (313) • Menu Varieties (313) • Make a Menu (314) • Eating Out (314) • Make a Multicultural Menu (314) • Multi-Ethnic Menu (314)

Suggested Recipes for the Classroom

Guacamole and Tortilla Chip Dip (314) • Fresh Fruit Salad (314) • Spanish "Old Clothes" (Ropa Vieja) (315) • Kabach (Frijoles Negro) (315)

• Frijoles Refritos (Refried Beans) (315) • Chocolate Caliente (315) •
Chili Con Carne (316) • Taco Chip Dip (316) • Heavenly Hash (Picadillo
del Cielo) (316) • *Resources* (316)

Reproducible Activity Pages   317

The Very Elegant Rooster (three pages) (*storytelling kit*)
The Talking Toucan Puppet (*storytelling*)
Old Turtle's Folk Tale Recipe (*preparing for writing*)
Quick! Mix Up the Papier-Mâché for Posada (*making a piñata*)
San Antonio Abad (*Mexican celebration*)
It's Carnival Time! (*celebration*)
Days of Independence (*research; visual reporting*)
Create a Mola Design (*art project*)
Create a Picasso-Style Face (*visual art*)
Oh, What a Beautiful Country Cart (*visual design*)
A Polar Bear in Mexico? (*geography*)
Chocolate Caliente (Hot Chocolate) (*food recipe*)
International Road Sign Language (*visual information*)
Do an Author Study—Latin America (*Spanish/English versions: Ruth
    Heller; Lois Ehlert*)

NORTH AMERICA: NATIVE AMERICAN CULTURES   335

Recommended Children's Books   336

Folk Tales   338

General Storytelling (339) • Trickster Figures (340) • The Purpose of
the Tales (340) • Variant of the Beanstalk Tale (340)

Suggested Activities for the Classroom

Storytelling (341) • Dioramas (342) • Create a Sound Story (342) •
Make an ABC Book of Native Dwellings (342) • Set Up a Trading
Station (343) • Learn Native American Vocabulary (343) • Write
Messages Using Picture Symbols (343) • Grinding Corn and Making
Cakes (343) • Good Medicine/Bad Medicine (344) • A Study of
Clothing (344) • Animal Study (344) • Where in the U.S.A. Are We?
(344) • Variants of the Cinderella Tale (344) • Looking for the Moon
(344) • Look for Colorful Language Examples (345)

Celebrations   345

The Green Corn Ceremony (345) • Harvest Ceremonies (346) •
Storytelling at Celebrations (346)

Suggested Activities for the Classroom

Let's Practice Storytelling with Paul Goble (346) • Let's Practice
Celebrations with Byrd Baylor and Peter Parnall (346) • General

Reproducible Activity Pages   421

AFRICA

RECOMMENDED CHILDREN'S BOOKS

This list is representative of the books that are available for African-American children today. Some settings are in Africa and some are in the United States. Some are picture books, some are folk tales, and some are written or illustrated by African-Americans and thus give an inside perspective of the culture. Others, such as poetry books, are to be enjoyed in many languages and cultures.

Aardema, Verna. *Rabbit Makes a Monkey of Lion*. Pictures by Jerry Pinkney. New York: Dial Books, 1989. To make a monkey of someone means to make him or her look foolish. This is a rollicking good tale about animals who are hungry for the honey from the calibash tree. Rabbit has a close call, but uses his wits to outsmart Lion. Delightful illustrations.

_____. *Anansi Finds a Fool, an Ashanti Tale*. Pictures by Bryna Waldman. New York: Dial Books for Young Readers, 1992. In this old African legend, lazy Anansi wants to fish with a partner who will do all the work. His clever friend, Bonsu, offers to make the fish trap *if* Anansi will get tired for him, because when work is done someone has to get tired. Anansi, not wanting to get tired, agrees to cut the palm fronds to make the fish trap. Is he outsmarted by Bonsu? Read on.

Anderson, Joy. *Juma and the Magic Jinn*. Illustrated by Charles Mikolaycak. New York: Lothrop, Lee & Shepard Books, 1986. This tale takes place on the island of Lamu, in the Indian Ocean off the coast of Kenya. It is here that Juma, a young boy, longs to be someplace where everything is new. He summons the magical figure from the jinn jar, and his adventures begin. Lovely illustrations.

Gray, Nigel. *A Country Far Away*. Pictures by Philippe Dupasquier. New York: Orchard Books, 1988. This is two books in one. The text is in the middle, and the illustrations at the top of the page show the action occurring in Africa while the illustrations at the bottom of the page show what is occurring in the USA. Bike riding, swimming, soccer, shopping, celebrations, and family portraits make a very interesting cultural contrast.

Greenfield, Eloise. *Grandpa's Face*. Illustrated by Floyd Cooper. New York: Philomel Books, 1988. A tender story about a girl, Tamika, who sees the world reflected in her grandpa's face. It is a wonderful face that can communicate without words. One day, Tamika sees grandpa practicing for a play before a mirror, and his face reflects anger. Seeing this new face makes "scared places in her stomach." After much anguish and a talk-walk, there is a peaceful resolution. Also read *Africa Dreams* and *Me and Nessie* by this author.

Grifalconi, Ann. *The Village of Round and Square Houses*. Boston: Little, Brown and Co., 1986. The setting is the village of Tos, at the foot of Naka Mountain in the Bameni Hills of West Africa. Here we learn about family traditions, and the good life until Old Naka, the volcano, begins to erupt. It is then that we learn why the men and the women live in separate houses.

Howard, Elizabeth Fitzgerald. *Chita's Christmas Tree*. Illustrated by Floyd Cooper. New York: Bradbury Press, 1989. Chita, affectionately named after the Spanish "muchachita" (little girl), is the daughter of one of the city's first black doctors. The setting is Baltimore and the joyous occasion includes getting the Christmas tree with Papa. Then, Chita and Mama bake cookies, the relatives come for Christmas Eve, and Christmas Day finally arrives. Beautiful illustrations give the reader a warm feeling about the family.

___. *Aunt Flossie's Hats, and Crab Cakes Later*. Paintings by James Ransome. New York: Clarion Books, 1991. On Sunday afternoons a visit to see Great-great-aunt Flossie's house means a trip to a house neatly crowded with many things, and boxes and boxes of hats! The hats are Aunt Flossie's memories and each one has a glorious story.

Isadora, Rachel. *City Seen from A to Z*. New York: Greenwillow Brooks, 1983. This ABC book brings to life the magic of the big city, with its skyscrapers and subways and the multi-ethnic faces of the young and old. It is a book to study carefully.

Lewin, Hugh. *Jafta—The Town*. Pictures by Lisa Kopper. Minneapolis: Carolrhoda Books, Inc., 1984. An introductory book to the ways of the people of South Africa. Jafta and his mother go to the crowded, hustling and bustling town where his father works in a factory. This book is one in a series of Jafta books. The sepia tone illustrations give a warmth to the book.

Moss, Thylias. *I Want to Be*. Illustrated by Jerry Pinkney. New York: Dial Books, 1993. This poetic book asks the question, "What do you want to be?" A child answers, "I want to be a new kind of earthquake, rocking the world as if it's a baby in a cradle." A fine book for exploring values, and an opportunity for expression through language. Lovely illustrations help enrich the book.

Onyefulu, Ifeoma. *A Is for Africa.* **Photographs by the author. New York: Cobblehill Books, 1993.** The photographs were taken in Nigeria, home of the author, and they represent warm family ties and traditional village life found throughout the continent. Although Africans may dress differently and speak different languages, this vast continent is home to them all.

Pinkney, Andrea Davis. *Seven Candles for Kwanzaa.* **Illustrated by Brian Pinkney. New York: Dial Books, 1993.** Kwanzaa, a holiday that historically celebrated the harvest season, is held from December 26 through January 1. Families light a candle during each day of the week to celebrate one of Kwanzaa's seven principles. A good learning opportunity, with fine illustrations.

Polacco, Patricia. *Chicken Sunday.* **New York: Philomel Books, 1992.** A powerful inter-racial story about a girl and two boys who spend every Sunday with the boys' grandmother, Miss Eula. They always attend church and then have fried chicken for dinner. Miss Eula longs for a new Easter hat from Mr. Kodinski's shop, and these loving children are bound to get it for her. A sensitive, heartwarming tale, with beautiful illustrations.

Pomerantz, Charlotte. *If I Had a Paka, Poems in Eleven Languages.* **Illustrated by Nancy Tafuri. New York: Greenwillow, 1982.** This book makes it easy to believe that the English-speaking reader can learn to speak and understand Swahili, Serbo-Croatian, Samoan, Indonesian, Japanese, and other languages. And, you can! For example, "If I had a paka, meow, meow, meow, meow, I would want a mm-bwa, bow wow wow wow" is understandable to the young reader. An excellent teaching tool.

Reingold, Faith. *Tar Beach.* **New York: Crown Publishers, Inc., 1992.** For a poor family who can't afford to go to a sandy beach, the roof of tar with a blanket spread across it will have to make do. But the stars are bright, and one girl dreams that someday she will rise above her lot and fly with the stars. Bright, bold colors and a good city view.

SanSouci, Robert D. *The Talking Eggs.* **Pictures by Jerry Pinkney. New York: Dial Books, 1989.** This tale is set in the south, and is adapted from a Creole folk tale from Louisiana. It's the story of two sisters, one who is spoiled and favored by the mother, and one who is expected to fetch and carry. The fate of the miserable girl is changed when one day she meets a witch-woman who shows her a wondrous world, and changes her life for the better. Winner of the Caldecott Medal and Coretta Scott King Award.

Winter, Jeanette. *Follow the Drinking Gourd.* **Pictures by Jeanette Winter. New York: Alfred A. Knopf, Inc., 1988.** This is a story about the Underground Railroad, a network of people and places that hid escaped slaves on their dangerous trip to freedom. The drinking gourd is the Big Dipper, which points to the North Star. Other clues, hidden in the song, are explained in the author's note about the story. The folk song is included at the end.

FOLK TALES

There is a rich, fertile legacy of folklore from Africa. On this vast continent, folk tales and myths serve as a means of handing down traditions and customs from one generation to the next. The storytelling tradition has thrived for generations because of the absence of printed material. Folk tales prepare young people for life, as there are many lessons to be learned from the tales.

Because of the history of this large continent, which includes the forceful transplanting of the people into slavery on other continents, many of the same folk tales exist in North America, South America, and the West Indies. These are told with little variation, for the tales were spread by word of mouth and were kept among the African population.

In addition to the folk tales, there are myths, legends, many proverbs, tongue twisters, and riddles.

Anansi, the Spider, is one of the major trickster figures in African folk tales. This spider can be wise, foolish, amusing, or even lazy—but always there is a lesson to be learned from Anansi. The spider tales have traveled from Africa to the Caribbean Islands. Sometimes the spelling is changed from Anansi to Ananse. In Haiti the spider is called Ti Malice. Anansi stories came into the United Stated through South Carolina. The Anansi spider tales are told as "Aunt Nancy" stories by the Gullah of the southeastern part of the U.S.

In the African folk tales, the stories reflect the culture where animals abound; consequently, the monkey, elephant, giraffe, lion, zebra, crocodile, and rhinocerous appear frequently along with a wide variety of birds such as the ostrich, the secretary bird, and the eagle. The animals and birds take on human characteristics of greed, jealousy, honesty, loneliness, etc. Through their behavior, many valuable lessons are learned. Also, the surroundings in which the tales take place reveal the vastness of the land and educate the reader about the climate, such as the dry season when it hasn't rained for several years, or the rainy season when the hills are slick with mud. The acacia trees swaying in a gentle breeze, muddy streams that are home to fish, hippos and crocodiles, moss covered rocks, and giant ant hills that serve as a "back scratcher" for huge elephants, give the reader a sense of the variety of life in this parched or lush land in this part of the world.

UNCLE REMUS TALES

These are very well-known folk tales from Africa. In the Uncle Remus stories, Bre'r Rabbit is the outstanding trickster figure. Hare, or Little Hare, appears in this role in the eastern part of Africa. The tortoise is a primary trickster figure in the Nigerian tales. Bre'r Rabbit and the Tar Baby is similar to Anansi and the Gum Doll of West Africa. The Tar Baby motif has been traced from India to America through Africa, Europe, and Spain.

TORTOISE AND THE HARE

In African versions of this tale, the tortoise wins because he uses his wits. In the European versions, on the other hand, the tortoise wins through sheer endurance and grit. The triumph of brain over physical strength is a common thread that runs through the trickster tales from Africa. The trickster figure is clever, witty, and unscrupulous, as are trickster figures all over the world, but the African trickster almost always wins out because of his brilliance.

A WEALTH OF PROVERBS

There are many thousands of proverbs from African folk tales. A single tribe may have as many as a thousand—or even several thousand—of their own. So there are proverbs in abundance from this continent. Many times, a proverb is spoken in a tale by a character, rather than being left for the end of the story. Some of the more familiar proverbs do not need a story context in order to figure out the meaning. For example, "Do not set the roof on fire and then go to bed"; "He who runs and hides in the bushes does not do it for nothing; if he is not doing the chasing, we know that something is chasing him"; and "Chicken says: We follow the one who has something."

DILEMMA TALES

Many stories are deliberately left without an ending. This leaves the ending wide open for audience discussion and participation. The ending of the tale would be determined by the group of people involved in the exercise. The ending, therefore, is flexible and might change depending upon who is participating.

STRING STORIES

Making a simple loop from string and telling a tale with the string by twisting and turning the string to represent different parts of the story, is one of the oldest forms of storytelling in the world. In parts of Africa, the native children who cannot speak a word of English can often communicate with an English-speaking foreign visitor via a string story. It is a way of getting acquainted without words, and is a form of communication as different cultures share string stories. Some of the African string figures are the same as those of Pacific Ocean islanders or Eskimos of the far north.

THE ROLE OF THE AUDIENCE IN STORYTELLING

Many of the folk tales have musical participation by the audience that adds much to the tale. It is common for the audience to answer questions aloud, to clap their hands in rhythm to word repetition (chorus), and to join in the chorus. The audience participation cannot be cut short, or the audience will let the storyteller know it. Some of the tales have a repetitive quality to them (such as, the same chorus may be used repeatedly) because the audience wants to enjoy the story and participate in the experience for as long as possible.

CROCODILE TALES

There are a wealth of crocodile tales from Africa. In parts of West Africa, a person attacked by a crocodile is said to be the victim of the vengeance of someone he has harmed. It is said that he who kills a crocodile becomes a crocodile. A South African Vandau proverb reminds us that, "The strength of the crocodile is in the water." In another tale, the fox claims to have the answer to killer-crocodiles who terrorize the people. He says the solution is simple. He eats their eggs. The ending proverb is, "Get rid of your enemy before he is stronger than you."

THE VOICE OF THE DRUM

Language can be conveyed by drums. The Ashanti and other West African tribes, just by the rhythms and intervals in beating their drums by their fingers, the flat of their hand, or the thumb, can convey messages and be understood over long distances. Many different tones can be made by the pressure of the arm under which a drum is held. The stick for beating the drum came later. We still refer to a turkey leg as the "drum stick."

THE KIND LION

This type of tale is from Africa, where lions live in the wild. It is the idea that the Lion, King of the Beasts, lets his victims go for one reason or another, and then this good deed is rewarded in the end by the victim saving the life of the lion. It is the "one good turn deserves another" motif. This kindly lion theme spread from Africa to Europe.

THE SACRED VULTURE

"Opete" is the Twi term for the vulture. This bird is believed to be an instrument of the gods by the Ashanti and other West African peoples. This feeling of the sacred bird has survived in the New World and in the Caribbean.

SUGGESTED ACTIVITIES FOR THE CLASSROOM

1. STRING SOMEONE ALONG WITH A STRING STORY

"The Cat's Cradle" is one of the most well-known string stories. No one knows exactly where it came from; the Chinese call it "well rope" and the Koreans call it "woof taking." The four most well-known figures are the Cat's Cradle, the Soldier's Bed (in France it's called "Scissors"), Cat's Eye (in England it's called "Diamonds"), and Fish-in-a-Dish. An excellent resource book is *Strings on Your Fingers, How to Make String Figures* by Harry and Elizabeth Helfman, with illustrations by William Meyerriecks (New York: Morrow, 1965).

2. A STUDY OF ANANSI THE SPIDER

Secure a selection of trickster tales in which Anansi plays the key role. There are many picture books available, including Gerald McDermott's Caldecott award-winning *Anansi the Spider*. Keep track of the transformations of the spider (changing shape and form), the way the spider plays its tricks to get what it wants, the other characters in the story, and so on.

3. THE DILEMMA TALE

Select a good story and read it just so far and then close the book. Have students suggest a variety of solutions. After the suggestions, read the ending that the book provides. This can lead to many versions of the same tale, and students can begin to get an inkling of why many tales are similar yet different. This can lead to "Story Starters" where just the first sentence or paragraph is given.

4. STORY DRUMS

Decorate cylindrical containers with story illustrations. A skin top can be made from chamois (available in the auto repair section of a variety store). Using their hand or hands (the heel of hand, fingertips, thumb) students can make a variety of sounds and learn to beat the drum as a story accompaniment.

5. AFRICA MAP SHAPE

Cut out a giant shape of Africa from orange paper and place it on the bulletin board. Students can learn the names of the rivers, major cities, crops, where various tribes live, etc., and can place this information on the sunny orange continent shape. Have them pinpoint locations of story settings from books they read. The ABC Book *Ashanti to Zulu* by Margaret Musgrove gives valuable information about the people.

6. CREATIVE WRITING

Have students create a trickster tale and write it on an oval shape (representing a spider body). Give them a story stem, such as: "Anansi has been promised a ride by crocodile to the other side of the river bank, only if he will ride on the nose of the crocodile." Make a colorful book cover, with four dangling legs on each side.

7. A BRE'R RABBIT FESTIVAL

Students can read a variety of Bre'r Rabbit tales and have a storytelling festival. They can make masks and puppets to embellish the stories.

8. ANIMAL STUDY

The stories about such animals as the rhinocerous, the hippopotamus, and the crocodile can lead to some spelling challenges. It also provides an opportunity to learn more about the animals, their habitat, whether they are predator or prey, and so on. Students can make an Animal Book for their study of real-life animals in nature.

9. INVITE A STORYTELLER TO CLASS

Invite a librarian or someone who enjoys telling stories for children to the class. If this is not possible, secure a videotape or a recording from the local library. Sit back and enjoy the tale.

10. REALIA

Contact the local Historical Society or the Department for African Studies at a nearby college or university, and arrange to have a guest speaker come to talk about this distant land. Often guests bring samples with them, such as kente cloth, masks, drums, batiks, thumb piano, wood carvings, dolls, and so on, for students to enjoy.

CELEBRATIONS

There are many different countries, tribes and clans in Africa. This information is by no means complete, but gives you an idea of some types of celebrations that are valued in this part of the world, and an appreciation of the African-American heritage.

EGYPTIAN NATIONAL DAY

Egypt is in the northern part of Africa. The capital city of Cairo is the largest city in Africa. Cairo is derived from the Arabic words "El Qahira," which means victorious city. On July 23, National Day is celebrated with parades.

ETHIOPIAN NATIONAL DAY

On the same date as the Egyptian National Day, the Ethiopians celebrate their national day in conjunction with the birthday of the Emperor Heile Selassie. While thousands of people gather outside the Emperor's Palace, the emperor greets them from a balcony. People wear their best clothing and sing their national anthem, "Ityopya hoy dass yiballish," which means "Let Ethiopia be joyful."

CELEBRATION IN KENYA

December 12 is a national holiday in Kenya when schools are closed, people sing their national anthem, and government officials make speeches. It is on this date that Kenya was granted its independence. **The anthem of the country is a lullaby tune that African mothers sing to their children.** The song was chosen, from among several, by a group of children to be the national anthem. People work in the spirit of "Harambe" (hare-AHM-bee), which means "let us all work together." This is the spirit that fills their villages, and helps members to build their schools. A good resource book is *National Holidays Around the World* by Lavinia Dobler (New York: Fleet Press, 1968).

CHRISTMAS IN KENYA

The holiday of Christmas is celebrated by some but not all of the people in this area, for it is a Christian holiday. A native Kenyan who lives in a village and celebrates his or her own cultural traditions may find the ways of Christmas to be strange. For example, when a foreign visitor in Kenya asks what children would like for Christmas, the answer is that "they are not taught to ask for things." The idea is that people do not need many "things" to be happy. The reasoning goes something like this: If a child asks for a new pair of shoes and you give him a pair, soon he is asking for another. If a person grows up getting all of the things that he wants and asks for, he is never satisfied. He will keep asking for something more, something bigger, something better. And so, it is best not to introduce this concept of asking for things when one is a child. The adults will see to it that the child does not do without; therefore, the child does not have to ask.

MASAII WALKING STICK

It is the custom that as soon as a Masaii (muh-SIGH) boy can walk on his own, he is given a walking stick. From then on, wherever he walks he takes the stick with him. Grown men carry their walking sticks with them and can be seen along the roadside leaning on them as they rest, or using them to brush tall grasses out of their path.

MARRIAGE CEREMONIES

A girl from the Sotho (SOO-too) tribe carries a beaded doll with her. It is customary for her to name the doll, and when her first baby is born that is the name given to the child.

The Ndaka (n-DAH-kuh) bride is wrapped in yards and yards of colorful cloth, and her head is encircled with cloth from which beads hang to cover her face. For interesting traditions and colorful pictures read *Ashanti to Zulu* by Margaret Musgrove, with pictures by Leo and Diane Dillon.

THE OUTDOORING

Among some people in West Africa, there is a celebration when a baby is brought outdoors for the first time. In Ghana, this takes place when the child is eight days old. In other places, the child may be a month old. The child is introduced to the sunshine, the scenery, and the surroundings. People gather to welcome the baby.

MEDICINE CUTTING DAY

Among the Galla people of Ethiopia, when a baby is five days old, the women of the village and the family members go into the woods and collect herbs. These are brought back to the village and boiled in a large pot. Later, when it cools, the mother and new baby are washed with the soothing herbal water.

SHAKING THE BABY WITH THE GRAIN

In some parts of Egypt where a child is born into a family that makes a living through agriculture, it is the custom to bring several large baskets into the home with different types of grain in each. A baby is then put into a large sieve, and surrounded with grains poured from the baskets. Then, the baby and the grain are gently shaken together in the sieve. After this, the baby is washed and named. This ceremony is performed in the hopes that the child will have a life of plenty.

HAIR CARE

It is the custom for the Masaii man to wear his hair long, and for the woman to shave her head. Hair is worn in different styles by different groups of people. Some men smear the red clay of the earth on their hair for certain occasions. Often, the twisting of a cloth on the head of a women reveals whether she is married or single.

Throughout the world, hair style has always been given attention. In Europe, the royalty wore powdered wigs—and to this day, magistrates and judges in courtroom attire wear wigs as part of their official garb.

CELEBRATION IN THE UNITED STATES—KWANZAA

This celebration is one that was begun in the United States during the late 1960's. Kwanzaa is celebrated in December. On the 26th day of the month, the seven-day festival begins with the lighting of a candle. Each night, a candle is lit at home and the family discusses one of the seven principles of African-American family life. These seven principles are: unity, self-determination, work and responsibility, cooperative economics, purpose, creativity, and faith.

CELEBRATION IN THE UNITED STATES—
MARTIN LUTHER KING, JR. DAY

In January, the birthday of civil rights leader, Dr. Martin Luther King, Jr., is celebrated as a national holiday. On this day, people gather together for singing and speeches, and for an assessment of life. Dr. King believed in gain through peaceful methods. A great orator, his "I have a dream" speech is often reenacted on this day at services held in his honor.

SUGGESTED ACTIVITIES FOR THE CLASSROOM

1. IN THE SPIRIT OF "HARAMBE"

Harambe means that everyone will work together to achieve a goal. This is the time to talk about cooperation in the classroom, and to set goals and the means to achieve them. It could be a simple beginning, such as good listening habits when someone else is speaking and sharing information. Work on this repeatedly, and then go on to another goal. Goals can be set in academic areas (spelling, math facts, etc.).

2. TAKING A GOOD LOOK AT HAIR STYLES

There are many activities that can be done using hair as a basis. Students can graph the colors of their hair, and the styles of their hair (pigtails, corn rows, where it's parted, length, curly/straight, color, etc.). Remember, the Masaii men wear long hair and the women shave their head.

Students can examine hair styles in picture books. For example, the book *Mufaro's Beautiful Daughters* by John Steptoe (New York: Lothrop, Lee & Shepard, 1987) can be compared to the hair styles of *The Egyptian Cinderella* by Shirley Climo with illustrations by Ruth Heller (New York: Harper Collins, 1989).

When people celebrate a special event, they often wear their hair in a special way, or go to a salon or barber shop to have it cut or styled. Have students discuss their experiences with hair care in conjunction with the celebration of an event.

3. KWANZAA CELEBRATION

This celebration is in December. Students can prepare for it in school by focusing upon one of the aspects of this holiday each day during discussion time. The topics include: unity, self-determination, work and responsibility, cooperation, purpose, creativity, and faith. Much can be done to boost self-concept during these discussions. An excellent resource book is *Seven Candles for Kwanzaa* by Andrea Davis Pinkney, with illustrations by Brian Pinkney (New York: Dial Books for Young Readers, 1993).

4. DR. MARTIN LUTHER KING, JR. AND OTHER AFRICAN-AMERICAN CONTRIBUTORS

In January for this national celebration, it would be a good idea to explore the contributions of many Black leaders in the world. Students can divide into teams to do library research. Martin Luther King, Jr. (played by a student) could invite George Washington Carver (played by a student) to tell of his work with peanuts. Then, Harriet Tubman (Underground Railroad leader) can be introduced to tell her story, and so on. A celebration of Black Americans often takes place in the United States during Black History Month in February.

5. CELEBRATE THE ANIMALS

Congratulations! Students in class have just won a trip to Africa. They will go on a safari to various game parks, and look for a wide variety of animals—lion, cheetah, hippopotamus, giraffe, gazelle, zebra, and so on. Students can send away to a local travel agency for information about safari trips, and plan their trip.

In one of the game parks in Africa, it is possible before going to bed at night to leave a "check list" of the animals that you want to be awakened to see in the middle of the night if they should happen to stop by the nearby watering hole. Then, a guard keeps watch and when the animal comes by, he checks his list and knocks on the doors of all of the people who checked that animal. They get up sleepy-eyed, and go to their balconies to get a glimpse of the wonderful animal. Students might want to make a list of ten animals, and check five that they would want to be awakened to see. Be sure to have plenty of library books with animal pictures so students can see these animals and learn about them. Plan to get a videotape from the local library on the animals of Africa. The National Geographic Society is an excellent resource.

Graph the animals by size and weight. Also, set up the easel with fresh tempera paint for some dazzling animal pictures. Have students outline the animals in black tempera paint when the painting is complete.

6. CELEBRATE THE DIVERSITY

Have students check a variety of African folk tales for stories about these peoples in Africa: Ashanti (Ghana), Bedouins (Egypt), Berbers (Morocco), Khosian (Botswana), Dinka (Sudan), Hausa (Nigeria), Kikuyu (Kenya), Masaii (Kenya), Swahili (Eastern Coastal countries), and Zulu (South Africa).

7. CELEBRATE THE RAIN FOREST

In Africa, as in other parts of the world, there is a rain forest with endangered species. Do a study of the rain forest and make a layered book that shows, from the bottom up, the four layers: (a) forest floor, (b) understory, (c) canopy, and (d) emergent layer. The *tropical* rain forests are found near the equator in Africa, Asia, Australia, and South America. Other parts of the world have *temperate* rain forests.

ARTS AND CRAFTS

The numerous tribes on this vast continent all have different styles of art. While much of African art is made for religious ceremonies, religion is also connected to daily living, so art plays a large part in the life of the Africans and the ancestors of the African-Americans.

Since many tribes live close to nature, the art reflects the natural world. Grasses and plant stalks are dried and woven into baskets so fine that some are used for carrying water. Intricate geometric designs are woven into the baskets by dyeing some of the grasses with bright colors made from berries, vegetable dyes, and the earth.

Clay is used for hand-molding of jugs and vessels that are used to store and transport water and food. Also clay figurines that represent the gods are finely molded by hand. Implements such as sharp bones and sharp plant stalks are used to help mold fine details.

Body painting and face painting is an art form. Red clay, made by mixing the earth with water (two natural elements), is a chief source of paint. However, many rich colors can be obtained by adding liquid dye made from berries and other fruits to a base of finely ground stones or dried plants. In some tribes the hair is caked with the red clay mixture as well. Painting of the body decoratively for celebrations is an age-old art form. It pre-dates the wearing of jewelry.

Ceremonial masks made from wood, plant fibers, animal skins and hides, and turtle shells that are decorated with natural fibers or small animal bones and teeth are considered to be works of art and are preserved and housed in many gallery collections around the world for all to admire.

Some masks represent animals, and some represent ancestral spirits or gods, and are used in the reenactment of stories. Masks can be worn over the face or on top of the head.

Bead work is a popular art form. In Kenya, for example, the women make coils of beads and wear them piled one on top of the other, high on their neck and chest, much like a collar. Also, strands of beads are attached to the neck collars in front and hang down to the mid-chest or waist. From this decoration it is possible to tell whether the woman is married or single, and her age range.

Wood carving, mainly of animals in the environment such as the elephant, zebra, lion, impala, rhinocerous, giraffe, and so on, are carved from mahuhu wood and sold to the tourist trade along with ebony carvings of family groupings, masks, and walking sticks.

Colorful batiks from Africa are representative of the environment and depict scenes of adults, children, and the beautiful animals. These batiks are now sold all over the world.

Egypt, located in the northern section of the continent of Africa, has a rich legacy of art in the form of its **architecture and sculpture**. The early carvings on buildings show the human figure from the front view. Later, the head was carved in profile while the rest of the torso remained in front view. Much later, people were shown with the head and feet facing to the left or right, and the torso still in front view.

Indeed, the fine arts and crafts from this area of the world are renowned for their workmanship, beauty, and ingenuity.

SUGGESTED ACTIVITIES FOR THE CLASSROOM

1. A SPLENDOR OF MASKS

Masks play a part in all African ceremonies. It is believed that a person who wears a particular mask can cease to be him- or herself for a time and become the spirit of the force within the mask. For most tribes a white mask is a sign of death.

Paint is used to decorate the mask, along with beads, plant fibers, seeds, shells, or small bones. Some are crudely made to be used only once, and others are very delicately sculpted from wood.

Students can make individual simple masks using colored paper of a heavy quality as a base. More intricate masks and much larger masks can be made using papier-mâché. Some of the masks are worn on top of the head, and some bird masks, for example, are six feet in length. This would lend itself to a cooperative classroom project in the arts.

2. SQUARE AND ROUND HEADED DOLLS

In Ghana, the Ashanti women tuck wooden dolls into the backs of their waistbands. The dolls are flat with very long necks. They are actually charms to ensure having good looking children. If a woman carries a doll with a round head, it means she wants a boy. If she carries a doll with a square head, it means she wants a girl. Boys and girls in the classroom can make their own doll construction from gold or tan paper strips glued onto a cinnamon or brown background. Use the appropriate Ashanti head shape for boy or girl.

3. ROCK PAINTING

Cave paintings are common in this part of the world, with scenes often depicting the tribe hunting a large animal. Later, others painted over these or added more detail. Some paintings are done on much smaller rocks, and add historical significance or beauty to a particular area.

Have students collect rocks. Turn them over and look at them from every angle. What do they resemble? If a shape brings something to mind, such as the head of an animal or the contour of a bird, then use paints to sharpen the image. If the shape of the rock suggests nothing, then use the flat rock to paint a design or a scene.

4. GOURDS AS ART

Cut open a gourd and clean out the insides. Allow it to dry in the sun. Then decorate it on the outside with a blunt instrument and rub black powdered paint into the crevices or lines. This gourd is transformed into what the tribes call a "calabash." It can be decorated with geometric shapes, people, birds, animals, or flowers.

5. BLUE INDIGO CLOTH

The main coloring dye for cotton fabric is blue from the leaves of the indigo plant. The knowledge of the plant and the process of making dye was brought to Africa from India. In the Americas, fields of indigo were planted in the southern parts of the United States, and this was the original dye used for "blue jeans."

Students can use a cold-water dye of blue to dye a small piece of white cotton fabric. They can then paint decorative patterns on the cloth with a black fabric crayon.

Another technique is to dye the cloth blue. Allow time for drying. Then dip an object of a particular shape into black tempera paint and place it on the cloth in a repeat design. In Ghana, the "combed pattern" is very popular. Take a comb with large teeth, dip it into the black tempera paint, and make a swirl pattern on the blue cloth.

An excellent resource book is *The Art of Africa* by Shirley Glubok, designed by Gerard Nook, with special photography by Alfred H. Tamarin (New York: Harper & Row, 1965).

6. BASKET WEAVING

Basket making is a fine art in Africa. In some areas, the baskets are woven so tightly they can hold water! Mostly, baskets were used for storage of dry food. Some baskets are oblong and have a cover, some are square and some are rounded with a flat bottom. Students can examine baskets (see the Native American section) and perhaps arrange to have a basket maker come to class to show his or her handiwork and to get the students started with basket making. Contact the local art gallery or historical society for resource people.

7. LEARNING HOW TO SKETCH

Teach students the art of sketching. Sketching is accomplished by holding a pencil or piece of charcoal between the thumb and fingers, and by making many, many lines rather than a solid line. Have students sketch basic shapes such as a circle, square, or oval. In sketching, they are aiming for an approximation of the shape; it does not have to be perfect.

8. SKETCHING THE HUMAN FIGURE/FOCUS UPON THE PROCESS

It is difficult to draw people, and much in the way of results depends upon the stage of art development of the student. For students over age seven, they can sketch a face from memory. Remember that the lines—and there are many of them—are lightly drawn. Even the ancient Egyptians had difficulty drawing the human figure in motion. Movement was shown by drawing the feet from the side, with the body standing straight in front. Ask for a volunteer model to stand in front, and have students experiment with sketching the face or feet from the side and the body from the front view. Remind students that a sketch is NOT a finished product. The artist often uses a sketch to record shapes, lines, size, form, and so on. (It can be likened to the rough draft of story writing.) This must be emphasized so that students will continue to sketch and not expect a beautiful final product all at once. The focus is upon the process rather than the outcome. Encourage students to keep a sketch book, and to sketch in it daily, much as one might write in a journal daily. Since the human figure is difficult, set up a sketching table that contains items such as a brick, rocks, nuts, leaves, shells, pencil, eraser, and so on. Special colored pencils, special paper, an artist smock, and beret may provide added inspiration.

9. MAKING NATURE'S JEWELRY

Collect a variety of seed pods, nuts, seeds, and tiny stones. Students can use twine, needles and thread, and glue to make bracelets. This activity teaches students that making fine jewelry requires time and patience, and it is a skill that is practiced for many years before people become adept at their craft. For a lesson in cooperative learning, have students share with each other the ways that they have found to attach and string items together. Then, have them try again using the new methods.

10. ANIMAL PICTURES

Obtain "fake fur" from the fabric shop, such as black and white stripes (zebra), brown spots on yellow (tiger), golden yellow (lion), and gray (elephant or rhinocerous). Cut the fur into irregular shapes and lay them out on a table. Have students study them and talk about the animals native to Africa that come to their mind. What part of the animal could the shape represent—a head, a part of the body, a leg, a foot? Then let students select a piece of fur, paste it on a colored sheet of paper, and fill in the rest of the animal with crayons or paint. (Another way to select the material is to gather all of the pieces together in a bag after the discussion, and have students reach in and draw one out.)

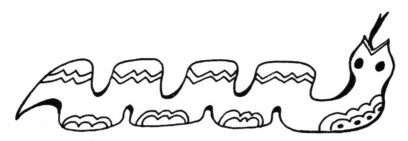

11. MAKE ANIMAL SHAPE BOOKS

Have students select an animal that they want to learn more about, or an animal that will be the main character in a folk tale that they plan to write. Using heavy paper or light cardboard, students can design the book cover in the shape of the animal. Add features using cloth, paint, or by gadget printing.

12. MAKING COLORFUL, FANCIFUL ELEPHANTS

In the picture book *Elmer* by David McKee (New York: Lothrop, Lee & Shepard, 1968), Elmer the Elephant has a patchwork hide of bright colors; all of the other elephants are gray. But, one day a year the elephants get all painted with bright stripes, flowers and designs, and Elmer gets painted gray. Students can make unusual elephants by making them from wallpaper sample books, with a mix-and-match approach. The toenails, ears, trunk, and tusks can be different from the body, head, and legs. When finished, decorate the door with these fanciful creatures.

13. EXAMINING AFRICAN-AMERICAN ART WORK IN PICTURE BOOKS

There are many excellent African-American artists illustrating picture books and using a variety of techniques. Here are two unusual techniques with which students may have success.

a. **Brian Pinkney—"Scratch Board Art."** The artist covers his paper with a variety of colors, covers the entire paper with a dark color, and uses a sharp implement to scratch the picture. See *The Dark-Thirty, Southern*

Tales of the Supernatural by Patricia C. McKissack, with illustrations by Brian Pinkney (New York: Knopf Books for Young Readers, 1992). Students can cover a 9″ x 12″ sheet of white paper with a variety of crayon colors. It is imperative that students press hard on their crayons and leave no white showing. Then, brush over the entire sheet with India ink or watered-down black tempera paint. Allow it to dry. Students can scratch their picture with the point of a compass or other blunt instrument. The joy is in watching the variety of bright colors that begin to appear when the black covering is scratched away.

b. **Floyd Cooper—"Eraser Art."** The artist covers his canvas with a wash of light brown paint, then uses an art gum eraser to remove the parts that he does not want. See *Grandpa's Face* by Eloise Greenfield (New York: Putnam, 1993) and *The Girl Who Loved Caterpillars* by Jean Merrill (New York: Putnam, 1992), both illustrated by Floyd Cooper. This is a reverse form of painting. Students can try this by using chalk and a slate or the chalkboard in the room. First, cover the entire surface with white chalk; then use the eraser to create (erase) the shape, scene or figure. It will take lots of practice. Later, colored chalk can be added to parts that were erased.

GAMES

Throughout the vast continent of Africa, there are many different tribes and a variety of games that children play. The games of childhood are pleasurable and include the traditional run-and-chase games, ball games, hide-and-seek games, string games, "it" games, and games that employ items made from nature. Game playing is often accompanied by rhythms, chanting, and hand clapping. One of the games seen in many villages across Africa is the game of "Mankala," which is played with pebbles by young and old. As in most cultures, young children imitate the work of the adults while at play. And through games, children gain a sense of honesty, sharing, teamwork, and competition, and learn to deal with the sweet taste of victory as well as the acceptance of defeat. It is a part of the growth process. Native children in villages do not play with commercially made toys, but are apt to make their own from sticks, twine, and other items from the outdoors. Children in large metropolitan cities have access to commercial games.

GOOSE FEATHER THROWING GAME

Five or seven goose quills are placed on the ground in a circle. A tree is designated as the target. A pebble is placed on the ground at the spot where each child stands when his or her turn comes. Then, each child picks up a feather or quill, and one by one, throws a feather at the tree. The winner is the one whose feather lands nearest to the tree. Feathers are then picked up, arranged in a circle, and the game begins again.

JAMOLIBANNA (PINCHING FOOT GAME)

One child is "it." Other players sit around in a circle with their feet stretched out in front of them. "It" is in the middle and chants:

> Nini nini kills twenty, nini nini kills thirty,
> Nini nini kills fifty. Once there was a chief—
> And one was king—Ogundele, the Blacksmith,
> Take in your foot.

"It" points to a child, who pulls in his or her leg and foot. "It" repeats this chant, pointing to each child one at a time, until just one person is left with a foot extended. At this point, everyone in the game gets the chance to pinch the toe of that person, who then becomes the next "it."

THE JUMPING GAME

The Masii of Kenya play a game to see who can jump the highest from a standing position. With practice, children can jump very high off the ground. This is accompanied by chanting. Each child has a stick that is used to thump the ground during the jumping, and to help gain momentum.

BOJUBOJU (HIDE OH!)

This is a type of hide-and-seek game. Children form a circle. One player is chosen to be "it" and goes to the center. "It" covers his or her eyes with hands and sings, "Hide, hide oh! Rich man is coming! Hide, hide oh!" The children scatter and hide, and when all is clear they call to the one who is "it" to uncover his or her eyes. "It" then sets off to find the players. If "it" tags them, they assist in helping to tag the other players. The last one to be tagged is the new "it."

KINI O NI IYE? (WHO WEARS FEATHERS?)

Each player has a large tree leaf in his or her hand. The leader, facing the group, begins to name things one by one that do/do not have feathers. It is put into the form of a question, such as: "Do crows have feathers?" "Do cows have feathers?" "Do lions have feathers?" If the answer is no, children answer "beko"; if the answer is yes, children answer "beni." The tempo can be speeded up by the leader. If a player becomes confused and gives a wrong answer, the other players hit his or her legs with the leaves. A new leader can be chosen at any time.

MAWIRA MAITU NI OGWO (THIS IS THE WAY OUR WORK IS DONE)

This is similar to the chant, "This is the way we wash our clothes, wash our clothes, wash our clothes. This is the way we wash our clothes, so early in the morning." Children sing and use accompanying motions.

In this version, players sing, "This is the way we chop our wood, here in the land of Kikuyu," and make appropriate motions. Other lines include, "This is the way we carry our water," "This is the way we oil our bodies," and "This is the way we grind our corn."

HAND CLAPPING GAME

The leader makes motions with arms high in the air, one arm in the air, then the other arm in the air, then a jump, etc., and all players must follow. Those who do not are out, and begin to clap to the rhythm of the leader's movements. The last one in the game is the next leader. (This game is similar to "Simon Says.")

Resource

Millen, Nina. *Children's Games from Many Lands.* (Ann Arbor, MI: Books on Demand, 1965)

SONGS, DANCES, RHYTHMS

Perhaps some of the oldest tribal instruments were made from hollow logs and struck with a piece of wood. Or, wood was struck with stone. Animal bones were used to create a rattling sound. "Talking Drums" refers to messages that were sent via drum beats to other members of the tribe or to a distant tribe. Often the message conveyed was one of danger.

THE VOICE OF THE DRUM

A hollow log with dried animal skin stretched across the opening may have been one of the first drums. For students to make drums, use a pair of embroidery hoops. Leather or other stretchable material can be secured between the hoops and placed over the top of an empty cylinder (coffee can, oatmeal can) that acts as a resonating column to intensify the sound of the drum. The drum can be struck with a stick, fingers, or palm of the hand in time to the beat of songs that are sung in your classroom.

Perhaps the drum is the beginning of what we call the percussion instruments. Early drums were used to give signals. Drums can express feelings, changing rhythms, signal a change in tempo, and explode in volume depending upon how hard the instrument is struck.

HORN-TYPE INSTRUMENTS

In ancient days, animal horns were hollowed out so that sound could be made by blowing air into a hole in the small end that traveled out the larger end. The sound from a horn is made by the reverberation of the air within the tube or column of the horn. This same effect (reverberation of a body of air) can be achieved by blowing gently across the open top of a soft drink bottle. A large bottle creates a deeper sound. Another way to change the sound is to vary an amount of water placed within the bottle. The more water in the bottle, the higher the pitch. The sound comes from the vibration of the air above the water in the bottle.

WE CAN MAKE A THUMB PIANO

In Kenya, thumb pianos are used today to help keep the rhythm and the beat as groups of people sing and move rhythmically together. Materials needed for this hand-held instrument are a block of wood and flexible strips of metal of varying lengths and thickness that are affixed to the wood at one end and free to vibrate at the other. The metal pieces are plucked by the thumbs to create the sounds.

PLAYIN' THE BONES, PLAYIN' THE SPOONS

In early Africa, animal bones were used as instruments to help keep the beat and rhythm of a song. The bones were held in each hand and clicked together, which requires manual dexterity and patience to learn. In the United States, African-Americans use metal spoons that they play while in a seated position, so that the spoons can be clicked and also slapped on the thigh and even elbows. Usually the techniques have to be learned from a person who knows how to "play the spoons," in the same manner that one would have to take lessons on the piano from one who can play and teach.

CEREMONIAL DANCES

Many dances were used at ceremonies where people gathered to pray for rain, to pray for a good hunt, or to pray for the return of the sun to help the crops grow. Some ceremonial masks were worn, but it was the custom for all to join in the celebration of the dance and to "move with the spirit" in a manner that we would call "improvisation." Young students enjoy being able to express themselves with body movement, so put on a recording and let them improvise. They soon pick up ideas from one another to add to their movement repertoire.

FEATURING THE DANCE SPECIALISTS

When people gather at celebrations, music and dancing are always a part of the festivities. People dance together as a group and then, in many cases, certain people do a solo. One person might excel with fancy footwork, one might be wearing ankle decorations and accentuate his or her ankle movements, and so on. This is done while the onlookers clap their hands in time to the rhythm, and enjoy the specialties of their friends. Encourage students to work on their own movement specialties, and practice, practice, practice.

IMITATION OF ANIMALS IN NATURE

Animals are depicted through dance movements, such as the imitation of the watchful, circling hyena; the graceful jumping movement of the gazelle; the ponderous, thundering walk of the elephant; the slinking movement of the leopard on padded feet; and the swooping wings of the magestic eagle.

These accentuated body movements can be emphasized as children listen to narrations of folk tales and reenact the action. They can be used to enhance their storytelling, too.

Resource

Video Anthology of World Music and Dance, Middle East and Africa IV, Volume 19, Ivory Coast/Botswana/Republic of South Africa. JVC, Victor Company of Japan.

FOOD

Because the continent of Africa is so vast, with hundreds of ethnic groups, it is difficult to put the food into simple categories. Therefore, this section is a representative sample of some dishes, and is not intended as a complete guide. Most of the people in the eastern and western section of the continent eat two meals a day—at noon and in the evening, with a snack in between. In other areas, three meals a day are eaten. Because of a lack of refrigeration in many areas, food is purchased fresh and eaten the same day. Most people eat fresh fruits and vegetables and the coastal people have a ready access to seafood.

SUGGESTED RECIPES FOR THE CLASSROOM

Peanut Sauce Dish

1 onion
2 tomatoes
1 small eggplant
2 tablespoons vegetable oil
1/2 cup smooth peanut butter
1/4 cup water

Peel and chop the onions. Cut the tomatoes and eggplant into small pieces. Heat oil in electric frypan for one minute, and saute onions. Add tomatoes and cook for 4 to 5 minutes. Add eggplant and cook for 4 to 5 minutes. In a separate bowl, combine peanut butter and water. Add this paste to the frypan mixture and stir well. Simmer until eggplant is cooked (approximately 10 minutes). Serve with potatoes or rice.

Sweet Doughnut Balls (Ghana Style)

1 egg
1/2 teaspoon salt
3 tablespoons baking powder
1/2 teaspoon nutmeg
1-1/2 cups warm water
3-3/4 to 4-1/4 cups all-purpose flour
vegetable oil

Combine egg, salt, baking powder, nutmeg, and sugar, and stir well. Add water and stir. Fold in flour so dough is stiff and slightly sticky. Clean and flour hands, and then roll dough into tiny balls the size of pecans. Prepare electric frypan by heating an inch of oil in pan. Place balls in oil, and fry until brown (3 minutes). Remove, drain, and serve warm. Makes three dozen sweet doughnut balls.

Fufu (Dough for Soups and Stews)

1 pound cassava (a starchy root)

Wash and peel the cassavas, and soak in water for four days. Cut out the hard cores. Place in a pan of water and bring to a boil, then simmer for approximately ten minutes. Remove the cassavas, put them into a bowl; and pound them until they form a soft dough. Place this dough on a dish, and serve with meat or stew.

Fufu (New World Version)

1-1/4 cups Cream of Wheat®
1 cup potato flakes
4 cups water
1 tablespoon margarine

Bring 2 cups of water to boil, then reduce heat. Bring another 2 cups of water to boil in a different saucepan, reduce heat to medium, and add Cream of Wheat®, a little at a time, stirring constantly. When mixture becomes too thick, add hot water from the first pan. Add potato flakes, a little at a time, stirring constantly, and adding hot water when mixture becomes too thick. Add margarine, and stir. Continue to cook and stir until mixture of fufu separates from the sides of the pan and forms a ball. Serve fufu in cups or bowls.

Fried Plantains

several large, ripe plantains
vegetable oil

Peel the plaintains and slice into thin round pieces. Place the slices in a medium-heat frypan (in 1/2-inch vegetable oil), and brown on both sides. Remove and drain.

Plaintain can be baked and boiled also. For variety, it can be baked and served with a topping of brown sugar, or boiled and served with tomatoes and onions.

Dovi (Zimbabwe)

peanut sauce
cooked chicken cut into small pieces
1 sliced onion
2 tomatoes cut into small pieces
2 cups water

Mix ingredients together and simmer for one hour to make a stew. Serve in small bowls.

Note: In many areas of Africa, it is normal to have a common pot of stew for supper. Then, every family member eats from this pot by dipping into it with cornmeal bread or chapatis, a type of bread. This is a time when the family is "one"; to be invited to join the group is considered an honor.

Coconut

The coconut is used as a part of many dishes. Shredded coconut is added to vegetables and is used as a dessert. Coconut milk is a refreshing drink.

Resources

Excellent resources include *African Food and Drink* by Martin Gibrill (New York: The Bookwright Press, no date); and "Easy Menu Ethnic Cookbook Series," *Cooking the African Way* (Minneapolis, Lerner Publications, no date).

REPRODUCIBLE ACTIVITY PAGES

African Storyteller Mask (*storytelling*)

Join the Folk Tale Adventure (*record keeping*)

"Anansi the Spider" Trickster Award (*reading selection*)

Anansi and the Frog Beauty (*creative writing*)

The Role of the Snake in Folk Tales (*research/writing*)

The Lion's Dilemma—An Original Tale (*story starter*)

Shaking the Baby with the Grain (*celebration of birth*)

Endangered Species Department. May I Help You? (*issues*)

In the Spirit of Harambe (*emphasis on cooperation*)

To Market, to Market in Africa (*research/writing*)

Baskets That Can Hold Water (*art design*)

Cronedag Is Hungry for Information (*geography: oceans and seas*)

Do an Author Study—Africa (*Verna Aardema; Robert San Souci; Brian Pinkney*)

JOIN THE FOLK TALE ADVENTURE

Keep track of the folk tales you read. Color the space on the balloon when you have journeyed to that area in a story. Enjoy your story trips!

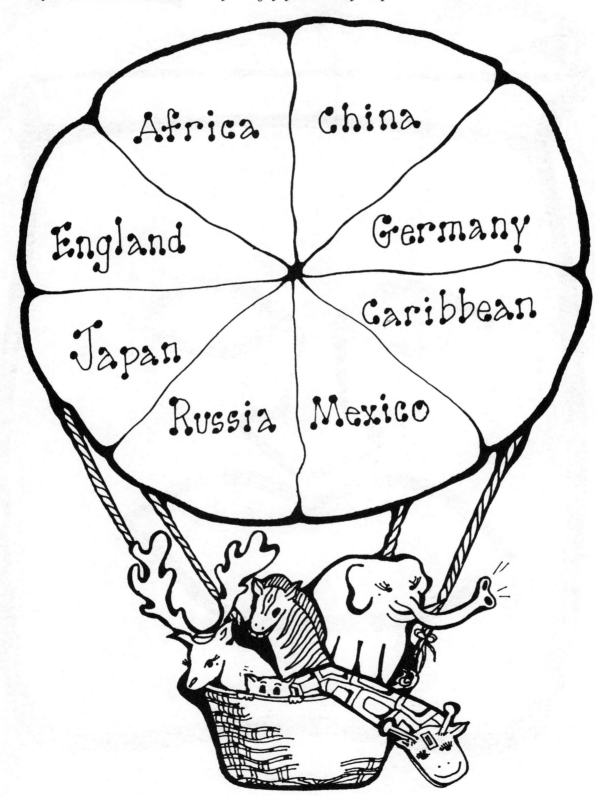

Name _____   Date _____

"ANANSI THE SPIDER" TRICKSTER AWARD

Anansi appears in many African and Caribbean folk tales, and is always playing tricks on people or animals. Sometimes the tricks backfire, but not always. Anansi is on the lookout for other characters who play tricks in folk tales, fairy tales, or short fables. Read some trickster tales and fill out the award below. (Sometimes Anansi gives the award to his own tales!) Enjoy a trickster storytelling festival in your classroom and share good books.

title	
author	
artist	
characters	
country	
story message	
why I gave it an award	

Name _____ Date _____

ANANSI AND THE FROG BEAUTY

Anansi, the trickster, sometimes does things that "backfire!" That means that Anansi doesn't get his way, but learns a lesson. Below is such a tale. You are the author. Write this funny story on the frog.

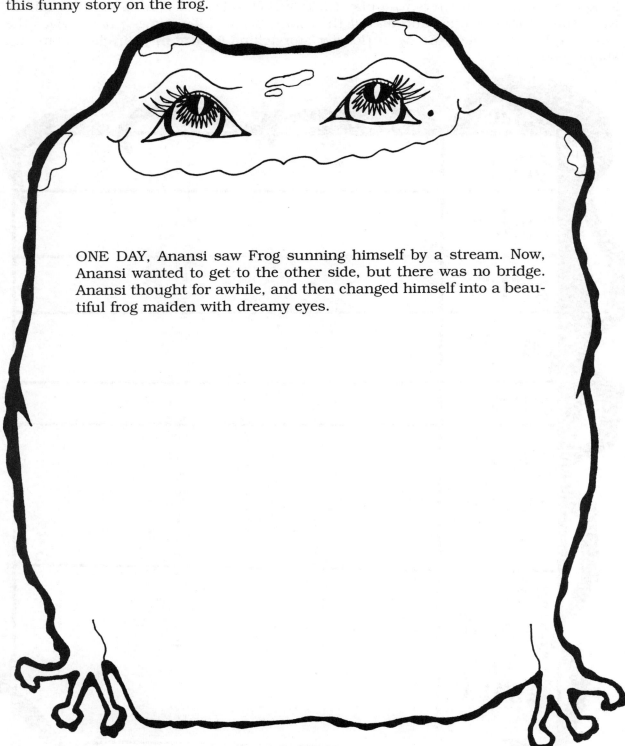

ONE DAY, Anansi saw Frog sunning himself by a stream. Now, Anansi wanted to get to the other side, but there was no bridge. Anansi thought for awhile, and then changed himself into a beautiful frog maiden with dreamy eyes.

Name _____   Date _____

THE ROLE OF THE SNAKE IN FOLK TALES

Around the world, the snake appears in folk tales—especially in warmer climates. Find a folk tale where the snake plays an important role and share the information in the space the snake provided for you. Watch out!

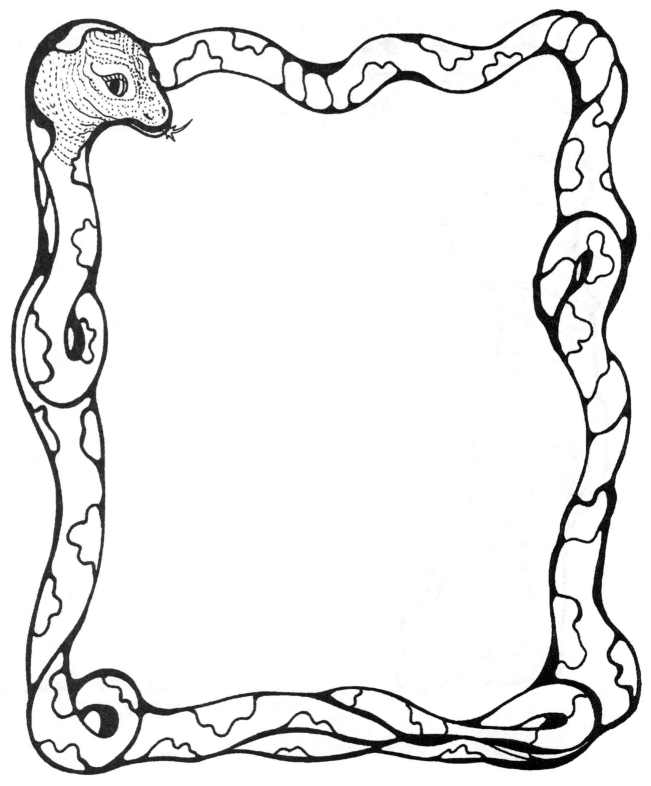

Name _____ Date _____

THE LION'S DILEMMA—AN ORIGINAL TALE

You are about to write a "dilemma tale." Lion has just sent his beautiful fur to the cleaners and it won't be ready for a week!

Ring! Ring! It's the Emperor! He's having a birthday party tomorrow for his son and wants Lion there at 2 o'clock. Lion is the son's favorite animal.

This is a real "dilemma." What will happen? Write your story below

Use your problem-solving skills. Remember, emperors don't like the word "NO"!

SHAKING THE BABY WITH THE GRAIN

In agricultural areas of Egypt, a baby is put into a large sieve with grains and gently shaken. The baby is then washed and named, and wishes are made for the baby's life.

What four things would you wish for a baby? Write them on the grain below. Then color this happy picture.

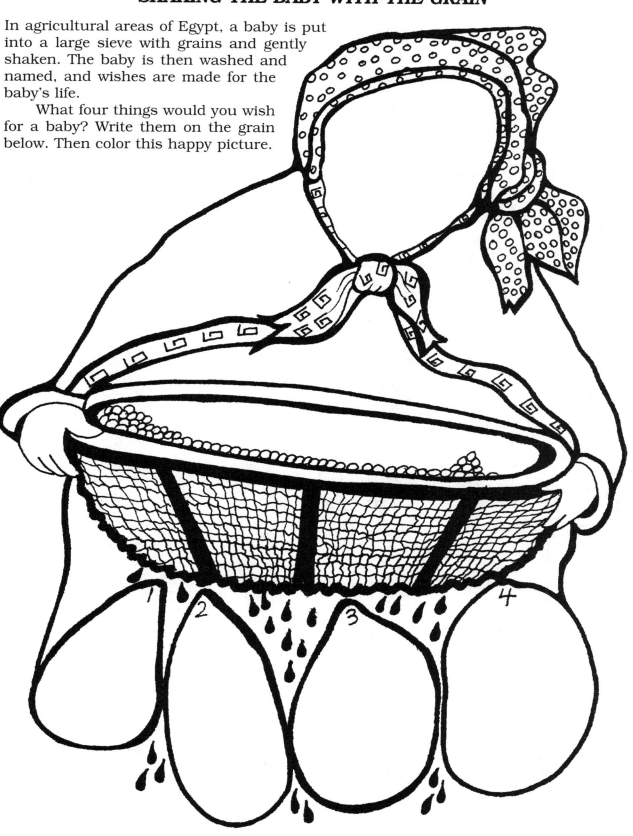

Name _____ Date _____

ENDANGERED SPECIES DEPARTMENT. MAY I HELP YOU?

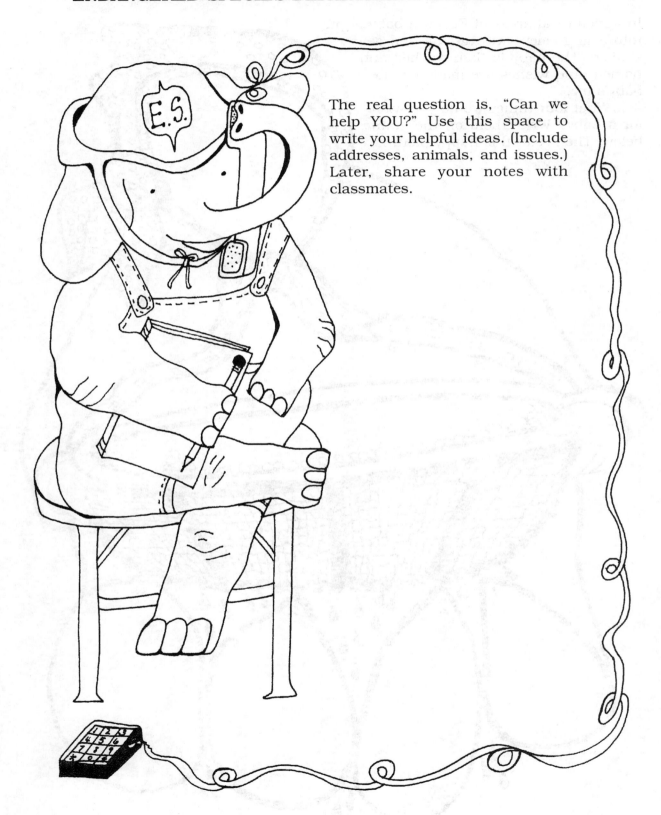

The real question is, "Can we help YOU?" Use this space to write your helpful ideas. (Include addresses, animals, and issues.) Later, share your notes with classmates.

Name _____   Date _____

IN THE SPIRIT OF HARAMBE

In Kenya, "Harambe" means that everyone will work together to achieve a goal. Let's set a goal of COOPERATION and begin with good listening habits.

Grade yourself daily by using the following symbols:

Things to Work On	M	T	W	TH	F
1. I will listen when others are speaking.					
2.					
3.					
4.					
5.					

TO MARKET, TO MARKET IN AFRICA

This young mother is walking to market in her red and yellow clothing. Fill her baskets with fruits and vegetables.

COUNTRY:

CLIMATE:

WHAT FRUITS MIGHT BE GROWN HERE?

WHAT VEGETABLES ARE GROWN HERE?

AHA! Along the way, Anansi the Spider is watching and waiting, and he is very hungry! What happens is up to you. Write your tale on the other side of this sheet.

Find an Anansi tale at the library and learn it by heart. Tell it aloud.

Name _____   Date _____

BASKETS THAT CAN HOLD WATER

In Africa, some baskets are woven so tightly they can actually hold water. This one will have beautiful nature designs (trees, birds, animals) woven into the basket.

Help the weaver. Use earth tone colors to finish the basket. Make it beautiful, so take your time.

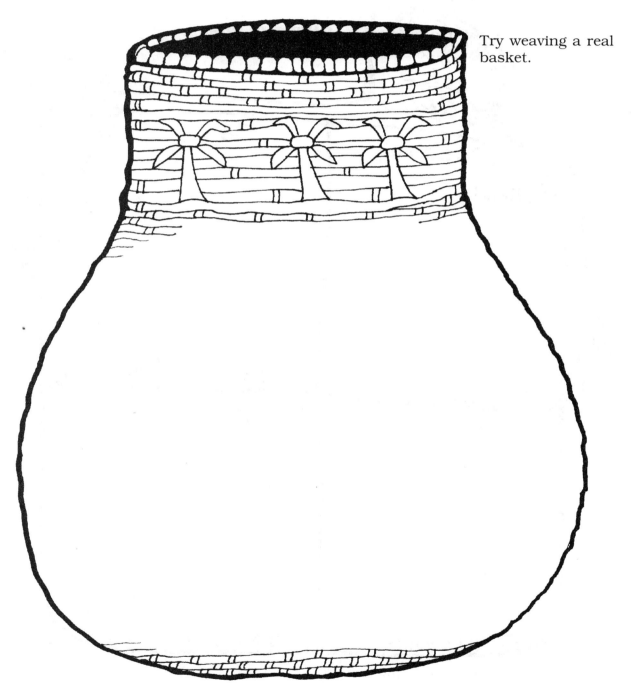

Try weaving a real basket.

Name _____   Date _____

CRONEDAG IS HUNGRY FOR INFORMATION

Message from Cronedag the Ogre: "I am trying to learn about Planet Earth. What is the difference between an ocean and a sea? I heard they both have salt water. Please list the information or I'll gobble up these giant tunas."

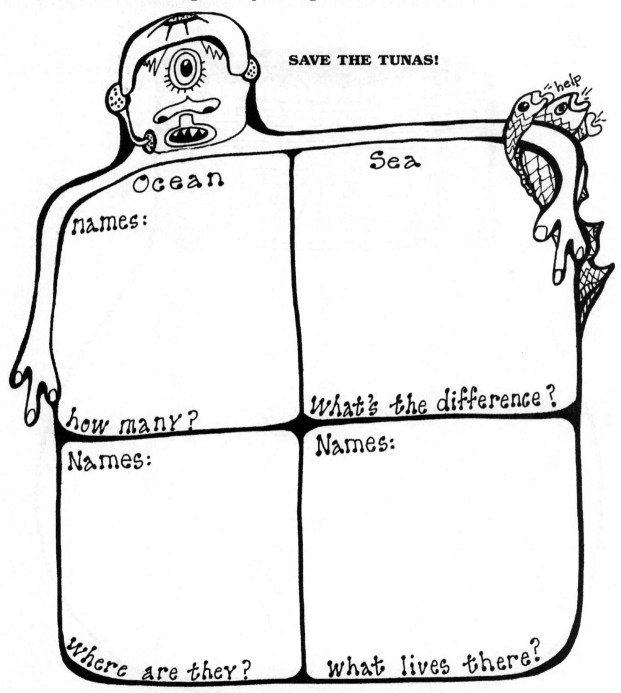

SAVE THE TUNAS!

Ocean — Sea

names:

how many?

Names:

What's the difference?

Names:

where are they?

what lives there?

Does a river have salt water, too?

Name _____ Date _____

DO AN AUTHOR STUDY—AFRICA

There are many African folk tales retold by Verna Aardema. Locate some in the library and read them. Also, locate picture books with tales retold by Robert San Souci and illustrated by Brian Pinkney, such as *The Talking Eggs* and *Sukey and the Mermaid.* Make journal notes about the colorful books. Books by authors Patricia McKissock and Eloise Greenfield will also add to your knowledge and pleasure.

Notes:

ASIA

RECOMMENDED CHILDREN'S BOOKS

There is an abundance of tales from this area of the world. The following list is representative.

Ai-Ling, Louie. *Yeh-Shen, a Cinderella Story from China.* Illustrated by Ed Young. New York: Philomel Books, 1982. This is the classic Cinderella story, and is believed to be the oldest one—even older than the more familiar European versions. In this tale, Yeh-Shen is the daughter of Chief Wu, who has two wives. One wife dies, and Yeh-Shen is raised by her stepmother. In this tale, the girl befriends a fish who helps her. The illustrations with the fish motif throughout are stunning.

Armstrong, Jennifer. *Chin Yu Min and the Ginger Cat.* Illustrations by Mary Grandpre. New York: Crown Publishers, 1993. A hauty Chinese woman, who is wealthy, greedy and unkind, meets up with a ginger cat who helps to provide for her when the woman's husband dies. She lives a selfish existence until one day when the ginger cat disappears and the widow has to fend for herself. It is never too late to have to learn a hard lesson, and it is never too late to change.

Bang, Molly. *The Paper Crane.* New York: Greenwillow, 1985. A new highway is built to replace the old one, and soon a restaurant is abandoned. One day a stranger appears and makes an origami crane figure in return for a meal. He instructs the restaurant owner to clap his hands to make the crane dance. The word spreads far and wide. This is an ancient Japanese folk tale in a modern setting.

Blia, Xiong. *Nine-in-One Grr! A Folk Tale from the Hmong People of Laos.* Adapted by Cathy Spagnoli. Illustrated by Nancy Hom. Chicago: Children's Book Press, 1989. Traditionally, the Hmong embroidery tells a story. In this tale, or story cloth, the land is in danger of being overrun with tigers. Can the land be saved? A high point of this book are the illustrations in the traditional embroidery motifs and styles.

Carpenter, Frances. *Tales of a Korean Grandmother.* New York: Doubleday, 1947. This is a collection of popular folk tales including "The

Rabbit That Rode on a Tortoise." Also by this author are collections of tales entitled *Tales of a Basque Grandmother, Tales of a Russian Grandmother, Tales of a Chinese Grandmother,* and *Tales of a Swiss Grandmother.*

Dee, Ruby. ***Two Ways to Count to Ten: A Liberian Folk Tale.* Illustrated by Susan Meddaugh. New York: Henry Holt & Co., 1988.** This retold tale takes place long ago when beasts of the jungle lived in harmony. The leopard, who is king, is looking for a successor, but first he must find an animal wise enough to rule. A clever ending.

Goom, Bridget. ***A Family in Singapore.* Photographs by Jenny Mathews. New York: Lerner, 1986.** This book is one in a series called "Families the World Over." Twelve-year-old Chor Ling and her family live in urbanized Singapore. Father eats with chopsticks while the rest of the family eats with forks, which is just one contrast between the old and the new. Also included in this series is a book about a family in Thailand.

Heide, Florence Parry and Gilliland, Judith Heide. ***Sami and the Time of the Troubles.* Illustrated by Ted Lewin. New York: Clarion Books, 1992.** Sami and his little sister, Leila, live in Lebanon but are like children everywhere. Their environment in Beirut, however, is one of violence and chaos. There are good memories to cling to, and always the hope that someday the fighting will stop. The beautiful watercolor illustrations are in themselves a visual education for children.

Hidaka, Masako. ***Girl from the Snow Country.* Translated by Amanda Mayer Stinchecum. New York: Kane/Miller Book Publishers, 1986.** Each winter, snow blankets Mi-chan's village. On this particular day as Mi-chan and her mother walk to the village, the girl brushes the snow from the statute of Jizo. Jizo is the protector of children and travelers. Through the pictures and text, the reader visits outdoor market stalls and the girl receives berries from a kind vendor. Mi-chan's mother says it is Jizo's way of repaying her good deed.

Ike, Jane Hori and Zimmerman, Baruch. ***A Japanese Fairy Tale.* Pictures by Jane Hori Ike. New York: Frederick Warne, 1982.** The beautiful Kyoko is married to a man who is frighteningly ugly. What an unusual pair; yet it is plain to see that they are very happy. What is the secret of this match? Is it possible to make a bargain in heaven? The illustrator is a third-generation Japanese-American, born in Los Angeles.

Kimmel, Eric. ***The Greatest of All, a Japanese Folk Tale.* Illustrated by Giora Carmi. New York: Holiday House, 1991.** In this retold tale, Chuko Mouse tells her father that she wishes to marry a handsome field mouse, but the father mouse insists that she deserves better than that. So he sets off to find her a more suitable mate. He goes to meet the Emperor, who sends him to the sun, who sends him to the cloud, who sends him to the wind, who sends him to the wall. Another variation of this cumulative tale is Gerald McDermott's *Stonecutter*.

Knowlton, Mary Lee and Sachner, Mark, eds. *Burma*. Photographs by Takashi Morieda. Milwaukee; Gareth Stevens, 1987. This book is one in a series entitled "Children of the World." The aim of the book is to interest children in the way of life in another culture—Burma, or Myanmar. We follow a boy through a typical day at home and school, and meet his family. There is a valuable resource information for further study at the end of the book.

Lattimore, Deborah Norse. *The Dragon's Robe*. New York: Harper & Row, 1990. Kwan Yin, a young weaver, decides to journey to the Emperor's Palace to find work. Along the way she meets an old man, too ill to perform his duties, so she helps him. This story uses the classic folk tale formula of rewarding good and punishing evil. The story ends happily for the good Kwan Yin.

Nomura, Takaaki. *Grandpa's Town*. Illustrations by Amanda Mayer Stinchecum. New York: Kane/Miller Book Publishers, 1991. A visit to grandpa's town includes a public bath in a steamy room, laughing and soaking with grandpa's friends, hooking little fingers with another person to make promises, and recognizing that although grandpa lives alone he has many good friends in the city.

Paterson, Katherine. *The Tale of the Mandarin Ducks*. Illustrated by Leo and Diane Dillon. New York: Lodestar Books, 1990. This is a retelling of a popular Japanese folk tale about a greedy lord who captures and cages a mandarin duck for all to admire. The kitchen maid takes pity upon the poor duck and sets him free. For this, she and another servant are sentenced to death. But on their trip through the forest, the grateful mandarin duck and his mate work their magic. The blue and gold illustrations in the style of eighteenth-century Japanese woodcuts enrich the book.

Tran-Khanh-Tuyet. *The Little Weaver of Thai-Yen Village*. Illustrated by Nancy Hom. Chicago: Children's Book Press, 1987. This is a touching story of a little girl, a Vietnamese refugee from a war-torn land. For one so little, she has suffered much; yet through her weaving, she is able to send blankets back to her village and keep the hope alive that one day she will return. The text is in both English (by Christopher N. H. Jenkins) and in Vietnamese so that children can see the languages.

Young, Ed. *Lon Po Po, a Red Riding Hood Story from China*. New York: Philomel Books, 1989. In this version of the Red Riding Hood tale, the granny ("Po Po"), comes to visit the three children who have been left by their mother with strict instructions not to let anyone in. But when Po Po, the wolf in disguise, comes to visit, how can they refuse? Most of the action in this exciting tale takes place within the setting of the house. A Caldecott Award winner.

____. **Adapted from the retelling by Leslie Bonnet.** *The Terrible Nung Gwama, a Chinese Folk Tale.* **Illustrated by the author. New York: Collins and World, in cooperation with the U.S. Committee for UNICEF, 1978.** This is a well-loved tale of a reluctantly brave folk-heroine, who saves herself and the rest of the countryside from a most horrendous monster. The girl has help along the way from many people who try to outwit the demanding beast.

FOLK TALES

Asia is a large continent and is often referred to by location, such as East Asia (including China and Japan), South Asia (including India and Sri Lanka), West Asia (including Turkey and Lebanon), Central Asia (including Afghanistan and Bhutan), and Southeast Asia (including Malaysia and Thailand). The archipelago of Indonesia is considered to be a part of the Asian culture. In the past, Northern Asia was the Soviet Union.

Many of the world's ancient civilizations can be traced to Asia, where great literature, poetry and sayings have been handed down through the centuries. Many of the old stories are anonymous. For example, most works of Old Javanese and Balinese manuscripts were etched on palm leaves. Illustrated manuscripts are known only from the end of the 19th century. For the most part, the Balinese literature is meant to be sung *and* recited.

"Wayang Kulit," the shadow theater of Bali, is one of the oldest forms of storytelling. Puppets are flat, and in any given performance over 50 puppets may be used. Characters are recognized by their outlines or costumes and there are always two types: "alus" (controlled) and "kasar" (vulgar and quick to anger). The master puppeteer is known as the "dalang," and the performances can last from two to five hours.

In Asia there is a fertile, richness of custom, belief and ritual that is quite complicated. While there is an abundance of written material about the various cultures, particularly China, it is a challenge to study the folklore because of the vastness of the area, the long period of time in history through which it extends, the mixture of cultures, the unfamiliarity with the language symbols, and so on. In this area of the world, the folklore is a vital and living force, with the teachings of ancient philosophers and holy men still relevant today.

MEET THE FOUR ANIMALS IN ASIAN LEGENDS

(1) The celestial dragon with its long tail and mist coming from its nostrils, (2) the giant tortoise, (3) the mysterious and beautiful phoenix bird that rises from the ashes, and (4) the fierce or kindly unicorn are in many Asian legends. You can find them again and again. The dragon often has the ability to live in the sea, in the sky, or on the land. If the sea dragon becomes angry, it can thrash its tail about and create tidal waves that have been known to overtake villages near the shore.

In a Chinese legend, the four creatures listed above were very helpful to a being named P'an Ku who made the universe. Then, when P'an Ku died, his body became the earth soil, his blood became the rivers, his hair became the trees, his breath became the wind, and his voice made the sound of thunder. One eye (left) turned into the sun, and the other eye (right) turned into the moon. This would be classified as a "creation myth" in literature.

DRAGONS OF THE EAST

One of the differences between dragons of the Eastern and Western societies is that dragons of the East usually breathe out mist and dragons of the West (Europe and North America) breathe out fire. Eastern dragons control the oceans, lakes and streams, and also make the clouds and rain. They have a tremendous amount of power, and can change in size from a monster (the size of a towering skyscraper) to the size of a person. Therefore, they can move about in the world and not be noticed because they look like an ordinary human and can speak the language. They are often wise and very wealthy dragons. Although they are not usually portrayed with wings, they are able to fly. From ancient times the dragon was considered the emblem of royalty and the symbol for greatness. It was a great honor to have the dragon's name associated with a family name.

INTRODUCING TANUKI AND KAPPA OF JAPAN

Tanuki is a fun-loving badger who can change shapes, like many of the characters from other cultures (examples: Anansi the Spider from African folklore, and Raven from Native American folklore). This magical beast is not ferocious but likes to play tricks on people.

The Kappa wears a tortoise shell on its back and has a face like a monkey, with webbed hands and feet. Its head is hollowed out on top (like a bowl) and filled with water. As long as it is filled with water, Kappa has all of its powers, but if the water runs out it loses its strength. Even though

Kappa does play malicious tricks on people, it is grateful for kindness shown to it and repays in full.

INTRODUCING THE ASIAN UNICORN

Unicorns in Asian folk tales are usually gentle but can be fierce if necessary. Supposedly the unicorn looks like the horse with the hind legs of an antelope, which explains its ability to jump as it runs. Their singular horn is magical, and if a unicorn dips its horn into stagnant water it becomes purified for drinking, and sea creatures flourish so abundantly that land animals can feed from the water.

THE PHOENIX RISES IN MANY CULTURES

The phoenix is a beautiful bird, larger than an eagle and with a sweet voice. In some cultures this bird lives for five hundred years; in other cultures, it lives for a thousand. When it reaches old age, it builds a nest of twigs at the top of a tall tree. A spark from the sun ignites the nest, burns it, and from the flames of the ashes a young phoenix springs forth to live a long life.

This bird is mysterious in China and Japan. He is kindly and gentle. His call consists of five sweet notes. (All Chinese music is based upon a musical scale of five tones, no matter what the instrument.) The phoenix also appears in tales from Egypt and the Arab countries.

MEET THE FOX

The Asiatic foxes live to a great old age, and when they reach one thousand their fur turns white and they no longer play tricks on people. In Japan the fox is a magical animal named Kitsune, who plays malicious tricks on people. In China, the fox keeps company with the fairies.

THE HIPPOGRIFF

This combination creature has the head, forefeet and wings of a griffin (bird) and the body of a horse. It can live in the mountains, although it enjoys grazing even with its large beak. This creature is found in the folklore of Asia Minor and also of Europe.

THE ROLE OF THE HARE

In some cultures there is the man in the moon, and in some Asian cultures there is a hare in the moon. This hare is busy pounding rice, or is busy sweeping to keep the moon clean. In Ireland and Wales the hare appears in tales to weave its magic. The hare also appears in Native American tales, often as a trickster figure.

ANCIENT CHINESE RECORDS

The *I CHING* (Book of Changes) shows a map of the heavens referred to as "Ssu Fang." Mythical animals control the four seasons of the year, as well as the four directions. The Black Tortoise is in charge of Winter and the North; the Blue Dragon represents Spring and the East; the Vermilion Bird (Phoenix) represents Summer and the South; and the White Tiger represents Autumn and the West.

THE ZODIAC TALE

As the story goes, when Lord Buddah lay on his deathbed, he summoned all of the animals of the kingdom to him. The faithful ox was plodding along when the rat asked for a ride on its back, and the ox gave the rat a ride to see Buddah. When they got to the gate, however, the rat jumped off and ran ahead of the ox and was the first animal to reach Buddah. So, as a reward, Buddah gave the rat first place in the zodiac. The ox has second place. In turn, the animals are as follows: Rat, Ox, Tiger, Hare, Dragon, Snake, Horse, Ram, Monkey, Cock, Dog, and Boar.

RAT: A symbol of prosperity in the Orient. Highly respected for his industriousness. Japanese proverb: "Getting rich means to invite the rat." Those born in the Year of the Rat are likely to acquire great riches.

OX: The water buffalo is revered for his patience and strength. Although he was outwitted by the rat, on rare occasions he can become ferocious. Those born in the Year of the Ox are alert, patient and strong, not impulsive and weak.

TIGER: Along with the dragon, the tiger holds a supreme place in Oriental folklore. The markings on his forehead resemble the Chinese character *wang*, meaning "royal." Those born in the Year of the Tiger are strong, brave, aggressive, and active.

HARE: Well known throughout Asia. The hare and the moon legend went from China to Japan, but in Japan the hare is put to work pounding rice on the moon. Those born in the Year of the Hare are always happy, but rather timid. They are generally well liked.

DRAGON: The only mythical animal in the zodiac, which shows how important it is, along with the tiger. The dragon's wisdom is supreme. Those lucky enough to be born in the Year of the Dragon are endowed with the four blessings (harmony, virtue, prosperity, and long life). They are healthy, energetic, and brave.

SNAKE: The snake (serpent) is associated with the sun. The snake represents deceit and cunning. Those born in the Year of the Snake are wise, determined, and persistent. They do not like to fail.

HORSE: The horse represents strength, intelligence, and sensitivity. In Buddhism, the horse is honored as one of the Seven Treasures. Those born in the Year of the Horse are cheerful, popular, and accomplish a great deal.

RAM: The sheep or goat represents cooperation, since it moves about in flocks. This animal holds an important position in Asian folklore. Those born in the Year of the Ram are considered to be more fortunate than those born in other animal years. They are tender-hearted, sympathetic, generous, unassertive, talented, and have good taste. They shun leadership.

MONKEY: The monkey plays an important role in early Chinese creation myths and is well known through Asia. The monkey is in the famous Japanese story, "See No Evil; Hear No Evil; Speak No Evil," carved at the Nikko shrines. Those born in the Year of the Monkey have outstanding memories, are curious, clever, skillful, and inventive.

COCK: The cock is the messenger of the sun goddess. The crown on his head is said to be a mark of literary spirit. He is also brave and sure. Those born in the Year of the Cock are always busy and tend to undertake more than they can manage. They are not in the least shy, and are blunt and outspoken.

DOG: Some dogs became such favorites of early emperors that they had an official rank and appropriate dress. Possessing a dog is to possess good fortune. The dog is a faithful guardian. People born in the Year of the Dog have a deep sense of duty, are honest, and get on well with people.

BOAR: Among Semitic people, the pig was considered sacred because it taught people how to plow by turning up the earth with its nose. It symbolizes courage and a ferocious nature. Those born in the Year of the Boar are thought to be courageous and headstrong. They are honest and pure but short tempered. Make friends with a boar and you have a friend for life.

Use the following time table to figure out: (1) the name and characteristics of the year in which students were born, (2) the current year and what forces are in operation, and (3) the name and characteristics of the year in which family and friends were born.

Rat	1972	1984	1996
Ox	1973	1985	1997
Tiger	1974	1986	1998
Hare	1975	1987	1999
Dragon	1976	1988	2000
Snake	1977	1989	2001
Horse	1978	1990	2002
Ram	1979	1991	2003
Monkey	1980	1992	2004
Cock	1981	1993	2005
Dog	1982	1994	2006
Boar	1983	1995	2007

LUCKY AND UNLUCKY DAYS

In India, the Hindus regard even numbers as unlucky. So it is common in the folklore for someone to have a lucky day where things go well, and an unlucky day where one has to be very careful. Lucky days are ruled by the moon and unlucky days are ruled by the sun. (Monday, Wednesday, Thursday, and Friday are lucky days.)

Many other cultures have certain days of the week designated as lucky or unlucky. For example, when the 13th day of the month falls on a Friday, it is considered to be exceptionally unlucky. In this old verse, we note that the day of the week on which a child is born helps to determine its fate:

> Monday's child is fair of face,
> Tuesday's child is full of grace,
> Wednesday's child is full of woe,
> Thursday's child has far to go,
> Friday's child is loving and giving,
> Saturday's child works hard for its living,
> And a child that's born on the Sabbath day
> Is fair and wise and good and gay.

Resource

Sun, Ruth Q. *The Asian Animal Zodiac* (Japan: Charles E. Tuttle Company, 1974)

SUGGESTED ACTIVITIES FOR THE CLASSROOM

1. MAGICAL CREATURES IN PICTURE BOOK ILLUSTRATIONS

Read and study a wide variety of Asian folk tales and be on the lookout for the magical dragons, turtle, unicorn, and phoenix. Note the different ways they are depicted by the illustrators. Students can work in teams to create their own large versions of these four creatures using mural paper and tempera paint. Cut out the giant creatures, hang them around the room, and surround them with 3 x 5 cards that each contain a summary of a tale that students have read.

2. A GIANT STORYTELLING DRAGON ROBE

During the study of the Asian cultures, have students make a giant papiermâché head of a dragon. Paint it with bright colors. Attach a flowing yellow or red cloth robe to the dragon's head. At least four or five students can stand under the robe (make head holes) to tell a single folk tale. Decide in advance which part each student is responsible for telling, and have them practice. Decide if the dragon will move rhythmically through the audience, or to another part of the room, as part of the action in the story.

When not in use, the dragon can be hung in an inviting section of the room that has a library of folk tales.

3. CREATE A MAGIC BEAST DICTIONARY (BEASTIONARY)

Find library books about magical beasts found in folk tales of many lands. On a large chart, record the beast's name, country, a short description and then make an illustration. A good resource book is Robin Palmer's *Dragons, Unicorns and Other Magical Beasts* with illustrations by Don Bolognese (New York: Henry Z. Walck, Inc., 1966).

4. YOUR BEHAVIOR IS BEASTLY!

Read Katherine Paterson's *Tale of the Mandarin Ducks* (see the children's books section) and note the beastly (uncivilized) behavior of the lord. Compare this beastly behavior to another beast tale such as *Beauty and the Beast* with illustrations by Mercer Mayer and Marianna Mayer. How do the beasts differ? Who are the major characters in each story? Learn to pronounce their names. How does "beauty" figure into each tale? How does the magic power of love figure into each tale? How do the royal settings differ? Make a chart to record your findings. Then keep reading beast tales from other countries to learn what motivates beasts to act as they do.

5. MAKE YOUR OWN VERSION OF A HIPPOGRIFF

Students can make a combination beast. The dragon has been described as having the head of a camel, horns of an elk, eyes of a rabbit, ears of a cow, neck of a snake, belly of a frog, scales of a carp, claws of a hawk, and feet of a lion. After creating this colorful dragon, students can write or tell a trickster story or a tale with a lesson, with the magical creature as a main character. Asian dragons are in control of lakes, rivers, seas, and the rain.

6. SILHOUETTE PUPPETS

The art of storytelling with flat puppets behind a sheet, with the light also coming from behind the sheet, is a high art in Indonesia and other parts of Asia. Students can work in teams to create the characters and the story dialogue from favorite Asian folk tales.

It is also possible for students to do silhouette storytelling but, instead of using puppets, *they* become the characters and move in and out from behind the white sheet that acts as a screen upon which the story is played out.

7. ENRICHING SOCIAL STUDIES

Making puppets that reflect cultures from many different lands naturally gets children involved with types of clothing, with shelter and climate relationships, and with coastal or inland locations, along with other information. A good resource book is *Folk Puppet Plays for the Social Studies* by Margaret Weeks Adair and Elizabeth Patapoff (New York: The John Day Company, 1974).

8. THE MAGIC PEARL

The Magic Pearl is said to be the dragon's most precious possession, which it guards like a hawk. It has the power to make things multiply. Also, the dragon has a voice like the clanging of copper pans. To learn more, read *The Dragon's Pearl* by Julie Lawson, with artistic illustrations by Paul Morin (New York: Clarion, 1993). Perhaps this tale will inspire students to write stories with sound accompaniment.

9. YIN/YANG

This term signifies balance as the law of existence. It is often represented as a circle that is half black and half white. Yin/yang represents positive and negative, heaven and earth, male and female. If something is not balanced, it causes trouble and requires attention. Students can compile a list of "opposite" characteristics in storybook characters (such as greedy/generous, kind/mean, and so on).

Select one of the unbalanced terms and begin to weave a story around this concept. The story will require at least two characters that display the opposite characteristics, the conflict, and a bit of magic to help with the solution.

10. A TASTE OF HONEY

In the New Year, the Kitchen God (an idol) is burned and ascends to heaven to report on the behavior of the Chinese and the Japanese family. So that he will speak only sweet words, the lips of the doll (or figure that represents the Kitchen God) are smeared with honey. It would make a good folk tale if a Kitchen God got away before the honey got smeared on its lips.

11. DRAGON EAST MEETS DRAGON WEST

If the dragons of the east breathe mist and the dragons of the west breathe fire, do they cancel one another out in their quest for power? Sounds like good material for a folk tale. Write the story on dragon shapes.

12. THE UNICORNS TO THE RESCUE

If unicorns can dip their horns into stagnant waters and the water becomes purified, what would happen if we could contact a unicorn about our water pollution problems? How do we write to a unicorn? How do we describe the conditions of our earth? How can we get help? Brainstorm possible solutions and set up a writing center for letters and for magical stories.

13. JAPAN'S NATIONAL FLOWER

The chrysanthemum is the national flower of Japan and a symbol of purity, perfection, and long life. Write a story about a chieftain who will give his daughter's hand in marriage to the one who can bring her a dozen chrysanthemums. Aha! But there is one catch. The flowers grow on the other side of the forest, which is filled with demons and ghosts!

14 THE ASIAN ZODIAC

Have students learn about the animals of the zodiac shown in this section. Also, help them to determine how they would be perceived if they were born into an Asian family, by figuring out what animal represents them in their birth year. What animal characteristics are at work in the current year? This study can lead to much research about family members, classmates, and can foster writing, language development, creative dramatics, painting, and so on.

CELEBRATIONS

Asia is a huge continent, and consists of many countries in Central, North, East, West, South, and Southeast Asia. In addition, the archipelago of Indonesia is considered an Asian culture, as are parts of the former Soviet Union. For this reason, there are celebrations taking place almost every day in this part of the world.

THE BONTEN FESTIVAL

This festival takes place in Akita in February. Each team of young men represents a district of the city and each has its own "bonten" (a ten-foot bamboo pole topped with a figure of the animal of the year). Every year is named for an animal according to the old Oriental calendar and twelve animal names are used. Each cycle begins with the Year of the Rat and is followed by the Years of the Ox, Tiger, Rabbit, Dragon, Snake, Horse, Sheep, Monkey, Cock, Dog, and Boar. If, for example, it is the Year of the Horse, all of the figures on the bontens are of the horse. The team members must race to carry their long bamboo pole up an icy slope and place it inside the temple. For the winners, it means good luck for that zodiac sign.

BOYS FESTIVAL—TIME TO FLY THE CARP

In late April and early May, boys are celebrated all over Japan. People buy kites shaped like carp, the fish that symbolizes strength, courage and determination, and place them in their yards to dart and dive in the wind. On this day, a Japanese family takes a traditional bath called a "shobu-ya." It is believed that water can wash away bad luck. The family members soap, scrub and clean themselves before getting into the tub to relax in the hot water. Papa soaks first, then mama, then each child.

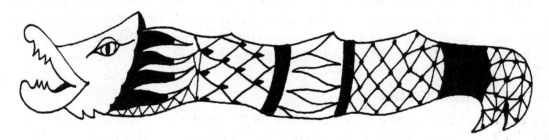

GENJITSU—NEW YEAR'S DAY

This is a special festival in Japan. On New Year's morning, the family dresses in new clothes. They eat soup, black beans, and seaweed (symbolizing happiness).

After the meal, children receive their special New Year's gifts, usually coins sealed in special gift envelopes.

On the second day, the "first writing" or *kakizome* occurs. Every family member uses the art of brush and ink to write a poem or proverb on a long piece of paper. They are shared, and some are hung in the home.

GIRLS FESTIVAL—HINA MATURI, OR DOLL FESTIVAL

This takes place on March 3. At one time, people rubbed themselves with paper dolls, as if rubbing out the evil spirits. They then threw the paper dolls into the river. Later, dolls were made of clay. Then, still later, the dolls were made in the image of the emperor and his family and became so stylized and lovely that today young girls acquire a doll collection. A traditional doll set includes 15 figures along with trees, furniture, and other objects. This is displayed on a rack of seven shelves that is covered with red cloth. A good resource book is *A Year of Japanese Festivals* by Sam and Beryl Epstein, illustrated by Gordon Laite (Champaign, IL: Garrard Publishing Company, 1974).

GUNG HAY FAT CHOY (CHINESE NEW YEAR)

This is a time for families to get together. The Chinese add a year to their age on New Year's Day, regardless of the day on which they were born. It's one big grand birthday party! It's a time for new clothes, time to fill the home with flowers and fruit, and time for families to remember their ancestors. There are money gifts wrapped in red paper for the children, called *lai see*, and firecrackers are set off to scare away any evil spirits.

At this celebration, the ceremonial dragon winds its way through the throngs of happy people in the streets. Those who are under the dragon are doing some fancy foot work to help hold it up. It is an honor to be chosen for this task.

CHINESE FESTIVAL CHARACTERS AND COLORS

The new year festival is named for one of the twelve animals of the Chinese zodiac, on a rotation basis. The symbols for the months are thousands of years old, and they include the monkey, rooster, dog, boar, rat, ox, tiger, hare, dragon, serpent, horse, and ram.

The joyous colors of the festival are orange and red, and people make pyramids of oranges and apples in their homes for good luck.

The celebration can last as long as a week. There are art exhibits, karate contests, dancing, and a parade with papier-mâché figures of the lion. The best part of the celebration is the Golden Dragon Parade, with

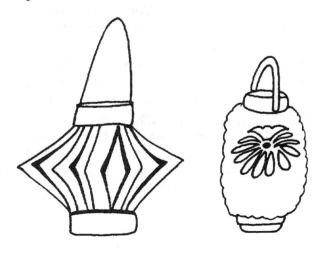

many people holding up the long dragon as it weaves back and forth along the street. The dragon is a symbol for goodness and strength.

INDONESIAN CELEBRATION

The natives of Bali celebrate a 210-day ritual cycle. This may be related to the rice growing cycle, since rice is an important part of the culture. During the holidays, offerings of fruit-of-the-earth are made to the gods and to ancestors. A procession of women, dressed in their finest native clothing, take artfully arranged food from their village to the Hindu temple by carrying the sculpture-like construction on their heads. The colorful food, beautifully displayed like a work of art, contains many fruits, rice cakes, and even roasted chickens, skillfully arranged in the foot-high displays. The women march in a procession through the temple grounds, remove the offerings from their heads, and place them in front of the statue at the temple. The priest purifies the offerings using holy water and incense. After the gods and ancestors have consumed the "essence" of the food, it may be eaten by the worshippers.

Each home has its own temple, called a "sanggah," and during this celebration, every family sets out an offering that consists of food, water, and fire (burning incense) on a palm frond.

BALI RITES-OF-PASSAGE CEREMONIES

The "manusa yadnya" (life-cycle) rites are designed for a baby's spiritual and material well-being. Among others, they include:

1. THE THREE-MONTH CEREMONY. When the baby is 90 days old, its feet may touch the earth for the first time. Prior to this time, the baby is carried around.

2. THE 210-DAY CEREMONY. The baby's first birthday (otonan) is celebrated. The baby's hair is cut for the first time, and the mother announces to the village that her child has arrived.

3. THE TOOTH-FILING CEREMONY. When a child reaches the age of puberty, the tooth-filing ceremony occurs. During the ceremony, both upper canine teeth are filed down slightly to symbolically erase the "animal nature" in a person. At this time it is expected that children should have control over their emotions.

THE FESTIVAL OF TOOLS (VISVAKARMA PUJA)

This religious festival is held in India and is dedicated to the Hindu Visvakarma, the patron god of all artisans. In every home and in every place of work, a pitcher is set in a place of honor (the pitcher represents the god). Then, people place their work tools by the pitcher—the artist places brushes, school children place a book, musicians place their instruments, tailors place their scissors and needle and thread, fishermen place their nets, and so on. A candle is lit and people bow and pray silently, giving thanks for the help of the tool in the past and asking for good service in the future.

SPRING FESTIVALS

Holi, The Fire Festival, is a major celebration in India. Another festival is The Poet's Spring. Since many poets have written about spring, young men wear yellow (the sacred color of India) and people wear something green (to honor the green earth). During the festivals there is fasting, feasting, bonfires, and dancing.

THE DOUBLE NINTH HOLIDAY

In Taiwan, there is a festival on the ninth day of the ninth month. This celebration is two-fold in that it is for those who enjoy strenuous activities and also for those who are of a more artistic temperament. Mountain-climbing expeditions and poetry writing activities are held.

DRAGON BOAT FESTIVAL IN TAIWAN

This festival usually occurs on the fifth day of June. Two boats, decked out with the head and tail of a dragon, race against each other at one time at various sites. In each boat, there is a person at the helm, a drummer, and the 20-member crew with oars for rowing. Other teams watch and wait for their turn as day turns to dusk.

For this special holiday time, homes are thoroughly cleaned, and herbs are added to foods to ward off disease. Children wear sachets of herbs and spices attached to their clothing to cast off germs. (There is a similarity here with the European and North American custom of "spring cleaning." Also, children in Italy wear garlic around their neck to ward off germs.) Today we know that garlic and herbs and spices *do* have medicinal value.

SUGGESTED ACTIVITIES FOR THE CLASSROOM

1. HAPPY NEW YEAR IN ANY LANGUAGE

Work with students to elicit the celebrations of the New Year in their family. Are there special foods served? Is the day or evening spent in a special way? Ask students to interview their grandparents (or an older person) to find out how they celebrated the New Year when they were growing up. Students can look for customs that have been retained, and some that may have been lost or weakened. *Holidays Around the World* by Carol Greene (Chicago: Children's Press, 1982) is a good beginning resource.

2. THAT LITTLE RED ENVELOPE

In China, children receive a red envelope with a money gift for the New Year. Perhaps students can receive a little red envelope (or any color) with a treasure message inside that gives them a choice of an activity. They can "spend" it any day during the month of January. (Some suggested treasure opportunities include looking through picture books, painting a picture at the easel, an extra half hour exploring at the science table, an extra half hour working with math manipulatives from the McMath-to-go Shelf, and so on).

3. THE ARMCHAIR VIDEOTAPE TRAVELERS

The National Geographic Society has a number of videotapes on Asia that can be secured from the local library. They have tapes of countries all over the globe.

Set up the monitor, and place the chairs as one would inside an airplane. Students enter with a "passport" and have it stamped. Then, the hostess asks for all seatbelts to be fastened (meaning "quiet") while directions are given. During the video, there can be a time when the hostesses and steward distribute small bags of popcorn. Since many of the tapes are an hour in length, perhaps the travel time could be spread over two days. These videotapes will enrich classroom discussion, story writing, and art work.

4. ELEPHANT DESIGNS

Students can trace a large pattern of an elephant on grey construction paper, and decorate it with colorful felt markers for a parade. These can be displayed around the border of the bulletin board on "Festivals." Sequins and other materials that can be glued onto the elephant add to the festive look.

5. THE GIANT DRAGON

This is the time to create the giant dragon, if you have not already done so. The head can be made from papier-mâché, and a long colorful cloth can be attached. The cloth can be purchased material, or students can decorate a yellow cloth with red felt markers. This mist-breathing dragon of the East, in charge of oceans, clouds, thunderstorms, and typhoons, will excite the imagination of the learners and spur them on in their study of the Asian cultures.

6. THE DOUBLE NINTH DAY

This is a wonderful opportunity to celebrate the poets and artists, and also the gymnasts and contact-sports players. Have students sign up for either one or the other, and on this double day set aside some time for both activities. This gives students with different learning styles and different learning capabilities an opportunity to excel.

7. SPEAKING OF DOUBLES, HOW ABOUT SEVENS?

Howard Gardner (Harvard University psychologist) has suggested that there are at least seven varieties of intelligences. These are: mathematical, verbal, musical, bodily, spatial, introspection, and interpersonal. Give students opportunities to develop all seven—on a regular weekly basis. Time can be built in for learning opportunities during the school day, during recess, and during free choice time. The following is a list of ideas to get you started, but keep adding to the list. Look for children's strengths (and build upon them) and look for areas of weakness (and build them up):

a. Mathematical—a wide variety of games, symbols, opportunity to use logical thinking, manipulatives, challenging puzzles

b. Verbal—opportunity to develop new ways to describe things, looking at an item and describing it in as many ways as you can, opportunities to speak and to listen

c. Musical—listening to music, exploring with sound, playing an instrument, listening to nature sounds

d. Bodily—moving with sports, creative interpretive movement in dance, opportunity for using large muscles

e. Spatial—puzzles, challenges of building items in 3-D, working with clay so that the whole figure must be developed, soap or wood carving

f. Introspection—identifying feelings, expressing self in writing, with art materials, with music

g. Interpersonal—working in groups as leaders and participants, valuing the ideas of others, showing respect for the opinions of others with statements of regard, "I like Carmen's idea that ..."

8. THE POET'S SPRING

Have each student select and memorize a poem that they can then illustrate with colored chalks. Play background music while listening to poetry. Have students read a wide variety of poems written for children (such as books by

X. J. Kennedy, J. Patrick Lewis, Shel Silverstein, Jack Prelutsky, Aileen Fisher, Myra Cohn Livingston, and so on). Then have students write their own poetry. *It Doesn't Have to Rhyme* by Eve Merriam (New York: Macmillan, 1986) is a helpful resource book.

ARTS AND CRAFTS

In the ancient civilizations of this part of the world, art has always played a major role. In Bali, for example, there is no separate word in the language for art because art is incorporated into daily life in terms of color, design, and even body movement. In other countries, art is used in a broader sense, such as the art of arranging flowers in a vase, or the art of carving food decoratively and arranging it artistically on a plate.

This area of the world has given us fine china, the art of making paper including rice paper, luscious textiles, batiks, and brush painting. Even the writing, done with brush strokes, is considered an art form.

The silk that is woven into fabric and made into clothing is exquisite. Woodworking is a fine art with carvings of intricate designs, and silver jewelry in Indonesia is delicately crafted from fine strands.

The world is enriched by the art work and the crafts from the many Asian cultures.

SUGGESTED ACTIVITIES FOR THE CLASSROOM

1. THE ART OF PAPER MAKING

During the Han Dynasty (202 B.C.-A.D. 220), the Chinese invented the art of making paper. For a student activity, paper can be made in the classroom.

Students can draw or paint on the paper, or use it as a background for a work of art that they make from cut paper.

2. THE PUZZLING FINE ART OF MAKING PORCELAIN

China dishes were developed and perfected in China as long ago as 3000 B.C. Secrets of porcelain making were so closely guarded that some have been lost and to this day are still unknown. For example, the art of painting fish, insects and animals inside of bowls in such a way that they can only be seen when the bowl is filled with water was a technique used long ago that is considered a "lost art." How was it done? What special combinations of ingredients were used? Students might want to speculate about this and experiment with clay and colored designs.

3. ASIAN POTTERY DESIGNS

In addition to its beauty, the pottery from this part of the world contains certain symbols. Four flowers symbolize the four seasons: Spring (peony), Summer (lotus blossom), Autumn (chrysanthemum), and Winter (flowering plum). The iris stands for strength and courage, and the dragon stands for supernatural power.

For a student activity, use two sizes of paper plates and a cup, and have students become designers by creating their special set of china. Blue is one of the favored colors, but any combination of colors can be used.

4. FACE PAINTING THE KATHAKALI WAY

For thousands of years, people around the world on almost every continent have painted their faces with designs. These designs represent gods, demons, or animals from myths and legends. In southwest India, the Kathakali Theatre performers are known by the faces they are "wearing." Katha means "story" and Kali means "play." It may take hours to make up the face, so makeup artists are used by the actors.

Inexpensive face-painting makeup can be found in bookstores, toy stores, drugstores, or variety stores. In the United States, face painting is popular at storytelling festivals, fairs, and on Halloween. An excellent resource book is *Painting Faces* by Suzanne Haldane (New York: Dutton Children's Books, 1988).

5. FACE MASKS

If it is inadvisable to use face painting in school for a storytelling event, have students devise a face mask to use. A paper plate can be used as the base. Use bright tempera paint or thick felt pens for the designs. Completely fill in the space so that no background is showing. These masks are works of art and can be displayed in an area of the room to encourage storytelling. For example, in Korea some masks are worn for protection against the evil spirits. In Thailand, a funeral mask is used to cover the face of the person during burial so that the personality will remain with the body. Knowing this can enrich the storytelling.

Paper plates, paper bags, and masks designed by the students and cut from heavy paper can add to the reading and writing connection in the classroom. Students can wear their disguise and write a powerful story from the point of view of the character depicted by the mask.

6. KITSUNE MASK

This fox mask in Japan is very popular. Fox masks are also popular in China. There is a belief that the fox is very powerful and magical, and can change into a human being after many hundreds of years. Students can design fox masks and add a variety of materials—from fake fur to sequins along with other available materials—to make a unique fox. Then, wearing their creations, have them go very quietly (as quiet as a fox) to the library on a fox hunt for books that have a fox as a major character, a fox in the title, or a fox shown in a picture book illustration. They can share the findings of their fox hunt back in the classroom.

7. SOUTHEAST ASIAN TEXTILE ART

The famous double-woven "ikat" cloths, sometimes referred to as "endek," are highly prized. Both the warp and the weft have designs, which makes weaving difficult. Dye is sometimes applied to the unwoven weft threads once the loom is dressed. The weaver then aligns the warp and weft colors during the weaving process. The range of designs includes birds, trees, flowers, snakes, and geometric designs.

For the fabric known as "Songket brocades," the weaver uses gold and silver threads to make the fabric look richer. For centuries, this cloth was used only by people from higher castes.

Black and white large checkered cloth is also woven. This is used during certain ceremonial times for dressing all the statues. The black/white represents the yin/yang or good/evil presence in man.

Students can make cardboard looms, if they have not already done so, and intersperse gold and silver threads into their weaving. Try partner weaving with black and white yarns. Or, after the loom is dressed, students can outline a simple design on the threads and color it in with felt-tip pens of different colors. Then, weave over the design, making sure to match up the colors.

8. PUPPETRY AND FOLKLORE

The Indonesians use hand-made marionettes and puppets for theater time. Through this medium, the children learn the stories that are handed down from generation to generation. There may be puppet shows weekly for children. And there can be puppet shows during the time of celebrations.

Shadow puppets on a long stick are also used. The light comes from behind a large white sheet, and the audience recognizes the puppet characters by their shapes. The narrative is added, and the fun begins. (Refer to the folklore section.) After reading a variety of folk tales, have a discussion of "silhouettes." What features are needed to make a shadow puppet look like a rabbit, a fox, or a tiger? Have students experiment with exaggerated ears for the rabbit or teeth for the tiger and create their flat shadow puppet. Set up the white sheet and the background light, and practice storytelling with these props.

9. THE ASIAN DRAGON

The dragon is used in many Asian arts and crafts. Bhutan is called "land of the dragon." The Chinese dragon is thought to be responsible for thunder and lightning. All dragons have four claws, except for the dragon of the emperor, which has five claws. Yellow is the color of the exceptional dragons! The dragon is a symbol of power from a supernatural source. Have students examine colorful dragons from picture books and information books. Spread mural paper on the floor, and have students sketch (with chalk) and paint (use sponge painting) a long, winding, colorful dragon. This can even be cut out and hung from the ceiling. Add ribbons for nostril steam.

10. THE ROYAL ELEPHANT

In Thailand, elephants appear in paintings, fabrics, and ceramics. In Thailand, along with other Asian countries, elephants travel in long processions. They are decorated with rich colors and patterns painted on their head, legs, body, sides, back, and down the front of their trunk. They often wear a decorative tapestry strapped onto their back. Some elephants, looking like a work of art, have been known to carry the royal family on their backs.

This is a day like no other at the easel. First, each student needs to paint a large gray elephant. After it dries, students can decorate their elephants with bright colors and designs. Have them use the gadget printing

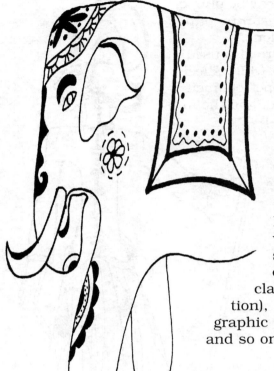

technique of dipping objects (paper clips, nail head, thread spool, toothpicks, and so on) in bright paint, placing the object on the elephant, pressing, and lifting. After drying, these elephants can then be cut out, backed with paper, stapled or glued around the edges, and stuffed with torn bits of paper to give them a rounded look. More decorations can be added if necessary. The elephants make a colorful procession around the classroom when hung on the walls. Also, they motivate students to seek out and read stories about elephants. Have the elephant "share" its story with the class by introducing itself (characterization), telling what book it is from (bibliographic information), where it lives (setting), and so on.

11. COUNTING

Count Your Way Through China by Jim Haskins, illustrations by Dennis Hockerman (Minneapolis: Carolrhoda Books, Inc., 1987) introduces the reader to the characters and pronunciations for the numerals 1 through 10. Each number is used to give factual information about the country in terms of its arts, food, location, government, and so on. Other books in this series are *Count Your Way Through Japan, ... Russia*, and *...the Arab World*.

TANGRAMS AND GAMES

The following games are representative of this area of the world, but are not intended to be complete in themselves. As for tangrams, these puzzles originated in China. According to legend, the original tangram was a beautiful 4-inch tile square that was accidentally dropped by a servant. The tile broke into seven pieces, or tans. In an effort to put it back together again, the servant began making many designs.

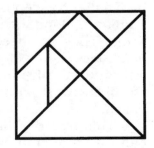

TANGRAM PUZZLES

Make sturdy tangram pieces and laminate them, or cover them with clear self-stick vinyl. Then, use the tangrams for a guessing game by having students use the seven pieces to create the shapes of birds, animals, houses, trees and other objects, while fellow students try to guess what they are. (See the reproducible activity pages.)

THE TANGRAM COVER-UP

Create a tangram bird or flower or tree from one color and paste it onto a sheet of paper that is a contrasting color, such as orange on blue. Then, make the same tangram shape and paste it onto another tone of the same color, so that there is very little contrast (for example, orange on red-orange). Have students compare the two sets.

Use the one that is more difficult to see to introduce the concept of "camouflage." Go on a camouflage hunt through picture books or science books that show jungle animals or woodland animals in their natural habitat. Have students make construction paper storybook illustrations showing magic creatures in their pictures that are camouflaged. (Examples: a green frog hidden by tall blades of green grass in a spring meadow; a large gray bird behind a gray rock on a dreary, rainy day background; or a witch in black on a dark blue cloudy night; and so on.)

TANGRAM FINGER PUZZLES

Students can work in pairs using two sets of tangrams. Spread one set of tangrams on the counter and keep the second set in an envelope. Student #1 can close his eyes and put his hands behind his back. Student #2 must place a tangram piece (from the envelope) in the hand of Student #1. With eyes closed, Student #1 feels the shape, and then opens his eyes and must point to the tangram shape on the counter that is exactly like the one he is holding. If correct, score one point. If incorrect, no point is scored. Students take turns with this exercise until the first one with 10 points win.

THE MAGIC SEVEN TANGRAM STORY

Seven is a magic number in many folk tales. Have students create a "Magic Seven Tangram Story." Somehow, the seven pieces have become separated (problem) and must find each other in order to live happily ever after. Illustrate the tale with seven pictures.

THE STICK HOP

This game can be played with two teams of 3 to 6 players. Lay out a row of sticks for each team, about 1-1/2 feet apart.

The first player on each team, at a given signal, hops on one foot over every stick, turns around, picks up the first stick, and hops back over the sticks. She taps the next player, who does the same thing. (The sticks are put in a container after each play.)

The object of the game is to be the first team to put all of the sticks in the container. If the person who is "it" jumps on a stick or moves it with the foot at any time, he or she must return to the first stick and begin the stick hop all over again.

CRAB RACE GAME

This game can be played with only two players, or with two teams of players. No materials are necessary.

This race is run on all fours and *backwards* from a starting point to a designated ending line. Backwards can mean on hands and feet with stiff legs, or, for variation, on hands and knees. Second player must be given a "go" signal when first player reaches the designated line.

LET'S GO FLY A KITE!

Kite flying is a favorite hobby in Japan. Kites can be made in a variety of shapes and sizes, and the carp shape is a favorite with boys. Students can bring kites to school, arrange to make kites, or purchase kites for a special international festival celebration at school. After displaying the kites in the classroom, students can become weather watchers and be on the alert for a breezy day that is just perfect for flying kites.

Folded paper "airplane kites" can be made by each student. Then, in the hallway, set up an airplane kite-flying station and have each student stand on a specified spot and project the kite forward. An assistant can measure and record the distance that the kite traveled. Graph the information. Make different kites and try again.

FUKUWARAI

Think of the game of "Pin the Tail on the Donkey," where blindfolded students are turned around three times and then have to pin on the tail. In Fukuwarai, an outline of a face is made and blindfolded students have to put the features on the face. Sometimes the blank face is worn, or it can be posted on a bulletin board.

SONGS, DANCES, RHYTHMS

CREATIVE MOVEMENT—KUNG FU

The Chinese martial arts, originally used in warfare, are a form of self discipline and rigorous body training that make for a physically and spiritually healthy person. The martial arts traveled from China to Okinawa to Japan and then to Korea. Many children receive training in school because it builds stamina, balance, and coordination. It is also a form of mental exercise (mind over body) and is said to lead to peace of mind. This is especially true of T'ai Chi training.

The Stance

A "stance" can best be described as what an athlete's body looks like just before or during a sport. A team of football players have a stance just prior to the time when the quarterback puts the ball into play; the tennis player has a stance just before swinging the racket to serve the ball; the swimmer has a stance just before diving off the edge of a pool. In Kung Fu, "the stance" is where the novice begins and there are several stances that can be practiced. Students can practice the stances they know, and play guessing games with them. On a volunteer basis, a student can "take a stance" for 20 seconds, then relax, and call upon students who have their hands raised to guess what game they were preparing to play.

The Horse Stance

Stand erect, arms at sides, feet apart, and bend knees. This is one of the first sets of exercises to master. Students can try it for one minute and keep adding time each day in an effort to get the muscles of the legs and lower back in shape. (Serious trainees may practice this exercise for as long as a year without being taught any other techniques, and can eventually stand in this position for as long as an hour.)

The Crane Stance

Stand erect, hold arms out from body (like wings), and stand on one leg with the other leg pulled up to the body.

The object of these exercises is to acquire body skill in coordination and balance, and to literally "be still." As one progresses, movement is added and a group of people practicing their exercises resembles a group of dancers moving simultaneously to the same rhythm. The martial arts are supposedly never used to attack, but always to defend oneself. A good resource book is *The Martial Arts* by Susan Ribner and Dr. Richard Chin (New York: Harper and Row, 1978).

BALI: THE GAMELAN

Gamelan refers to instruments as well as to the people who play them. The two are not separate. The bell-like tones of the gamelan can be heard at all celebrations. Music and dance are an integral part of the life of the people. Since emphasis is upon unity and cooperation, the songs are played with the cooperation of all the musicians.

The anklung, made from bamboo reeds, is played by shaking the bamboo construction with the hand. Large groups of people, again in the spirit of group unity, comprise an orchestra, and each person has one note or tone to contribute.

The concept may be understood more clearly if we liken it to the bell choir of the western world, where each person has one note (or tone) and rings the bell at the appropriate time to make a song complete.

For a student activity, select a familiar tune and distribute several simple instruments (bell, drum, rhythm sticks, jar of rice) to students and determine when each instrument should be heard singly and at the same time. This will take practice, but it is a rewarding activity.

THE MOVEMENT OF THE HANDS

In Asian cultures such as Indonesia, China, Japan, and others, the movement of the hands is very important in performance dancing for an audience. The hands help to convey the story. Boys and girls begin to practice at a very young age to control hand movements, to move hands slowly, to move fingers separately. For a student activity, begin to work with finger plays and motions of the arm, hands and fingers to help portray birds, birds in flight, and bird feathers ruffling in the breeze and in the wind. Have students begin to concentrate on incorporating hand motions while listening to music and with their storytelling experiences.

Resources

Secure videotapes from the local library or from a college collection so that students can view the folk dancing of different areas of the world. A good teacher resource is: *Video Anthology of World Music and Dance, Europe III,* Vol. 22, Romania/Yugoslavia/Bulgaria/Albania. Also, Soviet Union, Vol. 26.

FOOD

Rice is the staple food for this area of the world. Because of the diversity of the people and the religious differences, there is a wide range of styles of cooking and eating. For the coastal regions, there is an abundance of seafood which is boiled, baked, pickled, or dried. Many people use chopsticks, and it is acceptable to lift a bowl of rice to your mouth and push, or shove, the rice inside.

In China, there is a common pot (fan) and accompanying dishes (cai) of vegetables or sometimes meat. The Chinese are aware of the link between what a person eats and how the person feels. Foods are classified as hot (fatty meats, heavily spiced), cold (vegetables, citrus fruits), or neutral (rice) and have an affect on the body's "qi' (chee), or energy level.

In Japan, the meal is artfully arranged and is selected to appeal to the senses. The meal should be pleasing to the eye in its arrangement and different colors; it should have different textures of food; it should smell pleasant, taste good, and sound good. Portions are usually small. It is a compliment in some areas of Asia to make noises while eating crunchy foods and slurping soup. The food sounds are a compliment to the host and hostess and convey the message that the guests are enjoying the meal.

Visit an Oriental market or check at the supermarket for many ready-made items that can be used. For example, ready-to-fill wrappers make egg rolls easy to make. Prepared noodles can be boiled and used in soup that is familiar to children. And cookie and candy treats are available in packages so that students can try them too.

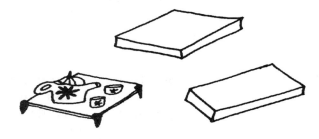

SUGGESTED RECIPES FOR THE CLASSROOM

Gohan (Rice)

1-1/2 cups short-grain white rice 2 cups water	Wash the rice. Put rice and water in saucepan. Cover, boil and simmer over low heat for 15 minutes. DO NOT LIFT THE LID. Leave the rice in the pan for 10 more minutes to steam.

Sushi Rice

1-1/2 cups short-grain white rice 3 tablespoons rice vinegar 2 tablespoons sugar 1-1/2 teaspoons salt	Cook rice, following the directions for gohan. Add vinegar, sugar, and salt to cooked rice, tossing lightly.

Kappa Maki (Cucumber Rolls)

The "kappa" is a mischievous frog creature who often appears in Japanese tales, and who happens to like cucumbers. This cucumber roll is named for him.

1-1/2 cups rice
1 cucumber
4 large sheets of "nori" seaweed
red pickled ginger
soy sauce
vinegar

Cut the cucumber in half lengthwise, scrape out the seeds, and then cut it into long, thin strips. Lay one sheet of nori on a cutting board (or a bamboo rolling mat that can be purchased at Oriental food stores). Spread sushi rice over half of the nori. Lay cucumber strips in the nori, and roll up the nori so that the rice encloses the cucumber. Seal edge with a bit of vinegar. Then cut into 6 slices with a sharp, wet knife. Serve with soy sauce and red pickled ginger.

Falafil in a Wok

1 cup dry falafil mix
1/2 cup water
salad oil
wok
tempura stand

Stir falafil mix and water together, and shape dough into small balls (about 1 inch in diameter). Place 1 inch of oil into wok, add tempura stand, and heat to 350 degrees. Place falafil on tempura stand to fry, turning occasionally, until golden brown. Drain, and serve. Makes approximately 30.

Almond Milk Jelly

This dessert is cut into 1-inch squares, the amount of dessert eaten after a meal—if dessert is served. An Oriental person who first comes to the United States, for example, is surprised to see the huge portions of cake or pie a la mode a person might eat after a regular meal.

This same person would be astounded at a "pot luck" gathering of friends (in the United States) where three or four desserts are placed on a table and an individual might sample more than one. But you might not know that the Oriental person is astounded, because emotions are kept private. You might see a trace of a smile and think that the person is enjoying himself or herself, when in fact the person could be hiding his or her embarrassment.

1-1/4 cup milk
1-1/4 cup water
1 package unflavored gelatin
3 tablespoons sugar
1 teaspoon almond extract

Boil half the water and place into a bowl. Add gelatin to hot water and stir until it is dissolved. Add sugar and stir. Add remaining water, milk, and almond extract. Place in a square pan and put in refrigerator to help it set. Cut this jelly into one-inch squares.

Fruit Kabobs

In Indonesia, many of the small pieces of lamb or beef are cooked on sticks and served hot. Fruit is also abundant in this area. Here is a way to combine the sticks and fruit to make kabobs.

pineapple chunks (fresh or canned)
bananas, cut into slices
fresh strawberries (rinse and dry)
fresh grapes (rinse and dry)

Prepare the fruit and put each fruit on a separate plate. Give each child a long kabob stick (or chopsticks can be purchased from Oriental markets or the supermarket). Have each child select the fruit to be eaten and "construct" a fruit kabob. (Encourage patterning, working slowly, and artfully designing the kabob. Begin eating only when everyone is ready. And, remember, it is not polite to bite the stick or to play with it.)

Rice from the East*

1 cup rice
2 cups cold water
1/2 teaspoon salt

Put rice, water, and salt in a medium saucepan, stir, and cover with a tight lid. Cook over medium heat for 20 minutes, without stirring or lifting the lid. Remove from heat and stir. Eat with chopsticks.

Morning Rice

1 cup cooked rice
dab of butter
1 teaspoon cinnamon
milk
brown sugar

Combine the cooked rice, butter, and cinnamon. Mix well. Then cover with milk and stir. Sprinkle with brown sugar before serving.

---

*Many people eat plain rice. But cut-up bits of meat and vegetable can be added if desired.

Dim Sum (A "Dot to the Heart")

Dim sum means a "dot to the heart," or an appetizer. It is a small portion, or a Chinese finger food, that is the equivalent of the French hors d'oeuvres. They are easy to prepare and usually served with tea.

Egg rolls are an example of dim sum. They are available in many varieties in the frozen food section of supermarkets or in Oriental specialty food stores. Cook according to the directions on the package.

Won Ton Soup

12 cups water
1 scallion, sliced
1 package ready-made won tons
1/2 pound barbecued pork
6 cups chicken stock
1 tablespoon light (in color)
    soy sauce
1/2 head bok choy (greens)
1 tablespoon sesame seed oil

Bring 12 cups of water to boil in a large pot. Add won tons and bring to boil again. When won tons float to surface, remove and strain. Rinse and drain. Bring chicken stock to a boil in the same large pot. Add bok choy and soy sauce. Boil. Slice the barbecued pork and add to soup along with scallions. Carefully drop won tons into soup. Add sesame seed oil and boil for one minute. Serve.

Sweet and Sour Sauce

1/2 cup sugar
1/2 cup catsup
2 cups water
1/2 cup white vinegar
4 tablespoons cornstarch (dissolved
    in 4 tablespoons cold water)
2 green peppers
    (chopped into small pieces)
4 tablespoons pineapple chunks

Combine first four ingredients and bring to a boil. Add cornstarch, stirring constantly, until mixture thickens. Add peppers and pineapple and mix. Use as a dip for fresh vegetables or with crackers.

Resources

Downer, Lesley. *Japanese Food and Drink* (San Francisco: Chronicle Books, 1993).

Shui, Amy, and Stuart Thompson. *Chinese Food and Drink* (San Francisco: Chronicle Books, 1993).

REPRODUCIBLE ACTIVITY PAGES

The Role of the Dragon in Folk Tales (*storytelling mask*)

The Hare in the Moon (*folk tale research*)

The Wayang Kulit Puppets (*making a moving puppet*)

The Folk Tale Fox (*research/book report cover*)

The Role of Food in Folk Tales (*research/record keeping*)

The Animal Winds Blow Through Four Seasons
(*drawing/creative writing*)

What a Refreshing Book Cover! (*visual design*)

Gung Hay Fat Choy (*Chinese New Year celebration*)

Design a China Set Fit for the Emperor's Dragon (*art design*)

A Japanese Carp Festival (*visual design*)

Yin Yang—Keep Your Balance (*language development: opposites*)

Dim Sum (A Dot to the Heart) (*food recipe*)

Hariette the Hot Air Balloonist (*geography*)

I'm Thinking of a Country (*study sheet*)

Do an Author Study—Asia (*Ed Young; Mitsumasa Anno*)

THE ROLE OF THE DRAGON IN FOLK TALES

Dragons of the east breathe mist. Dragons of the west breathe fire. Read several folk tales with dragon characters. Color this one, and cut out the mouth. Use it as a storytelling mask when you share your dragon story.

Cut Out

Name _____   Date _____

THE HARE IN THE MOON

In Asian folk tales, the hare is busy sweeping the moon or pounding rice. In Ireland and Wales, the hare is magical. In Native American tales, the hare is a trickster figure. Read a number of folk tales that include hares.

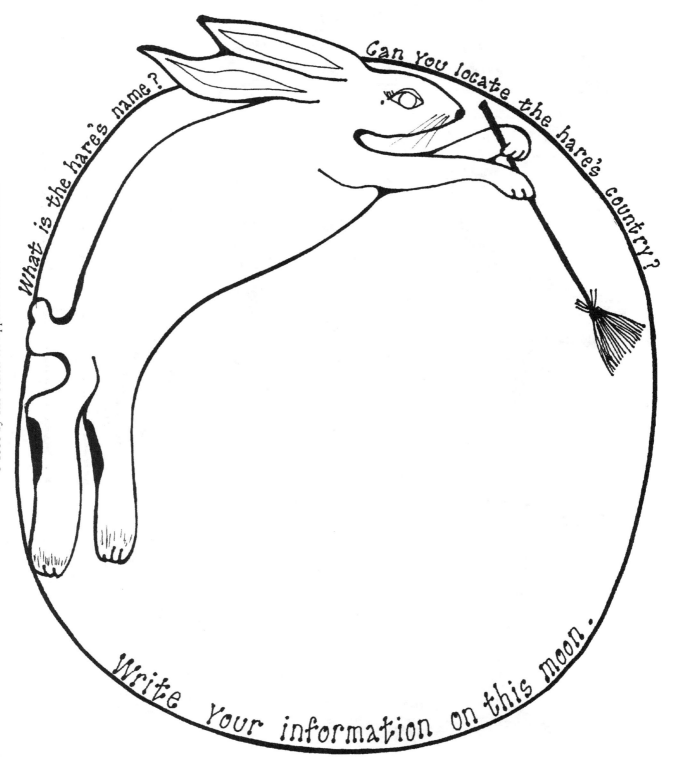

What is the hare's name?

Can you locate the hare's country?

Write your information on this moon.

THE WAYANG KULIT PUPPETS

The shadow puppets of Java and Indonesia are centuries old. The puppeteer moves the puppet behind a white sheet that is lit from the rear. Cut out the figure. Fasten the arms and hands with paper fasteners. Attach a string to each fastener and practice moving the puppet. Tell a story.

THE FOLK TALE FOX

The clever fox is found in folk tales around the world.

Read several stories that have a fox as a major character. Color and cut out this fox and use it as a book cover for your own clever fox tale.

In Asia, when the fox has its 1000th birthday, it turns white, and can no longer play tricks on people. Then what happens to the fox?

THE ROLE OF FOOD IN FOLK TALES

Carefully examine folk tale picture books from around the world. Then, draw and color four different foods from four different countries. Share the information with your classmates.

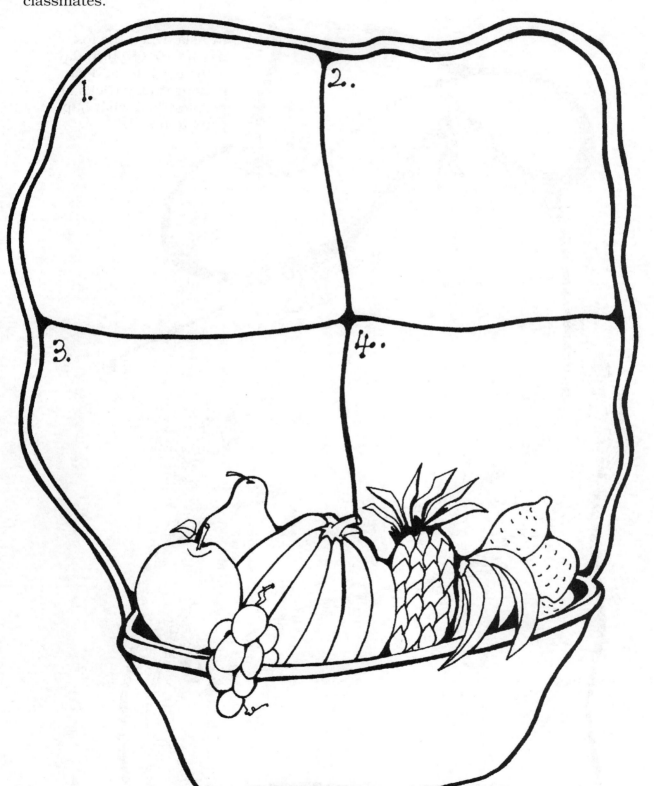

THE ANIMAL WINDS BLOW THROUGH FOUR SEASONS

In Asian stories, the four seasons and four directions are controlled by four animals. Draw each one below: *Winter*—black tortoise; *Spring*—blue dragon; *Summer*—red bird; and *Autumn*—white tiger.

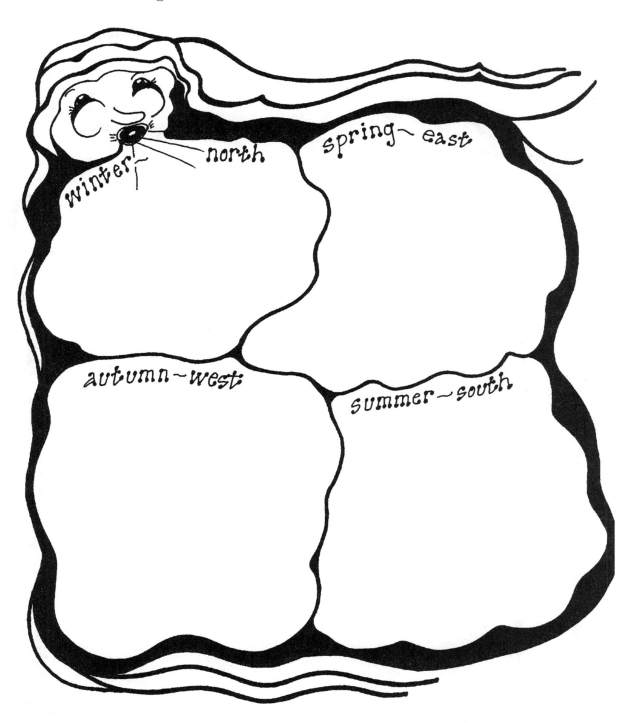

Make up a seasonal story about the wind, the direction, and the animals.

Name _____   Date _____

WHAT A REFRESHING BOOK COVER!

This elephant needs to design a brand new book cover for a favorite story. Select a good picture book and show what the cover would look like if you were the designer.

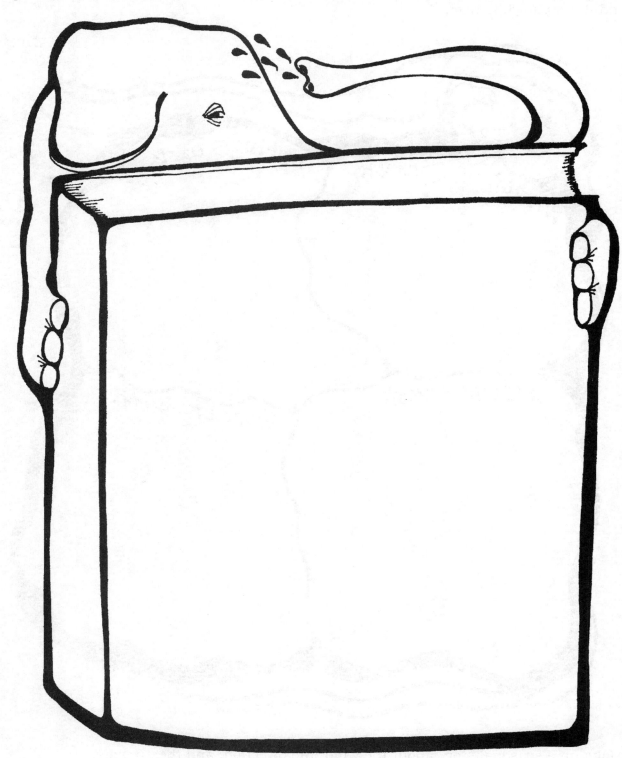

Name _____ Date _____

GUNG HAY FAT CHOY

Red and orange are happy colors for the New Year! Finish designing and coloring this New Year's dragon. Color in the Chinese symbols very carefully. Using a crayon, felt-tipped pen, or brush, practice making the symbols.

DESIGN A CHINA SET FIT FOR THE EMPEROR'S DRAGON

Pottery from Asia contains certain symbols. Flowers play an important part in the design.

Summer—lotus blossom
Autumn—chrysanthemum
Winter—flowering plum
Spring—peony

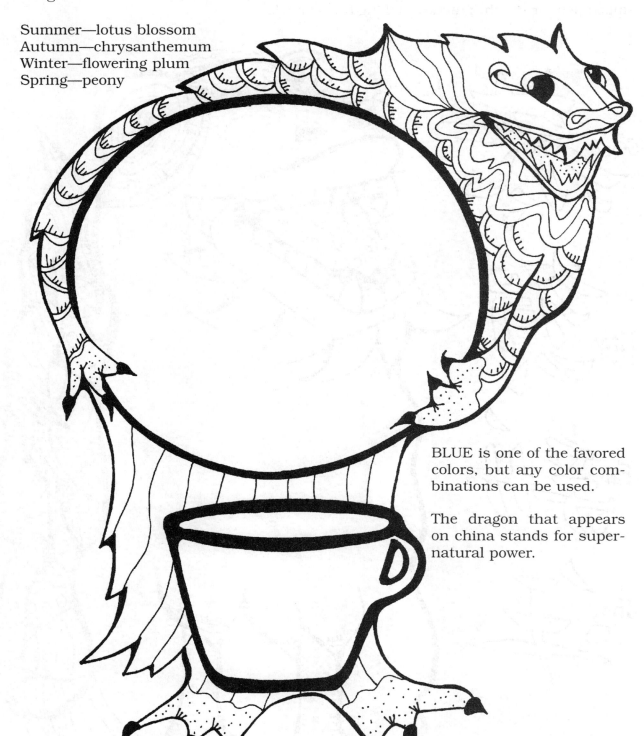

BLUE is one of the favored colors, but any color combinations can be used.

The dragon that appears on china stands for supernatural power.

A JAPANESE CARP FESTIVAL

Decorate this fish with bright, bold colors and shapes. Cut it out and use it as a design on a book cover. In Japan, the carp represents strength and bravery. A cloth carp, brightly decorated, is hung on a bamboo pole outside a house where there is a boy in the family. In some communities, schools of carp, or koinobori, are flown at outdoor spas. Plan a kite festival at your school.

YIN YANG—KEEP YOUR BALANCE

The symbol below represents "yin yang." That is the title given to the idea that there is a balance in the world of opposites.

On the lines below, list things that are the opposite of each other. Some are given to get you started. Compare your ideas with those of your classmates.

What would this proverb mean: "You can have too much of a good thing." (Talk it over).

day _____   night _____   winter _____   _____

hot _____   cold _____   _____   _____

up _____   _____   _____   _____

over _____   _____   _____   _____

north _____   _____   _____   _____

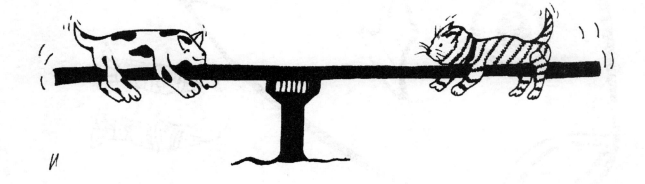

Name ______________________________ Date ______________________

DIM SUM (A Dot to the Heart)

Dim Sum is an appetizer, a small portion, a Chinese finger food that is the equivalent of the French hors d'oeuvres. This small bit of food is referred to as a "dot to the heart." Egg rolls are an example of dim sum. They are available in supermarkets or specialty stores. Try them.

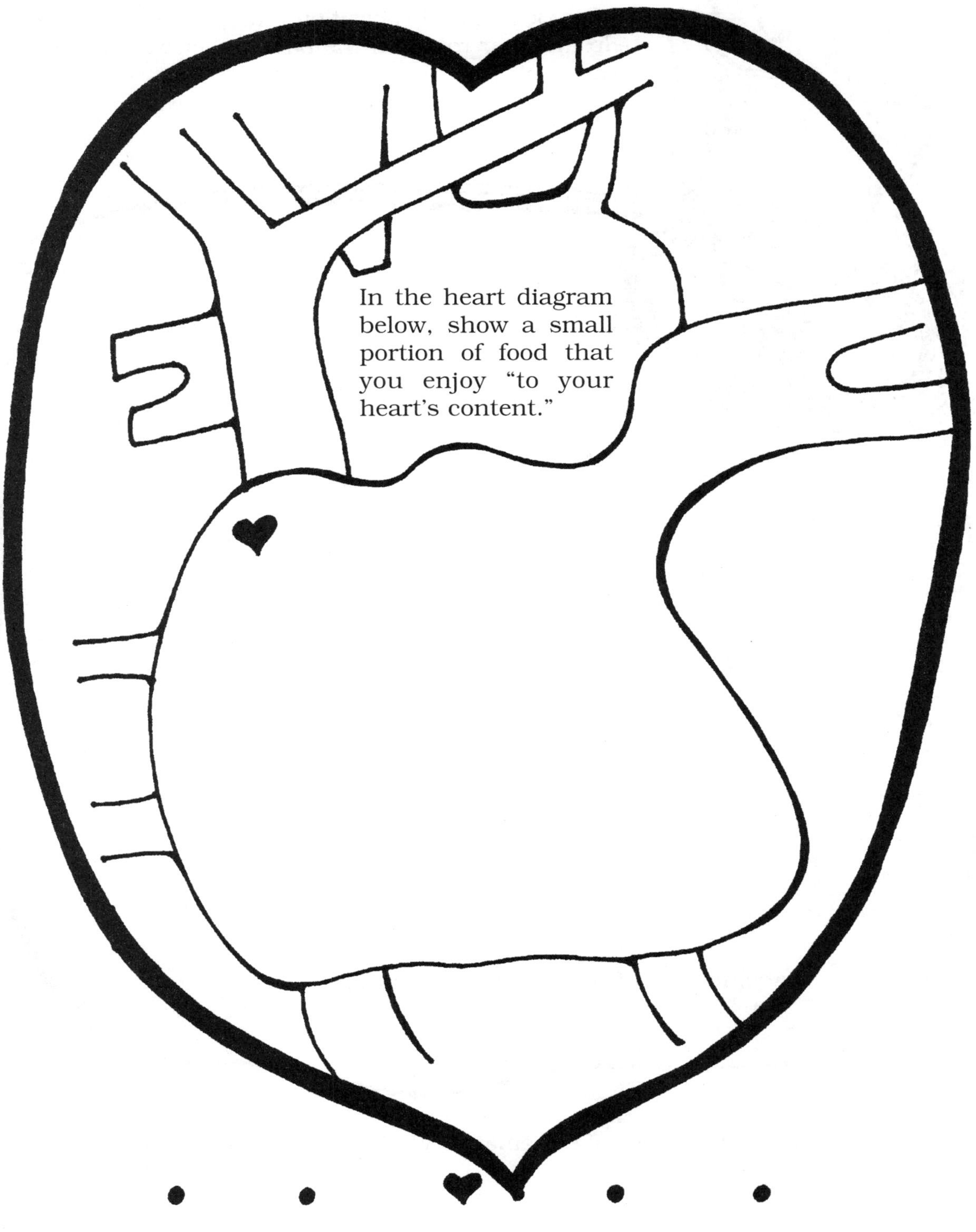
In the heart diagram below, show a small portion of food that you enjoy "to your heart's content."

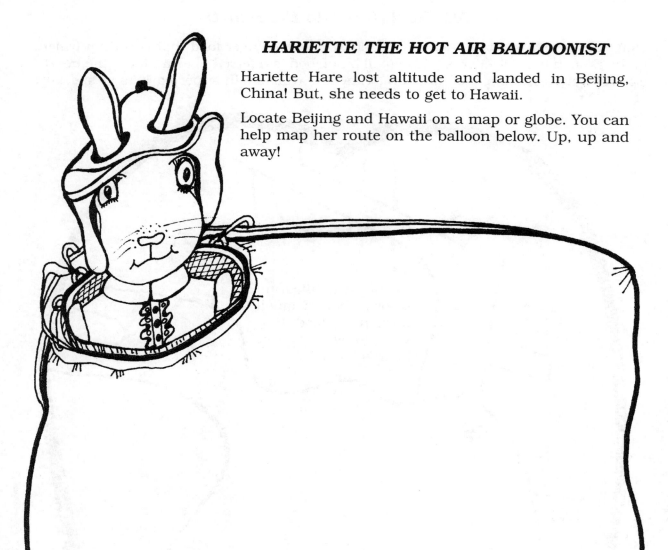

HARIETTE THE HOT AIR BALLOONIST

Hariette Hare lost altitude and landed in Beijing, China! But, she needs to get to Hawaii.

Locate Beijing and Hawaii on a map or globe. You can help map her route on the balloon below. Up, up and away!

Label major cities and bodies of water.

Compare your route with those of classmates. Work with a partner, too.

Name _____   Date _____

I'M THINKING OF A COUNTRY

THE COUNTRY IS _____.

Shape

Climate

Main Foods

Travel Poster Ideas

(Make your colorful poster on the other side of this sheet.)

Name _____   Date _____

DO AN AUTHOR STUDY—ASIA

Read *Lon Po Po* by Ed Young. It is the Asian version of *Little Red Riding Hood*. Make comparisons with the story with which you are familiar. Find a copy in the library and compare the characters and the illustrations. Find other stories written and illustrated by Ed Young.

Compare:	Red Riding Hood	Lon Po Po
Major characters		
Where does most of the action take place?		
Describe the wolf.		
How does the wolf make his entrance?		
How is the problem solved?		

RECOMMENDED CHILDREN'S BOOKS

Many of the stories from Australia and New Zealand have been handed down by storytellers in ancient times, and have not been set in print.

Anno, Mitsumasa. *All in a Day.* **Other illustrators: Eric Carle, Raymond Briggs, Nicolai Ye Popov, Akiko Hayashi, Gian Calvi, Leo and Diane Dillon, Zhu Chengliang, and Ron Brooks. New York: Philomel Books, 1986.** This delightful picture book, a contribution to the cause of world peace, visually shows the reader what is going on simultaneously in Chicago, England, Brazil, Kenya, Moscow, Tokyo, China and Sydney. It begins with December 31 and celebrates the New Year. Excellent message.

Baer, Edith. *This Is the Way We Go to School, A Book About Children Around the World.* **Illustrated by Steven Bjorkman. New York: Scholastic, 1990.** This book, in rhyme, takes the reader on a journey to school by way of school bus, ferry boat, cable car, skis, train, bicycle, and even by radio. At the end is a listing of 22 students and where they live, and then a visual map of the world that shows the information. An excellent teaching book.

Baker, Jeannie. *Where the Forest Meets the Sea.* **New York: Greenwillow, 1987.** This book offers the reader a visual feast as we travel through the tropical rain forest in North Queensland, Australia. "But will the forest still be here when we come back?" That's the question.

_____. *Window.* **New York: Greenwillow, 1991.** This hauntingly lovely wordless picture book by Baker, an English author/illustrator now living in Australia, gives the reader a view from a window. The scene through the window changes from a nature scene to the sprawl of a city as a baby boy grows up. When he is a man, he holds his own child and looks out the window. What does he see?

Fox, Mem. *Possum Magic.* **Illustrated by Julie Vivas. New York: Harcourt Brace Jovanovich/Gulliver, 1990.** Grandma Poss has made her granddaughter, Hush, invisible by a magic spell. Hush meets up with dingoes, wombats, kookaburras, and kangaroos found only on the island continent. Whimsical illustrations.

Gray, Nigel. *A Country Far Away.* **Pictures by Philippe Dupasquier. New York: Orchard Books, 1988.** Author Nigel Gray was born in Ireland and lives in Australia, while Dupasquier lives in England. This is a multi-ethnic story of two boys who wake, sleep, play, eat, and share in family life on opposite sides of the globe. They may be two different worlds, but they are similar stories.

Hathorn, Elizabeth. *The Tram to Bondi Beach.* **Illustrated by Julie Vivas. New York: Kane/Miller Book Publishers, 1989.** This is a fast-moving story about a boy named Keiran who loves the sound of the trams careening, rattling, flying down the hill to Bondi Beach. Right now he wants to sell papers, but he knows what he wants to do when he grows up. The illustrations bring the story to life.

Mahy, Margaret. *17 Kings and 42 Elephants.* **Pictures by Patricia MacCarthy. New York: Dial Books, 1987.** Oh what a wonderfully colorful journey, via batik illustrations, through the jungle with 17 kings and 42 elephants going on a journey through a wild wet night—in rhyme. The author is from New Zealand.

___. *The Horrendous Hullabaloo.* **Illustrated by Patricia MacCarthy. New York: Viking Penguin, 1992.** This is a rollicking sea tale about Peregrine the Pirate who goes off and leaves his Aunt and a parrot at home. Bored, they throw a hullabaloo of a party and feast on rumble bumpkins and dance a wild jig. Still another amusing tale by this author is *The Pumpkin Man and the Crafty Creeper.*

Roughsey, Dick. *The Giant Devil-Dingo.* **New York: Macmillan, 1973.** The author, an Aborigine, has written and illustrated some of the traditional tales of his people. This legend is about the dingo, or hunting dog, from the Cape York region. The book has won several prestigious awards in Australia.

Wheatley, Nadia. *My Place.* **Illustrated by Donna Rawlins. Brooklyn, NY: Kane/Miller Books, 1992.** From 1988 back to 1788, every decade is marked by a brief description of life in that year as told by a child of that era. One tale is told by an Aboriginal child, another by a young English convict deported to Australia, and others are told by German, Chinese, Irish, and Greek children. The book deals with environmental issues, and contains wonderful maps.

FOLK TALES

Australia is the world's smallest continent. New Zealand is composed of two islands, North and South, and is located to the southeast of Australia. Both countries were settled by the British and are referred to as the land "down under."

In Australia, the Aborigines are people who have lived "down under" for many thousands of years. Places with rhythmical names such as Tumbarumba, Woolgoolga, and Wagga Wagga came from the aborigine tribes. One such tribe is called the Gagga Ju. Their culture is linked to the "Dreamtime"—the beginning of time when their ancestors lived on earth.

The "Dreamtime" is the source of all art, song, dance, and stories. It is the memory of the race within each tribesman, and one who has been initiated into the tribe is taught how to tap into this resource by an elder. Unfortunately, the information is dying out as the tribes dwindle in size.

All societies have creation myths and Australia is no different. In this culture, god turned himself into a rock which now contains the life force. The earth (red clay) represents blood and vitality.

The New Zealand culture of today represents a number of people who have traveled to this part of the world from Europe and the Far East, via Indonesia. Original settlers were the Maori of Polynesia. It has many modern cities, and shares the same language as Great Britain and the United States as well as many of the same customs. New Zealanders enjoy a close relationship with the sea and families spend holidays at the beach, although most people live in modern cities. Both Australia and New Zealand are industrialized nations.

THE LIZARD TALE

The lizard was at one time human, but did not listen and ruined a very special ceremony. As punishment, the person was changed into a lizard so it would always be seen that way. When a tribesman sees the lizard it is a visual reminder to listen and obey the ways of the tribe, or suffer the consequences. Also, it may be viewed as a warning that one needs to begin paying attention, especially if an individual sees it when alone—for the spirit world is all around.

THE STRING STORIES

String stories are a favorite with the Aborigines. String stories can be found in ancient African cultures as well. It seems that all civilizations enjoy string stories. (See the African section.)

THE FLYING FOX MEN

Bats, referred to as flying fox men, are seen as dark and evil forces, perhaps because they only come out at night.

THE LEADING ROLES IN MYTHOLOGY

Animals play a big role in the tales. Because this area was isolated, the evolution of the animals is unique to this part of the world. There are archaic types of animals including egg-laying mammals such as the duckbill and spiny anteater; the marsupials like the kangaroo, bandicoot, wallaby and wombat; and flightless birds like the emu.

THE ROLE OF ANTS AND INSECTS IN STORIES

Ants and insects, because of their abundance, play an important part in world folklore. In Australia, there are tales about the revival of dead people by stinging ants. The scampering, buzzing, crawling, hopping insects are called "children of the earth."

Ants are viewed differently by various cultures. The Hebrews believe ants have wisdom. In Bulgaria and Switzerland, ants are a bad omen. In Estonia, ants are a good omen. To the Hindus, ants are sacred.

THE WISE AND FOOLISH BROTHERS

These tales, common throughout the world, are found in southern Australia and in New Zealand. Again, the purposes of the tales is to learn a valuable lesson.

THE "DREAMTIME"

This is called "Alchera" by the Aranda of Central Australia. It is the state from which everything flows. The artist may hold the brush in his or her hand, get into a dreamy state, and create the drawing through the brush. The same is true of the person who enters the dream state and tells stories. In a sense, the story is verbal art. At "story places," sacred spots, the ancestors created everything and then returned to the earth or sky, or transformed themselves into rocks. The role of the ancestors is extremely important.

THE ROLE OF FASTING

Abstaining from food on a voluntary basis is common among almost all peoples. In New Zealand, among the Maori, it is common for the women to fast for the welfare of the warriors while they are away, and this is reflected in the folklore.

EGGS IN FOLKLORE

Eggs represent the earth and life. In many cultures eggs play a role in the stories. In New Zealand, Maori buried their dead with an egg in one hand. In Europe, there are many tales that include eggs. Among Germans and Slavs, a mixture of eggs was smeared on the plow just before Easter to insure a rich harvest. There are many sayings that surround eggs, such as: "to remove a baby's birthmark, rub the mark every morning for nine mornings with a fresh hen's egg and bury the egg under the doorstep." In England, to dream of eggs means riches.

THE SWAN MAIDEN

There is a cycle of tales the world over about the maiden who is half swan (half supernatural, half human). The swan comes ashore, takes off its magic robe, and becomes the swan maiden. A youth finds and steals her swan coat on shore and hides it. He marries her and is able to keep this beautiful swan maiden with him in human form until she finds the robe, puts it on, and returns to the sea. This folk tale is found in Australia where there is the beautiful Black Swan, and is also found in Asia, Europe, Eastern Europe, Japan, Indonesia, Africa, and South America.

SUGGESTED ACTIVITIES FOR THE CLASSROOM

1. DO AN AUTHOR/ILLUSTRATOR STUDY—AUSTRALIA

Get books from the library by Australian-born Mem Fox, who was raised in Africa. Most of her books are illustrated by Julie Vivas. *Possum Magic*, a bestseller in Australia, gives the reader a feeling for the rhythm of words. Other books include *Wilfred Gordon McDonald Partridge; Koala Lou; Night Noises;* and *Guess What.*

2. DO AN AUTHOR/ILLUSTRATOR STUDY—NEW ZEALAND

Get books from the library by New Zealander, Margaret Mahy. Several of her books are illustrated in batik by Patricia MacCarthy, and others are by different illustrators. Compare the different styles. Mahy's amusing books include *17 Kings and 42 Elephants; The Horrendous Hullabaloo;* and *The Pumpkin Man and the Crafty Creeper.*

3. FINDING THE LAND DOWN UNDER

Help students locate Australia and New Zealand on a map or globe. They can use an atlas to help locate cities, ports, and rivers and information books to learn about the people, foods, and customs.

4. A POCKETFUL OF GOOD ANIMAL STORIES

Trace the shape of a kangaroo on large paper and tack it to a bulletin board. Then, for the pocket, use a real paper bag, or a bag made from cloth, tacked to the board. Fill the pocket with storybooks and information books about the unusual animals (the wombat, kookaburras, wallabies, and the dingo) found in Australia and New Zealand.

5. REMEMBER THE FOLK TALE FORMULA

If students have some difficulty in finding an abundance of tales from New Zealand and Australia, they can begin to create their own. Younger children can substitute an unusual animal for the wolf in "Red Riding Hood," for example. Older children can use the information about the unusual animals and change the setting in order to meet animals in other parts of the world. Which one will be the trickster?

6. GOING TO SCHOOL BY RADIO

In remote parts of the country, children "attend" school by listening to their lessons on the radio. Have students prepare lessons and make cassette recordings for them. Then, set up a study area and have students "go to school" following the directions on the tape. This provides an excellent opportunity to strengthen listening skills and to carry out verbal messages.

7. ANIMAL LANGUAGE CODES

Since we are learning about unusual animals in a different part of the world, we will have to "crack the code." This provides a good opportunity for students to work with coded messages (A=1, B=2, for example), and symbols that stand for letters. Students can create cartoon strips with language bubbles for short coded messages. They can work with their maps to make hidden treasure messages, and then exchange them and try to find out where the treasure is located.

8. G'DAY MATE

In Australia, there are many words or expressions that we can learn and use when writing stories. For example:

G'day	(hello)
mate	(good friend)
Ta	(thank you)
bonzer	(terrific)
postie	(postman)
walloper	(police officer)
Crissie	(Christmas)
joey	(baby kangaroo)

CELEBRATIONS

Many festivals remind people of a story or of an event that happened long ago. In fact, it is the purpose of festivals to remember and to honor the past, to relive memories, and to retell stories that relate to origin, or to beliefs, or to a specific time of year, and to share in the celebration once again.

CELEBRATING ORIGINS IN NEW ZEALAND

The Maoris of New Zealand, the original tribes that migrated from Polynesia, have intermingled and intermarried with the Europeans who later migrated to this area. However, today there is a resurgence of interest in "Maoritanga"—the Maori way. A new interest in traditions and celebrations is springing up. Old values like "whanaungatanga" (family relationships) and "aroha" (love, caring, and sympathy for each other) are coming to the forefront, as the original New Zealanders strive to maintain their links with other peoples who live in the Pacific—namely the islanders of Tahiti, the Cooks, Easter Island, and Hawaii.

CELEBRATING ORIGINS

The Australian Aborigines believe that the world was made by their ancestors. Each clan, or group, of people honors something in nature because it is believed that their ancestor took that form or shape. A clan may honor the rocks, or a particular bird, plant or tree, and so on. Dances honoring the ancestors come from the "Dreamtime," a time of collective memory. Throughout the world, there are many different beliefs about the origin of man. Today the Aborigines are dying out as a people, and the only way to prevent this is to have some of the people of Aborigine descent return to their living ancestors for knowledge and information about the old ways before they no longer exist. A father can only pass this information along to his son.

AUSTRALIA DAY

The Australians celebrate a national holiday on January 26. On this date there are colorful parades and ceremonies that mark the first settlement by Europeans of this land in 1788.

NEW ZEALAND DAY (WAITANGI DAY)

On February 6, the New Zealanders celebrate their national holiday. The celebration is held to commemorate the signing of the Waitangi Treaty between the Maoris and the British in 1840. The white people were called "Pakehas" in Maori language. There are parades and ceremonies for the festive occasion.

THE HUI IN AOTEAROA

A *hui* may be a wedding or a conference. It is a meeting of the Maoris that is held on the "marae," an open space in a village. People may stay at a marae for days. At this time, the Maori language is spoken, and the old culture is revisited and celebrated with speeches, dancing, singing, and eating. The Maori word for New Zealand is "Aotearoa."

THE MAORI GREETING

The "hongi" is a traditional form of greeting between Maoris. Especially at the hui, men will shake hands and press their foreheads together with eyes closed. It is a head-to-head greeting of respect for each other and a celebration of being Maori. An excellent resource is *The Maoris of New Zealand* by Graham Wiremu (Vero Beach, FL: Rourke Publications, Inc., 1989).

MELBOURNE CUP

This horse race is held on the first Tuesday in November. It is similar in scope to the Kentucky Derby in the United States. All over Australia people listen to the race on the radio or watch it on television.

NEW ZEALAND'S ANZAC DAY

This day, on April 25, is celebrated with the Dawn Parade to honor both the Australians and New Zealanders who served in the Army Corps during World War I. It is a memorial day with parades, bands, music, speeches, and flag waving.

SUGGESTED ACTIVITIES FOR THE CLASSROOM

1. TAKING A LOOK DOWN UNDER

Australia comes from "australis," a Latin word for "down under." People refer to Australia as the land down under because it is south of the equator. Have students locate this small continent on the map or globe, and note that it is the only island (surrounded by water on all sides) that is a continent. They can make size comparisons between Australia and the United States, or Africa, or South America which are also continents. Students can learn the bodies of water that surround the continent (Pacific Ocean and Indian Ocean) and learn its relationship to New Zealand in terms of distance and direction.

2. TAKING A CLOSER LOOK DOWN UNDER

The Great Barrier Reef is located off the eastern coast of Queensland and is the longest coral reef in the world. Coral is a hard, bony skeleton that is secreted by certain marine polyps. Try to locate real samples of coral for students to examine. Often, coral is used in making jewelry.

3. THE KIWI

For a nickname the New Zealanders have chosen "Kiwi." This is a bird found only on the islands. It is flightless, emerges at night, and is a relative of the chicken. Students can celebrate names! Discuss and list nicknames chosen for their country, city, or state. Also discuss personal nicknames and nicknames for pets.

4. THE COLOR OF CORAL

Coral is either a pinkish red or a yellowish pink. In the United States, the flower named coral bell flourishes in the southwestern United States, but can also grow elsewhere. Try to identify the beautiful shades of coral red and coral pink. Get sample strips from a local paint store. Mix colors and make a coral painting.

5. WORKING WITH NATIONAL FLOWERS

The flower for Australia is the "wattle" which is a member of the acacia family. The soft yellow flowers feel like light feathers. Do students know their state flower? The national flower? The flower of bordering states? Find this information in the library. Make a set of flower flashcards.

6. WHAT IS YOUR NATIONAL ANTHEM?

In New Zealand, the national anthem is entitled "God Defend New Zealand." Do students know their own national anthem? An "anthem" is a song of praise, so when it is sung it is meant to make the singers feel a sense of pride in their country.

7. LET'S EXAMINE FLAGS

All countries have a flag. Can students recognize the flag of their country? Secure a book of flags from the library (often the flags are in encyclopedias) and have students find the flag of Australia and New Zealand. Then, have them learn to recognize the flag of the countries of their ancestors. Students can make flag flash cards on 3″ x 5″ cards. Color the flag on one side with bright felt pens, and print the name of the country on the reverse side with pencil. How many flags can students name this week? How many can they name next week? Keep working at it. Classify the flags by countries within continents.

8. LET'S CELEBRATE THE ANIMALS

Australia has so many unusual animals with unusual names that this becomes a study in itself. MAMMALS include the platypus and echidna, and MARSUPIALS (develop in the pouch) include the kangaroo, wallaby, koala, and wombat. Animals of the Great Barrier Reef include the hammerhead shark, green sea turtles, and the sea wasp. The black swan is found only in this area of the world. An excellent resource book is *Amazing Animals of Australia*, National Geographic Society, Books for Young Explorers, 1984.

9. AN ANIMAL PARTY

Suppose a fictional character in a fairy tale or folk tale sent out party invitations to the animals in your neighborhood, but the mail got mixed up and was sent all the way to

Australia! Then, on the party day the wombat, kangaroo, platypus, and koala showed up. Now what? Do they "fit in"? What do they eat? How do they move? What is necessary in order for all of the animals to get along at the party? This would be a good discussion and role-play situation, using animals as a starting point and people at a later time.

10. THE BIRDS FOUND PARADISE AND CALLED IT "NEW ZEALAND"

The flightless kiwi, the weka, the takahe, the tui, the bellbird, the saddle-back, and native thrush are natives to this area. Other birds who found their way here include the oystercatcher, albatross, and parrot. Investigate these unfamiliar birds in information books about birds, and create a book such as, "Let's Celebrate the Birds." Learn more about this land through *Enchantment of the World, New Zealand* by Mary Virginia Fox (Chicago: Children's Press, 1991).

ARTS AND CRAFTS

The arts and crafts of this area of the world reflect the European influence, especially British. However, in Australia the Aborigines have their own specialized artwork that comes from the "Dreamtime"—a place in the mind where all knowledge and skills of the ancestors reside. In New Zealand, the Maori people, original inhabitants of this area from Polynesia, are having a resurgence of "Maoritanga"—a Maori renaissance in flax weaving, wood-working, pottery, and sheepskin products made by hand.

SUGGESTED ACTIVITIES FOR THE CLASSROOM

1. CREATING A DREAMTIME ATMOSPHERE

In the Aborigine tribes, not everyone does art work. Each person has a specialty, for the culture works together as a unit. For our purposes, we can suppose that everyone has access to art information.

To set up the activity, the students will have had to be exposed to a wide variety of art in picture books, perhaps a visit to the art gallery, and an awareness of color and design.

You will need background music for students to listen to, and then have them paint to the music. They can paint different pictures for different types of music. A march, for example, might call for repeated bold, straight lines, whereas a dreamy melody might call for wavy lines. Have students move their body to the music in response to how they feel. (The media can vary. Use chalk dipped into water, finger paint, water crayons, or watercolors.)

This can lead to setting up a center for painting in the classroom, so that students can go there when their work is finished. If possible, arrange to have them use a headset with a variety of music tapes to shut out classroom distractions and to inspire their works of art.

2. A NEW ZEALAND INVENTION THINK-TANK

New Zealanders are recognized as being inventive; that is, they have an uncanny ability to invent things on their own using basic materials and tools. An ideal student activity would be to set up a problem to solve (ecological, communication, transportation, etc.) and have students form their own groups. If they prefer working alone, that is fine as long as they are working on the problem.

Prior to this, set out a large box so that students can bring in all sorts of items from home, such as plastic bottles, pie tins, TV dinner trays, cardboard cylinders, twine, clothespins, paper clips, etc. Have them use the materials as they invent a new gadget for humanity. The sky's the limit in a think tank—no idea should be discounted. Encourage "playfulness" since it is part of the creative process. Students can later name their invention and explain it to classmates.

3. MAKE A "HEITIKI"

A Heitiki is a Maori ornament that was carved from pounamu (greenstone) and worn around the neck. Greenstone is a form of jade. Students can use modeling clay to create a heitiki that they can glaze and wear around their neck. (In the Maori culture, there was no information about metals and so greenstone was used for axes and chisels, as well as ornaments.)

4. BAA-BAA BLACK SHEEP, HAVE YOU ANY WOOL?

There are many flocks of sheep grazing in both Australia and New Zealand. The wool is used for weaving, and much of it is exported. The very coarse wool of the romney sheep is used in carpets.

Younger students can create woolen sheep by coiling strands of wool yarn around a cardboard cylindrical shape for the body, and adding a wool ball for the head. Use felt for ears, eyes, and hoofs.

Another activity is to use woolen yarn to make pictures. Outline shapes with glue, and carefully add the colored yarn.

Make a wool pompom. These balls of wool are attached to woolen yarn strands and used by the Maori women in their ceremonial dances. To make a pompom:

a. Cut two round doughnut shapes from cardboard.

b. Wind yarn around the two shapes until they are covered.

c. Cut the yarn around the edge.

d. Pull apart the cardboard, and tie the center part with a piece of yarn.

e. Carefully remove the cardboard pieces.

5. WEAVING THE MAORI WAY

The women wove beautiful patterns of zigzag colors, but they did not use a loom. Long pieces of yarn were tied around a long, horizontal bar or stick. This stick was tied on each end to sticks that were placed in the ground (or in something stationary). Then the weaving was painstakingly done with the over/under technique as the threads hung loose. The results were beautiful, and it took patience as well as a lot of time to complete an item. This type of weaving apparatus can be set up in the classroom so that all students can have an opportunity to experience weaving the Maori way.

GAMES

These games are representative of the cultures and are not intended as a complete resource. Because people in this climate spend a great deal of time outdoors, many games such as soccer, rugby, tennis, swimming, and squash are very popular. On the other hand, an excellent resource book for indoor games is *The World's Best Party Games* by Sheila Anne Barry, illustrated by Doug Anderson (New York: Starling Publishing Co., Inc., 1987).

FORCE BALL (ALL HANDS AND NO FEET TEAM SPORT)

This game is similar to Leg Relay, and can be played by 20 to 30 players. You will need two teams, a large space (indoor or out) and a basketball.

Have children line up in two rows, with about five feet between the rows. Children turn and face the opposing row or team. Standing side by side, each player needs to stand with legs apart and with feet touching the feet of the player on either side. To start the game, the ball is rolled between the two teams. Players bend over and—*using hands only*—try to bat the ball between the legs of the opposite team. No one is allowed to move his or her feet. Score one point for each time the ball goes through the legs of an opposing team member.

TAG RELAY RACE

You will need two teams. Players stand in a straight line. The first player on each team must run to a designated point (base, wall, around a circle) and return to the next player who has his or her hand extended. The first player must touch the hand of the second player, which sends the second player on his or her run before taking a place at the end of the line. Go through this procedure for the whole line. The first team to end up with the first player at the head of the line again is the winner.

TAG RELAY WITH BOUNCING BALL

You will need two teams (players stand in a straight line) and a basketball or large ball.

Follow the same procedure as for Tag Relay Race, only this time each player has to bounce a ball while running to the destination. The ball can either be bounced back or carried back, and handed off to the next person in line, prior to the first player taking his or her place at the end of the line.

Variation. Same as above, only the player carries the ball to the halfway point, bounces it a designated number of times, and carries the ball on the return run to the next player before going to the end of the line.

KANGAROO JUMP

Students line up and, one by one, they jump from a stationary position. The jumping distance is measured and the winner is the person who has jumped the farthest.

KANGAROO RUNNING JUMP

Students line up some distance from the starting point. At a given signal, they begin to run toward the starting point and then jump when they reach that point. Measure the jumps, and the winner is the person who has jumped the farthest. Compare the distance for the still jump and the running jump.

STRING GAMES

String games are found throughout the world and are a good form of communication when people speak different languages. The Aborigines of Australia have string games, and there are an abundance of string games from the Native American Indians. String games can be found in Asia, Africa, Europe, Canada, United States, and South America. They are found all over the world.

When playing string games, the hands are held with the palms facing each other and fingers are up straight.

Cat's Cradle is one of the more familiar ones in all cultures, and is believed to have originated in Asia and spread throughout the world. In New Zealand, the Maori people tell stories to match the string figures they make. In Germany, string games are called "Hexenspiel," and in Japan they are called "Ayatori." Resource: *The World's Best String Games* by Joanmarie Kalter (New York: Sterling Publishing Co., Inc., 1978).

FOLDING ARMS (A BALL GAME FROM NEW ZEALAND)

Any number can play. You will need a tennis ball. Have children line up, fold their arms, and face the person about to throw the ball.

The ball thrower can throw or pretend to throw the ball at a player. If the ball thrower does not throw the ball, and the person in line opens arms wide to receive it, the person in line is out. If the ball is tossed and the person in line is too late to open arms to receive it, the person in line is out. The last one standing in line is the winner. (This is a game of wits and skill.)

SONGS, DANCES, RHYTHMS

In parts of Australia, the Aborigines were cut off from the outside world for centuries, so they have their distinct forms of song and dance that are used for festivals and celebrations. In other parts of Australia, the cultural life has been influenced by Europe. The Sydney Opera House features well-known musicians and dancers from around the world. New Zealand, as well, has the folk music and dance of the Maori people. In the main, the cultural life is greatly influenced by the western world, mainly Europe and America.

This section will deal mainly with creative movement and exercise.

ABORIGINE DANCES OF THE ANIMALS

The Aborigines use their body to imitate the animals in their immediate environment. Some representations are as follows:

The *Kangaroo Dance* requires holding the hands in front with elbows bent, and hopping on the legs.

The *Butterfly Dance* requires the flapping of arms to represent the fluttering of the wings, and the graceful body movement of the butterfly.

The *Fish Dance* requires twisting and turning of the whole body as if moving through water.

The *Crane Dance* requires a high-stepping leg movement that represents lifting the long legs of the crane up and down, up and down as it moves on land searching for food.

Children enjoy moving to music and imitating animals. Face masks can be used for this type of dancing.

WHAT OTHER ANIMALS CAN WE IMITATE?

Since students enjoy moving to music in a way that represents animals, play music on the piano or on a recording, and ask children to listen. Decide what animal the music suggests (any suggestions are acceptable) and have students move in that fashion. Some suggestions:

Lion: Standing up, hunch up the shoulders and move the arms in a forward motion, one at a time. Good exercise for neck and shoulders.

Giraffe: Stretch the neck muscles up, up, up.

Fish: Pretend the fish are swimming in a small aquarium, so use hand and wrist motions as the two fish tumble, roll over and interact. Fingers of the hand can be stretched by starting with fingertips together, then opening wide, fingertips together, opening wide. This represents the mouth of the fish as it gathers its food.

Horse: Gallop, stretching the large muscle of the legs.

Elephant: Down on all fours, with back up. Move left side, then right side, as the elephant sways from side to side. Good back stretch and body twist.

HOW WOULD ANIMALS OF AUSTRALIA MOVE?

How can we move like a duck-billed platypus? How does the wallabie get around? And the wombat? The black swan on a smooth lake? This calls for some research about the animals and birds of Australia, and some creative movement, rhythms, and tunes.

CARTWHEELS AND BACKBENDS

Australian Aborigines have a great deal of space and freedom of movement. Take the students outdoors for some creative movement in large spaces.

Designate an area for cartwheels and backbends. Encourage running and jumping along the perimeter of the playground area for some good old-fashioned exercise.

PLAYGROUND MAPS AND GAMES

Get permission to make a large world map (with chalk) on the playground blacktop. Parents can help with this project. Then have students jump from Australia to New Zealand and back again. They can jump from continent to continent and name them as they go.

Another good use of the playground at recess is to toss a beanbag onto the blacktop and, wherever it lands, a game will be played from that area of the world. Organized games are enjoyed by children the world over.

If the beanbag is tossed and lands on an area where no game is listed in this book, and if you have no immediate resource available, it is a good opportunity for students to do some research on this area later so that they can learn about the people and their culture and the games they play—and play one another day.

Resource

The JVD Video Anthology of World Music and Dance, Oceania I, Volume 29, Victor Company of Japan.

FOOD

People who live in rural Australia are referred to as "bushmen," and they call their food "tucker." A tucker bag carried by a "swagman" (hobo) usually contained some flour. Flour mixed with water makes "damper" (dough). Damper was cooked on a stick over the campfire, or even baked in the fire's ashes just as it was done in very early civilizations in other parts of the world. Thus, we have another thread that connects the early civilizations of man.

Two foods that are very popular with native-born Australians are Vegemite and meat pies. Vegemite is a salty black yeast extract that is thickly spread on bread or toast, just like jam. It is often the first solid food for young children. The meat pie (hot meat and gravy inside rolled up pastry) is a snack food, like the American hot dog.

In New Zealand, the native Maori people have feasts at their get-togethers (hui) that are prepared in an earth oven (hangi). Meat and vegetables are steamed, and many kinds of seafood, such as eel and shellfish, are included.

New Zealanders eat large quantities of meat and dairy products, with the favorite meat being lamb. Sweet potatoes, or kumara, are regular fare. The Maoris brought the kumara with them from Hawaiki (Polynesia), and it is an important staple in the diet. Today, the favorite drink is tea.

SUGGESTED RECIPES FOR THE CLASSROOM

Lamingtons (Cakes)

This favorite cake was named in honor of Baroness Lamington, originally from England. It is a teatime favorite.

Cake:
1 package yellow cake mix
  (2-layer size)

Icing:
1/3 cup cocoa
3 cups powdered sugar
3 tablespoons melted margarine
3 cups shredded coconut
1/2 cup boiling water

Bake cake as directed in rectangular pan. Cool. When cake is cooled, remove from pan. Cut cake into 2-1/2-inch squares. Set aside. Sift the cocoa and sugar into a bowl. Add melted margarine and boiling water to cocoa mixture and blend. Put shredded coconut into a shallow bowl. Dip each square of cake into: (a) the warm cocoa icing (using two forks to hold it securely), and then (b) the coconut until all sides are covered. Place each lamington on a wire rack. Allow lamingtons to cool. (Makes one dozen.)

Tomato and Mint Sandwiches

Trim the crust from ten slices of bread. Butter the bread, and make a sandwich from thinly sliced tomatoes. Add tiny bits of mint sprigs (fresh, if possible). Cut the sandwiches diagonally to make triangles. You now have tiny sandwiches to arrange on a plate for a tasty treat.

Kiwi Fruit

This fruit is native to New Zealand, and at one time was called the "Chinese gooseberry." It was renamed to make it known as a product of New Zealand. The kiwi fruit is yellow-gold on the outside, and green on the inside. It can be peeled and sliced and used in fruit salads.

Wheat Bread and Wheat Crackers

Wheat is the principal crop of Australia. Wheat is also grown in the United States. A variety of wheat crackers (whole wheat, cracked wheat, whole grain, etc.) makes a good mid-morning snack. These can be served with peach, apricot, or plum jam.

An Abundance of Fruits

In Tasmania, the climate is cool with quite a bit of rain; apples grow so well here that it has been nicknamed "The Apple Isle." Australia has a rich crop of peaches, plums, and apricots with canning factories nearby, so much of the fruit can be exported.

Canned Peaches: Serve over vanilla ice cream for a tasty treat.

Canned Plums: Cut up and serve along with cut up pieces of real plums for a contrast in texture, color, and taste.

Canned Apricots: Cut up and serve with dried apricots for taste comparisons.

Peach, Apricot, or Plum Topping: Jams made from these fruits make a tasty topping on a scoop of vanilla ice cream. It is one way that students will experiment with new tastes.

Since peaches, apricots and plums are available in most grocery stores across the United States, a sampling of these fresh fruits is a healthy snack. Serve to students while they are listening to a story that takes place in Australia or New Zealand. (See the Children's Literature section.)

A Macadamia Nut Treat

Macadamia nuts are grown in Australia. These nuts are exported all over the world and are usually quite expensive. They can be cut into slivers and baked on top of muffins.

Pikelets (Australian Pancakes)

3/4 cup flour
1 tablespoon sugar
1/2 teaspoon baking powder
1/2 teaspoon baking soda
1/4 teaspoon salt
1 egg, beaten
1/2 cup milk
vegetable shortening

Mix flour, sugar, baking powder, baking soda, and salt in a bowl. Mix egg and milk together, and slowly stir into the dry mixture. Heat shortening in the electric frypan on medium low. Drop the batter (by the tablespoon) onto skillet. Brown on both sides. Serve with jam. Makes approximately 16 pancakes.

Resources

Fox, Mary Virginia. Series, "Enchantment of the World," *New Zealand* (Chicago: Children's Press, 1991).

Garrett, Dan, and Warrill Grindrod. Series, "World in View," *Australia* (Madison, NJ: Raintree Steck-Vaughn, 1990).

Germaine, Elizabeth, and Ann L. Burckhardt, with colored photos by Robert and Diane Wolfe. *Cooking the Australian Way,* (Minneapolis: Lerner, 1990). One in a series of easy-menu ethnic cookbooks.

REPRODUCIBLE ACTIVITY PAGES

Pocket, Pocket, What's in the Pocket? (*porquois tales*)

The Role of the Horse in Folk Tales (*comparisons*)

Pardon Me, Are You a Hippogriff? (*following directions*)

The Octopus Story Mapper (*highlighting eight story components*)

G'day, Mates! Am I on Time? (*mammal study*)

I'm a Kiwi. Who Are You? (*nicknames*)

Maoritanga (*family relationships*)

Tomato and Mint Sandwiches (*food recipe*)

Camelopard Meant to Say Africa But It Came Out "Australia" (*geography*)

Ulak Is Hungry for Information (*geography: iceburgs and glaciers*)

Baa Baa Black Sheep's Big Bag o' Wool Award (*feelings*)

Do an Author Study—Australia (*Mem Fox*)

POCKET, POCKET, WHAT'S IN THE POCKET?

Can you find a tale where the main character is a kangaroo? You can write a porquois (por-kwa) tale about why Kanga has a pocket.

This kangaroo is playing a game. She is touching three items in a real pocket (without peeking). She can have three guesses. You, too, can play this game.

THE ROLE OF THE HORSE IN FOLK TALES

After you have read many folk tales and examined many picture books, you will notice that the horse plays an important role.

I found these horses in two different folk tales:

1. _____ Country: _____
   (name of horse)

Role of the horse in this story:

2. _____ Country: _____
   (name of horse)

Role of the horse in this story:

PARDON ME, ARE YOU A HIPPOGRIFF?

Barnaby Bear operates a Check Point Station. The hippogriff is a combination beast or dragon with the following characteristics:

Head (camel), Horns (elk),
Eyes (rabbit), Ears (cow), Neck (snake),
Belly (frog), Scales (carp),
Claws (hawk), Feet (lion).

Make your version of the hippogriff. Does it pass inspection?

THE OCTOPUS STORY MAPPER

Amy Octopus has a challenge for you. Read a folk tale from any culture. Then, break the story down into eight pictures from beginning to end. Draw the pictures in the suction circles. Then, using this story map as a guide, tell your folk tale.

Name _____   Date _____

G'day, Mates! Am I on Time?

Well, look who just opened the door—the Duckbilled Platypus from Australia! Does she belong at a party for mammals? This calls for some detective work at the library.

DEFINITION OF MAMMAL:

INFORMATION ABOUT THE DUCKBILLED PLATYPUS:

THE DUCKBILLED PLATYPUS (DOES/DOES NOT) BELONG AT THIS PARTY BECAUSE . . .

Mammal

Party

2 o'clock

she lays eggs!

Oh! Oh!

Name _____ Date _____

I'M A KIWI. WHO ARE YOU?

New Zealanders have chosen "kiwi" as their nickname. The kiwi bird is found in New Zealand and is flightless, comes out at night, and is a relative of the chicken. Let's take this opportunity to explore nicknames. Nicknames give us information about people or things.

PET NICKNAMES FOR PEOPLE YOU KNOW.
What does it tell about them?)

PET NICKNAMES FOR PEOPLE IN THE NEWS.
(A football player might be called "The Rock," a figure skater could be called "Ice Princess," and so on.)

MY NICKNAME IS _____
(What does it tell about you?)

PET NICKNAMES FOR ANIMALS.
(What information do we get from the nickname?)

SELECT A NICKNAME FOR EACH OF THE FOLLOWING.
(Explain why.)

MAORITANGA

Maoritanga means "The Maori Way." When the Maori people of New Zealand use the word "whanaungatanga," it means family relationships. "Aroha" means love and caring for others.

In the space below, draw your family members in a situation that shows they love and care for one another.

TOMATO AND MINT SANDWICHES

Try this tasty New Zealand treat! Draw and label your favorite sandwich on the other side of this sheet. Find out what five classmates chose.

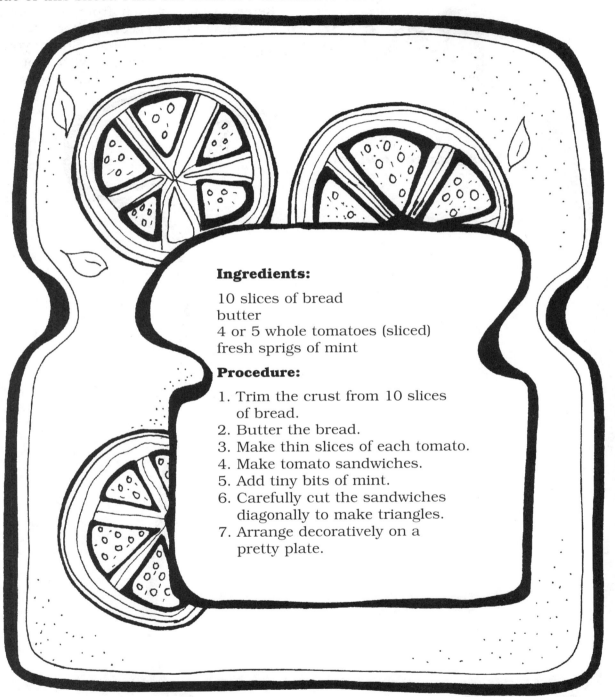

Ingredients:

10 slices of bread
butter
4 or 5 whole tomatoes (sliced)
fresh sprigs of mint

Procedure:

1. Trim the crust from 10 slices of bread.
2. Butter the bread.
3. Make thin slices of each tomato.
4. Make tomato sandwiches.
5. Add tiny bits of mint.
6. Carefully cut the sandwiches diagonally to make triangles.
7. Arrange decoratively on a pretty plate.

Can you find a picture book where someone is shown eating a sandwich? Go on a sandwich hunt!

Name _____   Date _____

CAMELOPARD MEANT TO SAY AFRICA
BUT IT CAME OUT "AUSTRALIA"

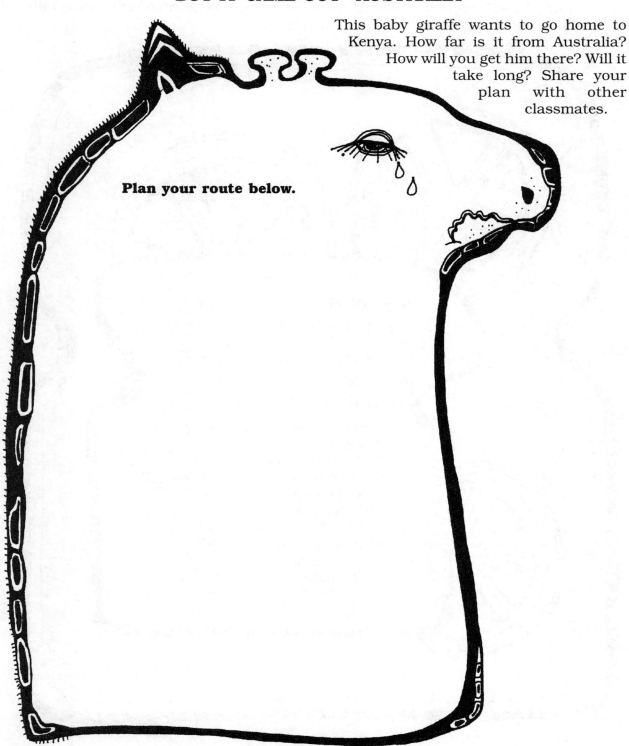

This baby giraffe wants to go home to Kenya. How far is it from Australia? How will you get him there? Will it take long? Share your plan with other classmates.

Plan your route below.

© 1995 by The Center for Applied Research in Education

Ancient Europeans called the giraffe "camelopard" because they believed that it was a cross between a camel and a leopard.

Name _____   Date _____

ULAK IS HUNGRY FOR INFORMATION

Ulak the Ogre is the winner of last year's GEOGRAPHY CONTEST ON CITIES. This year he is entering a contest on Iceburgs and Glaciers. He's hungry for information and will eat this penguin for a snack IF you don't feed him as much information as you can write down (and remember).

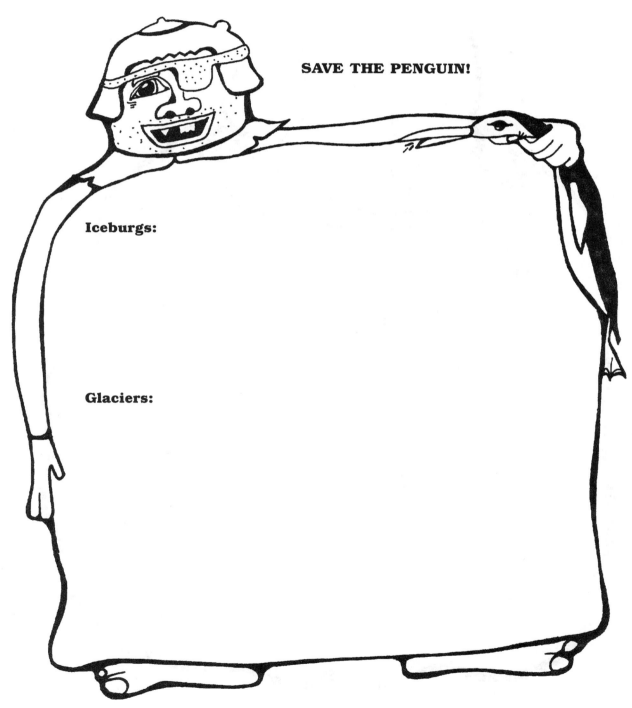

SAVE THE PENGUIN!

Iceburgs:

Glaciers:

Name _____   Date _____

BAA BAA BLACK SHEEP'S BIG BAG O'WOOL AWARD

This award goes to the book that made me feel warm all over. It was "sheer" pleasure!

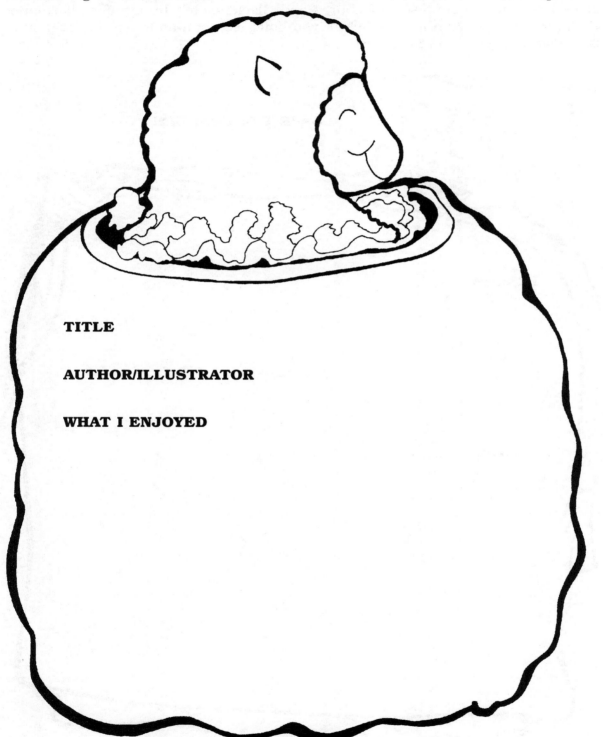

TITLE

AUTHOR/ILLUSTRATOR

WHAT I ENJOYED

DO AN AUTHOR STUDY—AUSTRALIA

Mem Fox is a noted Australian author who was raised in Africa. Her words have a rhythm and a beat to them. Locate several in the library and read them for the humor and the message. What is the author trying to tell us? Outline one of the books below. Some titles to look for are *Wilfred Gordon McDonald Partridge*, *Possum Magic*, *Hattie and the Fox*, and *Night Noises*.

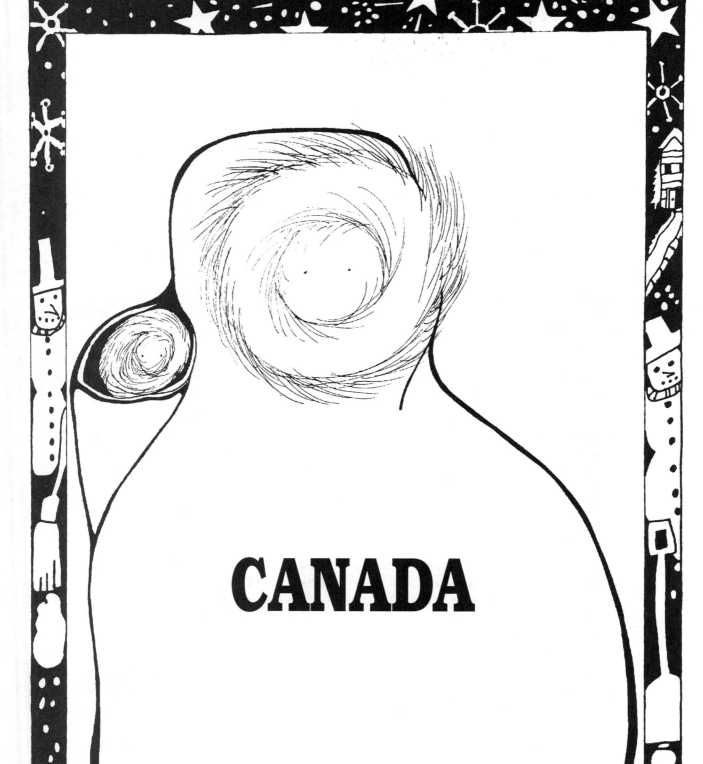

CANADA

RECOMMENDED CHILDREN'S BOOKS

Children's stories from this multicultural land include Eskimo and North American tales.

Carlson, Natalie Savage. *The Talking Cat: And Other Stories of French Canada*. Illustrated by Roger Duvoisin. New York: Harper & Row, 1952. This volume includes seven stories of the pioneer life in the city of Quebec. They give the reader good tales and a good perspective.

DeArmond, Dale. *Berry Woman's Children*. New York: Greenwillow, 1985. Eskimo animal stories combine myth, folklore, and daily life. The stories are enhanced by the illustrations from real woodcuts.

Hewitt, Garnet. *Ytek and the Arctic Orchid, an Inuit Legend*. Illustrated by Heather Woodall. New York: Vanguard Press, Inc., 1981. This legend tells of the time when the caribou became less plentiful and food was scarce for the harsh winter. A young Inuit boy, Ytek, son of the aging shaman, Owljut, is in training to become the leader of his people. But he is only twelve years old, and he must face his final test of worthiness. Spectacular illustrations.

Joosse, Barbara M. *Mama, Do You Love Me?* Illustrated by Barbara Lavallee. San Francisco: Chronicle Books, 1991. This universal story is set in the Arctic, and is unique because the characters are Native American, and the pages are filled with exciting animals such as whales, wolves, puffins, and sled dogs. Stunning, sophisticated art work. A helpful glossary at the end.

Kusugak, Michael Arvaarluk. *Baseball Bats for Christmas*. Illustrated by Vladyana Krykorka. Ontario, Canada: Annick/CN/, 1990. A true tale of a boyhood Christmas on the Arctic Circle. It's too far north for trees to grow, so when a supply plane brings six evergreen trees for Christmas, no one can figure out what they should be used for. The boys refer to them as "standing ups." With the scarcity of wood for toys, they make great baseball bats when the branches are cut off. A good multicultural story to foster understanding.

Martin, Eva. *Tales of the Far North. Illustrated by Laszlo Gal. New York: Dial, 1986.* Twelve tales from English and French-Canadian lore. Many of the tales are variations on the Perrault and Brothers Grimm tales.

Poulin, Stephane. *Ah! Belle Cite/A Beautiful City ABC.* **Bilingual ed. Plattsburgh, NY: Tundra, 1985.** Montreal is a cosmopolitan city; yet it is a cluster of ethnic neighborhoods, like many large cities. The city includes monuments, shops, busy avenues, and quiet side streets. It is a good view of the city in both French and English.

Wallace, Ian. *Chin Chiang and the Dragon's Dance.* **Seattle: Douglas & McIntyre, 1984.** Chin Chiang, a small boy who lives in Vancouver's Chinatown, has dreamed of the New Year's Day when he will be old enough to join with the dragon dancers. But, when the time comes, Chin Chiang is so frightened that he runs to the rooftops to hide. Can he find the courage to dance with the dragon?

Wallace, Ian and Angela Wood. *The Sandwich.* **Ontario, Canada: Kids Canada Press, 1975.** Vincenzo Ferrante brings out his favorite lunch of mortadella and provolone cheese on fresh Italian bread, but the other children hold their noses and say "Vincenzo eats stinky meat!" Should he eat peanut butter and jelly sandwiches like the others do? Not after his talk with Dad. And soon everyone wants "stinky" meat for lunch.

Wheeler, Bernelda. *Where Did You Get Your Moccasins?* **Illustrated by Herman Bekkering. St. Paul, MN: Pemmican Publications, 1986.** Jody's kindergarten classmates admire his new moccasins and ask where they came from. His "kookum" made them. Children ask about that and learn that "kookum" is his word for "grandmother." This leads to more questions and answers. A good multicultural awareness book.

FOLK TALES

Canada is a vast country with a wide variety in temperature and a wide variety of ethnic groups. The northern part of Canada, home to the Eskimo (Inuit) culture, is frigid in winter. The elders in the Eskimo culture instruct the young children through the oral tradition of storytelling. In addition, there is a large Native American (Indian) population. In both of these groups, values, beliefs and traditions are passed down from one generation to the next via the oral tradition. Because of the isolation of the Inuits and because of their oral tradition, there are few tales written down.

The two predominant cultural and linguistic groups are French and English. There is a large French population in Quebec, so there is a rich legacy of French folktales in this area. Many Europeans, Orientals, and people from the Middle East have settled in the larger cities, and there is a rich tradition of folklore that each group has brought with them.

Canada, then, like the United States, has a rich mixture of many cultures under the same roof. Unlike the United States, however, it has never in its history become a "melting pot" but has continued from early times to be more of a multicultural mosaic. The government has an active Multicultural Program and seeks to have minority groups maintain and develop their ethnicity, while at the same time promoting understanding of all groups through the arts.

THE NATIVE PEOPLES

There are over 50 different languages or dialects in Canada. The people belong to 10 major linguistic groups: Algonkian, Iroquoian, Siouan, Athapaskan, Kootenayan, Salishan, Wakashan, Tsimshian, Haida, and Tlingit.

The Tlingit culture has Raven, the bird, as its hero figure, because Raven stole the light from the heavens and gave it to the people. He is an important folklore figure who is credited with bringing light to the world. In cultures the world over, there are folk tales to explain how people got light from the sky.

THE POTLATCH GET-TOGETHER

The Native Americans in the Vancouver area have the same potlatch customs as those in the Pacific Northwest region of the United States. This was a time of great feasting, celebrations, naming-of-babies, weddings, storytelling, games, and so on. The potlatch celebration could last for weeks. When this was over, it was the custom for the visiting tribe to be given the wealth of the host tribe. This "sharing of the wealth" concept discouraged warfare. It also motivated the receiving tribe to hunt well and to create fine items from the hunt and from the land, so that when it was their turn to give the potlatch within the next year or two, the first tribe's wealth would be increased. In this way, the tribes cooperated and their storehouse of goods became more abundant through the years.

THE BRITISH INFLUENCE

Since English is one of the two official languages of Canada, and since almost half of the population speaks English as their first language, many of the beliefs and tales from England are told in Canada. Very young children are brought up on Mother Goose nursery rhymes and on fairy tales such as "Goldilocks," "Red Riding Hood," and "The Three Bears," which are also common in the United States.

British folklorist, Joseph Jacobs, can be likened to the Grimm Brothers in Germany. His purpose in collecting tales was different, however. The Grimm Brothers were students of the language, but Jacobs collected and "adapted" tales so that they would appeal to young children. He took out the crudity and violence in many of the tales and, because of his work, children are able to enjoy such favorites as: "Three Little Pigs," "Henny Penny," "Johnny Cake," and "The Story of the Three Bears."

THE FRENCH INFLUENCE

Charles Perrault was another collector of tales who made an enormous contribution to literature. Perrault revised many of the tales and made them lively with conversation and dazzling with magic. In his version of "Cinderella," for example, the pumpkin coach was introduced along with the glass slipper and the clock that struck midnight when everything returned to its normal state. These are some of the tales that Perrault and his son, Pierre, collected and revised:

"La Petite Chaperon Rouge"	("Little Red Riding Hood")
"La Belle au Bois Dormant"	("The Sleeping Beauty")
"La Barbe Bleue"	("Blue Beard")
"Le Maitre Chat, ou	("Puss in Boots")
Chat Botte"	

"CATCH TALES"

The catch tales are found in folk tales the world over. A story is told in just such a way as to trick the listener into responding, and ending up looking foolish. The "just like me" formula is a familiar one. The first person asks the second person to respond with the three words "just like me." It may go something like this:

"I met a school chum."
   "Just like me."
"She had brown eyes."
   "Just like me."
"She wore a blue dress."
   "Just like me."
"She was a monkey."
   "Just like me."

THE IMPOSSIBLE TASK

Many folk tales have tasks that are just about impossible for the character to carry out, unless the character meets up with a magic figure (toad, frog, hag, fairy, gnome, fox) who helps him or her out. Some of the impossible tasks include making the princess laugh, catching a man's breath, finding berries in the dead of winter, and carrying water in a bucket with holes.

SUGGESTED ACTIVITIES FOR THE CLASSROOM

1. MULTICULTURAL EXTRAVAGANZA

Since Canada thrives on its multiculturalism, get folk tales and informational picture books from the library that represent the large English, French, Native American, and Eskimo populations. Have students read one story from each of these cultures and look for similarities/differences. Then, let's remember, that Canada also has a large representation of Oriental, Ukranian, Hungarian, Greek, Egyptian, and many other cultures. This calls for more folk tales!

2. THE UNIVERSAL APPEAL OF FOLK TALES

From their study of folk tales of different cultures, students may begin to note that they have a universal appeal because the tales value the same things: honesty, hard work, good will, kindness, and so on. Students can make a list of characters from different cultures who have these qualities.

3. HOW DO WE SOLVE PROBLEMS?

With a nation as vast as Canada and with many diverse cultural groups represented, have students note how problems were solved in the folk tales. Do we use any of these methods today? Students can work in teams to solve a common problem and come up with a list of potential approaches.

4. THE FAIRY TALES

Secure a collection of tales by Charles Perrault. Have students compare them with other versions in terms of text and especially conversation. Make a comparison between Perrault's version of "Cinderella" and other versions of the same tale. It is in Perrault's version that we first find the pumpkin coach, the glass slipper, and the importance of the clock at the stroke of midnight.

5. MOTHER GOOSE

Make a giant goose shape from fabric and sew and stuff it. Have students make a hat from construction paper (or use a real hat) and glasses from pipe cleaners. Tie a big bow around the neck and label her "Mother Goose." The goose can be set on a cozy rug, with a pile of good Mother Goose rhymes which students can read for enjoyment. They can memorize the verses and act them out, or improvise with background music fitting for the rhyme.

6. A TALE TIMELINE

Select a good tale. Then, cut a long strip of paper or tape many pages of 8-1/2″ x 11″ paper together in a row, and make an illustrated timeline of events that happen in the tale.

7. MATCH THE TALES

Students can take a piece of paper and cut it in half. On one half, illustrate a character from a specific tale. On the other half, illustrate another character or an event from the tale. Be sure to put the name of the tale somewhere on the paper. When all students have finished, spread the papers out upside-down on a grid. Students turn over the sheets one at a time in an effort to match the tales. This will encourage talking about the tales and help with language development.

8. IN A NUTSHELL

On small oval nut shapes, students can print proverbs they find in a tale, or the moral of the story in one sentence. Put these in a large basket that students take to their seats to read and categorize.

9. LET'S INVESTIGATE BRIDGES

Between Canada and the United States is a "Peace Bridge." Have students locate it on the map between Buffalo, New York, and Canada. This bridge is a tribute to two nations that live side by side in peace along miles and miles of border land.

10. WHERE IS LONDON BRIDGE?

This famous bridge is actually located in the United States because it was taken apart and moved to Arizona. Get a copy of Peter Spier's picture book, *London Bridge is Falling Down.* In this book is a history of the famous bridge, and all of the verses that go with the rhyme. Divide the class into two groups and do choral reading, with group 1 saying the verses that ask the questions (left side of page) and group 2 saying the verses that respond (right side of page).

11. AND THEN THERE ARE OTHER BRIDGES IN FAIRY TALES AND FOLK TALES

The "Three Billy Goats Gruff" are involved with a troll under a bridge. Drawbridges often lead to castles, and sometimes ogres hide out under bridges. Have students keep track of the bridges that play a part in folk tales.

12. BUILDING BRIDGES

"Bridging the gap" and "building bridges" are phrases in our language that denote cooperation between one side and another, one team and another, one country and another. Have students construct bridges from cardboard tubes, boxes, and other shapes. They can make a puppet figure at one side representing one country, and a puppet figure at the other side representing another country. Students can look for the similarities in the stories that would help these two to "bridge the gap." Write the stories and similarities on a 3 x 5 card and set it on the bridge.

CELEBRATIONS

Because Canada is a multicultural nation, many holidays represent beliefs, traditions, and customs that ethnic groups brought with them. In addition, there are national holidays that are Canadian in nature. The name "Canada" is an Iroquois word that means "village." Canada, then, is representative of the global village concept.

CHRISTMAS CELEBRATIONS

This holiday has a special flavor all its own for the various ethnic groups in Canada. In the Ukranian tradition, Christmas Eve is January 6, and a candle is lit and placed in the window of Ukranian homes. This serves as a symbol of light to guide the Holy Family. Hay or straw is placed under the tablecloth when the table is set as a reminder of the humble beginnings of Christ. A variety of dishes are served, and they are all meatless and have no milk. Since Christmas is one of the most widely celebrated of all holidays, there are variations of these customs throughout Canada. December 25 is the official day of Christmas.

DOMINION DAY

The birthday of the dominion of Canada is July 1. People celebrate with picnics, parades, and sporting events.

THE VISIT FROM NALUYUK

In Labrador, which is far to the north, the Eskimo culture has the equivalent of the "boogey man" who visits in early January. This person is a member of the group who disguises himself in a big shaggy coat of animal skins and goes from house to house to question the children regarding their behavior. After what seems like a very long time, the children are given a gift—usually a sweet treat—from Naluyuk's bag.

WINTERLUDE

In February, there is a winter sports celebration that lasts for ten days, which celebrates the joy that snow brings. People engage in activities such as skating, skiing, sleigh riding, sledding, and so on. One exciting aspect of this festive time of year is the vast array of snow and ice sculptures.

The Carnival in Quebec City, held in February or March, is another opportunity to take advantage of the snow. Tons of snow are transported into this city with a large French population, from which a large snow castle is built. It also provides an opportunity for smaller ice sculptures and contests.

VICTORIA DAY

May 24 is the birthday of Queen Victoria and is a day of sporting events and parades. The traditional May Pole celebration is sometimes held on this day, with dancing and the crowning of the King and Queen of May. This same holiday is celebrated in New Zealand.

THE CHINESE NEW YEAR

Toronto has a large population of Chinese. In "China Town," the street name signs are printed in both English and Chinese symbols. There is a celebration of the New Year (Gung Hay Fat Choy) with dancing in the streets and the traditional Chinese dragon. (See Asian Celebrations.)

HAPPY NEW YEAR!

Many Canadians celebrate the end of the old year and the ringing in of the new year on December 31. The Coptic New Year celebration is held in Canada on September 11. This is when Egyptian-Canadians celebrate the return of Sirius (star) to the sky. It was a signal for the Egyptians that the River Nile would soon overflow.

A YEAR-ROUND WONDER!

Niagara Falls, which borders the United States and Canada, is a special attraction for visitors from all over the world. At night colored spotlights shine on the Horseshoe Falls, Bridal Veil Falls, and the American Falls.

There are boat rides and other activities in the summer. Many newlyweds choose this spot for their honeymoon. During the summer, people drive for miles to picnic at the Falls and to enjoy the spectacular view.

SUGGESTED ACTIVITIES FOR THE CLASSROOM

1. OUR NEIGHBOR TO THE NORTH

Locate Canada on a map or globe. Canada is divided into provinces; have the students name and locate them. Have students make passports from construction paper for their travel throughout Canada. Note the area near Detroit, Michigan, where Canada dips to the south of the United States.

2. THE LAND OF NORTHERN LIGHTS

The Eskimos live in this country in the far north. "Eskimo" is an Algonquin name for the tribes who live to the north, who ate raw meat. The Cree word is "askimowew"—and it also means that food is eaten raw. This is a good time to discuss what foods we eat (in terms of fruits and vegetables) that are "raw" or uncooked.

3. THE COLDER, THE SAFER

This presents an opportunity to discuss refrigeration. Why is it possible for the Eskimos to eat raw meat and to store it for long periods of time without cooking? Why, on the other hand, would it not be possible for someone from a hot climate, such as Mexico, to eat raw meat? Explain to students why it is inadvisable for them to eat raw meat, especially if they are preparing their own food at home. (Meat harbors bacteria that spreads rapidly in warmth, and it requires cooking at a high temperature in order to make it safe for human consumption.)

4. WINTER SPORTS

If you are located in a cold, snowy area, take advantage of the snow and have a "sports day" in the afternoon. Talk about snowy-day activities that students can engage in if they do not have sporting equipment. They can build snowmen, make snow sculptures, play fox and geese, make snow forts, and so on.

5. WINTERLUDE POETRY

Students can write "winter words" on snowflake shapes, cut them out, and hang them in the classroom. When they have an abundance of winter words, they can write cinquain poetry about winter or winter activities. Use the following cinquain format:

one subject word
two words that describe subject
three words that end in "ing" that relate to subject
four-word sentence about the subject
an "oomph!" word to sum it up

Examples:

Snow
White, light
Glistening, falling, showering
It blankets the street.
Wonderland!

Skating
Smooth, graceful
Gliding, swooping, falling
I have new skates!
Fun!

6. THE MAPLE LEAF

The maple is a hardy tree that grows well in the northern climate. The flag of Canada has the symbol of the maple leaf in the middle. Sugar maple candies in the shape of a leaf are sold at stores. The professional hockey team from Toronto is called the "Maple Leafs." Discuss the concept of symbols and find out what the maple leaf stands for, or represents, to the people. Does Canada have other symbols? What are they? Then do a study of symbols from other countries. Have students look up the symbol(s) that represent the United States (Uncle Sam, Liberty Bell, Flag, Eagle, and so on). Also, have them identify two countries that they would like to know more about, and check their symbols in a world atlas.

7. HARNESSING NIAGARA FALLS

Have students locate Niagara Falls on the map between Buffalo, New York, and Canada. A Peace Bridge has been built over the falls that enables traffic to move between the two countries with relative ease.

When the word "harness" is used in conjunction with Niagara Falls, it means harnessing the tremendous power of the waterfalls to generate electricity. Students can do a scientific study of waterfalls and how the power is actually harnessed. On the lighter side, this calls for a festival of tall tales to see who can "harness" the falls, who can go over the falls in a barrel, who can tame the falls, and so on.

8. COLOR-CODED MONEY

When people attend parades, festivals, or celebrations, they often buy souvenirs, balloons, food, and so on. In Canada the paper money changes color with each denomination. This is unlike the United States, which has "greenbacks" whether the denomination is one dollar, five dollars, ten dollars, twenty dollars, fifty dollars, or one hundred dollars. In which country would it be easier to keep track of the money in your wallet? Get samples of Canadian coins and paper money at the bank and examine it for its color and for the symbols.

ARTS AND CRAFTS

Canada has a multi-ethnic population, so the art of this country reflects the ethnicity of the groups (English, French, Asian, Middle Easterners, and a wide variety of European countries). Canada is home to the rich arts and crafts of the Eskimo culture. Many wooden items are carved from the rich timber. Also, ice sculpting has reached an art form in Canada.

SUGGESTED ACTIVITIES FOR THE CLASSROOM

1. ESKIMO ARTS AND CRAFTS

The art of the Eskimo culture consists of items that are often worn and/or used. That is, functional items for everyday use are artfully decorated with bits of bone, leather, and animal hair. Beadwork is sometimes sewed onto clothing. In this harsh climate and environment, art is not something that is hung on the wall, but rather is linked to everyday life.

For example, in James Bay, the people make duck decoys from twigs and twine. These are functional because when they float on the water, they attract ducks and help the hunter get his dinner. On the other hand, people from other cultures gather these decoys, pay a minimum price for them, and sell them as folkart in the United States and other parts of the world. They are perceived by the native people as a function of their everyday life, and they are perceived by other cultures as works of art. Help students make this distinction.

Use twigs and grapevines, along with twine, to sculpt ducks, birds, dolls, and so on for a student activity. Soak the vines until pliable and then gently bend them. If students are not having much luck with figures, perhaps a wreath or a crude basket is an easier way to begin, since the twigs and vines seem to have a mind of their own! Through this process, students can gain an appreciation for the works of art that the native people are able to produce with little effort. The focus here can be upon the experience (process) rather than the outcome (product).

2. LANDSCAPE AS ART

In parts of Canada, the flower gardens have reached a high art form. In Vancouver and in Victoria, British Columbia, the flower gardens are a major tourist attraction. In some parks, there are sections for Japanese Gardens, Italian Gardens, French Gardens, English Gardens, and so on. In Toronto, flower beds of begonias are planted in such a way that they make colorful geometric designs. At Niagara Falls, a large flower clock is planted and colorful flower designs border the parks.

Students can plan a garden landscape with flowers of different heights and colors. Also, a bouquet of real flowers can be brought into the classroom for students to carefully examine, sketch, and then paint with watercolors or tempera paints. Be sure to study flowers in picture books to see how the illustrators are portraying flowers with line, color, shape, and design. Younger children do well at the easel with flower paintings. Read *The Reason for a Flower* by Ruth Heller (New York: Putnam, 1992) and *Planting a Rainbow* by Lois Ehlert (San Diego: Harcourt Brace Jovanovich, 1992).

3. SAWDUST ART

Canada is the land of lumbermills, which means an abundance of sawdust. Sawdust can be used to create interesting art works. Students can make a sketch of an item or landscape on a 9″ x 12″ sheet of dark construction paper. Then, they can outline their design or picture with glue. Carefully sprinkle the sawdust over the glued area. Allow to semi-dry, then lift and gently shake the paper to remove excess sawdust. Students can do several of these to try different techniques. Sawdust can be obtained from a building construction company or from the vocational education teacher in the school district.

4. MODELING WITH SAWDUST

Sawdust can be modeled in a manner similar to clay. Bits of material can be added to the basic piece by moistening and sticking them together. For one cup of the modeling material for this project, you will need:

1 cup fine sawdust
1 cup thin paste (paper paste)
old newspapers

Procedure:

1. Mix sawdust with paste to form a dough.
2. Knead thoroughly until mixed.
3. Spread old newspapers on modeling surface.
4. Model. Add pieces by moistening with glue.
5. Allow to dry until sculpture is hard (2-3 days).
6. Woodgrain surface can be sanded or sprayed with shellac (optional), which must be done only under adult supervision.

5. BR-R-R! LET'S BUILD AN ICE CASTLE

For building a castle, you will need a collection of molds (do not use glass) such as muffin tins, funnels, plastic bowls, yogurt containers, etc. In cold areas, these may be filled and left outside overnight to freeze.

1. Fill molds and freeze.
2. Select a cool place to work indoors (not by a sunny window).
3. Put on warm, woolen gloves.
4. Unmold ice shapes by dipping containers into warm water.
5. Make a solid foundation (use ice slush to help).
6. Build the castle. Put parts together with ice slush or a spray of warm water.

6. HIBERNATION MURAL PAINTING

Create a mural that shows life above ground and below ground. Students can work with chalk to create a line about one third of the way up on large light blue mural paper. The land below the line can show animals that are hibernating for the winter in their holes or dens (bears in a cave, turtles under the water in the ground, beaver dam with beavers under the water, and so on). Use white paint for mounds of snow above ground. Use black or brown for trees; when dry, paint white snow on the tops of the branches (or use cotton). Then, paint several animals that appear above ground in winter (spotted deer, snowshoe hare, and so on). Birds made from construction paper or paint that do not migrate can be added to the mural. This makes a very effective art mural for January or February.

7. A SNOWY DAY MURAL

If you live in an area where it snows, hang a wide piece of blue mural paper on the wall or bulletin board and wait. Wait for what? Wait for a snowy day.

When the snow begins to fall, have three or four students at a time paint an item on the mural *using white paint only* because everything is covered with snow. They can paint snowmen, houses, trees, and so on. This makes a very effective snowy day art experience.

8. CANADA, A HORIZONTAL AND VERTICAL EXPERIENCE

Canada has many large metropolitan cities with tall skyscrapers. At the same time, Canada has vast amounts of relatively flat land for miles and miles. Have students paint city scenes on tall, skinny sheets of paper, and country scenes on long, wide, thin sheets of paper. A helpful picture book resource is *Town and Country* by Alice and Martin Provenson (New York: Crown, 1984).

GAMES

The games are representative of this area of the globe and are not intended to be all inclusive.

PTARMIGANS VS. DUCKS (ESKIMO TUG OF WAR)

The Eskimos use a seal skin rope, but any rope will do. The Ptarmigans represent those students who were born in the winter and the Ducks represent those students born in the summer. So, line the teams up on either side of the rope accordingly and *pull*. (The contest is helpful in deciding how severe the winter will be—so if the Ptarmigans win, we're in for a blustery winter.)

ESKIMO SKIN TOSS

Do this with stuffed animals on a trampoline. Jump and toss the stuffed animal high in the air and try to catch it. In the Eskimo culture of Canada and Alaska, the skin toss game is played by people holding a large, circular animal skin tightly in their hands. One player gets into the middle of the skin and begins to jump up and down, getting the rhythm and motion going faster and faster until the combination of the people moving the skin up and down and the person jumping finally catapults the jumper high in the air.

FOX AND GEESE

This game can be played in fresh snow. One person is designated as "it" (fox) and the rest are geese. The geese follow the leader and must stay in the path of beaten down snow, but the fox can get out of the ruts made by the footprints and snatch one of the geese if it's not careful. When the fox makes a catch, this person is "it" and the game can continue on fresh snow.

FOLLOW THE ANIMAL TRACKS

Students can make a game of identifying tracks in the snow, and follow them to determine where the small animal or bird might be. Also, students can make their own snow track route to a buried treasure and try to confuse the followers by having the tracks disappear along the trail and then reappear.

SNOW SCULPTURE

Snow that is heavy and wet is very good for modeling. Balls can be rolled for snowmen, that can then be decorated with hat and mittens, etc. Snow can be packed into boxes and transported for making big forts or an igloo. Large figures of storybook characters or favorite animals can also be made. This is an outdoor activity for a day when the snow is "just right" for packing.

AN AFTERNOON OF SNOWY DAY SPORTS

In certain parts of the world, and in certain parts of the country, an entire school can plan for an outdoor winter sports day. Outdoor areas need to be designated for specific activities and age groups. The playground can be "flooded" during the week of the winter sports day so that students can bring their skates and enjoy this area. In addition to skating, there can be sledding and snow sculptures. Plan to have each group stay outdoors for about one hour; then return to a toasty classroom for hot chocolate with marshmallows melted on top, a snack treat, and a good story for listening.

SONGS, DANCES, RHYTHMS

Canada has a rich mixture of songs, rhythms, and dances because of the many cultures that make up this vast nation. The bagpipes of Scotland, for example, can be heard throughout the land, along with the spirited varieties of folk music from Europe. Sounds from the Middle East and Asia can be heard, along with the more formal music of French and English composers. Because of its proximity to the United States, the music of the U.S. is also quite popular in Canada.

The Winnipeg Music Festival is a yearly event with Canadian orchestras, soloists, and choirs performing from various regions throughout the land. Scholarships and prizes are awarded to foster the talented young musicians. And the Stratford-on-Avon yearly summer festival keeps the work of William Shakespeare alive.

CUMULATIVE SONGS SHARPEN YOUR MEMORY

"The Twelve Days of Christmas" is an example of a cumulative song, which is enjoyable for children to sing and act out as well. The creative dramatics can be done with sound effects or with large pictures that students have created. Another example of a cumulative song for students to enjoy is "I Know an Old Woman Who Swallowed a Fly."

THE INUIT WAY OF COMMUNICATING

Stories, songs, and legends about life in the past and in the present are ways that the Inuits communicate. The songs are accompanied by rhythmic drumbeats. Simple movements and steps may also be employed as a person tells about an event. Encourage students to practice this method so that their storytelling of folk tales and fairy tales may be enriched.

DID YOU EVER SEE A LASSIE?

This song can be continued for a long time. The movements may vary with the words "go this way and that way" every time a new person leads the tune. Here are the words to this familiar rhythm:

> Did you ever see a lassie, a lassie, a lassie,
> Did you every see a lassie, go this way and that (demonstrate).
> Go this way, and that way, go this way, and that way (all join in).
> Did you ever see a lassie, well how do you do (bow).

RAILROADS IN CANADA AND IN THE U.S.A.

The railroads played such an important role in the expansion of these two countries that it is no wonder there are many popular songs about the railroad. Here is a favorite.

"I've Been Working on the Railroad"

I've been working on the railroad,
All the live long day.
I've been working on the railroad,
Just to pass the time away.
Can't you hear the whistle blowing?
Rise up so early in the morn.
Can't you hear the captain shouting,
"Dinah, blow your horn!"

Dinah, won't you blow,
Dinah, won't you blow,
Dinah, won't you blow your hor-or-orn?
Dinah, won't you blow,
Dinah, won't you blow,
Dinah, won't you blow your horn!

Someone's in the kitchen with Dinah,
Someone's in the kitchen, I know o-o-oh!
Someone's in the kitchen with Dinah,
Strummin' on an old banjo!

He's strummin'
Fee fi fid-dl-ee i o,
Fee fi-fid-dl-ee i o o o o ,
Fee fi fid-dl-ee i o,
Strummin' on the old banjo. HEY!

"PUFFING BILLY" DOWN BY THE STATION

The steam locomotive helped to do the work and was referred to in England as "Puffing Billy" or "Puffer Belly." Young children can sing the following with accompanying motions while standing in a row, and then go shuffling down "the track" in time to the tune as they sing it once again.

Down by the station
early in the morning
See the little puffer bellies
all in a row.
See the engine driver
pull the little throttle,
Puff, Puff! Toot, Toot! Off we go!

SONGS THAT REFLECT WOMEN'S LIFE—THE LAUNDRY AND HOUSEHOLD WORK SONGS

To the tune of "The Mulberry Bush" this song has been sung with accompanying motions by young children for decades. These songs were developed before the luxury of electricity to help with household chores. It's a good "sing and stretch" song.

This is the way we wash our clothes, wash our clothes, wash out clothes
This is the way we wash our clothes, so early Monday morning. (*scrub board motions*)
This is the way we iron our clothes, iron our clothes, iron our clothes

This is the way we iron our clothes, so early Tuesday morning. (*ironing motions*)

This is the way we scrub the floor, etc. (*on hands and knees, scrubbing*)

This is the way we mend our clothes, etc. (*hand sewing motions*)

This is the way we sweep the house, etc. (*broom sweep motions*)

This is the way we bake our bread, etc. (*kneading motion*)

This is the way we go to church, etc. (*hands folded*)

THE RED RIVER VALLEY

This song refers to the Red River which flows through Manitoba in Canada and then south into the United States. It is a wistful song.

From this valley they say you are leaving,
We will miss your bright eyes and sweet smile.
For they say you are taking the sunshine,
That has brightened our pathway a while.

MY BONNIE LIES OVER THE OCEAN

The trip to Canada from Scotland, Europe, and other lands was very far indeed and immigrants left their families behind for a new life. Yet all people get homesick for loved ones and familiar sights that they might never see again. This song united people on that common ground.

My Bonnie lies over the ocean,
My Bonnie lies over the sea,
My Bonnie lies over the ocean,
Please bring back my Bonnie to me.
Bring back, bring back,
Oh bring back my Bonnie to me, to me.
Bring back, bring back,
Oh bring back my Bonnie to me.

FOOD

Just as Canada has a multicultural society, it follows then that it would have a wide array of ethnic foods. There is a heavy English and French influence, along with Asian, Indian, and European style cuisine, among others. In a major city, such as Toronto, it is not unusual to find neighborhoods with bakeries, fresh fruit and vegetable stores, and meat markets that cater to specific ethnic tastes. In the downtown area, restaurants of every ethnic group are represented. It is a gastronomical delight!

SUGGESTED RECIPES FOR THE CLASSROOM

Sourdough Starter

During the days of expansion in Canadian territory, and also in the United States, travelers often took along a small pot with sourdough in it for making biscuits. People in search of gold were given the nickname "sourdoughs." Sourdough is believed to have originated in Egypt thousands of years ago. Here's a recipe for sourdough starter:

1 teaspoon active dry yeast
1 cup warm water
1-1/2 cups flour
4 cups very warm water
6 cups flour

Stir yeast, water, and flour (first three ingredients) together in a bowl with a wooden spoon. Let this mixture sit uncovered for 6 days. Stir daily. It will begin to bubble and smell sour. After 6 days, store in refrigerator.

To make pancakes or biscuits from this dough:

Add the remaining water and flour, and mix well. Remove 1 cup of this lumpy mixture for the next "starter" and store in refrigerator, covered. Use this dough to make your breakfast or luncheon biscuits or pancakes.

Sourdough Biscuits

3/4 cup sourdough starter
1 cup milk
3 cups flour
1/2 teaspoon salt
1/2 teaspoon baking soda
1 tablespoon sugar

Use the procedure for making biscuits from any cookbook.

Also, each child can be given a half cup of sourdough starter to take home with a recipe. Ask parents first if they would like to engage in this activity at home.

Gingerbread

Gingerbread served as a home "barometer" for the weather in Germany. A gingerbread cookie cut-out of a soldier was hung by the entrance. Upon leaving in the morning, if the gingerbread was soft (absorbed water), it was apt to rain that day. If the gingerbread was dry, it was supposed to be a dry day. Gingerbread is often used as a holiday treat at Thanksgiving and especially Christmas.

1 cup butter (softened)
1 cup sugar
1-1/4 cups molasses
4 eggs
2 tablespoons dry ginger (spice)
3 teaspoons cinnamon
5 teaspoons baking soda
1-1/2 cups boiling water
5-1/2 cups flour

Cream butter. Stir sugar, molasses, and eggs into creamed butter. Add ginger, cinnamon, and baking soda and continue to stir. Stir in half the water. Stir in half the flour. Stir in remainder of water and flour. Grease two 9″ x 13″ baking pans. Bake in (toaster) oven (in the classroom) at 350 degrees until center springs back when touched, approximately 25 minutes. These can be baked one at a time—cool the first one, cut into portions, and eat it while the second one is in the oven. Serves 32.

Try the gingerbread experiment and hang a piece by the doorway. Does it get more moist and more dry as the weather changes? Could this actually be used as a weather predictor in your area?

Hot Chocolate for a Br-r-r! Day

6 cups water
4 ounces unsweetened chocolate
1 cup sugar
9 cups milk
tiny marshmallows (optional)

Bring water to boil in medium-size pan on hot plate. Add chocolate and stir until chocolate melts (low heat). Add sugar and stir until smooth. Stir in milk, a little at a time. Sprinkle marshmallows on top. Serves approximately 16.

Grilled Cheese and Canadian Bacon Sandwiches

2 slices of bread per child
1 slice of cheese per child
1/2 slice of canadian bacon
    per child
margarine
mustard

Fry bacon in electric frypan until slightly crisp. Set aside. Clean the pan. Make cheese sandwiches, and add bacon to each. Place some margarine in frypan and cook sandwiches until golden brown on both sides. Add mustard to taste.

Poires Helene (Pears Helen, France)

chocolate syrup
vanilla ice cream
canned pear halves, drained
strawberry jam
hot water (to thin the jam mixture)

Place one tablespoon chocolate syrup in the bottom of a little bowl for each person. Place one scoop vanilla ice cream on top of syrup. Place one pear half over the ice cream. Put a spoon of jam mixture on top of pear.

Nanook's Home-Made Ice Cream (From Long Ago)

This recipe is made in a pound coffee can with a lid, and then placed inside a larger tin can and surrounded with ice.

1 cup whipping cream
1 cup milk
1/2 cup sugar
1/2 teaspoon vanilla extract
ice
rock salt

Put smaller can inside larger can and surround with ice. Place rock salt over the ice. Place whipping cream, milk, sugar, and vanilla in inside can and secure lid. Secure lid on outer can. Roll can back and forth on an even surface for at least 10 minutes. (Students enjoy taking turns.) Then, open the large can and remove the inner can. Drain ice water. Open inner can and stir. Replace lid. Reinsert smaller can into large tin can. Repack with ice a second time. Secure lid on outer can. Roll for 10 more minutes, taking turns. Open and spoon into little cups.

Resource

Foodworks: Over 100 Science Activities and Fascinating Facts That Explore the Magic of Food. Ontario, Canada: Ontario Science Center, 1987.

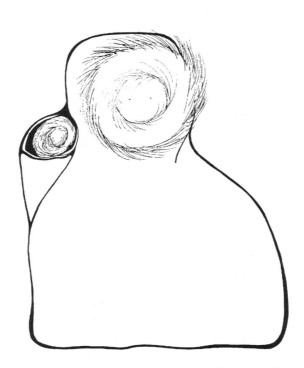

REPRODUCIBLE ACTIVITY PAGES

Tales from the North (*dependence upon animals*)

M. M. McMoose Takes Up Winter Sports (*information books*)

The Role of the Goose in Folk Tales (*storytelling*)

The Role of the Tree in Folk Tales (*comparisons*)

Unicorn Pollution Control Center (*gathering information*)

Make a Pride Badge (*awareness of heritage*)

Why the North Sky Sends Snow in Winter (*porquois tales*)

Catch Me If You Can—Gingerbread Man Recipe (*food recipe*)

Sea Tales and the Cheese Rat (*bookmarks*)

Cypress Is Hungry for Information (*geography: ponds and rivers*)

I Went Backpacking and Wound Up in Canada (*geography*)

Jack Horner's Purple Plum Award (*motivation for reading*)

Do an Author Study—Canada (*Ted Harrison and others*)

TALES FROM THE NORTH

The people in northern cultures depend upon animals in many, many ways. Read some northern tales, and, in the space below, diagram several ways that animals aid people.

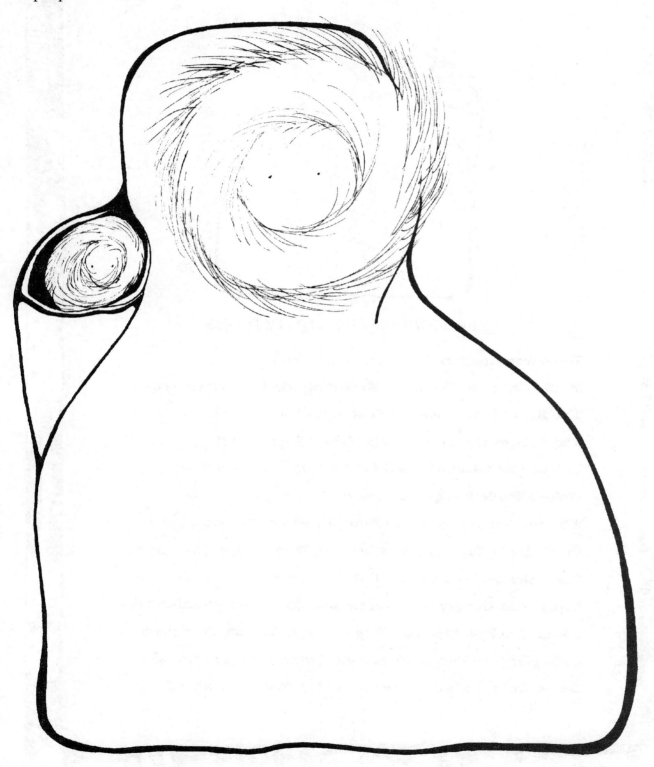

Name _____ Date _____

M. M. McMOOSE TAKES UP WINTER SPORTS

M. M. McMoose is busy skiing today and needs your help. Write the names of eight winter sport activities

1.

2.

3.

4.

5.

6.

7.

8.

Select a sport you would like to know more about. Find information books about the sport. Take notes on the other side of this sheet. Share the information with classmates.

THE ROLE OF THE GOOSE IN FOLK TALES

The goose is associated with magic and golden eggs in all parts of the world. There were sacred geese in Greek temples. In China, geese are given as a wedding present because geese are faithful. The Goose God of the Ostyaks of Siberia lives in a special nest of fur and skin.

   Enjoy a folk tale about a goose and be prepared to tell it. Practice it while you color this page.

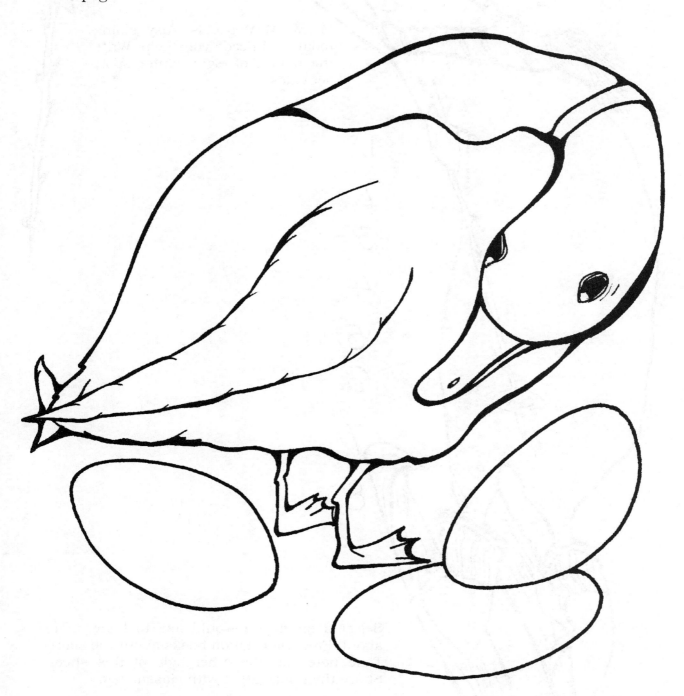

Name _____   Date _____

THE ROLE OF THE TREE IN FOLK TALES

Many tales have talking trees and helpful trees. The evergreen is forever faithful. The tree-of-life is often an apple tree or a date tree. Search through folk tales and find trees that play a powerful role in the story. Share the information below.

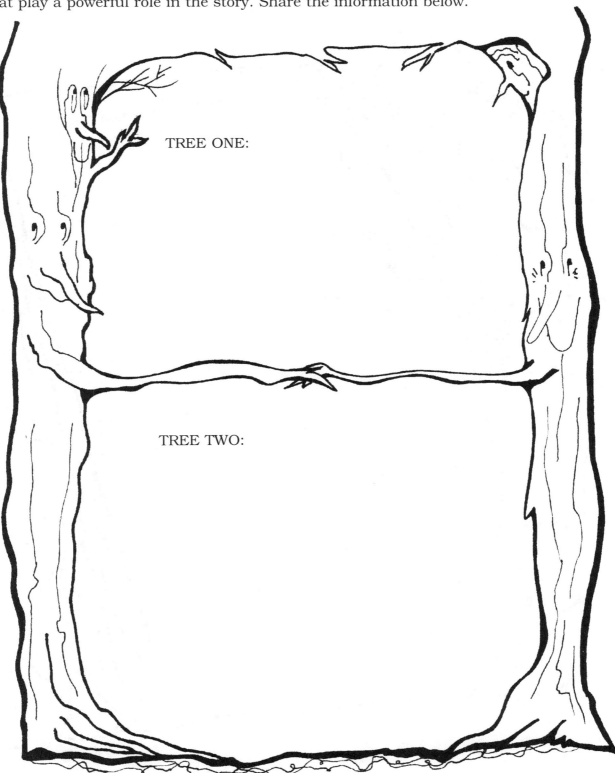

TREE ONE:

TREE TWO:

UNICORN POLLUTION CONTROL CENTER

Pollution is a worldwide problem. In legends, the unicorn dips its horn into stagnant water, and it magically clears up. Write to the unicorn about a pollution problem.

Pay Attention to Pollution Problems

HELP!

MAKE A PRIDE BADGE

Design it, color it, cut it out, and wear it with pride! Do your research by asking family members or by reading library books.

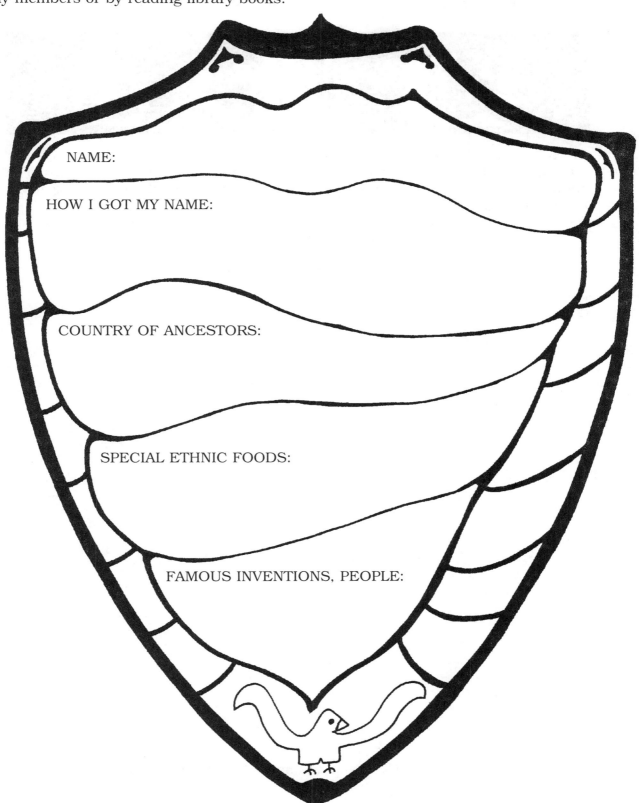

NAME:

HOW I GOT MY NAME:

COUNTRY OF ANCESTORS:

SPECIAL ETHNIC FOODS:

FAMOUS INVENTIONS, PEOPLE:

WHY THE NORTH SKY SENDS SNOW IN WINTER

In French, the word *porquois* (por-kwa) means "why." Many tales have the word *why* in the title. Read a variety of them, and then you can write your own. The ending is done for you. Now you need a beginning and several events that lead up to this ending.

... and that is why the North Sky sends snow in winter.

CATCH ME IF YOU CAN—GINGERBREAD MAN RECIPE

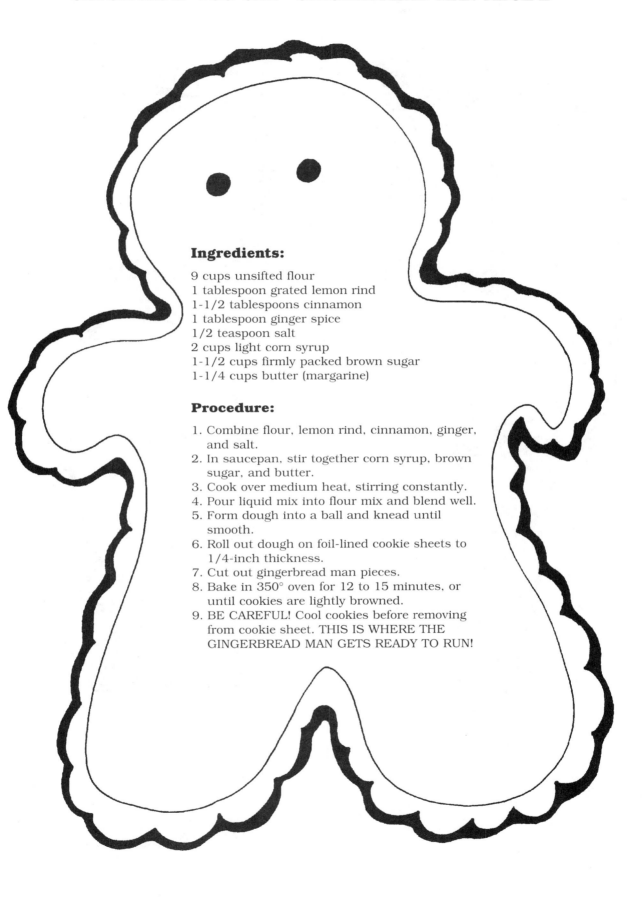

Ingredients:

9 cups unsifted flour
1 tablespoon grated lemon rind
1-1/2 tablespoons cinnamon
1 tablespoon ginger spice
1/2 teaspoon salt
2 cups light corn syrup
1-1/2 cups firmly packed brown sugar
1-1/4 cups butter (margarine)

Procedure:

1. Combine flour, lemon rind, cinnamon, ginger, and salt.
2. In saucepan, stir together corn syrup, brown sugar, and butter.
3. Cook over medium heat, stirring constantly.
4. Pour liquid mix into flour mix and blend well.
5. Form dough into a ball and knead until smooth.
6. Roll out dough on foil-lined cookie sheets to 1/4-inch thickness.
7. Cut out gingerbread man pieces.
8. Bake in 350° oven for 12 to 15 minutes, or until cookies are lightly browned.
9. BE CAREFUL! Cool cookies before removing from cookie sheet. THIS IS WHERE THE GINGERBREAD MAN GETS READY TO RUN!

name

Put Your Nose In A Good Book

Sea Tales

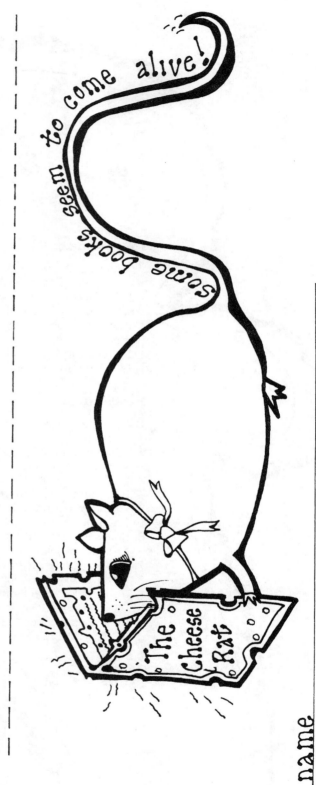

some books seem to come alive!

The Cheese Rat

name

Name _____   Date _____

CYPRESS IS HUNGRY FOR INORMATION

Have you heard of a Spelling Bee? The Ogres are having a Geography Bee! Message from Cypress: "I need all the information you can write down (and remember) about ponds, rivers, and gulfs OR I'll have the ducks for dinner. Be neat, too."

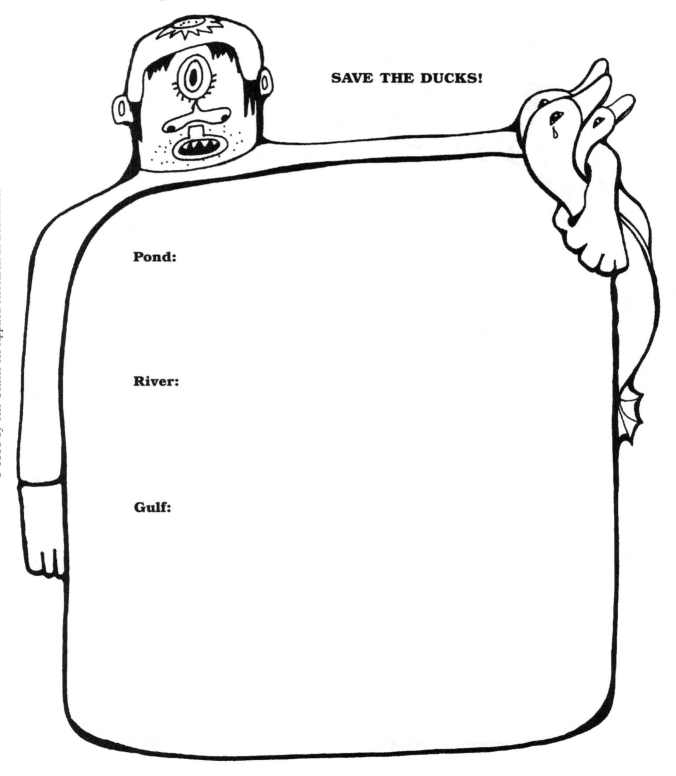

SAVE THE DUCKS!

Pond:

River:

Gulf:

Name _____ Date _____

I WENT BACKPACKING AND WOUND UP IN CANADA

I'm from the Caribbean (Jamaica), and before you knew it I was in Montreal," announced C. F. Turtle. Can you map out a return route for her in the space below? Is it far? Can she walk? Good luck with your mapping!

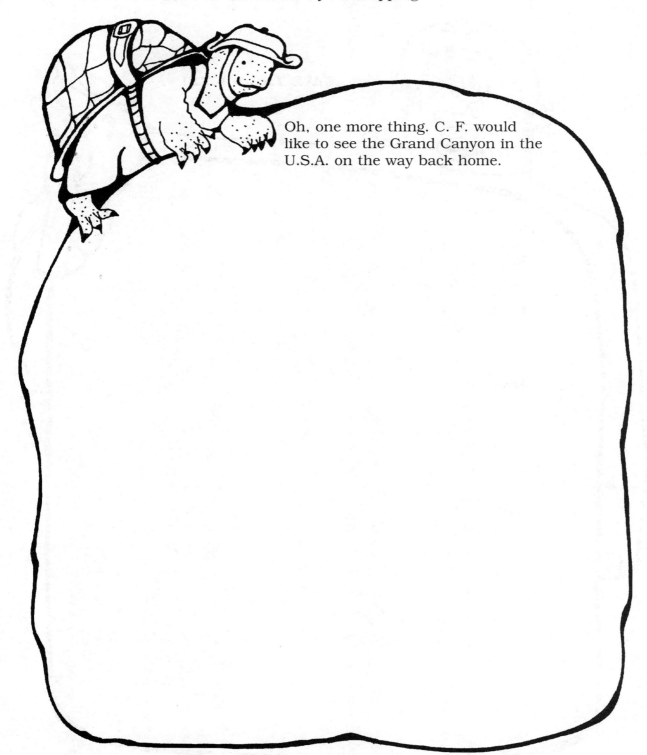

Oh, one more thing. C. F. would like to see the Grand Canyon in the U.S.A. on the way back home.

Name _____   Date _____

JACK HORNER'S PURPLE PLUM AWARD

This award is given to a book that's a real plum! "Plum good" means REALLY good!
This book is so good, it made me want to read more!

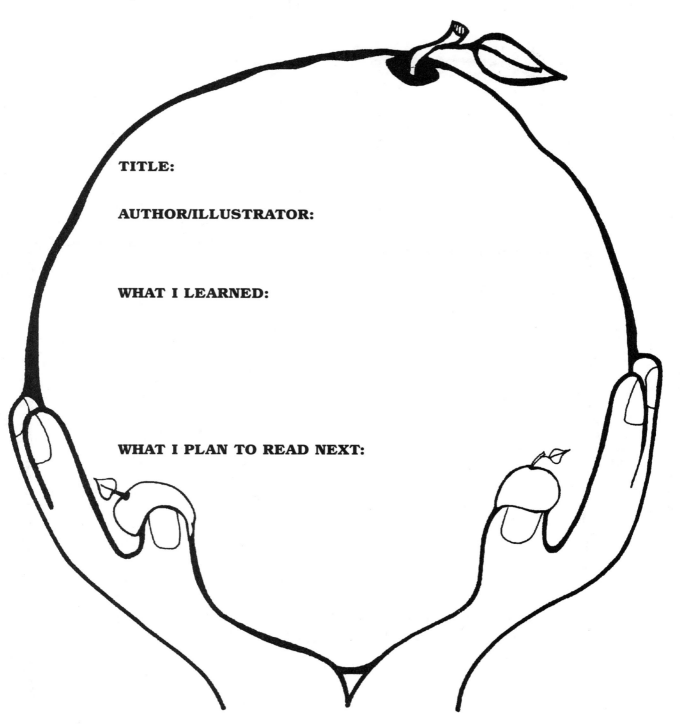

TITLE:

AUTHOR/ILLUSTRATOR:

WHAT I LEARNED:

WHAT I PLAN TO READ NEXT:

Name _____ Date _____

DO AN AUTHOR STUDY—CANADA

Locate a variety of books about Canada, and a variety of authors. One introductory book is *O Canada* by Ted Harrison, with words and music to "O Canada" and information about each province. In the space provided below, give three information facts about Canada.

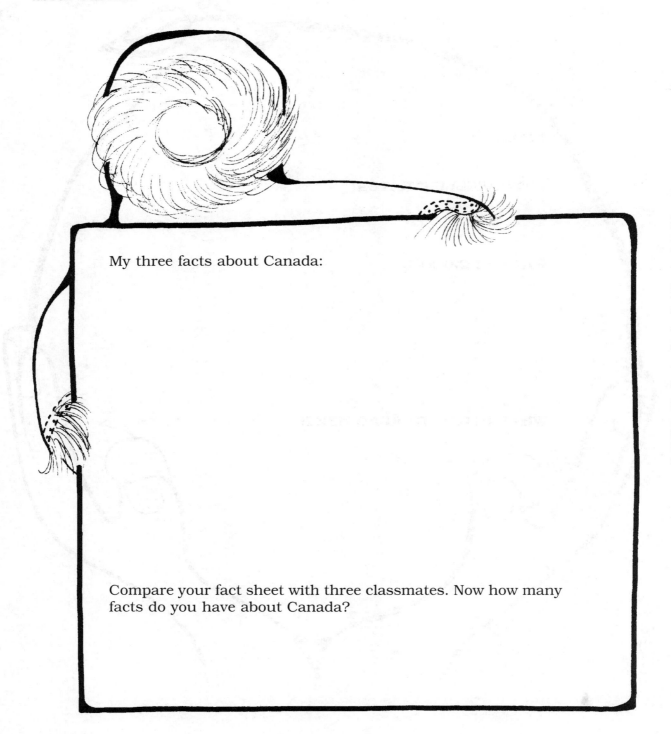

My three facts about Canada:

Compare your fact sheet with three classmates. Now how many facts do you have about Canada?

CARIBBEAN and OTHER ISLANDS

RECOMMENDED CHILDREN'S BOOKS

This section focuses upon the Caribbean Island Cultures, which have more books in print than Pacific and Indian Ocean Island Cultures.

Agard, John. *The Calypso Alphabet*. Illustrations by Jennifer Brent. New York: Holt, Rinehart, and Winston, 1989. This book introduces the cultures and customs of the peoples of the Caribbean. It is a poetic journey, and the scratchboard illustrations with vibrant colors give the book an energy of its own.

Belpre, Pura. *Perez and Martina*. Illustrations by Carlos Sanches. New York: Viking: 1932, 1992. This re-released cumulative folk tale from Puerto Rico is about the tragic romance between a refined cockroach, Martina, and a gallant mouse, Perez, who is accidently cooked in Martina's Christmas pudding!

Burgie, Irving. *Carribean Carnival: Songs of the West Indies*. Illustrations by Frane Lessac. New York: Tambourine, 1992. This book contains a collection of Calypso songs by composer Burgie, and includes "Day-O" along with other rhythmic tunes that make a fine collection. The illustrations are done in primitive style.

Gittins, Anne. *Tales from the South Pacific Islands*. Illustrated by Tom Kealiinohomoku. Owings-Mills, MD: Stammer House Publishers, Inc., 1977. A variety of folk tales collected from the South Pacific including Fiji, Rotuma, Tonga, Samoa, and other islands. Meet the two-headed giant and Ulu-Matua ("Wisehead") who was taller than a coconut tree!

Joseph, Lynn. *A Wave in Her Pocket; Stories from Trinidad*. Illustrations by Brian Pinkney. New York: Clarion Press, 1991. This book contains six stories remembered from a childhood in Trinidad. The tales, based on traditional folklore, include the blood-sucking soucoyant. There is family history to be enjoyed also.

___. *An Island Christmas*. Illustrations by Catherine Stock. Boston: Houghton Mifflin, 1992. In this selection Rosie is busy helping her mother and Tantie prepare the traditional black-currant cake, sorrel drink, and soursop ice cream.

Keller, Holly. *Island Baby.* **New York: Greenwillow, 1992.** A young boy named Simon helps nurse a baby flamingo back to health, and in the process learns a lesson in independence.

Makhanlall, David P. *Folk Tales of the World: Brer Anansi and the Boat Race—A Folk Tale from the Caribbean.* **Pictures by Amelia Rosato. New York: Peter Bedrick Books, 1988.** Brer Anansi, one of the most popular characters of West Indian and West African folk lore, has made his way into the Caribbean culture, and is known as one of the most famous of the tricksters. Brer Rabbit and Brer Bear challenge Brer Anansi to a boat race—but watch out! This is one in a series of folk tale books from this publisher that include *What Made Tiddalik Laugh?*, an Australian Aborigine folk tale, and *The Wizard Punchkin*, a folk tale from India.

Myers, Walter Dean. *Mr. Monkey and the Gotcha Bird.* **Illustrated by Leslie Morrill. New York: Delacorte Press, 1984.** The author combines African and Caribbean folk tale motifs with playful, rhythmic language. Be careful if you don't keep your word, especially if you have a monkey by the tail.

Powell, Pamela. *The Turtle Watchers.* **New York: Viking, 1991.** A leatherback turtle lays her eggs on the beach as three island sisters, who have stayed up all night, watch this spectacular event. But, turtle eggs are appealing to hungry sea birds, a boy looking for a snack, and even to an untrustworthy customs officer. The turtle watch begins!

Rohner, Harriet and Jesus Guerrero Rea. *Atariba and Niguayona: A Story from the Taino People of Puerto Rico.* **Illustrated by Consuelo Mendez. Chicago: Children's Book Press, revised edition, 1988.** A bilingual text of a moving legend about a young boy, Niguayona, and his search for the red fruit of the caimoni tree that will save his best friend's life. A helpful pronunciation guide to names is included.

Sherlock, Philip. *Anansi the Spider Man, Jamaican Folk Tales.* **Illustrated by Marcia Brown, New York: Thomas Y. Crowell, 1954.** When things go well, Anansi is a man, but when he is in danger, he can transform himself into a spider and hide in a web. When the great migrations to the islands of the Caribbean took place years ago, the Africans brought with them the stories they loved about Brer Anansi and his friends Tiger, Crow, Moos-Moos the mouse, and Kisander the cat. These tales are filled with wisdom and good humor.

Wolkstein, Diane. *The Magic Orange Tree, and Other Haitian Folk Tales.* **Illustrations by Elsa Henriquez. New York: Knopf, 1978.** A rich and varied collection of 27 different stories gathered by the author while traveling through Haiti. An excellent read-aloud book.

FOLK TALES

The folk tales from this part of the world are a rich mixture because of the variety of backgrounds of the people who live there (Native American, African, Chinese, Hispanic). The Native Americans were the inhabitants before many of the islands were claimed by the Europeans, primarily Spanish, French, and English. Slaves were brought to the islands from their homeland in Africa. And many Chinese went to the islands as indentured servants.

The languages that are spoken, then, are of a great variety. For example, many of the islanders speak English (Bahamas, Jamaica, Virgin Islands, Barbados, Trinidad), many speak Dutch (Curacao, Aruba, St. Eustatius), several speak Spanish (St. Thomas, St. Croix, Puerto Rico, Cuba), and some speak French (Guadeloupe, Haiti, Martinique). With the rich cultural background and the rich mixture of language, the folk tales take on a distinct flavor all their own.

However, many of the African-New World tales keep their own style and message intact; this section deals mainly with this information.

DAY NAMES

In West Africa it was common for children to be named according to the day of the week on which they were born. This custom prevailed in Jamaica, and the following names representing the days of the week, are common as characters in the folk tales:

Day of the Week	Male	Female
Sunday	Quashe	Quasheba
Monday	Cudjo	Juba
Tuesday	Cubena	Beneba
Wednesday	Quaco	Cooba
Thursday	Quao	Abba
Friday	Cuffee	Feeba
Saturday	Quamina	Mimba

TORTOISE THE TRICKSTER

In Cuba, as in Nigeria, Tortoise remains the primary trickster figure, whereas in other parts of the New World, Anansi the spider is the trickster figure. There are trickster figures throughout the Caribbean in a variety of forms, some human and some divine.

KONI-KONI

This is a rabbit-like animal, similar to Cunnie-Rabbit of Sierra Leone. Koni-Koni is associated with many proverbs, and his name is used as a preface. Some of the forms used, for example, are "Koni-Koni says . . .," or "Koni-Koni says that one must not . . .," or "Koni-Koni says therefore . . ."

PRAISE NAMES

Known as "kirari" among the Hausa and "isibongo" among the Zulu, the praise names were recited in honor of important individuals. An example of this greeting in a folk tale where the lion is the king, might be as follows: "Oh King of Beasts, Oh Golden-Haired One, Oh One of Great Strength."

THE ZEST OF PROVERBS

In African cultures, proverbs are included in everyday conversation to add flavor. There are thousands of them, and they are used liberally. Several examples for one who cannot make up his or her mind are, "A person does not finish washing his hands and then say that he will eat some more," or "A person does not put on his party hat and then go to bed," or "A person does not wish for rice and then go hunting." (See Spanish proverbs below.)

THE SHARPENING OF THE MIND

Riddles in African culture have long been regarded as a means of sharpening a child's wits. They have animals, objects from nature, and people at their core and require concentration, analysis, and critical thinking.

They also serve another function—they teach lessons with regard to social etiquette and proper behavior. An example is, "Who goes down the street past the King's house but does not salute?" (*Answer:* Rain water) Parents use riddles to teach the young children, and eventually these give way to the proverbs for the older children.

THE SPANISH PROVERBS

These are to be found in abundance, and were spread throughout Europe and the New World. Some of them include:

- To accomplish anything, work is necessary.
- Too many gifts spoil the child.
- A rich man has many friends and many relatives.
- He who has a full stomach does not believe anyone is hungry.
- Hugs and kisses do not break bones.

TALKING HEADS, WALKING HEADS

These are familiar characters in folk tales. One belief is that they originated from people who walked among crops that grew up to their necks. Their movement, then, and the fact that they talk give the illusion that the head is disconnected from the body. Talking heads appear in folk tales in many areas of the world. In some tales, a person takes off the head, fixes the hair, and puts the head back on again. See *The Talking Eggs* by Robert San Souci, illustrated by Jerry Pinkney, a Caldecott Award Winner (New York: Dial Books for Young Readers, 1989).

ANANSI THE SPIDER TALES

Anansi the trickster figure came to the islands from Africa. (Sometimes the spelling is changed to Ananse.) In Haiti, the spider is called Ti Malice. These tales reached the United States through the sea islands around South Carolina, and are often referred to as Aunt Nancy Tales. (See the African-American section.) The Anansi trickster is one of the major trickster figures in island stories. Other favorite tricksters are the hare, jackal, and the mongoose.

THE RED GEM

In Spanish astrology, the sun is represented by red. It is considered to be the color of sacrifice. In Greece, wearing red is believed to help protect a child from drowning. Red rubies were often worn on ornamental breastplates in Europe. The color has important meaning the world over. In some cultures it is considered the color of life (blood red).

SUGGESTED ACTIVITIES FOR THE CLASSROOM

1. DAY NAMES

Have students do some research at home to find out on which day of the week they were born. Using the information about Jamaican day names in this section, they can find out what their name would be in that culture. Then, they can use that name for the main character in a folk tale who is invited to a party given by Anansi the Spider.

2. KONI-KONI SAYS

Students can rewrite their classroom rules using the "Koni-Koni says" style. For example, "Koni-Koni says you must not run in the hall." This may cause a renewed interest in doing things the right way, in a manner that appeals to the imagination of students.

3. RIDDLES

Aside from being fun, riddles do cause creative and critical thinking. Have students get books of riddles from the school library and learn to write their own. They can create a class Book of Riddles with the riddle on one page, and the answer on the back of that page. Make a bright, bold cover, and colorful illustrations.

4. WHAT'S IN A NAME?

In the Caribbean, "Mooma" is a term for "Mother" in some of the eastern-most islands. "Tanty" is a term for "Aunt," from the French "la tante." Have students share pet names for mother, father, and other family members. They can also share their own nickname. Secure a book on the origin of names from the library, and students can find out the meaning of their given name. Also, how does that name translate into Spanish or another foreign language?

5. MORE ABOUT NAMES

Since students will be reading a wide assortment of folk tales from different lands, have them begin a classroom chart of boys' names and girls' names. List them and the story title of the book. Students may want to keep a list of animal names as well. Some popular names from other cultures are:

Country	Girl	Boy
Spain	Maria	Carlos
	Carmen	Pedro
Israel	Rachel	Benjamin
	Rebecca	Jonathan
China	Liu	Cheng
Nigeria	Binta	Ado
	Ayo	Bola

6. ISLAND HOPPING

Secure a large map of the Caribbean Sea region, or use the opaque projector to make a map larger and trace the islands on blue paper. Color the islands lush green and learn the names. Which are large? Which are tiny? What products do they grow? What is life like on these different islands?

Students can make a passport, and travel from island to island by way of information books. On the passport page, put vital information about that particular island. Some of the islands include Bahamas, Jamaica, Haiti, Dominican Republic, Puerto Rico, Virgin Islands, Antigua, Dominican Republic, Martinique, Barbados, Trinidad, Cuba, etc. Write to various cruise lines that advertise in the Travel Section of the local newspaper for information about cruises to these special islands.

7. POETRY AND FOLK TALES

Set up a poetry nook in the classroom, and have students select poems that could "complement" a folk tale. A poem about a sly fox, for example, would be a good match for "Little Red Riding Hood," and poems about pigs would be a good match for "The Three Little Pigs." There are many poems about giants, ogres, and unicorns.

CELEBRATIONS

These islands are home to Native Americans, African-Americans who were brought over as slaves from Africa, African-Americans who escaped to the islands from North America, Chinese indentured servants, Spanish, Europeans, and other cultures. There is a wide variety of customs and celebrations that vary from island to island, and within a particular island. This list is not intended to include every celebration, but gives the reader some idea of festivals in this part of the world.

WHAI OH! JAMAICA INDEPENDENCE DAY

This national festival is held on the first Monday in August. In Kingston, the capital, there is a parade as a young girl is crowned Miss Jamaica. There are arts and crafts competitions with prizes and certificates. There are also floats, parades, and dancing in the streets. English is the spoken language. ("Whai oh!" is a Jamaican exclamation, similar to "Wow!" or "Wow-ee-ee!")

HAITI INDEPENDENCE DAY

January marks this festival, which coincides with the New Year festivities. Haiti is the only French-speaking republic in the Americas. Most people speak a dialect known as Creole. On this day people gather in the capital, Port-au-Prince, for parades, singing, and dancing. Major Christian holidays of Christmas and Easter are celebrated in Haiti.

PUERTO RICO

This island is a territory of the United States, and was at one time the most European of the islands. Many of the holidays and celebrations on this island are similar to those celebrated in the United States. At Christmas time, roving singers go from home to home singing carols. At Easter there are sunrise services at different points on the island beaches.

TRINIDAD CARNIVAL

Two days before Lent, a Carnival known as "Mas" (Mask) is held with singing, dancing, and festivities. Carnival costumes are sometimes outrageous, with head pieces as large as 6 feet high representing life-sized biblical characters, primitive-looking people, or present-day famous people. A Queen of the Carnival is chosen, and there is a competition for the best band. The integration of so many strains of people (African, Chinese, Indian, Venezuelan, Portuguese, and so on) has made the Trinidad Carnival quite unique in the world.

SUGGESTED ACTIVITIES FOR THE CLASSROOM

1. MAP AND GLOBE SKILLS

Locate the Caribbean Islands on the map or globe. Have students make shape flashcards, with the island name on the reverse side, so they can memorize the names.

2. CALYPSO MUSIC

Play this music as background when students are reading about folk tales and celebrations on these islands.

3. TOURISM, A MAJOR SOURCE OF REVENUE

There are many people from all over the world who go to the Caribbean for a vacation in the land of sea and sun. Get the "Travel" section from a Sunday newspaper or a travel magazine from the library, and have students check the information about cruise ship travel to this part of the world. Write for information.

4. PLAN A CRUISE

Students can use the information they receive from cruise lines to plan a Caribbean cruise for the classroom. What is the cost of airfare to the point of departure? Is it more expensive to go at celebration time, just before Lent, or during off-season? What is the cost per person and what does this include?

Students can divide into cooperative teams and work together to learn about a particular island. They can try to persuade others, through travel posters that they make, to come to their island. For this, they will need to dig for information in the library.

5. A CELEBRATION OF WATER SPORTS

This area of the world provides an excellent opportunity to study water sports such as snorkeling, water skiing, boating, swimming, surfing, and so on. Students can investigate a sport and find an interesting way to relate the information. Having a guest speaker who has been snorkeling or boating in this area will enrich the learning experience.

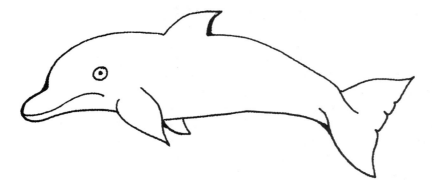

6. A CELEBRATION OF SEA LIFE

Get a videotape of underwater life from the library and go on a glorious visual expedition. Create a bulletin board of colorful sea creatures, covered over with blue cellophane.

7. CHANGING SEASONS

If students live in an area of the country where there is a change of seasons, have them "discover" that this brings with it a change of scenery, clothing, and different sports, whereas in the island culture the weather is the same all year. Have them discuss how the seasons affect our thinking and our living in many ways. What does it mean when some people from northern states say, "It just isn't Christmas without snow." Is it?

8. A CELEBRATION OF POETRY

Have students go to the library for poetry collections about the sea, sun, nature, colorful birds in the tropical islands, swashbuckling pirates, and so on. Be on the lookout for *Earth Verses and Water Rhymes* (New York: Macmillan, 1991) and *Fat Cats at Sea* (New York: Macmillan, 1992) by J. Patrick Lewis.

ARTS AND CRAFTS

One way that you can learn a great deal about a culture is by examining its legacy of art. Ancient civilizations of these islands created works of art from gold and silver because it was so plentiful in the environment. Earth was molded into figures of gods or animals for decoration, or for vases, bowls and jugs for everyday use. These were then dried in the hot sun. Later, the clay was fired in ovens (kilns) so that it was less porous and could be used longer. Early people made items that could be worn or used in their ceremonies, such as masks, jewelry, drums, and rattles.

SUGGESTED ACTIVITIES FOR THE CLASSROOM

1. THE SUN GOD

The sun is depicted in the folklore and in the art of the people since it played such an important role in their life. The sun was the giver of life in the sense that it enabled the rich, lush foliage to grow, which gave the people an abundance of fresh fruits and vegetables. The sun, then, is painted with a wide variety of lines that are filled in with bright orange, yellow, and red hues. For a student art activity, have them look through colorful picture books for different ways that the sun is depicted. Students can create their own large sun designs using black crayon, and color them in with bright watercolor crayons or tempera paint. Lines can be straight or circular, and the face of the sun god can appear in the center. These can make a lovely border for a bulletin board, or can be hung from the ceiling fixtures.

2. STARFISH TESSELATIONS

The sea star has a hard, spiny skeleton and five or more arms, or rays, that are arranged like the points of a star. In art, they can be painted with any color—blue-green sea tones, orange tones, or black and white. The star pattern lends itself to a repeat interlocking pattern of itself, or *tesselation*. (Have students examine picture books or calendars that show the art work of M.C. Escher for this concept.) They can work on 12″ x 18″ paper for their starfish designs.

3. MULTI-COLORED MOLAS

The women of Panama invented the mola, a type of applique. The multi-colored design is created by using layers of cloth of different colors; then cutting through the layers with tiny scissors, and turning the cloth under with tiny stitches. This takes time and patience. Originally, the people used this method to decorate their clothing, but it became so popular when visitors traveled to the islands that molas are now made and sold as works of art. People frame them and hang them in their homes.

Younger students can make mola-type designs by using a 9″ x 12″ felt background piece of black or red or yellow. Then they can cut their design (usually a bird, fish, flower, or a person) from smaller pieces of felt and glue them onto the background piece in layers. Older students might want to try their hand at a simple mola design using a bird or fish motif. (Also see the Latin American reproducible activity pages.) A good resource book is Judith Hoffman Corwin's *Latin American and Caribbean Crafts* (New York: Watts, 1992).

4. CARIBBEAN SEA MURAL

Carribean Canvas is a colorful book of paintings and poems and rhythms compiled by Frane Lessac (Philadelphia: Lippincott, 1985), and is an excellent resource book for children. Have them examine the shapes and colors of the plants and the fish, and drink in the vibrant colors that surround the people. Then have students create their own Caribbean Sea Mural of colorful fish, using a bulletin board backing of vibrant blue. Each student can contribute a strikingly colorful fish with stripes or polka dots or both! Students can then write stories or poems about their underwater world.

5. MASTER PAINTERS OF STILL LIFE

The islands have luscious fruits with colors heightened by the bright sun. Bring in a sample of four or five fruits and place them in a bright plastic bowl of pink or purple. Be sure to include a sunny yellow banana, a bright green lime, a large colorful orange, and a slice of melon. Have students create masterpieces of the still life using pencil sketches. Then use felt-tipped pens or tempera paint that has a phosphorescent quality to fill in the shapes. Frame the paintings by stapling them to a large construction paper sheet of brilliant orange or bright aquamarine. Hang them on your bulletin board gallery.

6. DID YOU EVER SEE SUCH A PARROT?

Parrots in this part of the world are bright and beautiful with many colors. Students can create large-sized parrots from brightly colored construction paper. Use an oval shape for the body, a rounded shape for the head, and then add a large beak, eyes, feet, and "feathers" of different colors. Encourage students to use a wide range of colors for the birds; mix orange, red, and yellow together for brighter feathers, rather than using a solid color. Arrange this display on the classroom door for a warm welcome.

GAMES

Because of the multicultural nature of the people in this area of the world, the games are similar to ones found in African, Spanish, and Asian cultures. Often the items used from nature are different and the rhythms may vary, but the games remain basically the same. Many of the games are games of skill, games of imitation of elders, games of run-and-chase, hide and seek, and the ever popular "it" games.

A LA RUEDA RUEDA (RING AROUND THE ROSY)

Children join hands and move around in a circle, jump, and then all fall down to this chant:

Circle, circle, circle
Bread and cinnamon.
Along came the teacher,
Give we a WHACK   (children jump)
What a smart CHILD   (children jump)
MARIPE, MARIPE*   (children jump)
I sat down PAT!   (all sit down)

*pronounced Ma-REE-pay

THE JUMPING CLOCK

This is a jump rope game. Two players hold the rope (or vine) at the end and keep it swinging. One player runs through for "zero," the next jumps once for "one," the next jumps twice for "two," and so on until the clock strikes twelve.

FOLLOW THE LEADER

Children form a line and must do exactly as the leader does. Often the leader does subtle movements such as turning his or her ankles so that the toes face outward or inward, or shifting a shoulder ever so slightly. Everyone must pay close attention.

CATCH THE BAG OF SAND

Sand is placed in a container (could be a big leaf) and wound with twine. Children stand in a circle and throw the bag of sand to each other. The one who "catches" the bag when it bursts open must run to the nearest tree and touch it before being tagged by a member of the circle.

TOSSING THE BALL

A lightweight ball is tossed into the air. It must be kept in the air by the players who can hit it with the sole of their foot, or with the heel of the foot. This requires considerable skill and develops as children continue to practice. In some cultures this is played by the men and the boys.

STICKS AND STONES

With a stick, a circle is drawn in the earth or in the sand, and two sticks are placed upright within the circle. Each player has two stones, and two throws in an attempt to knock over the sticks. A point is given each time a stick is knocked over.

Resource

Millen, Nina. *Children's Games From Many Lands* (Ann Arbor, MI: Books on Demand, 1965).

SONGS, DANCES, RHYTHMS

There is a rich mixture of songs, dances, and rhythms in the Caribbean because the people are from a variety of cultures. Not only did new arrivals (African slaves, Black slaves from the Americas, indentured Chinese, French, and Spanish people to name a few) bring their own music, but eventually it blended with the rhythms of the Native Americans who were already present. For this reason, the music has its own flavor with a variety of tempos.

The rumba is a fast, lively dance that originated in the West Indies. The conga and the cha cha originated on the island of Cuba. The tamborito is the national dance of Panama, and the merengue is a popular dance in the Dominican Republic and in Haiti. People enjoy listening to the music of the marimba, which resembles the xylophone. A good resource book is *American Neighbors* edited by John P. Augelli (Grand Rapids, MI: The Fideler Company, 1986).

LIMBER UP WITH THE LIMBO

Two people hold a long rope (or colorful scarves tied together) and dancers line up to move under the rope. The music begins, and the dancers who are lined up (one by one) go under the rope. Then, when the dancers have gone under the rope, the rope is lowered a bit, and dancers line up to move under the rope. The music begins and the dancers who are lined up go under the rope one by one. Then when the dancers have gone under the rope, they line up again. It is possible to get further down by leading the body movement with the hips and legs first. This is an art—successful limbo dancers can align their body parallel to the ground. The last one to go under successfully without stumbling and falling or touching the rope is the winner! Then, line up because the fun begins all over again. Try this with appropriate background music on a cassette player.

JAMAICAN RHYTHMS

The music of these islanders is composed mainly of folksongs, digging songs, and Mentos. The folksongs tell a story in rhythm and words, the digging songs are sung by the workers in the fields, and the Mento is a distinct music and dance form similar to the rhumba (Cuba).

CALYPSO RHYTHMS

Calypso music has a distinct sound. The rhythm is African and the melody is Spanish. Audiences jump, stomp, hum, and clap their hands to the 2/2 or 4/4 beat of the rhythms. Secure a recording of this famous music at the public library and, after listening to the catchy tunes, let the students join in by clapping, humming, and stomping.

Calypso music began with the "Chantwells." Chantwells were slaves who entertained plantation owners with songs during colonial days. The songs were about people they knew and things that happened to them. It was a way of passing along news, since most of the islanders could not read and write. It would be a challenge for students to pass along information of the day through rhythm and words.

STEEL DRUMS

The steel drums of the Caribbean Islands are fashioned from discarded oil drums that are considered no longer useful. The native islanders used their creativity to make them into something that brought beauty into their lives. An orchestra of the barrel drums, each tuned differently, can produce a variety of effects that resemble the guitar or piano. Bands can play the island music as well as popular tunes and symphonies. The player strikes various parts of the drum's surface with different parts of the hand or with an instrument. The drums are cut in varying lengths to produce different tones. Secure from the public library a recording or an audiocassette of the famous fast-paced music of the steel bands so that students can listen to the music and identify it whenever they hear the sounds.

This is a good opportunity for students to make drums from unusual materials that have been discarded or relegated to the scrap heaps. What can be done with old hub caps, jar lids, and other discarded items?

MAKING A MUSICAL RATTLE

Give students the opportunity to create a variety of musical instruments from scrap materials. One example is to make a rattle instrument by pounding a long nail through soda bottle caps onto a thick stick. Sounds will vary according to the number of caps, number of nails, and thickness of the wood.

The maraca is a popular instrument made from dry gourds and filled with seeds that rattle when the musician shakes them. Try making rattles with different seeds and different-sized cardboard containers if you do not have access to gourds.

TRINIDAD CARNIVAL

This festive event symbolizes the way of life in song and dance. People get ready for the event right after the December holidays. The parade features life-sized headpieces of biblical characters and legendary figures. Early bands in Trinidad were called "bamboo" bands because they consisted of bamboo poles struck against each other to make sounds. Students can decorate dowel rods with designs put on with paint or felt pen, and use them as rhythm sticks.

CREATE A RHYTHM BAND

Make instruments from heavy-duty paper plates. Place one plate upside down on top of another. Decorate the exterior with designs made from felt-tipped pens or paint. In between the two plates (like a sandwich) insert small materials (uncooked rice in one, dried peas in another, sand in another, and so on). Glue the edges, and then staple the edges when glue is dry.

This type of instrument, along with the rhythm sticks and other hand-made instruments, can be used by students to accompany recorded music. Have from three to five students work together to perform.

Variation: Students can get ready to go home while being entertained by the music of the rhythm band. Select from three to five class members to accompany the recorded music while students are cleaning up, and getting their sweaters or coats and hats at the end of the day. It is a good way to end the day on a happy note. Students can take turns being rhythm band members.

FOOD

The food from the islands is as varied as the people who inhabit the islands. The people came from many parts of the world and, in addition to bringing their folklore, celebrations and religions with them, they brought their special methods of preparing food. The wide variety of food served on the islands represents the variety of cultures—mainly African, Asian, Native American, and Spanish.

Some of the methods of preparing food and the food itself has been mixed with vegetation found on the islands, and so we find variations of original recipes. For example, cornmeal mixed with the tropical coconut and bananas turns into "boija" or coconut corn bread. And "pasteles," a very special dish in Trinidad, is a combination of cornmeal and meat wrapped in banana leaves. Bananas, rich in potassium, are important to the islands and are exported all over the world.

Some of the important exports are sugar, coffee, bananas, cocoa, and citrus fruits.

SUGGESTED RECIPES FOR THE CLASSROOM

Figues Bananes Fourrees

6 large bananas
14 tablespoons butter or margarine
2 cups confectioners' sugar
6 tablespoons chopped peanuts
    (unsalted)
4 tablespoons raisins
6 tablespoons lemon juice
glazed cherries (jar)

Peel the bananas. Then cut them into halves (both ways) and sprinkle with lemon juice. Cream the margarine and sugar. Scoop out a tiny groove through the middle of each banana piece and stuff it with the margarine mixture. Decorate with peanuts, raisins, and cherries. Refrigerate before serving. Makes 24 dessert servings.

Pineapple Drink

12 cups boiling water
peelings and fruit of two
    pineapples
1 teaspoon nutmeg
4 cloves

Place the pineapple peelings and fruit into a large, deep pan. Carefully cover with boiling water (an adult should do this). Cover and let it stand for 24 hours. Strain and add spices. Serve over ice cubes.

Lemonade

Squeeze juice from one dozen lemons. Add one quart water. Serve over ice. (This can be fortified with frozen lemon concentrate and more water.) In the Caribbean, the lemons are green and small, like limes. This juice is rich in vitamin C.

Plantain

Peel, cut, and boil the plantain until soft. Then add to your favorite soup.

Callaloo

This is what the leaves of the taro plant are called (known also as Chinese spinach). They are boiled and used in soups.

Pineapple Coconut Balls

1-1/2 cups dried uncooked pineapple (6 ounces)
2 cups shredded coconut
2/3 cup sweetened condensed milk
confectioners' sugar

Grind pineapples in a blender, or chop into tiny pieces. Add coconut to pineapple mixture. Add condensed milk and stir. Pour 1 cup confectioners' sugar into a separate bowl. Shape pineapple mixture into balls, and roll in sugar one at a time. Number depends upon the size you make them.

Shrimp Boats

1 cup cooked shrimp
several celery stalks
1/4 cup mayonnaise
frankfurter rolls (boats)

Mix together shrimp and chopped celery. Add mayonnaise. Spread shrimp mixture onto frankfurter rolls. (Can make a hearty sandwich or a thin one, depending upon amount of filling.)

Bananas

With bananas in abundance, there are a variety of ways to fix them, aside from peeling them and eating them. They contain potassium and are very good for you.

Banana Split:
bananas sliced in half lengthwise
ice cream
cherries
whipped topping

Each person gets a banana slice. Add a scoop (or little scoops) of ice cream of any flavor. Top with cherry halves and a dab of whipped topping.

Morning Bananas:
bananas
milk

Cut banana slices into a bowl and cover with milk.

Fried Bananas:
bananas
vegetable oil

Cut bananas into slices (can be thick or as thin as chips). Brown in vegetable oil in an electric frypan. Drain before eating.

Cuban Black Bean Soup

1 pound dried black beans, washed and drained
8 cups water
2 garlic cloves, crushed
2 medium onions, diced
1 green pepper, diced
1/2 cup olive oil
salt and pepper to taste
2 tablespoons wine vinegar

Bring beans to a boil for 2 minutes in large kettle of water. Remove from heat, and let stand for 1 hour. Saute onions, garlic, and green pepper in oil. Add salt and pepper. Add onion mix to beans, bring to a boil, and simmer for 2 hours. Add vinegar and cook 5 minutes longer. Serve with side dish of rice or bread and butter. *Optional:* Can be served over half a hard-boiled egg.

Frozen Fruit Sticks

2 cups fruit (any kind), cleaned and cut up
1/4 cup corn syrup
waxed paper cups
wooden ice cream sticks

Puree drained fruit and corn syrup in blender. Pour into paper cups (sizes are 4 oz., 6 oz., 8 oz.) until half full. Insert a stick in the center of each cup, being careful not to puncture a hole in the other end. Place in freezer until firm. Peel off cups and serve this treat on a stick.

An Abundance of Fresh Fruit

Because there is a wealth of fresh fruit on the islands, fruits can be fixed in a variety of ways.

Frying: Fruit such as pineapple or bananas can be fried in a small amount of butter and used as a pancake filling, with toast, or as a side dish.

Stewing: Fresh fruit can be peeled, cored, and quartered—seeds and pits removed. Add enough water to steam the fruit over low heat. Simmer until fruit softens. Remove and add a few drops of lemon juice. (Fresh fruit usually will not need a sweetener. If fruit is relatively unripe, sugar may be added.)

Gelatin Dessert: Stir your favorite gelatin flavor according to directions on the packet and add peeled, cut-up fruit. Pour into individual molds or into an oblong glass dish. Allow to cool and set. If an oblong dish has been used, students can count and measure to determine how many pieces need to be cut evenly for everyone.

Date and Nut Bars

1 cup pecans (or walnuts), chopped
1/2 cup dates, pitted
3/4 cup flour
3 eggs
1-1/2 cups brown sugar (packed)
1/4 teaspoon salt
3/4 teaspoon baking powder

Grease 9-inch x 12-inch baking pan. Mix dates and nuts together. Add one tablespoon flour and mix again. In another bowl, beat eggs. Add sugar gradually to eggs, stirring constantly. Sift together the rest of the flour, baking powder, and salt. Add to egg mixture. Stir date and nut mixture into egg mixture. Spread in greased pan and bake in 350-degree oven for approximately 20 minutes, or until cake springs back when touched. Makes 40 bars.

Caribbean Chocolate Sponge

8 ounces dark, sweet cooking chocolate
2 tablespoons butter
1/4 cup evaporated milk
4 eggs, separated
1/4 cup water
1 teaspoon unflavored gelatin

Melt chocolate with butter and milk over low heat. Remove from heat and cool. Add beaten egg yolks and stir. Return to heat and cook slowly for 1 minute, stirring constantly. Mix gelatin and water and let stand for 5 minutes. Add to chocolate mixture. Beat egg whites and fold into the mixture. Chill and serve. (Can be served with sprinkled nuts or cream on top.)

Resources

Paraiso, Aviva. *Caribbean Food and Drink* (San Francisco: Chronicle Books, 1993).

Paul, Aileen, and Arthur Hawkins. *Kids Cooking, First Cookbook for Children* (Santa Fe: Sunstone Press, 1982).

Paul, Aileen, and Carol Inouye. *Kids' Cooking Without a Stove: A Cookbook for Young Children* (Santa Fe: Sunstone Press, 1985).

REPRODUCIBLE ACTIVITY PAGES

Sail Along with a Good Book (*encouraging reading*)

I'm a Poetry Animal, and Proud of It! (*reading poetry*)

The Trading Game (*learning through play*)

Victor Manuel Paints by Color (*Spanish/English color words*)

You Can't Afford Not To! (*research/advertising*)

Weather Tracker (*keeping track of weather around the world*)

Celebrate Sea Creatures (*identification; practice through play*)

Put Some Color Back Into My Life! (*visual design*)

Caribbean Tasty Treat Recipe (*food recipe*)

Biklak Is Hungry for Information (*geography: islands*)

Gertrude M. Mouse Got Washed Ashore (*geography*)

Do an Author Study—Caribbean (*Anansi the Spider and others*)

Name _____   Date _____

SAIL ALONG WITH A GOOD BOOK

You can go anywhere in the world with a good book. Here are TEN free tickets to spend in your classroom library. Enjoy your journeys. Tell your friends so they can go there too!

Get your tickets here↓

ADMIT ONE	ADMIT ONE
ADMIT ONE	ADMIT ONE
ADMIT ONE	ADMIT ONE
ADMIT ONE	ADMIT ONE
ADMIT ONE	ADMIT ONE

Name _____ Date _____

I'M A POETRY ANIMAL, AND PROUD OF IT!

Marlo, the Caribbean Monkey, likes the rhythm and rhyme of poetry. Find a poem for each animal below. Copy it in the space provided. Say it and JUMP to the rhythm.

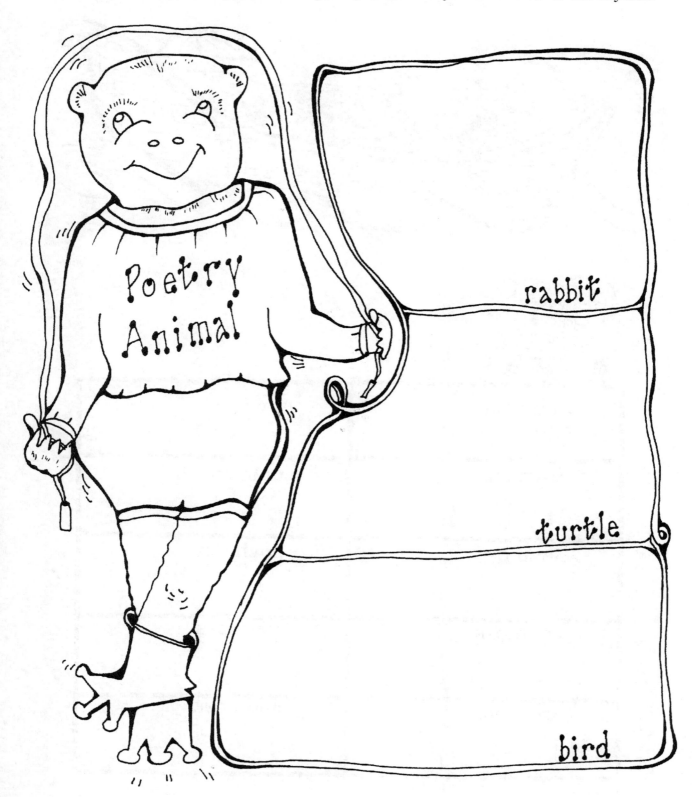

rabbit

turtle

bird

THE TRADING GAME

Prior to the use of money, people used many of the items here in exchange for goods and services. Color the page, laminate it, and cut apart the cards. They can be used for a classroom trading station. Or, two players can shuffle their cards together and turn them over in a pile. Each player draws a card, taking turns. The first one to get four matching cards is the winner.

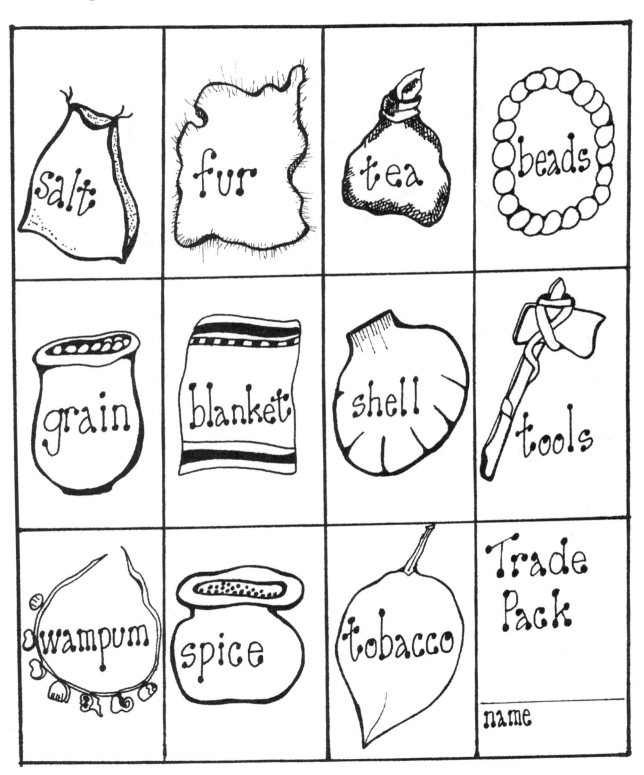

VICTOR MANUEL PAINTS BY COLOR

Did you ever hear of painting by number? This handsome bird is painting by color words . . . Spanish color words. Help him make a great painting, and he can help you with your color words in two languages.

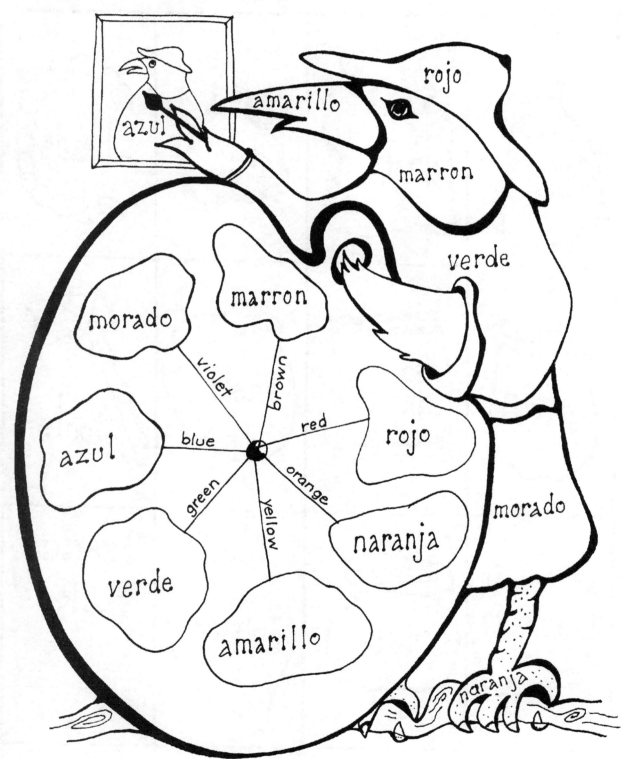

Name _____   Date _____

YOU CAN'T AFFORD NOT TO!

In the space provided, make an appealing travel poster for a visit to a special place—at rock-bottom prices. Convince your customers with attractive pictures, text, AND bargain prices. Bon voyage!

Name _____ Date _____

WEATHER TRACKER

Select three different cities in your state (or in the world) and compare their temperatures. Do this twice a week for three weeks. What are the highs and lows? The newspaper is a good resource. Listen to your local weather reports daily. What can you learn by doing this?

	Week #1		Week #2		Week #3	
	H	L	H	L	H	L
City 1						
City 2						
City 3						

CELEBRATE SEA CREATURES

Color and identify the sea creatures below. You can add two more in the blank boxes. Then, cut them apart. **DIRECTIONS:** Place the cards face down in a pile. Use them to write a rebus story. Or, shuffle them and place them face down in a pile. Turn them over one at a time. Tell two important facts about the sea creature in order to keep the card. This game can be played with two friends. (Have books handy to help you learn information about the creatures.

Name _____ Date _____

PUT SOME COLOR BACK INTO MY LIFE!

These Caribbean birds posed for a photo but it came out black and white. They want their beautiful, bright colors back. Their feathers are lemon yellow, startling lime, bright blue, and vivid green. They were promised a colorful background, too.

Can you get your colored pens and help? Check picture books for fancy designs.

CARIBBEAN TASTY TREAT RECIPE

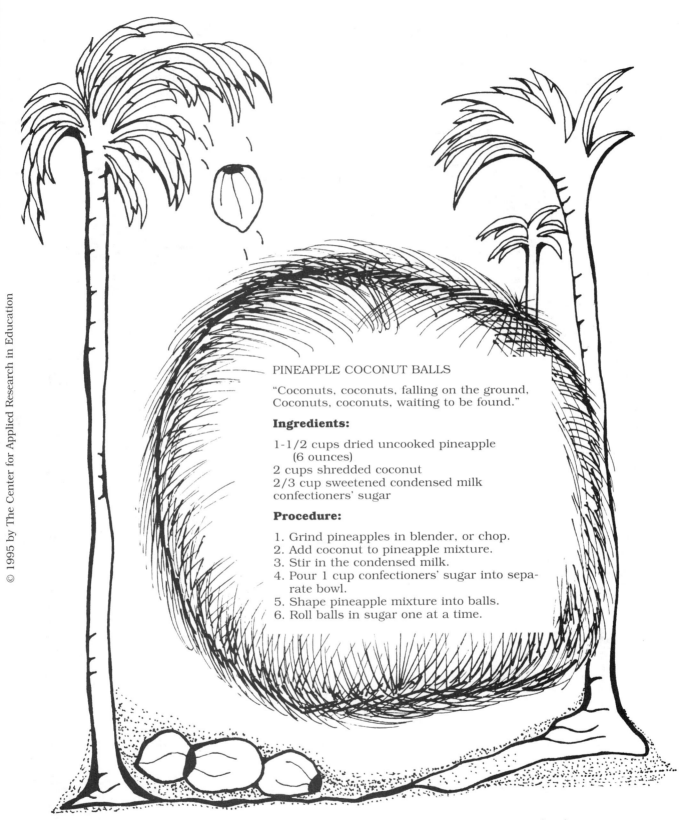

PINEAPPLE COCONUT BALLS

"Coconuts, coconuts, falling on the ground,
Coconuts, coconuts, waiting to be found."

Ingredients:

1-1/2 cups dried uncooked pineapple
   (6 ounces)
2 cups shredded coconut
2/3 cup sweetened condensed milk
confectioners' sugar

Procedure:

1. Grind pineapples in blender, or chop.
2. Add coconut to pineapple mixture.
3. Stir in the condensed milk.
4. Pour 1 cup confectioners' sugar into separate bowl.
5. Shape pineapple mixture into balls.
6. Roll balls in sugar one at a time.

The number made depends upon the size you make them.

Name _____ Date _____

BIKLAK IS HUNGRY FOR INFORMATION

Message from Biklak the Ogre: "See this chicken? Not for long! I'm starving for the information that you can look up in nonfiction books. I want words and diagrams, or I'll devour the chicken."

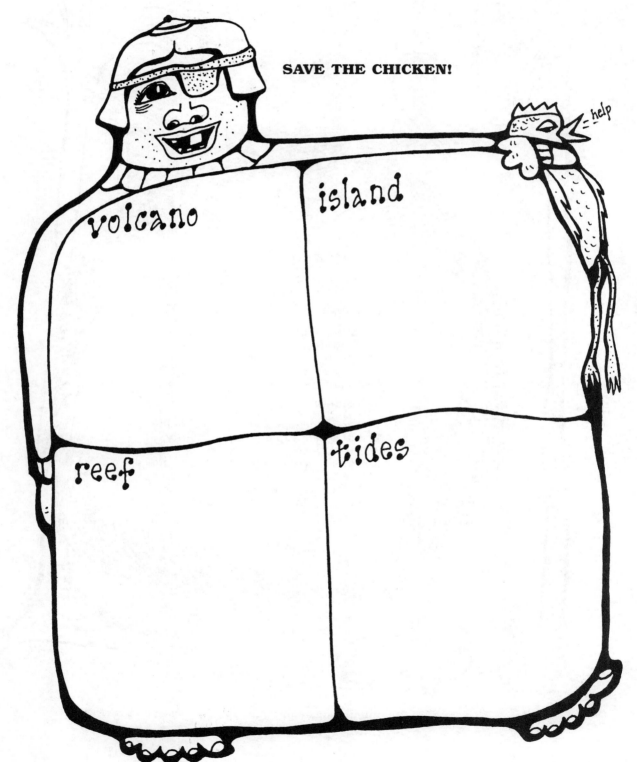

SAVE THE CHICKEN!

volcano

island

reef

tides

help

GERTRUDE M. MOUSE GOT WASHED ASHORE

This deep sea diver has Egypt as her destination. Her equipment got tangled and she got washed ashore in Puerto Rico. Can you help? First locate Puerto Rico on a map or globe. Then locate Egypt. How can she get to her destination? She wants to travel on oceans, rivers, and lakes as much as possible. Map her route on the diving capsule.

Share your route with classmates. How are they alike/different?

Name _____ Date _____

DO AN AUTHOR STUDY— CARIBBEAN

Locate a variety of tales that have the Caribbean as a setting. Many of the Anansi tales made their way from Africa to the Caribbean and to the Americas. Note the colorful illustrations of birds and flowers! Can you find any similarities in the tales? Record your information below.

A JOURNAL OF WORDS AND DRAWINGS ABOUT THINGS I NOTICED:

EAST EUROPE

RECOMMENDED CHILDREN'S BOOKS

The stories listed below are representative of the tales from this part of the world.

Aoki, Hisako and Gantschev, Ivan. *Santa's Favorite Story*. Boston: Neugebauer Press, 1982. Santa Claus falls asleep in the forest and the animals assemble to awaken him. Santa tells them that Christmas has nothing to do with him, and he relates the story of the first Christmas. The best present ends up being Christmas itself. Charming illustrations by the Bulgarian artist.

Asch, Frank and Vagin, Vladimir. *Here Comes the Cat!* New York: Scholastic Books, 1989. This book is written in both Russian and English, but the main words throughout are "here comes the cat" or "suy-DAH ee-DYOT kot." The book, which takes place in a land of mice, is an adventure in two languages as the word is spread about the coming of the cat. In the end, the mice are in for a surprise. This book is a collaborative effort between a Russian and an American.

Bider, Djemma. *A Drop of Honey, An Armenian Tale*. Illustrated by Armen Kojoyian. New York: Simon & Schuster, 1989. "Don't let trifles spoil your day" is the message given to Anayida by her mother. Anayida, who has just quarreled with her brothers, falls asleep and begins to dream about a journey. This cumulative tale sends out a valuable lesson. At the end, there is a written recipe for baklava.

Hirsch, Marilyn. *I Love Hanukkah*. New York: Holiday House, 1984. This book takes the reader along as a young boy learns the customs and traditions of the Hanukkah holiday. It is an excellent teaching/learning book.

Kimmel, Eric. *The Chanukkah Guest*. New York: Holiday House, 1990. An old woman is busy cooking to prepare for a feast when there is a loud knock at the door. Since she has poor eyesight, when she opens the door she believes it is the rabbi, when in fact it is a bear who has followed its nose to her wonderful smells. What follows is a hilarious dinner, with the bear grunting and gobbling, while she's wondering about his manners.

Finally, after the bear leaves, the worn out woman is surprised by a knock at the door...the real rabbi coming for dinner!

Langton, Jane. *The Hedgehog Boy, A Latvian Folk Tale*. Illustrated by Ilse Plume. New York: Harper & Row, 1985. The Forest Mother gives to an old childless couple a young baby covered with sharp prickles, like a hedgehog. This baby grows into a hedgehog boy who tends pigs. One night out in the forest he saves a beautiful young princess, and his love for her grows. Later, the King becomes lost in the woods and the boy bargains with him for the hand of his daughter. The message of this tale is a bargain is a bargain.

Lewis, J. Patrick. *The Czar and the Amazing Cow*. Pictures by Friso Henstra. New York: Dial, 1988. An old peasant couple in a Russian village have a faithful cow, Buryonka, who one day speaks to them and tells them to drink her magic milk. This takes them back to the "green time of their lives," and a chance to live things over again. Touching tale.

Polacco, Patricia. *Thunder Cake*. New York: Philomel Books, 1990. The story of how a little girl's wise grandmother (Babushka), who came from Russia many years ago, helps her to overcome her fear of thunder. A delightful and tender story with a recipe for real Thunder Cake at the end. The author/illustrator's illustrations reflect the Russian influence in the home.

___. *The Keeping Quilt*. New York: Simon and Schuster, 1988. This is a touching story of immigrants arriving in the United States, and the way in which the memories of the people from "backhome Russia" were kept alive through their swatches of clothing sewn onto a quilt. The colorful quilt is used for all important events in this Jewish family, and a very real sense of belonging is conveyed as the author/illustrator takes us from one generation to the next.

Tornquist, Rita. *The Christmas Carp*. Pictures by Marit Tornquist. New York: Farrar, Straus and Giroux, 1990. Thomas is spending Christmas day in Prague, Czechoslovakia, with his grandfather. This year there will be just the two of them. They go to the outdoor market to buy their tree and the carp for Christmas dinner. The fish, still alive, is kept in the bathtub and named Peppo, but can they kill it and eat it? The resolution is satisfying for all.

Williams, Marcia. *Greek Myths for Young Children*. Cambridge, MA: Candlewick Press, 1991. This is an introduction to some of the best-loved heroes and heroines of ancient Greek mythology through a unique, comic-strip format, with voice balloons. A rich collection to read and study.

Zabar, Abbie. *Alphabet Soup*. New York: Workman Publishing Co., 1990. This is a multicultural food book from A through Z. A is for antipasto, B is for borscht, C is for couscous, and so on. The 26 colorful illustrations help with the introduction of the varieties of food.

FOLK TALES

Folklore has played an important and productive role in the cultural life of all Eastern European peoples. The effect of this area has been felt in neighboring countries. For example, Western Finland was influenced by Russian lore, Lithuanian tales were influenced by Byelo-Russian lore, and there is much evidence of the Slavic influence in Greece and Romania. **NOTE:** Although Finland is a part of Europe, it is included in this East Europe section because of its great influence on Eastern European folklore (and vice versa). Finland has played a leadership role in the study of folklore.

The puppet drama and farce is well developed in Czech tradition. Novelettes, rather than fairy tales, are prevalent in the Slavic folklore. In Eastern Europe lore there is an abundance of proverbs, riddles, and rhymes. In the Ukraine and in the western part of the Balkans, many stories were accompanied by the use of stringed instruments. Russia is among the countries richest in animal tales, along with Romania and parts of Finland.

ROMANY FOLKLORE

Romany is the name given to a group of people, who are referred to in English as "gypsy." Other names are Zigani (Russia), Cigány (Hungary), Bohemians (Spain). The language of the gypsies is Indo-European, but the Romany tribes have not recorded their history because they are the wanderers. That is, they do not stay in one place very long. It is felt, however, that they have kept a number of the folk tales alive through the oral tradition. They have taken the tales with them from place to place, and have told them over and over. Gypsies are famous for their music and dancing, and have spread folk songs from one country to another.

THE LAUREL

This evergreen shrub appears in many Eastern European tales. In some cases, the laurel can cause forgetfulness, or a person can be transformed into a laurel. In a Romanian version of "The Slippers of the Twelve Princesses" the cowherd hero grows laurel and the branches produce magic clothing.

THE MAGIC OF THE MOON

In Romanian tales, the moon is the sun's sister, and the sun is forever chasing the moon. She hides when he rises, and appears only when he sets. Thus, they never do meet. The moon is very prominent in the folklore of almost every culture. The *waxing moon* is the right-hand moon, for the curve of the right-hand index finger and thumb follow the curve of the crescent. The *waning moon* is the left-hand moon. The light of the moon is the best time for growing crops that grow above ground, and the dark of the moon is the best time for growing crops with roots that reach under the ground. In Europe, it is said that bad luck will come from seeing the moon over one's left shoulder. Noodleheads (see below) grow confused by the new moon.

In a Lithuanian tale, the Sun and Moon lived together in one small house, fell in love, and had a daughter they named Earth. After some time they began to quarrel and agreed to separate. It was decided that in the daytime the Sun could look after the daughter, and the Moon could take up the task at night.

NOODLEHEAD STORIES

The noodlehead is a person who appears dimwitted, but who ends up doing the absurd thing at just the right time and is rewarded in the end. This genre (category) of tales appears throughout the world. A good resource book is *Noodlehead Stories From Around the World* by M. A. Jagendorf (New York: Vanguard Press, 1957) with noodlehead tales from 36 different countries. Some stories are from England, Russia, Africa, and Puerto Rico. Many Jewish noodlehead tales are included also.

THROWING SHOES AT A WEDDING

The peoples of Europe and India believe that throwing shoes at a wedding will bring good luck and many children. Today, in the United States, we have the custom of tying old shoes to the back of the car that carries the bride and groom.

Shoes also enter into the funeral ceremony. In Russia, for example, a new pair of shoes is placed on the feet of the dead for the long journey that is to follow. There is much in the folklore of all people about shoes.

DIFFERENT LANGUAGES

In practically all mythologies there is a "porquois" (why) tale about "Why People Speak Different Languages." Usually it is an act of punishment for breaking a taboo, or for being disobedient. From Siberia to Indochina, from Europe to South Africa to Australia, people were punished with a "confusion of tongues." In some tales warriors are involved. One tale is about an old woman who walks among people with a stick, scattering night fires. When she dies, the people rejoice and devour her, and depending upon what part they ate they then spoke with different tongues.

GOING "BERSERKER" OVER BEARS

The word *berserker* or *berserkr*, in Old Norse, means "bear shirt." Warriors were capable of assuming the shape and attributes of bears or wolves. They went into a savage frenzy and would swoop upon the enemy.

In Russia, the bear is a symbol of strength. Among the Finno-Ugric people, the bear is sacred. In many cultures the bear is a god, ancestor, sacred animal, guardian spirit, and a curing spirit. The bear enters into many North American Indian myths, ceremonies, and beliefs.

In Europe there are many folk tales that deal with the bear as a foster parent, the bear's son, the bear who is mistaken for a cat, the bear who whispers in man's ear, and the bear woman.

"BEAUTY AND THE BEAST"

There are Basque, Swiss, German, English, Italian, Portuguese, Lithuanian, and Indian versions of this tale, among others. In the Lithuanian story, for example, the beast is a white wolf. These belong to a cycle of beast-marriage stories in which the prince, magically transformed into beast or a monster, can be saved only by the love and devotion of a beautiful woman.

"PORQUOIS" (WHY) TALES

The animal tale is one of the earliest forms of the folk tale. The countries richest in animal tales are Russia, Finland, and Romania. In its earliest form, the animal tale is usually a tale that gives an explanation of why things are the way they are. For example, "Why the Bear Is Stumpy Tailed," "Why the Rooster Has a Red Comb," "Why the Cat Meows," and so on.

FABLES

The oldest fables come to us from Greece and India. Aesop, a slave in Ionia, is associated with a large collection. The fables probably circulated by word of mouth. The fable is short, to the point, and has a message usually in the form of a lesson to be learned. It is told in two parts: first, the story with a moral; and, second, the explanation of the point of the story—often in the form of a proverb. The characters are usually animals who talk, think, and act like human beings.

HIDDEN IN THE TREES—THE ELEMENT OF FIRE

Throughout the world the myths indicate that the original fire of man was stolen from the gods and was hidden in the trees. That is why man has to rub this wood to produce fire. Fire is a purifying element. In some tribal cultures if a person died inside the house, the house was burned down and another was built. The Olympic Games begin with the lighting of the torch by fire brought from Olympia, Greece, by overland runners and ships. The symbolism of the torch being passed from hand to hand is familiar.

CHURCH BELLS

Originally, church bells were rung before services in Jewish temples and Christian churches to drive away the evil spirits. In parts of Europe, church bells were rung to try to ward off hailstorms. A bell hanging over the door of a shop that rings when the door opens lets in the person and scares away the evil spirits lurking nearby. Today, many shop owners have a bell that rings when a customer enters. The original purpose has been forgotten or lost, but to this day it does put the shopkeeper on the alert.

WHERE IS RUGIO BABA?

She is the old woman of the rye field in Lithuania. She is the Kormutter (corn mother) in Germany. These spirits promote growth of crops. In Indian legends and tales from Central and South America, there is worship and sacrifice (Aztec) to the gods who keep the corn growing. Many dolls are made from corn husks and corn cobs. Today little girls play with them, but at one time they were made to represent the corn god and to bring a good harvest.

KNOCK ON WOOD

Loud knocks from wood are thought to be from spirits enclosed in the wood. To "knock on wood" is a common superstition in many, many cultures and is often done after boasting about something.

SUGGESTED ACTIVITIES FOR THE CLASSROOM

1. GOING BERSERK OVER BEARS AND BEASTIES

Read a wide variety of tales and poetry about bears and other beasts. Make comparisons between *Beauty and the Beast* by Jan Brett and the version by Marianna and Mercer Meyer in terms of story and illustrations. Have students look for the ferocious bears, the gentle bears, and the helping bears and beasts. What are the names given to them? On a huge beast-like shape, students can record their information. They can also make an ABC Book of Beasts, using fake fur for the cover.

2. CREATE A BEASTLY CLASSROOM MURAL

Students can make large cut-out illustrations of the monsters from *Where the Wild Things Are* by Maurice Sendak to represent the hosts and hostesses of the study of Storybook Beasts. One can be placed on the door with a sign that reads "Welcome to the World of the Wild Things." Another can be placed on the mural with a speech bubble overhead containing the written message "Introducing the Wild Things from All Over the World." Students can paint the Loch Ness Monster from Scotland, the giant Cuchulain from Ireland, and so on. With the lights out, and only a lamp lit, students can tell the tales in front of the giant mural. Invite another classroom of students to listen to the tales in the beastly setting. A world map can be nearby to show the beast's homeland.

3. LETTER WRITING

Read aloud *The Jolly Postman* by Janet and Allen Ahlberg (Boston: Little Brown, 1986). Classify the different types of written communication (business letter, party invitation, postcard, etc.), and using this format set up a friendly postman mailbox in the classroom that can house correspondence. Use a huge rural mailbox, or a large box decorated to look like one. This activity leads to opportunities for reading, writing, and drawing. It can also lead to finding pen pals in another classroom, another city, another country.

4. PISKIES, SPRIGGINS, SNACKERS, AND SMALL PEOPLE

Using the descriptions in the European folk tale section (see "Meet the Droll Teller"), have the students create one of these characters using felt markers and construction paper. We have a set of clues, but we really don't know what these characters look like so there are no right or wrong representations. Cut out the figures and use them as a bulletin board border.

5. AND THAT IS WHY THE BEE GOES B-Z-Z-Z!

The "porquois" (why) tales are short, to the point, and contain a good message. Read aloud a wide variety to students, who can then go in search of them at the library. After being exposed to these tales, students have an opportunity for creative expression through writing by creating their own tales.

6. ON A KING'S HUNT

The King's messenger is on the hunt for common elements in folk tales—such as the use of the number 3 (three wishes, three brothers, three sisters, three days); the use of magic (spells, items); the impossible task (trying to guess the name of Rumplestilskin, trying to make the princess laugh); good vs. evil (Snow White, the Cinderella tales), and so on. How many of these elements can students find in folk tales and fairy tales? Older students can document the information by bibliographic notation including the page on which this common element first appears in the text.

A rollicking good read-aloud treat for the whole class is the chapter book *The Search for Delicious* by Natalie Babbit (New York: Farrar Straus Giroux, 1969). This is a hunt ordered by the King.

7. TIME FOR BOOKMARKS

Students can use their imagination to make a bookmark that represents a character, setting, or a shape (witch hat, giraffe neck, elephant trunk, etc.). Laminate the bookmarks.

8. THE UNSEEN HELPER

In many tales, the unseen helper makes life easier for others. Suggest to students that today is the day of the unseen helper. Ask them to do good deeds for others (picking up a pencil, letting someone else go ahead in line, hanging up a jacket that has fallen to the floor). Ask them to do it very quietly. But, if someone should see them, this is the signal. They are to place their right forefinger on their lips and wink. The other person is to wink in return. At the end of the day, let's count up the good deeds! Perhaps this can be tried one day per week.

CELEBRATIONS

This area of the world represents a diversity of cultures. This section does not attempt to include every celebration, but is designed to give the reader an indication of the types of celebrations that are valued in this part of the world.

THE FIRST OF MARCH

In Greece, there is a celebration on this date because Spring is just around the corner. March is considered a changeable month in terms of weather; that's because, according to folk belief, Mars has two wives. One wife is friendly, so that is when March is pleasant; but the other wife is disagreeable, and that is when March huffs and puffs.

GREECE INDEPENDENCE DAY

On March 25, the Greek nation celebrates its independence. There are many festivals throughout the country where people dance and sing. Music is provided by flutes, clarinets, castanets, and bouzoukis (a type of stringed instrument). People dress in bright costumes, the aroma of lamb being roasted awakens the appetite, and the day ends with fireworks that illuminate the sky.

TURKEY

There are many ancient celebrations that people enjoy to this day. In many towns and villages, there are wonderful puppet shows. The famous Karagoz puppets are made from thin, translucent animal skins that have been painted. The puppeteers move the puppets in such a way as to reenact the antics of the jesters of the thirteenth and fourteenth centuries, much to the delight of the audiences.

HARVEST FESTIVALS

There are harvest festivals the world over, and in this part of the world they are celebrated in the autumn. People gather for feasting, singing, and dancing after the crops have been brought in and tended to for another year. It is a festival of thanks for a bountiful harvest, and a time to relax after the hard work has been completed.

In the United States the "Octoberfest" is a time when there are regional celebrations with singing and dancing. The good food includes sausages and cheese. This celebration takes on the flavor of the harvest celebration of Germany. In the United States, handwork and crafts are on display at many of the harvest celebrations.

After the harvest festival in Switzerland, turnips are often dried and later made into lanterns.

In India, people celebrate the harvesting of rice with a rice festival. Rice is put into a pot to boil; when it first bubbles, it is time for the ceremony to begin. Food made from the new rice is then eaten.

FATHER FROST COMES TO RUSSIA

In January, Father Frost makes his visit with his sack of presents slung over his shoulder. In Leningrad, there is a giant sculpture of Father Frost that is brought outdoors in December for children of all ages to enjoy as they walk by. He looks down at the passersby with a hint of a smile. At this time, Russians in Moscow are busy buying small fir trees that they carry in their arms along busy streets as they head for home. The trees are stored outside of the apartments on little balconies, and when passersby glance at the massive gray housing development buildings, the little green trees give a hint of the holiday season to come. Later, they are brought into the home and decorated for the season.

CELEBRATE THE BIRDS AND ANIMALS IN DECEMBER

On the eve of Christmas in Finland, children leave food—such as nuts, corn, and suet—outdoors in the trees for the birds and animals; then the children set about the business of decorating the indoor tree. In some countries, the tree is decorated for a time after it is set outside. Then, piles of trees are burned, and along with it all of the past year "goes up in smoke" and people turn over a new leaf for the new year.

CELEBRATIONS FOR GUESTS

In Russia, when groups of foreigners visit schools they are always met ceremoniously by the principal who explains the background of the school. Then, guests visit classrooms and are treated to a performance by the students. The entertainment may be in the form of a choral group, or dancing and singing, or the reenactment of a familiar children's story. Children are considered to be their "national treasure."

Far to the north in Murmansk, Russia, which is in darkness during the winter months with only a few hours of daylight, the same type of ceremony occurs when visiting schools. After school hours, visitors are taken to a grand room and greeted by students in native costume who have a silver tray of bread and salt. The visitor "breaks bread," dips it into the salt, and eats it. It is a gesture of good will. Visitors are served Russian tea from an elaborate samovar that has been placed on each table. A variety of delectable pastries, made by the teachers, is also served to the visiting guests. For the entertainment, the teachers may sing, and then ask the visitors to sing as a group—so be prepared!

ESTONIA

The city of Talinn has always maintained its link to Christianity and celebrates the Christmas season. Talinn is sometimes celebrated as the new fashion capital of this area of the world, with beautiful, fresh fashion designs, some of which contain a folk-like quality, and some that are thoroughly modern.

FINLAND

In Helsinki, Finland, during the festive pre-Christmas holiday season, the city is aglow with lights strung over the streets, and with department store windows that have animated figures from Christmas legends and stories of the land. There are elves, reindeer, cottages, and children within forest settings, home settings, and natural settings. When it snows, the effect is euphoric! It is as if you stepped into a picture book setting for blocks and blocks. People have their own inner celebrations as they window shop through this wonderland.

FINLAND INDEPENDENCE DAY

This is a day of celebration on December 6. The Fins refer to their country as "suomi" which means "swamp." Finland has many swamps, rivers, and lakes, and Helsinki, the capital, is a harbor city. It is located between Russia and Sweden.

Each summer in Finland, there is a music festival held at an outdoor amphitheater. Thousands of choirs come from all over to sing in the festival and to be part of the audience as well. The singing can be heard for miles and miles.

HANUKKAH CELEBRATIONS

This is a Jewish holiday that is observed during mid-winter, in early December. It is known as the "Festival of Lights" because candles are lit in homes and synagogues (places of worship) in observance of a feast. The celebration covers a period of eight days, and the family lights a candle in the menorah, a type of candle holder, until eight candles are lit. In some families, children receive a little gift each day at dinner time. There are special games to play and special food to eat. A good resource book is *Jewish Holiday Fun* by Judith Hoffman Corwin (New York: Simon & Schuster, 1987).

SUGGESTED ACTIVITIES FOR THE CLASSROOM

1. HAVE A HARVEST OF PUPPETS

Celebrate an event by having students make puppets for the occasion. This can be for a national holiday, a seasonal holiday (Christmas, Easter, Halloween, Thanksgiving), a folk tale festival, and so on. Set up a puppet theater in the room that students make from a cardboard box covered with prepasted paper. A dowel rod across the opening can hold a curtain. Students can perform with the puppets for small groups or for a visiting class. They can even travel from classroom to classroom with a traveling puppet show.

2. MAKE A "SZOPKA"

A szopka is a small theater made from a cardboard box and brightly colored paper. Polish peasants are adept at making a szopka. Traditionally, they are carried at Christmas by the carolers and have moveable puppets.

3. OCTOBERFEST OR SPRINGFEST

During this time of year, students can display their arts and crafts work in the main hallway or foyer of the school. This helps to give a festive atmosphere to the school building. If this activity is held in the Spring, save art work during the year that will be on display.

4. DECORATE FOR THE BIRDS

During the winter months, if students are in an area where it is cold and there is a bitter frost, they can set food outside in the trees for the birds. String popcorn, pieces of apple, and leftover bread together and carefully hang it in the tree. Students can make little balls of peanut butter and wrap them in nylon netting to hang on the tree. Also, a big soup bone or a piece of suet from the butcher counter in a local supermarket can be wound around and around with heavy twine and hung from the tree. Some small plastic feeders can be affixed to classroom windows. With these, students can get a close look at the birds who pay a call.

Then, students can keep track of the birds that visit the feeder. Have field glasses available and bird books for identification. Have rules for bird watching (how long students may stay in this area, slow movements so as not to frighten the birds away, and so on).

5. GREETING GUESTS

How are guests greeted in your classroom? Is there a person who opens the door to greet visitors? Are students designated as "tour guides" around the classroom to show visitors what they are learning? Is there a guest book for signing?

Students can discuss possible ways that guests can be greeted in home situations. How are guests greeted at parties? What obligations do the

guests have for certain behaviors? This is a splendid opportunity for a review of good manners.

6. WHAT IS THE WEATHER LIKE IN EAST EUROPE AND IN RUSSIA?

Students can engage in some newspaper work to locate temperatures of major cities around the world. An excellent resource is the last page of Section A in the newspaper *USA Today*. Keep track of temperatures in various cities around the world for a period of time to make comparisons.

Read the book *Cloudy with a Chance of Meatballs* by Ron and Judi Barrett (New York: Macmillan, 1978). This book refers to spaghetti, hot dogs, hamburgers, and other foods from the United States. But, let's put this book in a different cultural setting. In Russia, for example, the food might be borscht, cabbages, and a stalled pattern of red beets. In parts of Europe, it could be raining sausages and snowing kuchen, with a stalled pattern of haloopki (hamburg and rice rolled in a cabbage leaf). What might the weather be like in Africa? China? Spain? This is an excellent way for students to learn different types of food from a variety of cultures.

7. MORE WEATHER LORE

Tying the wind in a knot is a part of folk belief among fishermen in Lapland and Finland. Then untying the knot to get a wind for sailing is the next step. People have been known to buy a handkerchief with knots (buying the wind) from an older person who is wise about the ways of the weather. Seven knots and twice seven knots are especially forceful. Perhaps students can read to find out more "weather lore" (e.g., "red sky at night, sailor's delight," and "red sky in the morning, sailors take warning"). Do any of these beliefs or superstitions hold true? Students can test them for accuracy.

8. HANUKKAH CELEBRATIONS—MAKING A CONNECTION

There are many festivities for this Jewish holiday in December. People celebrate by attending services and having family dinner at home during this period. Boys and girls are sometimes given token gifts each day. Children play the dreidel game, and students can learn to play too.

Hanukkah is also called the "Festival of Lights." At one time, there was no electricity for people and they used candles, then oil lamps and kerosene lamps. Eskimos used whale oil for their lamps. Today, we take the light and power from electricity for granted. How is it used in our homes? Make a large blueprint of a house and have students go from room to room telling how electricity is used in each room of the house. Make illustrations of appliances, for example, on the blueprint.

Write a group story about "The Day We Had No Electricity" at school, and see what happens with the day.

9. PLAYING THE "JONGLEUR" FOR OUR DAYS OF CELEBRATION

In the Middle Ages a strolling performer who could juggle, do acrobatics, sing, and play a musical instrument was called a "jongleur." Perhaps students could practice putting these four activities together for a talent show. (Maybe students could team together for this.)

ARTS AND CRAFTS

In this part of the world, there is much history in the art that one sees in the cathedrals, with the onion-shaped domes and ornate glass windows and statues. The parks and gardens are rich with statues of poets and beloved leaders. As in all cultures, art plays an uplifting role.

SUGGESTED ACTIVITIES FOR THE CLASSROOM

1. CREATING WITH MOSAICS

Mosaics have been used since ancient times to cover walls, ceilings, and floors of palaces. Making a mosaic is like putting together pieces of a puzzle. First, students can make a light sketch of an object and then cover it with bits of paper or other objects. Gluing can be done after the pieces have been moved around to the satisfaction of the artist. Here are some ideas for creating mosaics:

- **Paper Mosaic**—Cut pieces of construction paper or bright glossy paper from magazines. Then, tear them into small pieces that are no bigger than the end of a thumb. Outline the desired shape (bird, flower, tree, person) with a dark color such as black or brown. Fill in the space with colors, using a repeat pattern.

* **Shape Mosaic**—Cut the paper into triangular or square shapes to make a mosaic quite different from the one above.

* **Seed Mosaic**—Gather a collection of seeds that are quite large, such as beans and corn. Sunflower seeds are also effective. Students can create flower designs using seeds of many colors.

* **Tile Mosaic**—Small pieces of tile can be placed upside down in a plastic lid or pie plate. Then grout can be slowly poured around the pieces and allowed to dry. When dry, the works of art can be removed from the container and turned right side up so that the design shows. Grout can be obtained from the local hardware store. Often, tile pieces are yours for the asking or for a modest fee at linoleum and tile centers.

2. WE CAN PRESS FLOWERS

This art was practiced in Europe hundreds of years ago. It was common for people to press flowers between the pages of a book. Sometimes the flowers were saved from a special occasion, or perhaps they were picked and dried to be enjoyed during the long, dark winter months.

For a student activity, the materials needed are:
    flowers (a flat flower, such as a pansy, picked on a dry day)
    paper toweling (or blotter)
    a large, heavy book
    bricks
    cardboard backing
    glue

Procedure:
    a. Place the paper towel (or blotter) on top of a piece of cardboard.
    b. Arrange flower(s) and leaves carefully so that they are flat.
    c. Carefully place another paper towel on top of the arrangement.
    d. Place a heavy book or books carefully on top of the toweling.
    e. Put bricks on top of the book(s).

It will take at least two full weeks for the leaves to dry. When dry, remove the flowers carefully and store them in a dry, flat box until they are ready to be used. For framing, use a piece of stiff cardboard as a backing. Arrange a flower design or bouquet with the dried flowers. Carefully glue each piece individually (use a toothpick). Make a frame from cardboard or posterboard. (A real picture frame with glass is very effective for this project.)

3. COLORING EGGS FOR EASTER

Hard-boiled eggs, or eggs with the insides blown out, can provide a unique art experience. Students can decorate eggs with tempera paint in bold zigzag lines. Eggs can be covered with small pieces of tissue paper and glue. In the children's picture book *Chicken Sunday* by Patricia Polacco (New York: Putnam, 1992), the children engage in the art of making "pysanky" eggs, a method whereby designs are put onto the egg shells with hot wax, dyed, and then the wax is melted off the eggs. This process is repeated again and again for a variety of colors.

4. NESTING DOLLS

In Russia, children play with small dolls, usually made from wood, that fit inside each other. That is, the small doll is usually made from a whole piece of wood and does not come apart. It is placed inside a larger doll whose head is the lid. Together, the two are placed inside another doll, still larger, whose head is the lid, and so on. Usually, there are from three to five dolls in a set, but there can be any number of them. To make a set of nesting dolls, students can use cylindrical tubes of graduated sizes. The dolls can be brightly painted with flowers and patterns of numerous designs. (See the reproducible activity pages.)

5. BRING ON THE CIRCUS CLOWNS

The Russian circus, along with the European circus, has long been a popular form of entertainment. Students can make happy clown faces from paper bags or paper plates. The standard attire is the big bow tie, with polka dots made from circles of colored paper collected from a three-hole paper punch. A styrofoam ball, cut in half and glued to the surface, serves as a big round nose. Hair can be made from yarn, and buttons can be used for shiny eyes. Use other gadgets for the clown also, and decorate with paint or felt pen.

6. THE NOODLEHEAD CHARACTER IN FOLK TALES

Cut 18" x 24" sheets of heavy colored paper in half lengthwise so that the sheets are 9" x 24" in size. On these vertical sheets, students can make the noodlehead character found in folk tales, using real noodles to glue onto a circular head shape. A variety of noodle shapes and sizes will add interest to the noodlehead figure. The remainder of the body can be placed on the page with cut-out construction paper. Students can name their noodlehead and, after listening to many noodlehead tales, they can retell one or write their own. (**Reminder**: The noodlehead is rather a dimwit, but ends up doing the right thing, winning in the end no matter how ludicrous his behavior may seem.)

7. DOG-HEADED PEOPLE

In Eastern European tales, there are characters with the head of a dog and the body of a person. Have students go on a hunt through old magazines for pictures of dogs and people. Cut them out, and then put together this unlikely combination. Combining a glossy magazine picture of a dog head and drawing the body of a person is effective. Have students discuss the character they have created and look for combinations of animals/people in picture book illustrations.

8. BEAR'S TALES

Students can use fake fur to make a cover for their journal or record-keeping pages about the bear books they have read. There are many bears in folk tales, and in Russia one of the nation's symbols is the mighty bear. Glue felt eyes, nose, teeth, and other features on the book cover. Also, use the excess fake fur to cover a medium-size cardboard box. All information books about bears can be kept in this furry container.

GAMES

These games are representative of the area and are not all inclusive. Hiking is a popular sport in many parts of Europe, and students enjoy setting out with backpacks. In Greece, the national sport is grease-wrestling, with championships held in July. Contestants smear themselves with oil before the contests.

FLAPPING BIRDS

This is a game similar to "Simon Says." Everyone, including the leader, must flap his or her arms like wings. The leader calls out names of things that move in the air, or fly—such as "airplane"—and flaps his or her arms like wings and children do likewise. Other names include ladybug, fly, bluejay, crow, bee, jet plane, and so on. The leader at any time can insert another word of something that does not fly *and still keep flapping*, so children have to listen attentively. If children flap their arms like wings on a word of something that does not fly, they are out until the next round. (This can be played at holiday time by inserting festive names.)

NUT RELAY

This game can be played with two teams of players. Each team needs a spoon and a nut.

At a given signal, the first player of each team must place the nut on the spoon and hold the spoon in one hand while walking briskly to a designated spot, turning around, and returning to hand off the spoon and nut to the next player. During the relay, if the nut drops off the spoon, the player must scoop it up with the opposite hand and hold it in that hand while continuing the journey. The team to complete the relay first is the winner.

In many celebrations there are performances of the "spoon dance." Performers click wooden spoons held in each hand.

BUILD A "SZOPKA"

A szopka is a small theater box. Students can make a puppet theater stage from a box by covering it with paint or self-stick paper. A small curtain can be put along one side with a spring rod. Students can use the theater to make scenes from favorite folk tales, or make scenery and props from clay and construction paper and reenact favorite folk tales.

THE BEAR IS "IT"

The "it" game is common in many cultures all over the world. This is a game of run-and-chase. You need a stick to draw the boundaries of the bear's den, or pebbles to outline the bear's den.

The bear is "it" and is inside its den. All other players are in the field or on the court. The bear shouts, "The bear is coming!" and runs out to catch a player. When a player is caught, they lock hands and both go back to the bear's den. Then they shout, "The bears are coming!" and both go out together to catch one more player. They lock hands, forming a line, and shout, "The bears are coming!" and go out of the den to catch another player, one at a time. Finally, when almost all of them are joined together and all yell, "The bears are coming!" the last player to be caught is the next "it" (bear) and the cycle begins again.

THE WILD GOAT CHASE

The goat who is "it" is in the middle of the circle of players who may be standing or sitting. All other players start the chant, and the goat acts out what is said about it. "At one o'clock the goat is asleep, at two o'clock the goat is asleep, at three o'clock the goat is asleep," and so on until the seventh hour when the chant changes to, "at seven o'clock the goat wakes up," "at eight o'clock the goat yawns," "at nine o'clock the goat washes," "at ten o'clock the goat dresses," "at eleven o'clock the goat opens the door," "GET

READY—at twelve o'clock the goat runs." When the last word (runs) is spoken, the children scatter in all directions while the goat runs and chases the players until one is caught. That one becomes the next goat, and the cycle begins again.

SONGS, DANCES, RHYTHMS

The following is a representative sampling, and is not intended to be complete.

WHISTLING TO MUSIC

In Romania, whistling to music is popular. This can be done in time to the rhythm or as a form of accompaniment at the end of a phrase or stanza. For an activity, students can practice their whistling skills by whistling along to a well-known tune. Or they can start a tune by singing, whistle the middle part, and end up singing the last line.

CIRCLE DANCING

Circle dancing is one form of folk dancing that is used repeatedly for many different stories and with many different steps. One popular form is to move slowly with simple steps and end up dancing faster and faster as the music is sped up.

For an activity, have students form a circle (alternating boys and girls) and face the middle. Students can join hands and step to the right by moving the right foot, moving the left foot behind the right foot, and moving the right foot again (*pattern*: right, left, right, left). Practice this several times. Then, have the circle of students move to the left by moving the left foot, moving the right foot just behind the left foot, and moving the foot again (*pattern*: left, right, left, right). The foot they start out on determines the direction they will go. Practice this several times. Then add a recording that has a slow tempo so students begin to move to the rhythm.

Students can circle dance to different recordings at different speeds, and go to the right or to the left by following the teacher's commands.

THE BULGARIAN WEDDING DANCE

In this culture, the bride in a long white dress and veil dances with the groom who has paper money pinned to the front of his suit coat. The money is pinned to his coat by well-wishers at the reception.

For an activity, students can role play by facing each other, extending their arms toward each other, joining hands, and swaying their arms to music. The props of the coat, paper money and pins, and a white sheet for a veil add to the festive occasion.

RUSSIAN DOLL DANCE

One popular step with folk dancers in long skirts is to move the feet so smoothly that the audience has the illusion that the dancer is drifting on a cloud. Students can practice this by standing tall with feet and knees together. Keep the knees together and the heels together. Move both feet to the right (rotating on the heels), then move the heels to the right (rotating on the toes). Students can practice this foot movement in the circle dance formation until they gain a sense of balance and uniformity in movement.

STREET MUSICIANS

Street musicians play instruments such as accordions, drums, bells, flutes, lutes, Jew's harps, and balalaikas. Some groups play and sing. For a student activity, students might be interested in dressing in colorful costumes (use donated clothing, scarves, shoes, and hats from the prop box) and becoming strolling musicians. For those not interested in singing and/or dancing, they can be the appreciative audience. (This activity can be used as a culminating activity in a multicultural celebration within the classroom. Some students might read a story, tell a tale, recite a poem, or become a member of the strolling musicians.)

FANCY LEG WORK

In Russia, folk dancers cross their arms in front of their chest and, while they keep their back straight, they lower their body into a squatting position. Then they kick their legs out straight in front—first the right, then the left. For an activity, students can practice doing this fancy leg work that is very difficult and a challenge to master.

WORK SONGS

There are many songs that people sing as they ride in open trucks to work in the fields, and as they hoe and work in the fields during the day. It seems to make the work go easier. For a student activity, perhaps singing together at the beginning of the day, at the ending of the day, and in between as well may unite the group and help make the day go a little better.

PLAY THE CLASSICAL MUSIC OF GREAT COMPOSERS

During rest time, or for quiet listening, play the music of Tchaikovsky so that students become familiar with this type of music. The "Piano Concerto No. 1" is a favorite and is recognizable to the students after a short time.

FOOD

In Eastern Europe, we find many of the same dishes that are served in Europe; however, each country adds its own distinct touch and calls dishes by different names. Included in this section are Russia, the Slavic countries, and Finland.

SUGGESTED RECIPES FOR THE CLASSROOM

Salata

1 head lettuce
4 small tomatoes
2 small onions
mayonnaise

Wash lettuce thoroughly, drain, and dry with paper towel. Slice onions paper thin. Cut tomatoes into wedges. Cut lettuce into chunks. Toss the lettuce, tomatoes, and onions. Add mayonnaise. This tasty salad serves 8.

Haloopkie (Cabbage Rolls from Czech Republic & Poland)

Cabbage is used in many dishes from this area. This famous dish requires many steps, but it is so delicious that it is well worth the effort. Children who don't usually eat cabbage will eat haloopkie. It is called by different names in different regions (such as gowumpki or golabki), but everyone knows the term "cabbage rolls."

Filling:

1 pound ground beef
1 medium onion, chopped
1 egg
3/4 cup cooked rice or barley
1/2 teaspoon dried parsley flakes

1/2 teaspoon basil
1/2 teaspoon oregano
1/2 teaspoon salt
dash pepper
1 cabbage head

Sauce:

1 6-ounce can tomato paste	1 minced garlic clove
1 tablespoon flour	1 12-ounce can tomato juice
1-1/2 teaspoons sugar	1-1/2 teaspoons olive oil
1/2 teaspoon each of pepper, basil, oregano, dried parsley	

Part One: Cook rice or barley according to package directions. Combine beef, egg, cooked rice, spices, half of the chopped onion, and pepper, and mix well. (May need to knead it with hands; if so, wear plastic baggies.) Wash and core cabbage. Place in very large kettle of boiling water until outer leaves are tender (approximately 10 minutes). Remove cabbage from water (careful!) and gently (!) pull off the tender outer cabbage leaves, being careful not to tear them. When as many cabbage leaves as possible can be gently removed, place cabbage back into pot of water and boil until inside leaves become tender. Repeat until you have about 10 to 15 cabbage leaves.

Part Two: Combine tomato paste, flour, sugar, the other half of the onion, spices, and garlic. Mix thoroughly. To this, add tomato juice, stirring until smooth (add a little at a time). Add olive oil. Cut vein from larger cabbage leaves. Lay out cabbage leaves and place about 1 tablespoon meat/rice filling in the center. Fold over the two sides of the leaf and roll the little loaf. Place cabbage rolls (tightly fit and layered) into casserole dish that has approximately 1/2 cup of sauce. Pour remaining sauce on top.* Cover and bake at 350 degrees for 45 minutes. (Makes 20 rolls.)

*Do not layer more than 1/2 way up the casserole dish. Some natives pack the rolls and tomato mixture into the cooking pot and cook it on top of the stove for approximately 1-1/2 hours.

Polish-Style Cauliflower

1 head cauliflower
4 tablespoons margarine, melted
bread crumbs
dill weed
ground ginger (optional)

Wash the cauliflower thoroughly. Remove greens. Place whole, floret side up, in large kettle that has enough water so that it comes up to the bottom section of the cauliflower. Cover, and cook until tender (10-15 minutes). Remove and place in serving dish. Cover with melted margarine, and sprinkle with bread crumbs and dill weed. Sprinkling with ground ginger is optional. Serve hot (slice or scoop with a spoon).

Chai (Russian Tea)

Russia is one of the leading tea-drinking nations. The samovar (a type of water boiler) is used to help make tea. Tea is drunk with lemon or sugar, or sometimes with a dab of jam as sweetener. It is often served with a sweet cake. Russia, England, and Asia top the list as tea-drinking nations. At mealtime in Poland and Czech Republic, children often drink tea from tin cups with milk added.

Pappilan Hatavara (Bread Pudding

12 slices whole wheat bread
2 eggs
1-1/3 cups milk
4 teaspoons sugar
1/2 teaspoon salt
jam
whipped topping

Tear bread into tiny pieces. Beat the eggs, and mix them together with the milk, sugar, and salt. Soak the bread in this mixture. Coat 8 custard cups with vegetable oil spray. Spoon a layer of bread mixture in the bottom of each, then a layer of jam, then bread, then jam, etc., topping with bread. Bake at 350 degrees until top is crispy (approximately 40 minutes). Serves 8.

Zupa z Dynia (Pumpkin Soup)

1 16-ounce can pumpkin
1 quart milk
3/4 teaspoon allspice
1 cup cooked rice
2 tablespoons margarine
salt and pepper to taste

Mix pumpkin and milk together. Add allspice, pepper, and salt. Then place in a saucepan and bring to a boil. Stir in cooked rice and margarine. Simmer. Makes about 8 servings.

Zupa Jablkowa (Apple Soup)

6 large apples
1 quart water
3/4 cup sugar
1/2 teaspoon cinnamon
1/2 cup lemon juice
1 cup whipping cream

Peel and core apples, and cook in water until soft. Puree mixture in a blender to make applesauce. Combine apple mixture with sugar, cinnamon, and lemon juice. Chill. When chilled, fold cream into applesauce mixture. Makes about 8 servings.

Mazurkas (Dessert)

1 cup butter
3/4 cup eggs (beaten)
2 cups ground, blanched almonds
1-3/4 cups all-purpose flour
1 cup sugar
jam

Cream butter and eggs. Mix together the almonds, flour, and sugar. Add flour mixture to butter mixture, a little at a time, and beat or knead each time. Roll out dough onto a greased jelly roll pan. Bake at 350 degrees until golden brown (approximately 20 minutes). Spread jam over the top. Cool Cut into 2-inch squares.

Borscht (Ukraine)

3 quarts beef stock
2 potatoes, peeled and cut into pieces
1-1/2 cups shredded cabbage
2 8-ounce jars pickled beets
4 tablespoons butter
2 onions, chopped
2 carrots, chopped
4 tablespoons tomato puree
2 bay leaves
4 tablespoons cider vinegar
1 garlic clove, crushed
4 bacon slices
4 tablespoons parsley
1-1/3 cups sour cream
salt and pepper

In large saucepan, bring beef stock and potatoes to a boil. After 7 minutes, add cabbage and beets. Simmer over low heat. Melt butter in frypan and add carrots and onions. Stir in tomato puree. Add the carrots, onions, and tomato puree to saucepan mixture. Add the remaining ingredients EXCEPT SOUR CREAM. Cook for approximately 20 to 25 minutes with lid on saucepan. Serve with a dab of sour cream. Serves 12.

Potato Latkes

This traditional food is served at Hanukkah, a Jewish celebration.

3 cups grated, drained potatoes
2 tablespoons crumbled crackers
2 eggs
1 teaspoon salt
1/2 cup margarine
1/4 teaspoon pepper
4 tablespoons grated onion

Beat the eggs. Add potatoes, onion, salt, pepper, and crackers. Stir. Heat margarine in electric frypan and drop potato mixture in by tablespoons. Fry until brown on both sides. This can be served warm with a covering of applesauce or milk.

Wassail

2-1/4 cups sugar
1 quart water
12 cloves
4 cinnamon sticks, chopped
1-1/2 tablespoons ground ginger
2 quarts cider
2 cups lemon juice
3 cups orange juice

Boil sugar and water for 10 minutes. Then add spices and let stand for an hour. Strain. Add cider and juices. Place in punch bowl and float oranges and apples on top.

Resources

Bauer, Carolyn Feller. *Celebrations Read-Aloud Holiday and Theme Book Programs.* Drawings by Lynn Gates Bredeson. (New York: The H. W. Wilson Company, 1985.) Filled with holiday tips, stories, recipes, games, and jokes.

Jacobson, Michael, and Laura Hill. *Kitchen Fun for Kids: Healthy Recipes & Nutrition Facts for 7-12 Year Old Cooks* (New York: Holt, 1991).

Lapenkova, Valentina, and Edward Lambton. *Russian Food and Drink* (San Francisco: Chronicle Books, 1993).

Zamojska-Hutchins, Danuta. *Cooking the Polish Way,* "Easy Menu Ethnic Cookbooks" (Minneapolis: Lerner, 1984).

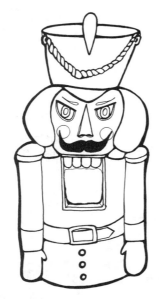

REPRODUCIBLE ACTIVITY PAGES

Cinderella's Fairy Godmother Compares Versions
   (*story comparisons*)

The Christmas Angel (*creative storytelling*)

Folk Tale Cottage Shoppe (*identifying folk tale elements*)

Piskies, Knackers, and Spriggins (*finger puppets*)

Matroshka Dolls (*bookmarks*)

You've Got the Beauty, Let's Make the Beast (*four beast versions*)

Beauty and the Beast (*art design*)

The Ugly Ogre Cover-Up Mask for Storytelling
   (*language development*)

The Giant Venn Diagram Comparison (*analyzing two giants*)

The Dragon Storyteller (*puppet making; language development*)

Kasha the Dancing Bear (*researching information about dance*)

Greetings from the Nutcracker (two pages) (*paper figure; music*)

Hanukkah—Focus Upon Lights (*modern-day lights*)

Do an Author Study—East Europe (*Jewish folk tales*)

Name _____   Date _____

CINDERELLA'S FAIRY GODMOTHER COMPARES VERSIONS

Hello. Did you know that there are over 400 versions of the Cinderella tale in Europe? And the story is in China, Africa, Korea, Egypt, and Native American tales. That keeps me very busy!

Grant me a wish. Compare two of the Cinderella tales from different cultures. Make notes on my magic cloak.

	Tale #1	Tale #2
Title		
Country		
Author		
Artist		
Name of main character		
Describe the problem		
Describe the shoe		
How is the problem solved?		

Name _____ Date _____

THE CHRISTMAS ANGEL

Color these three items, then think about how to link them together in a satisfying Christmas story. Share your story at a Storytelling Festival.

Christmas Angel

Surprise Package

Poor Family

Name _____   Date _____

FOLK TALE COTTAGE SHOPPE

Let's go shopping for a folk tale. Folk tales have specific characters and elements. Color those that apply.

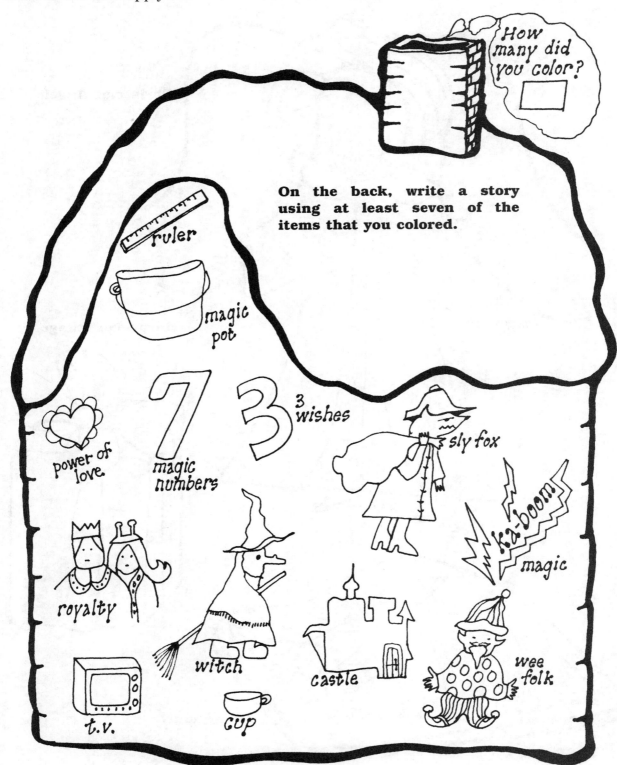

How many did you color?

On the back, write a story using at least seven of the items that you colored.

ruler

magic pot

power of love.

7 magic numbers

3 wishes

sly fox

Ka-boom magic

royalty

witch

castle

wee folk

t.v.

cup

PISKIES, KNACKERS, AND SPRIGGINS

The "wee folk" appear in many folk tales around the world. They are often in bright red, green, and yellow clothing. They will vanish rather than meet you face to face. Often, they have different jobs to do to help people. Look for the wee folk in folk tale picture books. What names do they have? What countries are they from?

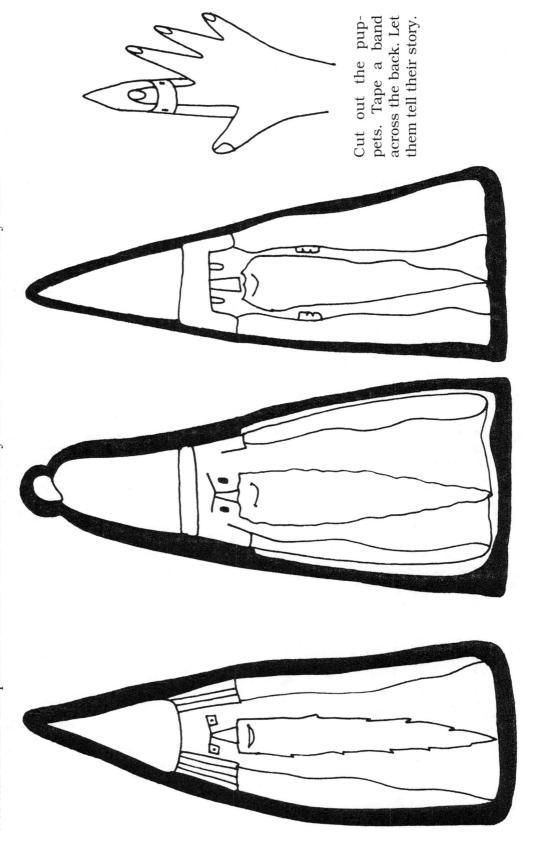

Cut out the puppets. Tape a band across the back. Let them tell their story.

A book is like a Matryoshka Doll

many treasures within

Name _____

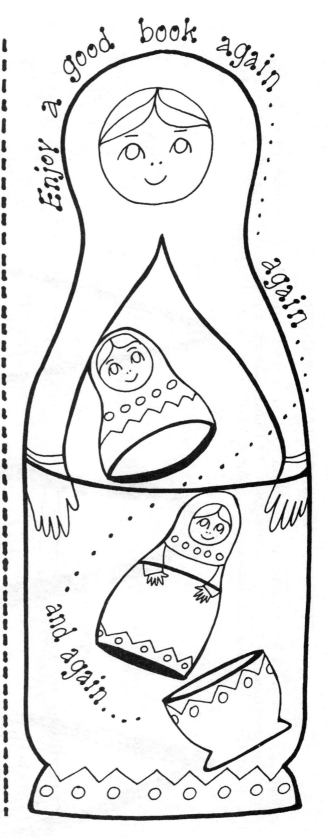

Enjoy a good book again...

...again...

and again...

Name_____

Name _____   Date _____

YOU'VE GOT THE BEAUTY, LET'S MAKE THE BEAST

There are many versions of the *Beauty and the Beast* tale all over the world. The beast takes many shapes, forms, and colors. Aha! Use your crayons to make a dazzling show of beastly beasts in the spaces below.

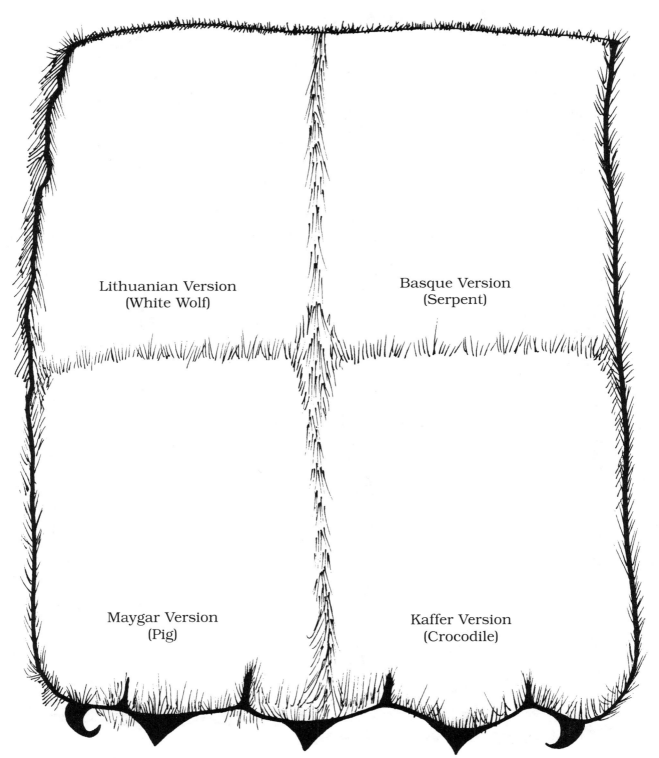

Lithuanian Version
(White Wolf)

Basque Version
(Serpent)

Maygar Version
(Pig)

Kaffer Version
(Crocodile)

Name _____   Date _____

BEAUTY AND THE BEAST

Beauty has agreed to marry Beast. Use your crayons to show their wedding portrait *just before* Beast is transformed into the handsome prince. Then, tell the story.

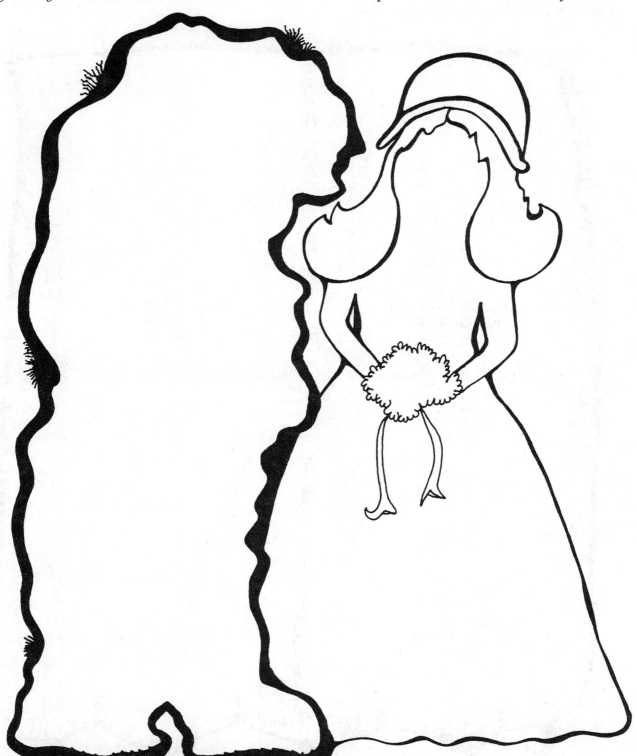

THE UGLY OGRE COVER-UP MASK FOR STORYTELLING

Color this ogre mask with dark splotches of purples and greens. Cut it out. Tie a string in each hole and wear it when you tell a story about the scariest ogre in the whole world.

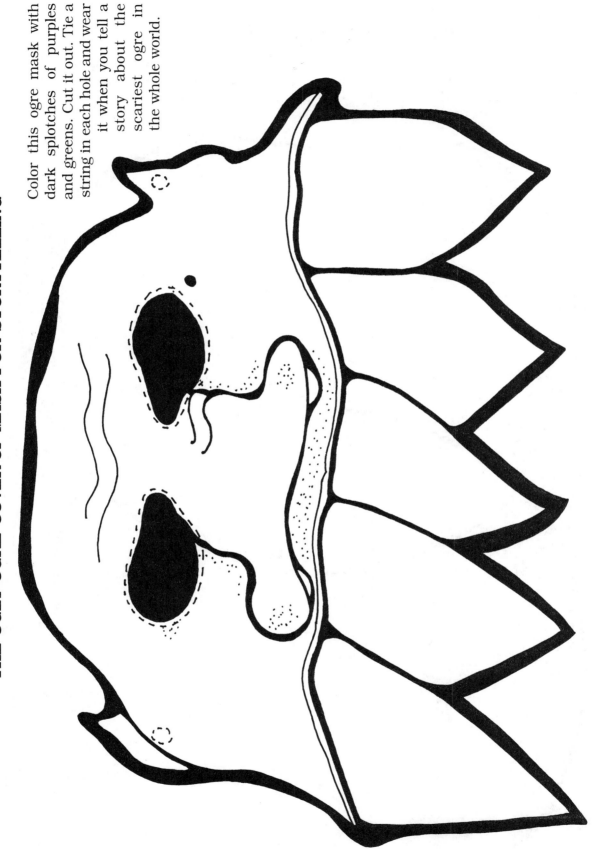

Ogre does brush these big teeth every day, even though they don't look it! What color will you choose for Ogre's teeth? Give him some good tips for taking care of his teeth.

THE GIANT VENN DIAGRAM COMPARISON

Giants appear in folk tales of many cultures. Read stories that have giants as major characters. What are they like? SELECT TWO. Use words that describe "Giant A" in his space and words that describe "Giant B" in his space. If they are alike in any way, those words go in the middle space.

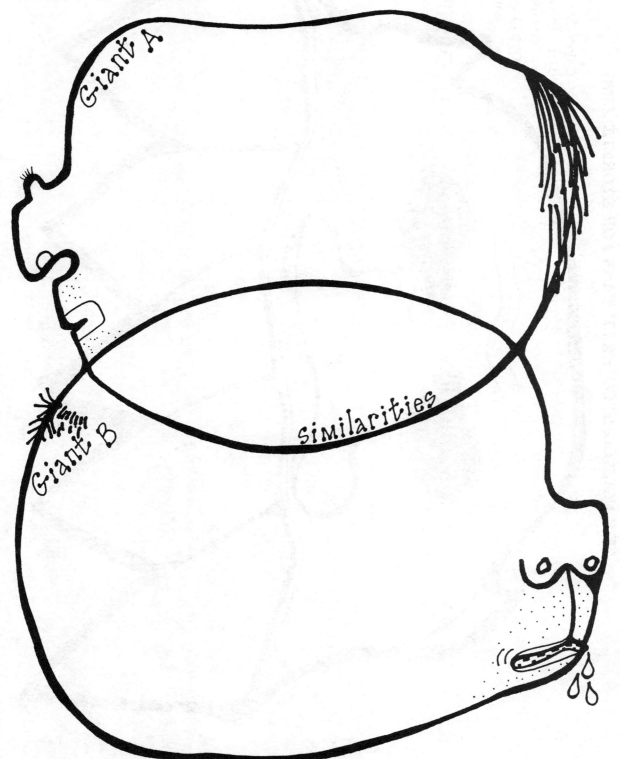

THE DRAGON STORYTELLER

Color and cut out this dragon. Mount it on a cardboard handle. Use it for storytelling. You can trace this dragon and make two. Dragons of the East breathe mist and dragons of the West breathe fire. Make up your own story about when they meet.

KASHA THE DANCING BEAR

Do you know what you want to do when you grow up? Kasha dreams of being a dancing bear in a circus. Meanwhile she is studying daily. You can help her. She needs information about three different types of dance (tap, ballet, square, folk, rhumba, Charleston, improv, and so on). Help her out! Write information in the spotlights.

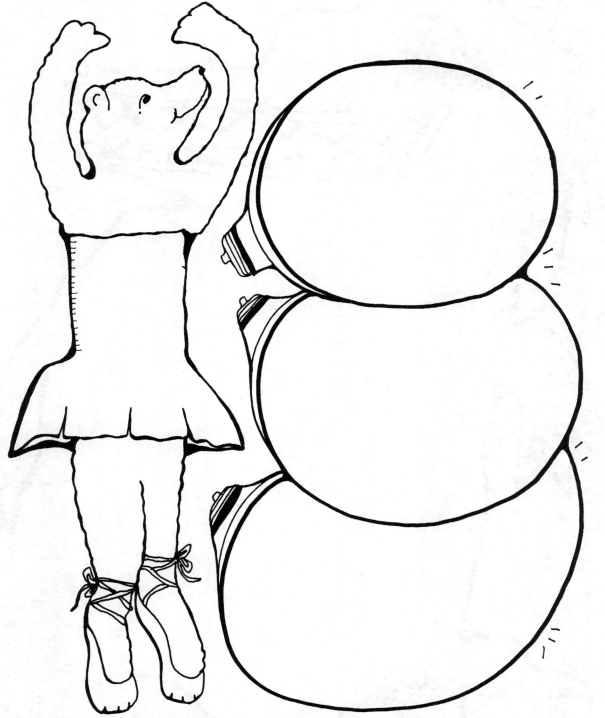

What do you want to be when you grow up? _____

What are you doing about it today? _____

GREETINGS FROM THE NUTCRACKER

The Nutcracker and the Mouse King was written by E. T. A. Hoffman. *The Nutcracker Suite* was composed by Peter Tchaikovsky. Carefully color and cut out this top half of the Nutcracker and combine it with the bottom half.

It can be pasted on a long, vertical piece of colorful construction paper.

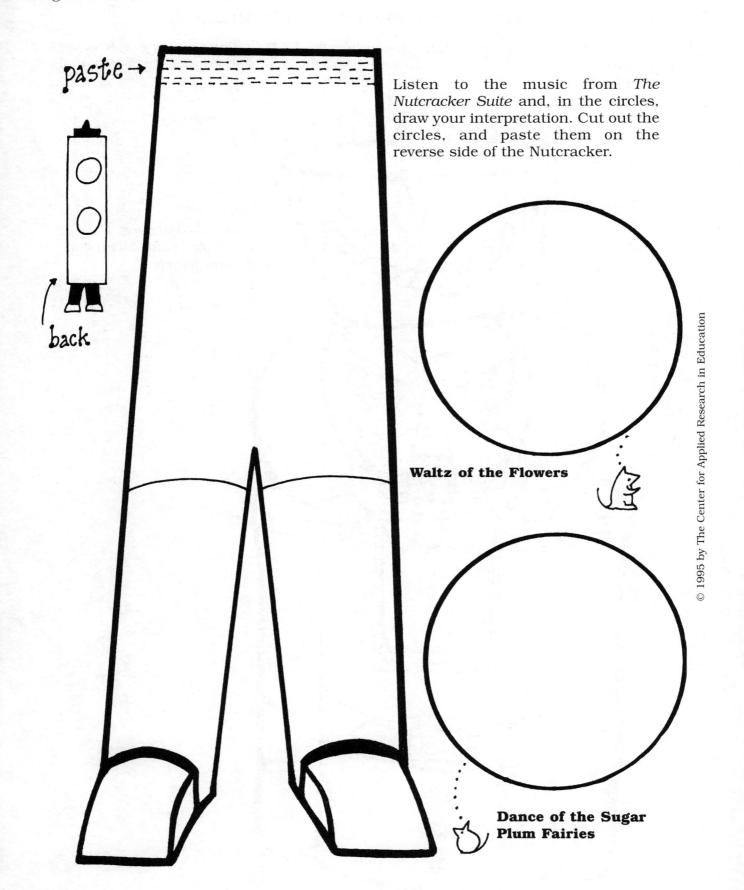

paste →

back

Listen to the music from *The Nutcracker Suite* and, in the circles, draw your interpretation. Cut out the circles, and paste them on the reverse side of the Nutcracker.

Waltz of the Flowers

Dance of the Sugar Plum Fairies

Name _____   Date _____

HANUKKAH—FOCUS UPON LIGHTS

This holiday is celebrated in early December and is known as the Festival of Lights.

Today we burn candles, but we no longer have to rely upon oil for light. In the shape below, draw a floor plan of the classroom (or a room in your home) and show where the lights are.

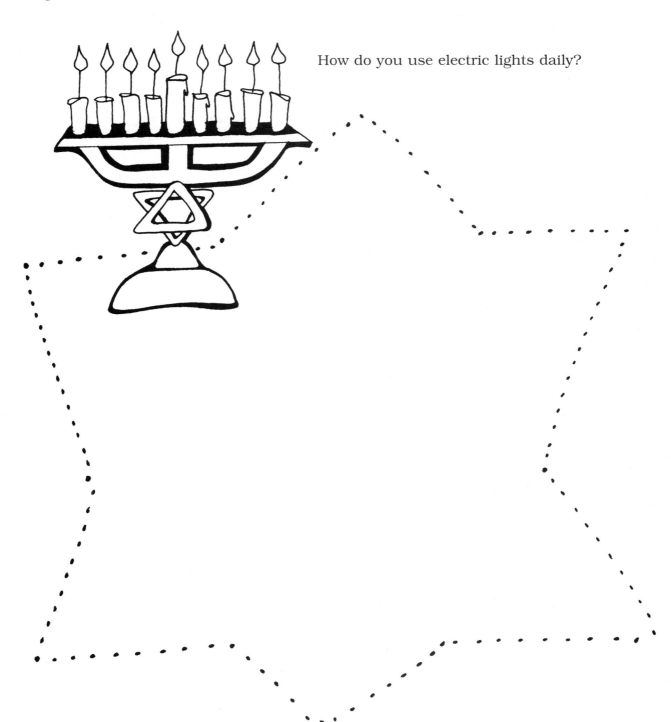

How do you use electric lights daily?

DO AN AUTHOR STUDY—EAST EUROPE

Read a variety of folk tales from Russia, Poland, Czech Republic, and a number of Yiddish (Jewish) folk tales. Analyze the books in terms of the theme (what is the author's message) and the plot (in what way did the author get the message across). Enjoy these timeless tales!

	Book 1	Book 2
TITLE		
AUTHOR & ILLUSTRATOR		
COUNTRY		
WHAT'S THE MESSAGE?		
WHAT WOULD YOU LIKE TO KNOW MORE ABOUT?		

EUROPE

RECOMMENDED CHILDREN'S BOOKS

This area of the world is extremely rich in stories from all cultures. The following list is only representative of the literature for children that is available.

Andersen, Hans Christian. *The Emperor's New Clothes*. Retold by Riki Levenson and illustrated by Robert Byrd. New York: Dutton Children's Books, 1991. This classic tale from Denmark is about vanity and foolish pride. In this version, all of the characters are magnificently dressed animals, rather than people. The emperor ROARS, so we know which animal portrays him. Same message, different style of delivery.

Anno, Mitsumasa. *Anno's Flea Market*. New York: Philomel, 1984. This Japanese author/artist takes the reader on a visual journey through a flea market. The setting resembles that of European outdoor markets, and each page is filled with old tools, old furniture, pots and kettles, lamps, musical instruments, masks, and a collection of other items. Events are going on at the market, as people walk through and get their photograph taken in the stocks or watch a performance. An excellent teaching book.

_____. *Anno's Journey*. New York: Philomel, 1983. The author/artist guides the reader through a variety of European settings from villages and towns to cities. The landscape changes as one approaches the city. A good book for discussions of story settings. Other books by the author include *Anno's England* and *Anno's Italy*.

Arnold, Tedd. *Mother Goose's Words of Wit and Wisdom, A Book of Months*. New York: Dial Books, 1990. A Mother Goose collection of 80 cross-stitched illustrations and samplers crafted by a variety of people. It gives a warmth to the favorite rhymes and may inspire students to try their hand at stitchery.

Asbjornsen, P. C. and J. E. Moe. *The Man Who Kept House*. Illustrated by Svend Otto Sorensen. New York: Margaret K. McElderry Books, 1992. This is a favorite Nordic tale. A grumpy husband who thinks he works too hard in the fields all day complains to his wife, so she suggests that they "swap jobs." He readily agrees, and is in for quite a surprise as he tends to the household the next day. Everything is in a state of disarray until the wife comes back. Never again do we hear a complaint from the husband!

de la Mare, Walter (retold). *Mollie Whuppie.* **Illustrated by Errol LeCain. New York: Farrar Straus Giroux, 1983.** This is a European version of *Jack and the Beanstalk.* Mollie Whuppie, a clever, hungry, poor girl from a large family goes out in search of food and ends up at the giant's doorstep. She uses her wits to outwit the giant more than once, so that he yells, "Woe betide ye, Molly Whuppie, if ye e'er come back again!" Does she?

dePaola, Tomie. *Fin M'Coul: The Giant of Knockmany Hill.* **New York: Holiday House, 1981.** This retelling of an Irish folktale is about Cucullin, the strongest giant in the land, and Fin M'Coul, another popular Irish giant. In this version, M'Coul's wife proves to be the heroine. When Cucullin comes thundering up to the cottage looking for M'Coul, it's the wife's cleverness and bravery that saves her frightened husband. *Jamie O'Rourke and the Big Potato* is another Irish tale by this author.

____. *Strega Nona.* **New York: Simon & Schuster, 1975.** In an Italian town named Calabria, an old lady called Strega Nona ("Grandma Witch") has a magic touch. She needs help with her little house and garden, so she puts up an ad in the town square. Big Anthony, who does not pay attention, gets the job. The fun begins when he is left in charge.

Edmonds, I. G. *Trickster Tales.* **Illustrated by Sean Morrison. Philadelphia: JB Lippincott, 1966.** Tricksters have been around for a long time. These tales are a collection from Thailand, India, Japan, England, and France. Tricksters include Reynard the Fox from France, Tyl Eulenspiegel from Germany, Brer Rabbit from the United States, and Hodja from Turkey, along with many other tricksters.

Green, Norma. *The Hole in the Dike.* **Illustrations by Eric Carle. New York: Thomas Y. Crowell, Co., 1974.** On his way home, Peter, a little Dutch boy in Holland, hears a frightening noise. He sees a hole in the dike where the sea water is just beginning to rush in, and his quick thinking saves the day. This familiar tale about a brave boy is about a hundred years old, and is retold by this author.

Jarrell, Randall, translator of a tale from The Brothers Grimm. *Snow White and the Seven Dwarfs.* **Pictures by Nancy Eckholm Burkert. New York: Farrar Straus and Giroux, 1972.** The familiar tale of Snow White is made all the more enjoyable by the beautiful, realistic illustrations. The authentic realism makes the tale believable and the seven dwarfs seem real. The drawings deserve to be studied carefully to learn more about the time during which the story was written. A Caldecott Award Winner.

Lurie, Alison. *Clever Gretchen and Other Forgotten Folk Tales.* Illustrated by Margot Tomes. New York: Thomas Y. Crowell, 1980. This collection of retold tales includes those of women who were not weaklings, but heroines who can fight and hunt, who solve riddles, who are not only beautiful but also brave, clever and resourceful. Meet Mollie Whuppie, Maid Maleen, and Kate Crackernuts, among others. An excellent resource, and good short stories.

McCully, Emily Arnold. *Mirette on the High Wire.* New York: G.P. Putnam, 1992. The setting is Paris, and the illustrations have a European flavor. This story takes place in a boardinghouse, where one guest, the Great Bellini—master wire-walker—is secluded because he has lost his nerve. But he has yet to meet Mirette, a plucky young girl, who helps him. A Caldecott Award Winner.

Nygren, Tord. *The Red Thread.* New York: R and S Books, 1987. In this wordless picture book by one of Sweden's popular illustrators, the reader follows a red thread on a journey from one fanciful page to the next. A listing at the end of the story gives some of the popular children's literature figures hidden within the illustrations, such as Winnie-the-Pooh, Little Red Riding Hood, and others.

FOLK TALES

Europe has a rich source of folklore, although the professional entertainers of the Middle Ages preferred prose and poetry. Many of the tales reflect the experiences and beliefs of the common folk and many were preserved in writing. Unlike the African or Native American culture, where the telling of stories is limited to certain times of the day or to certain seasons, it seems that there are no such taboos in Europe.

Many of the most archaic variants of fairy tales are found in Ireland and Scotland, and *not* in Russia as many believe. The reason for this is that Ireland, Scotland, Wales, and Iceland have been relatively insulated from foreign influence.

Fairy tales abound in Europe, and the fairy (fee) is French in origin. In northwest France, fairies are common in local tradition and are assumed to have originated in Brittany; then diffused over England, Germany, Italy, and Spain. Vampire tales are more Slavic in origin.

The European folk tales enjoy a strong popularity in the United States because the first immigrants who came to the country were mainly of European origin; thus, they brought their rich, entertaining, colorful tales with them.

THANKS TO THE BROTHERS GRIMM!

Jacob and Wilhelm Grimm were German "philologists," not storytellers. (A philologist is a "student of the language.") The Grimm Brothers roamed throughout the land, mostly Germany, and wrote down the tales that the common folk were telling. They were more interested in the dialect, and in compiling a German Dictionary than they were in the tales. So these famous tales, then, were not written by the Grimm Brothers, but rather they were *recorded* by them. We are fortunate that they undertook their language study; otherwise, the famous Grimm Brothers tales may have been lost to generations of people.

"JACK AND THE BEANSTALK"

There are numerous variations of this tale all over the world, including Europe and Africa. The most familiar version is a German tale, and many of the items are **symbols** that represent people or qualities. For example:

- Ladder or road: symbol of journey to the heavens
- Jack: symbol of man
- Giant: symbol for heavenly figure

The three treasures are also symbolic. For example, the bag of riches is a symbol for rain, the golden egg is a symbol for the sun, and the magic harp is a symbol for wind.

In a New Guinea version of the tale, a boy and his mother climb the beanstalk to kill Tauni-kapi-kapi, a man-eating giant that represents storms, such as tornadoes, hurricanes, and torrential rains.

Mollie Whuppie, retold by Walter de la Mare and illustrated by Errol LeCain (New York: Farrar Straus Giroux, 1983) is the female version of *Jack and the Beanstalk*. It originated in Aberdeen, Scotland—not in Spain. The rhyme that Molly uses to taunt the giant, "Never again I'll come to see'ee, Though so be I come to Spain," is thought to be the Scottish equivalent of "Rover, red rover, once more I'll come over."

Jack the Giant Killer is found in a variety of tales. In English folklore, the stupid, greedy giant, Blunderbore, is tricked into killing himself.

MEET THE DROLL TELLER OF CORNWALL

The droll teller was like a peddler who traveled from village to village, from house to house, and traded stories for cider and supper. His story, called a "droll," would either be told or sung. Here are some of the characters used by the droll teller.

Piskies:

Funny little men, no bigger than hedgehogs. A piskie wore a shoulder-length wig of gray moss, topped off by a pointed red hat. His clothing was brown, with stockings as green as grass. Piskies were cheerful and impish, and could never be caught. You'd be lucky to catch a glimpse of one. (Every home should have a hole in the outer wall, about the size of a mouse hole, so that a piskie can go in and out at will.)

Spriggins:

Tiny, but mean and ugly. They were the guardians of the giants' buried treasure. They had spindly legs, frog-like feet, and long arms that hung down to their knees. It was said that they had six fingers on each hand. (To keep a spriggin from getting into your house, leave a glove or a hat or a piece of clothing turned inside out.)

Knackers:

Elves who lived deep within the tin mines. They got their name from the "tap tap" tapping noises they made as they worked. They were friendly, but did not like to be spied upon.

Small People:

Elegantly dressed tiny people, or fairies about 12 inches tall. They ate honey and blackberries and lived in the woods.

For more information about the Cornish folklore, refer to *Piskies, Spriggins, and Other Magical Beings, Tales From the Droll-Teller*, retold by Shirley Climo, and illustrated by Joyce Audy dos Santos (New York: Thomas Crowell, 1981).

CATS, CATS, AND MORE CATS

There is an old Irish legend that tells of Trusan, a huge cat, as strong as an ox, who ruled over all the cats and lived in a cave at Knowth-in-Meath. To kill or to mistreat a cat is considered bad luck in European, African, and American Negro tales. In Transylvania, the cat is a fertility symbol and about a month after the wedding the cat is brought inside the home in a cradle and rocked back and forth before the newlyweds.

Here are more cat tales:

- A cat washing its face is a sign of rain.
- A cat looking out the window is looking for rain.
- You can tell the time of day by the size of a cat's pupils.
- Bathing a cat brings rain (Indonesia).
- A kitten born in May will never be a mouser (England).

THE STRENGTH OF IRON

In folklore, most people used iron to ward off evil spirits. Charm bracelets were put on newborn infants to protect them because of the strength it radiates. If a Scottish fisherman should forget himself and sputter something that he shouldn't say (swear), it is the custom to call out, "Cold Iron!" and grasp the nearest piece of iron and hang on tight. An iron horseshoe was hung on a nail over some doorways to keep evil spirits out of the house. Throughout Europe, iron is a powerful charm against witchcraft, yet witches use the iron vessels to prepare their brews. In India, the genie fears iron, and in China even the dragons fear iron. In China, some believe that in times of drought, you can throw a piece of iron into the dragon pool of water, and the dragon gets angry and may repay you with a good rainstorm! In parts of Ireland, even thieves won't steal anything made from iron.

IRISH "HELPERS"

The Irish have a grand tradition for telling stories and love to embellish them. As in all cultures, there are the helpers who assist the hero. In the folk tale "King of Ireland's Son," there are several helpers, such as:

- *the marvelous runner:*   had to keep one leg tied up from running too fast
- *the remarkable hearer:*   he could hear the grass grow
- *the mighty blower:*   had to hold a finger to his nose to keep from blowing down houses
- *the mighty stonebreaker:*   had to break stones without a hammer so they wouldn't end up pulverized

In tales of every culture, there is the unseen helper who assists the good and kindly person who has been wronged.

BONES, BONE FIRE, BONFIRE

The bones, or skeletons, of people are believed to be the residence of the animal nature of man. In a Brothers Grimm tale, "The Singing Bone," a bone is taken from the body of a murdered brother and made into a flute. Then, when it is played, it accuses the murderer. In the Asian Cinderella tale of "Yeh-Shen," there are magic powers in the bones of the dead fish. In parts of Africa, the monkey bone is thought to hold magic powers. In Indonesia, the "bone fire" is built for destroying corpses and bones by fire (cremation). This has been handed down through various cultures as the "bonfire" and is generally built today as an expression of cheerful feelings, such as at times of celebrations.

Today, in the United States, the skeleton and bones surface at Halloween time. Children dress in skeleton costumes, and paper skeletons are hung from the ceiling to scare us. This is what remains in our culture of any mention of bones as fearsome.

"BEAUTY AND THE BEAST" IN REVERSE—LOATHLY LADY

The reverse of "Beauty and the Beast" is the story of the handsome man and the hag. This is a universal tale in many cultures, and in some European tales she is called the "loathly lady."

BABIES BORN WITH TEETH

While this is common in all cultures, the reaction is either extremely negative or positive. In France and Italy, it is believed that the baby born with teeth will have a wonderful future. In many Asian cultures, and in southern African-American culture, it is considered bad luck. In some cultures, the tooth is immediately pulled and the baby is then considered harmless.

SPEAKING OF TREES

Planting a tree when a baby is born is common in many European cultures. This is called the "life tree." In Switzerland, an apple tree is planted for a boy and a pear tree is planted for a girl.

The apple tree (or apple) is considered a love charm in English, German, and Danish folk tales. There are many sayings associated with apples, such as, "An apple a day keeps the doctor away."

THE MESSENGER OF SPRING

The cry of the cuckoo at springtime is familiar in the Old World and is greeted with a great deal of excitement. In Germany, people roll on the grass with joy and their greeting is, "Der Kuckuck hat gerufen!" If there is money in their pocket, it is turned over for good luck.

THE CAULDRON, OR MAGIC POT

There are many stories that include the magic pot. In Celtic myth the cauldron of Annwfn would not boil a coward's food, and the cauldron of Cerridwea gave inspiration. Witches are often associated with the pot. The witches in Shakespeare's *Macbeth* stir up the pot with their famous lines, "Double double, toil and trouble, fire burn, and cauldron bubble." Iron is often used to guard against witches, such as the custom of hanging a horseshoe over the door, and yet the witch is associated with the iron cauldron.

PROTECTION FOR THE YOUNG

In Ancient Rome, Cardea, goddess of the door hinges, protected little children against attack at night by vampires and witches. The Otovolo Indians of Ecuador, South America, still tie a red ribbon around the wrist or neck of infants to protect them from harm. In most cultures, there are a variety of chants, names, and devices used to protect the young.

"CINDERELLA," THE MOST POPULAR AND WIDESPREAD TALE

There are over 500 versions of *Cinderella* in Europe, with more tales still being found and recorded. This is called a "universal" tale, with the step-mother who favors her own children over her stepchild. It is the best-known folk tale in the world—from South Africa to Korea, from Europe to Indonesia, from South America to Alaska. The tale appears in almost every culture, but it is believed that the tale originated in the Orient.

The Cinderella tale has been studied in detail. These are the elements of the tale:

1. The flight of the girl (from the wicked stepmother, or from the father). Here are just a few of the names of the heroine:

    Aschenputtel (German)
    Cendrillon (French)
    Cenerentola (Italian)
    Cenicienta (Spanish)
    Rhodopis (Egyptian)
    Yeh-Shen (Chinese)

2. The heroine wanders, disguised by unusual clothing:

    Mouse skin (Russian, Slavic)
    Cat skin (Irish, English)
    Pig skin (Italian, Finnish, Sicilian)
    Ass skin (French, Spanish)
    Turkey feathers (Zuni)
    Fur (Germany)
    Wood (Greek, Portuguese, Swedish)
    Crow skin (Swedish)
    Rags, tatters, boys' clothes (variants)

3. The heroine takes up a menial position in a home:

> tending the hearth
> scullery maid (cleaning, cooking)
> goosegirl
> shepherdess
> turkey girl

4. The heroine is discovered by a young prince:

> at a ball
> at a dance
> at a gathering of people

5. The escape by the heroine before she is discovered
6. The lost shoe and the search for the tiny foot
7. Recognition by the prince
8. Marriage
9. Punishment of the father or stepmother, stepsisters

Is the Emphasis upon the Foot Size a Cultural Clue?

The emphasis upon the tiny glass slipper (in some versions the slipper is made from squirrel fur) makes one look to the culture that reveres small feet. In the Orient, the feet of the royals were bound and tied so that they would not grow large. This strengthens the case for the tale having originated in Asia. Also, it strengthens the argument that Cinderella is of royal birth and is returned to her rightful place in society. Justice prevails in the end in tales.

Fairy Godmother

This person is found in the Charles Perrault version of the Cinderella tale, but is rarely found in the world tales. Mainly it is the dead mother who helps (in the form of a spirit, or a tree growing from the mother's grave, or from a cow or goat).

Also, the Perrault version introduces the glass slipper. In the Chinese and Egyptian versions, it is a golden slipper. In some cultures, it is a fur slipper.

Many Versions

Read a variety of the Cinderella tales to students. Be sure to include *Yeh-Shen, a Cinderella Story From China* by Ai-Ling Loui; *The Egyptian Cinderella* and *The Korean Cinderella* by Shirley Climo; *The Rough-Face Girl, An Algonquin Indian Tale* by Rafe Martin; and *Princess Furball* retold by Charlotte Huck, among others.

In *The Talking Eggs*, a folk tale from the American South and retold by Robert D. San Souci, we have some of the Cinderella elements—the mean mother and sister, the abused and overworked girl, the witch-woman who appears as helper, the element of magic with the talking eggs, the riches, the happy ending, and the punishment. Although this is not classified as a Cinderella tale by any means, there are versions of this type of tale in all world cultures, where one child is favored and another is badly mistreated.

Common Elements in Folk Tales

Once students have heard or read a number of fairy tales or folk tales, they can begin to see characteristics that make up the folk tale formula. This understanding will help them to gain a "sense of story," to make predictions, to use their imagination, and to write their own folk tales. Some characteristics are:

- a swift beginning
- quick introduction to setting and characters
- colorful language (descriptive words help to paint the picture)
- stating the problem or conflict
- the attempt to solve the problem
- use of magic
- the resolution
- the lesson to be learned

Some characters include:

- king/queen, prince/princess, fisherman/wife, farmer/wife
- youngest brother or youngest sister (often overlooked in terms of potential)
- wicked stepmother
- witch
- talking animals
- helpers (many forms)

Some devices used in folk tales are:

- magic numbers (3, 7, 11, 12)
- unlucky numbers (13)
- magic things (pebbles, ring)

- things happen in three's (third time is a charm)
- the long journey (under the sea, through the woods)
- making a promise, then breaking it

Some overriding themes of folk tales include:

- justice prevails in the end
- wicked are punished/good are rewarded
- wishes come true after a task (or test)
- the power of love
- honesty wins out

SUGGESTED ACTIVITIES FOR THE CLASSROOM

1. A "CINDERELLA" STUDY

Divide the students into teams to do an in-depth study of the Cinderella tale. Secure copies of the variants of the tale, some of which are listed in this section, from Europe as well as the Chinese, Egyptian, Native American, and Korean versions. Have students make a huge comparison chart for the wall. List the bibliographic information, name of main character, setting, type of magic, how Cinderella's problem was solved, the ending, and student reactions.

2. A MULTITUDE OF MULTICULTURAL CINDERELLAS... BEFORE AND AFTER

Use large kraft paper and have students trace the outline of several volunteer students. These outlines can be transformed (by paint, fabric, feathers, jewelry, etc.) into a life-size set of multicultural *Cinderella* characters. "Before and after" versions can be made by using both sides of the paper, or by cutting out double figures and gluing them back to back. Students can use these dramatic figures as props for a storytelling festival and creative dramatics.

3. THANKS TO THE BROTHERS GRIMM!

Read many of the Grimm Brothers tales to students and have picture books available for students to read on their own. Include a wide variety. This presents a splendid opportunity for storytelling. Always begin with "I'd like to thank the Brothers Grimm for this tale..." (give the title and tell the tale) and end with "Thanks to the Brothers Grimm, we have this tale to tell."

4. RETOLD TALES

The updated modern versions of tales are amusing to students, such as *Jim and the Beanstalk* by Raymond Briggs (New York: Putnam, 1989) and *The True Story of the Three Little Pigs! By A. Wolf*, as told to Jon Scieszka, and illustrated by Lane Smith (New York: Viking, 1989). Many other tales are retold also. Help students to locate, read, and enjoy these versions. Then, students are ready to do some modernizing of their own. Select a tale that has not been retold and help students enjoy the language experiences that retelling the tale provides.

5. AN AESOP FABLE MESSAGE BOARD

The Aesop fables are short, to the point, and contain a lesson. Students can read a wide variety of them and then report to the class. They can write the moral, and post it on a colorful classroom chart shaped like a fox, for example. Keep referring to the list daily as it grows.

6. "THE UGLY DUCKLING" PUPPET THEATER

It is said that Hans Christian Andersen created a puppet theater and puppets as a young boy, and then acted out the stories he developed. Students can create "The Ugly Duckling" Puppet Theater by painting and decorating a box (large or table-top size) where they can practice storytelling with puppets they make from a variety of materials.

7. JOURNAL WRITING

After being exposed to a variety of folk tales and even Mother Goose rhymes, students can keep a diary from the point-of-view of a character. What, for example, is Snow White writing in her diary each night? What is a specific Giant writing? What are the daily thoughts, as written from their point-of-view, of characters like the shoemaker, the elves, Little Bo Peep, Jack Sprat, and so on?

CELEBRATIONS

People have celebrations all over the world. The following celebrations do not represent every holiday nor every country in Europe, but serve as a general idea of the celebrations in this area of the world.

HAPPY NEW YEAR!

The new year is celebrated in Europe with special songs, greetings, and gifts. In France, for the New Year (The Peille Fete) the children write New Year's letters and send them to their mother with good wishes and apologies for any wrongdoings during the past year.

In Great Britain, part of the festivities includes the "burning of the bush," or burning up the past year. Also, there are the "first footers," the persons who are first to cross the threshold in the New Year. They should arrive bearing gifts, usually food. At midnight, on the stoke of ONE the back door is opened to release the Old Year. Then the door is locked to keep in the luck and the front door is opened at the stroke of TWELVE to let in the New Year.

First visitors on New Year's is important in Greece, also. And in Scotland, the first footers should bring gifts of bread, salt, and coal.

CANDLEMAS

In December, this procession of people carrying candles to lighten the way is a part of the Christian tradition. It is celebrated in Austria, France, Germany, Greece, and Spain.

BOXING DAY

This is the first work day after Christmas in Great Britain, where there is an old custom of filling boxes with gifts for those who are less fortunate. Sometimes money is given.

SCANDINAVIAN CHRISTMAS

This is a long holiday celebration. At this time of the year the days are short and nights are long, so there are candles and lights shining weeks before Christmas to brighten the landscape. On December 13, the holiday season officially begins with St. Lucia's Day, Queen of Light. A favorite part of the season is the traditional use of straw animals. The straw symbolizes grain, which represents food and prosperity. The **Julbock**, a big straw goat with braided hair, is a favorite. Also to hang on the tree are other straw favorites such as **Julgrisar**, the Yule pigs, and **Julbockar**, the Yule goats.

There is a splendid smorgasbord on Christmas Eve. The traditional codfish is served and, of course, the rice porridge (risgrynsgrot) is a part of the meal. Hidden inside the rice porridge is a single nut (almond); it means good fortune to the one who gets it.

Jultomten, a small gnome-like creature, arrives after dinner with a sack of gifts. The Scandinavian Santa Claus is not fat and jolly, but thin and small. He has a cap, gown, fur boots, and a long beard. He asks the question "Are there any good children in this house?" and is then invited in.

See the book *Holidays in Scandinavia* by Lee Wyndham, illustrations by Gordon Laite (Champaign, IL: Garrard Publishing Co., 1975).

NEW YEAR'S EVE TRICKERY

In Denmark, this is a night of pranks and jokes for young people. Children ring the doorbell and run. Finally, at the end of the evening the children are "caught" and brought indoors for treats.

SHROVE MONDAY AND SHROVE TUESDAY

In Bulgaria, the week before Lent is called "Cheese Week." All cheese, milk, and lard are used up in baking before the fasting of Lent begins. In Great Britain on Shrove Tuesday, just before Lent, women hold races while baking a pancake in a frypan. They must flip it over and catch it three times. The first woman to reach the church and feed the bellringer is the winner.

ST. PATRICK'S DAY

March 17 is the day for the wearin' of the green. Ireland has lush green landscapes because of the sea mist and favorable climate, and on this day people wear green. In some cities in Ireland and in the United States there are parades, bands, and great celebrations. It is a time for storytelling, dished up with corned beef and cabbage. Even green food coloring is used for small cakes and for drinks. In some areas of the United States, people celebrate this holiday by painting a green stripe down the middle of the highway, instead of the usual white or yellow.

SPRING CAPPING IN SWEDEN

In the city of Uppsala, it is the tradition on April 30 for thousands of students to assemble in front of the university library. Then at 3 o'clock, an official gives a short speech and waves his cap. This is the signal for all graduates to take their caps from their pockets and wave them in the air, then put them on their head. Swedish men and women keep the caps that they earned in school (gymnasium) and wear them throughout their life for special occasions. This is a day of celebration with a mock student battle, music, dancing, and fireworks.

MAY DAY

There are celebrations throughout Europe at this time of year. Officially, Spring growth has returned, the long winter sleep is over, and people rejoice. There is the traditional May Pole, with dancers holding onto ribbon streamers that weave over and under as they dance around the pole. Children gather flowers in little baskets and hang them onto the doorknob of homes in the neighborhood. A King and Queen of May are crowned, and good food is served. Archery is a popular sport for May Day events.

BASTILLE DAY

In France, July 14 is Independence Day (like Fourth of July in the United States). This is a time for military parades and marching bands. People hold bicycle races and boat races. In the evening are dancing and fireworks.

HAPPY EASTER

Germany is home to many of the customs and celebrations that have found their way to the United States. Easter is a particularly happy event that is celebrated throughout Germany, Europe, and the Christian world. Eggs (a symbol of life and growth) are decorated and hidden in tall grasses, and children go on a merry hunt for them. At one time, people gave decorated eggs as gifts. Also, young girls decorated eggs with red coloring and then rubbed them against their cheeks for color.

Today, in the United States, coloring eggs is customary at Easter, and they are placed in woven baskets lined with artificial grass and filled with candies. In some cities there are Easter Parades, and people wear their new clothes and Easter hats (bonnets). Chocolate eggs and candies are given as gifts.

The rabbit (representing spring and abundance) has become a symbol of Easter in the United States, and usually surprises children by leaving baskets of goodies for them. At the White House in Washington, D.C., a traditional Easter egg hunt is held on the lawn.

SUGGESTED ACTIVITIES FOR THE CLASSROOM

1. MAP IDENTIFICATION/LIBRARY RESEARCH

Have students trace a map of Europe on a large sheet of kraft paper. Use an atlas for help with identifying the names of countries. Then, have students divide into teams. Each team selects (or is given) a country to "study" at the library in terms of finding a special holiday for that country. Have students report their findings.

2. FOLK TALES THAT SHOW CELEBRATIONS

Have students also check through folk tales written about their assigned country to see if there are special celebrations in the story. (Even birthdays may give information about food or the custom of meeting with friends.)

3. THE FIRST FOOTERS

Make a "threshold" in the classroom (even a pillow can be used as something to step over). Discuss the idea that the New Year "first footers" (those first over the threshold in the new year) are symbolic of what is to follow. So, you want to put your best foot forward. Have each student step over the threshold with a personal New Year's resolution or a resolution that a famous storybook character might give.

4. SPRING CAPPING

Students can wear a hat on a designated day in the spring when everyone will identify them as the "Students in Room..." Perhaps the hats can be kept at school and worn for birthday celebrations and other special occasions. It may be possible to have each student bring in a plain white t-shirt, and stencil the logo of the class on it. This is also a means of group identification and pride.

5. EASTER CELEBRATIONS

Work with parents so that fresh eggs can be purchased at a supermarket, brought to school, washed, and hard boiled. When cool, students can print their name on an egg with a wax crayon, and dye the egg in food coloring. Later in the day, the egg can be eaten (precautions should be taken for food allergies). Read *Chickens Aren't the Only Ones* by Ruth Heller (New York: Putnam, 1993) during this time, and have students design colorful eggs with felt pens and construction paper oval shapes.

6. PRIDE BADGES

Have students identify (with the aid of parents) a country of their ancestors. Students can make a "pride badge" in the shape of that country and wear it proudly. Where in the world are the children from as a group? This calls for some world map work.

7. MAY DAY CELEBRATIONS

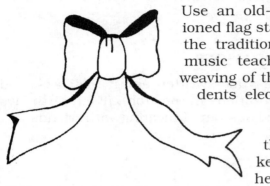

Use an old-fashioned clothes tree, an old-fashioned flag stand, or a stand from the gym to make the traditional May Pole. Enlist the aid of the music teacher in helping with the music and weaving of the ribbons over and under. Have students elect a King and Queen of May. Why? Because this is a celebration that has been carried on for centuries throughout Europe and we aim to keep traditions alive and to preserve the heritage of all people.

8. IT'S A DAY FOR THE WEARIN' OF THE GREEN

St. Patrick's Day, on March 17, is a day of celebration that can be used as a celebration of the color green. Have students wear something green to school. Students can make a shamrock-shaped name tag and print their name with an "O'" or "Mc" prefix, such as Susan O'Kolwicz (for Susan Kolwicz) or Diane McTurso (for Diane Turso). To help celebrate green, students can prepare a lime punch with green sherbet or make lime gelatin. This can be a day for Irish music in the background, storytelling, and folk tales from Ireland.

And, don't forget the leprechauns who like some very quiet times during this happy day. They especially like the game "Hide the Potato." (Everyone knows where it is except the one who is "it" and has to search the room for the hidden potato. When "it" is close, the class starts humming softly.)

9. IT'S A DAY FOR CASTLES

Throughout Europe, there are many castles that date from the Middle Ages. Students can investigate castles, and the book *Castle* by David Macaulay (Boston: Houghton Mifflin, 1982) is a good place to begin. On this day, the classroom can be turned into a castle, and students can search through folk tales and picture books for stories and pictures of castles from Europe. Perhaps castles can be constructed from cylinders, tubes, cardboard boxes, etc., and used as stages for story reenactment with puppets.

10. BUILDING CASTLES IN THE AIR

When we use the expression "building castles in the air," we mean that someone has come up with an idea that is far-fetched. It's a dream, and will never happen. But suppose it could happen? This might be a good way to begin a type of "Tall-tale Castle-in-the-Air Day" with a focus upon the impossible invention that works. This nurtures creative thinking and fosters scientific inquiry.

11. CHRISTMAS AROUND THE WORLD

On a large bulletin board, students can trace a map of the world and place a red dot on the areas that celebrate this holiday, since it is the most widely celebrated holiday in the world. Next to the red dot, have students make a cut-out drawing of the gift-bringer (Russia—Father Frost; USA and Canada—Santa Claus or St. Nicholas; Sweden—Jultomten the gnome; Turkey—Yule Baba, and so on). What is going on in other parts of the world at this time? Students may find that different festivals do occur around the world in late December. This information can also be represented on the map.

12. CHRISTMAS SYMBOLS

Students can list items that are associated with this season and then find the meaning behind their use. Record the information on a large chart in the room. Here are some to get you started:

mistletoe . . . . symbol of hope and peace
trees . . . . evergreen, promise of spring to come
candles . . . . guide the way for weary travelers
poinsettia . . . . red flower from Mexico associated with this holiday

Students enjoy singing carols, so make a cassette recording of their songs. The cassette can be gift wrapped and sent as a goodwill present to a local children's hospital, to a hospice, or to a nursing home with a cheery message.

ARTS AND CRAFTS

Many art movements were begun in this part of the world and spread to other cultures. For years, Paris has been regarded as the art capital of the world, drawing artists from all over the globe to perfect their craft in a creative and accepting atmosphere. Students can be introduced to different types of art, such as Expressionism (Vincent van Gogh with bright colors), Impressionsim (Renoir, Manet, Monet), and other styles of art such as

Cubism and Pointillism, to name a few. The work of artists in Florence, Venice, and Rome (Michelangelo and Leonardo da Vinci) is unsurpassed. The new world (United States and Canada) was enriched and influenced by the art that emerged from this section of the world.

SUGGESTED ACTIVITIES FOR THE CLASSROOM

1. MEET THE MASTERS

Share the work of master artists with students. There are many library books available for young children that introduce a particular school of art or an individual artist. Locate some of these and bring them to the classroom so that students can pour over them. Call upon the expertise of the art teacher, who may have 35mm slides of the works of well-known artists.

2. CELEBRATE THE ARTISTS IN THEIR STYLE

The intent is not to "copy" an artist, for each person is unique, but it is enjoyable for students to create a work of art in the style of a master. In fact, in many European schools of art, students are sent into the art galleries to copy from famous paintings in an effort to gain knowledge about perspective, the artist's use of color, where the light and dark shapes appear in a composition, and so on.

Seurat's "pointillism" (small colored dots of paint) makes students aware of shape and color; thus, it provides a good student art activity. Begin by lightly sketching one object (bird or flower) and slowly and carefully fill it in with small dots of paint. To make it simpler, when doing a bird, for example, use only three colors—blue, green and yellow. When the blue and yellow dots are placed close together, the eye sees them blending as green when held at a distance. This also happens with dots of red and yellow (orange) and dots of blue and red (purple).

3. THE CUBISTS

Have students make a colorful felt-pen drawing of a face on 8-1/2″ x 11″ paper. Then cut it out. Next, cut it in half lengthwise. Select a background color and paste the left half onto the paper. Then, position the right half slightly askew, either higher or lower than the half face on the left. After it is pasted, fill in the hair and chin to make it common for both sides. Have students experiment with this technique. Show them works by Miro and Picasso, who took liberties with facial features (juxtaposition of facial features, profile of face but two eyes looking front, and so on). Why do artists do this? Artists are always experimenting and looking for new ways to express themselves. Foster this attitude in the children's own art work.

4. IN THE STYLE OF MONDRIAN

Mondrian, a French painter, has a recognizable style. Secure works of Mondrian from a library resource book or book of art posters. Work with 12″ x 18″ sheets of stark white paper. Students will need to cut five thin strips from black paper and position two strips in a vertical position (they do not have to be straight) and three strips in a horizontal position (slightly askew or straight). Students can experiment with this line placement until it "feels right" to them. Then, glue it down. Next, select three colors (red, blue and yellow work well). Students need to make two decisions: (1) Of their 12 spaces, which 7 will they fill in with color, and (2) which color will they select for the spaces, making sure to use all three shades. They will need to cut the colors and paste them in the spaces. (For younger children, you can use 8-1/2″ x 11″ paper. After the lines are done, they can use felt pens to color in the spaces, rather than cutting the shapes.) Mount these on sheets of black and display in your gallery.

5. EXAMINE PICTURE BOOK ILLUSTRATIONS

While many of the artists/illustrators working in this field are from the United States, many have European ancestors. Examine their picture book illustrations, and try working in that particular style. For example:

Maurice Sendak ....crosshatching (*Where the Wild Things Are*)
Eric Carle ....fingerpainting, then cutting out shapes (*Have You Seen My Cat?*)
Tomi dePaola.....................folk art motifs (*Strega Nona*)
Brian Wildsmith ....watercolors (*Squirrels*)
Ezra Jack Keats ....colorful collage of wallpaper and solid colors (*A Snowy Day*)

6. CASTLES! CASTLES! CASTLES!

One thing we know about Europe is that there are many castles. An entire bulletin board, a wall of the room, or even the entire room can be made into a part of a castle. Use grey backing paper for the stone look.

If students are going to build a large castle, use a cardboard box (dishwasher size) for the base. Then paint the box and add features (windows that swing open, etc.). When it is finished, "furnish" the inside so that students can go in there for quiet work.

If students are going to build individual castles, start collecting cardboard boxes in many shapes and sizes. Foil wrap can be used to cover cylinder shapes and to sculpt details. First tape, then glue the shapes together.

7. SUNFLOWERS AND IRISES

Van Gogh made these two flowers popular. Have students go on a hunt for them in art books. Plant sunflower seeds in a school garden setting. When they grow, study them, draw them, and paint them. The same can be done with the iris.

Have students be on the alert for ways flowers are depicted in art books and in story picture books. Perhaps they can devise some new ways to make flowers (potato prints, gadget printing, wallpaper, cloth swatches, and so on). Make a large wall mural of nothing but flowers.

GAMES

Children the world over enjoy playing ball games. An excellent resource book is *The Marshall Cavendish Illustrated Guide to Games Children Play Around The World—Ball Games* by Ruth Oakley, with illustrations by Steve Lucas (New York: Marshall Cavendish, 1989).

MONDAY, TUESDAY

This is a British wall ball game for seven players, each of whom takes one day of the week as his or her title. Equipment needed are a ball and a wall.

"Monday" begins the game by throwing a ball against a wall and calling out another day of the week, for example, "Saturday." "Saturday" must try to catch the ball before it bounces. If successful, then he is next to throw the ball against the wall. If not successful, the ball goes back to "Monday" who then throws the ball and tries to hit a player. If a player is hit, "Monday" gets another chance to bounce the ball against the wall. If no player is hit, the turn shifts to "Tuesday" and so on through the seven days of the week.

SHERLOCK AND WATSON

This is a circle game for a large number of players, and focuses upon listening as a skill. Equipment needed is a blindfold.

Students sit in a circle. "It" (Sherlock) is blindfolded in the center of the circle. "It" calls out "Watson," and one member who has been designated as Watson, answers by calling out "Sherlock." The blindfolded Sherlock moves toward the voice and may say "Watson" again, and Watson answers "Sherlock." Finally, when Sherlock touches Watson, the game is over. Watson then becomes the new Sherlock and is blindfolded in the center, and a new Watson is selected quietly by the previous Sherlock who sits in the circle and joins in the fun.

PROVERB RUMOR

This is a variation of the all-time classic "Rumor Game." Divide the class into two teams with a leader for each team. You might want to have a list of proverbs.

The two leaders decide upon a proverb, or a sentence, and write it on a piece of paper. The leaders then whisper the message to the next person, who whispers it to the next, and so on until the last person on each team receives the message and stands up. When both team members are standing, they first say the message they received, and then read aloud the printed message that was sent. The team closer to the original saying gets one point. Begin again, with the last players now serving as team leaders.

IRISH HOT POTATO GAME

This is a variation of the "Circle Game," and students sit in a large circle. A player in the middle is "it." Equipment needed is a small potato or an object.

A small potato is passed from player to player in the circle while "it" sits with eyes closed and head down in the center. Keep the potato moving. When "it" yells out "HOT!" the person holding the potato is the new "it" and the game begins all over again. (The person holding the potato when "HOT!" is called can also be considered out, and the game can be played until only one player is remaining, who is then designated as the winner.)

FORFEIT

This is a very old game, at one time played by adults as a parlor game. One player is designated as the "judge."

Each player decides to forfeit a piece of clothing, jewelry, or other item. These are placed on the floor behind the "judge." One person holds an item over the judge's head, and chants: "Heavy heavy hang over your head, the owner must do whatever is said." Then the judge pronounces a sentence (not knowing who the owner is) and the owner must do that in order to get the item back. When all items are returned to rightful owners, begin again with a new judge. (Some suggestions for the judge are: bounce a ball ten times, juggle three erasers, keep yawning until someone else yawns, move like an elephant, gallop like a horse, hop like a rabbit, name six blue items in the room, and so on.)

THREE-LEGGED RACE

This is an outdoor game that can be played as a team game, or as a game that students can enter on the playground while other activities are in progress. You need a sack, twine, and a clock.

Two students, side by side, must place the leg closer to their partner into a sack. The sack is then tied and becomes the "third leg." Partners need to work as a unit by moving their "outside" and "inside" legs in unison to get them to the designated goal line. Their time is then recorded. Players with the shortest time are the winners. (As the year progresses, players may want to practice and compete again to decrease their time.)

LES BOULES (FRENCH)

You will need a set of "bowls" (balls), about the size of tennis balls (heavy balls used for croquet would be good). One ball is designated as the "jack." This game is played outdoors on the playground.

One player begins the game by throwing the "jack" into a cleared space. Each player, thereafter, tosses *or* rolls the "bowl" to try to hit the "jack." When the game is over, the winner is the one who has hit the "jack" or is nearest to it.

This is a version of the bowl game that is taken quite seriously. Perhaps the term "balling the jack" derived from this game.

SONGS, DANCES, RHYTHMS

Much of the orchestral music that is enjoyed the world over originated in this area of the world. Great symphonies, melodic waltzes, and sweet lullabies are still played by master musicians. An appreciation of this music was brought to the United States by the founding fathers, and to this day the concert halls in the United States and many other lands are filled with people who enjoy the experience of listening to the classical music that originated in Europe.

It seems appropriate to use this section for the study of the orchestra, its instruments, and for listening enjoyment. The following material can assist, but it is not intended as a complete list.

AN INTRODUCTION TO THE ORCHESTRA THROUGH CHILDREN'S BOOKS AND LISTENING

A very good resource book for young children is *Meet the Orchestra* by Ann Hayes and illustrated by Karmen Thompson (San Diego: Harcourt Brace Jovanovich, 1991). The rabbit plays the flute, the koala bear is the cellist, the alligator plays the timpani or kettledrums, and so on. The instruments are clearly shown and the sounds are described. A multicultural array of animals from all over the world make up this delightful orchestra.

A fine listening resource is the recording of *Peter and the Wolf* by Prokofiev, which should be available at the public library. It is a good introduction to the sounds of various instruments.

A good visual resource in terms of describing the instruments as well as showing them is *What Instrument Is This?* by Rosemarie Hausherr (New

York: Scholastic, 1992). This includes questions for each instrument pictured, such as "What instrument looks like a shiny boa constrictor with a wide-open mouth?" (sousaphone) "What instrument is long and black and has keys, rings and rods?" (clarinet).

AN INTRODUCTION TO INSTRUMENTS OF THE ORCHESTRA

Instruments are generally classified in seven categories. These are:

- Stringed Instruments (examples: violin, viola)
- Woodwind Instruments (examples: flute, clarinet, saxophone)
- Brass-Wind Instruments (examples: trumpet, trombone)
- Percussion Instruments (examples: drums, cymbals, xylophone)
- Harp
- Piano
- Modern Acoustical Instruments (example: computer-as-instrument)

Arrange to have the music teacher visit your classroom with an assortment of instruments that can be shown and explained to the students. Perhaps the teacher can play an instrument, or have music samples (recordings) of several of the instruments. Recordings are available from the public library.

AN INTRODUCTION TO COMPOSERS

We have a rich heritage of music from composers such as Beethoven, Brahms, Strauss, Mozart, and so on. Play this music during quiet times so that students can listen to the melody, bass, and rhythm, and try to identify some of the instruments of the orchestra.

PAINTING TO CLASSICAL MUSIC

Students can fingerpaint to music. Encourage them to make broad sweeping motions and short pointy repeat lines in time to the rhythm. Also, children can use battery-operated headsets and enjoy symphonic music while painting at the easel.

LET'S HEAR IT FOR THE TUBA

The tuba provides the very low sounds heard in band or orchestral music (bass). The tuba was invented by Adolphe Sax in the mid-19th century. He also invented the saxophone. The tuba is made up of a curved tube, hence the name "tuba." It produces a deep, deep tone. Encourage students to listen for the sounds of the tuba on recordings made available in the class-room. Often the distinct sound of the tuba can be heard on marching band recordings. Perhaps students can imitate the tuba with their own low tones, and determine the storybook characters that might have this low, low sound.

CHIMES RING OUT

Metal tubes of 1″ to 2-1/2″ diameter and from four to six feet long are called "chimes." They resemble the church bells that ring throughout Europe. The German "glockenspiel" sounds like bells. Children can listen for bells in their environment and list them. Some starters are: small bells that jingle, doorbells, clock bells and clock chimes, and so on. An assortment of bells can be brought into the classroom for examination. **Children can investigate the topic of bells by asking these questions:** In what ways do we use bells and chimes in our home environment, school environment, in shopping malls, in big cities? Do people wear bells? Do animals wear bells? Some dancers in various cultures wear bells around their ankles to jingle as they dance. Perhaps the students can compose a rhythm using bells, much like a bell choir.

THE ROYAL TRUMPET

For hundreds of years trumpets were used in the service of royalty. Trumpeters announced the entrance of the royals when they entered a huge banquet hall, or when they rode in their closed carriage through the town. Students can imitate the sound of the trumpet as they blow through their closed fist. This can be used in their creative play, or to trumpet the way to a section of the classroom for an important announcement.

A SYSTEM OF KEYS AND LEVERS

The flute used today was developed by Theobald Boehm, a German. It was originally made of wood. The flute resembles bird notes, and is the soprano of the orchestra. The flute is used in many South American countries. A flute combo of three or four flute players often performs at gatherings in

Ecuador and Peru. The piccolo is related to the flute, and is called "little brother." It has a shrill sound, and is referred to as the "imp" of the orchestra. When discussing imps, students can be asked to think about storybook characters or animals that could be represented by this imp instrument.

BOWS AND STRINGS

The violin, viola, violoncello, and double bass are all stringed instruments. During the 16th century, the violin center of the world was in Cremona, Italy. Stradivarius was the greatest violin craftsman of his time, and many of these valuable instruments are still in use. Students can identify the sound of stringed instruments by listening to recordings. Simple string instruments can be made with a block of wood as a base. Pound from three to five nails into each end, and string wire from the nail on one end to the nail on the opposite end. Students can learn to "strum" and "pluck" the strings. Perhaps they can invent a bow for their string instruments.

FOOD

There are many countries in Europe, each with its own flair for cooking. The following recipes are meant as a sampling from this region of the world, rather than a complete reference.

West Germany claims to have the greatest variety of breads in the world—more than 200 from which to choose! One variety is the Brezel, or large pretzel, with which westerners are familiar. Also, the Schwarzwalderkirschtorte, or Black Forest cherry cake, is internationally acclaimed.

In England, teatime is a daily custom at 4 p.m. That is when, in many households, the fine china is brought out and the wonderful cakes, small sandwiches, and mints are served. (At this same time of day, the Costa

Ricans in Central America are enjoying their Cafe Sita, a time when the table is set with china cups and dishes, and rich, brown Costa Rican coffee is brewed and served with fine desserts.)

France is known for its fine cuisine, Italy is renowned for its pasta, and other countries have their specialties as well. It is a gourmet's delight to have such a wide variety of dishes from this area of the world.

SUGGESTED RECIPES FOR THE CLASSROOM

Irish Buttermilk Oat Bread

1-1/2 cups oatmeal
1-1/2 cups buttermilk
1-3/4 cups flour
1-1/2 tablespoons sugar
1-1/2 teaspoons baking soda
1 teaspoon salt

Mix oatmeal and buttermilk, and let stand overnight in refrigerator. Sift the dry ingredients (flour, sugar, baking soda, salt), and stir into the oatmeal mixture. Knead the mixture into a soft ball of dough. Roll out onto floured surface into a round loaf, 1-1/2" x 6". Make a rounded shape by cupping it with your hands. Score the bread into quarters with a floured knife but do not separate the sections. Place on lightly floured cookie sheet and bake at 350 degrees for 50 minutes or until well browned.

Spaghetti al Aglio e Olio

This is Italian spaghetti with oil and garlic, rather than a red tomato sauce. It is a rich source of carbohydrates for long-term energy. Try the recipe for a change of pace.

spaghetti
3 garlic cloves
olive oil
freshly chopped parsley
salt and pepper
water

Bring large pot of water to a boil; then add spaghetti. Boil for 10 minutes until firm ("al dente"). Crush garlic cloves and brown in oil in electric frypan. Add drained spaghetti to garlic and oil and stir. Serve with sprinkled parsley.

Himmel und Erde

This is a German side dish that means "heaven and earth." The himmel is grown above ground and the erde is grown underground. In other words, it is a dish of mashed potatoes and bits of apple. Ummmmmm-good!

Kartoffelpuffer (Potato Pancakes)

Germans have many ways to fix leftover potatoes. Bratkartoffeln is fried leftover potatoes and onion, and Bauernfruhstuck is a hot dish made from leftover potatoes fried with bacon and eggs. Here is a recipe for potato pancakes.

4 pounds potatoes
4 eggs
2 onions
2 teaspoons salt
vegetable oil
lemon juice
cold water

Peel potatoes and place them in a bowl of cold water into which a bit of lemon juice has been added. This keeps them from turning brown. Grate the potatoes and chop the onions. Blot any excess water from the potatoes and onions, then add eggs and salt. Mix all the ingredients. Heat oil in electric frypan. Carefully drop spoonfuls of the mixture into the pan when oil is hot. (**CAUTION:** This should be done only by an adult.) Press the pancakes with a metal spatula and fry until a golden crisp on both sides. Remove and serve warm. (Can be reheated in a microwave.)

French Toast

1 egg
1/3 cup milk
1 tablespoon sugar
6 slices white bread (cut in half diagonally)
1/2 stick butter or margarine
1/2 teaspoon vanilla
jam or maple syrup
confectioners' sugar

Break the egg into a bowl, and add milk, sugar, and vanilla. Beat until blended. Put electric frypan on medium heat, and melt 2 tablespoons butter. Dip bread into egg mixture (use tongs) and place in frypan. Fry until golden brown, then turn over and fry other side. Add more butter as needed. Serve with jam or syrup, and a sprinkling of confectioners' sugar on top.

Tomatensoep Met Balletjes (Tomato Soup with Meatballs)

5 onions
5 celery stalks
5 carrots
6 cups tomatoes
beef bone
30 cups water
salt
1/2 pound ground beef
1/4 cup bread crumbs
2 eggs

Chop onions, and slice celery and carrots. Add to water and beef bone in large pot and bring to a boil. Simmer until vegetables are cooked (1-1/2 hours). Remove bone, and strain soup. Put soup and vegetables back into pot and add more water and salt to taste. Bring to a boil, then simmer. To make meatballs, mix ground beef, bread crumbs, and eggs together. Mold into small meatballs (makes about 30). Add meatballs to simmering soup, and cook until meatballs are done (20 minutes). Serves 25.

Svaskon Cram (Swedish Prune Pudding)

In Sweden, the smorgasbord is a table that has a variety of good foods— from appetizers to desserts. Try this dessert that serves 8.

1 pound prunes
5 cups water
6 tablespoons sugar
5 teaspoons lemon juice
1 teaspoon cinnamon
2 tablespoons flour

Cook prunes in water until tender (30 minutes). Drain and save the water. Remove prunes, cool, and remove pits. Put prunes and one cup of the prune water (add water if necessary) back into pan. Add sugar, cinnamon, lemon juice, and flour. Stirring constantly, cook until thick. Remove from heat, cool, chill. (Can be served with cream topping.)

Ice Cream Sandwiches

1 pint vanilla ice cream
24 large chocolate cookies

Soften ice cream for easy spreading. Lay out 12 cookies. Spoon ice cream onto 12 cookies and spread evenly. Place remaining 12 cookies on top of the first 12. Place sandwiches in freezer to firm the ice cream.

Murbe Keks (German Soft Cookies)

1/4 pound butter (1 stick) at room
  temperature
1/2 cup sugar
1-1/2 cups flour
1 teaspoon baking powder
1 teaspoon vanilla
1 egg

Preheat oven to 350 degrees. Grease and flour a cookie sheet. Cream the butter. Then add sugar and other ingredients to make a smooth dough. Set aside. Place flour on a cutting board or counter. Flour a rolling pin and your hands. Roll out the dough to 1/4-inch thickness. Cut out shapes with cookie cutter. Sprinkle with sugar and bake for approximately 10 to 12 minutes.

Pain au Chocolate (A Dessert Snack from France)

French roll
1/2 chocolate candy bar

Slice the roll in half (horizontally). Place chocolate in the middle and broil in toaster oven until chocolate has melted.

Lorenzo's Foot-Long Italian Submarine Sandwich

loaf of fresh Italian bread, sliced
  lengthwise
Genoa or hard salami, sliced
baked ham, sliced
provolone cheese*, sliced
tomatoes, sliced
lettuce, shredded
onion, optional
bottled Italian salad dressing

After slicing the bread, make layers of salami and ham on the bottom half. Add a layer of sliced cheese and sliced tomatoes. Sprinkle shredded lettuce over the top. Sprinkle with salad dressing. Cover with wax paper and place in microwave oven for one minute *or* eat cold. Slice diagonally into several small sandwiches. **Note:** Smaller individual sandwiches can be made on Italian submarine sandwich rolls or hot dog rolls.

A word about cheese: France and Italy have the greatest variety of cheeses in the world. Some available Italian cheeses are *parmesan* (good for grating over pasta or soup), *provolone* (a creamy white cheese), *ricotta* (the cottage cheese of Italy), *mozzarella* (usually eaten raw), and *gorgonzola* (similar to the French roquefort). In both France and Italy, people make a meal of fresh bread, cheeses, and a beverage.

Pease Porridge Soup

"Pease porridge hot, pease porridge cold, pease porridge in the pot, nine days old."

small onion
1 tablespoon butter
1 celery stalk, chopped
1-3/4 cups split peas
6-1/2 cups cold water
1 ham bone
salt and pepper

Saute chopped onion in butter. In a large pot, add together the remaining ingredients. Bring to a boil, then simmer until peas are well done (about one hour). Press through a sieve. Add ham from bone to the mixture. Serve warm.

Resources

Birch, Beverly. *Let's Look Up Food from Many Lands* (Morristown, NJ: Silver Burdett, 1984).

Hill, Barbara. *Cooking the English Way* (Minneapolis: Lerner, 1982).

Parnell, Helga. *Cooking the German Way* (Minneapolis: Lerner, 1988).

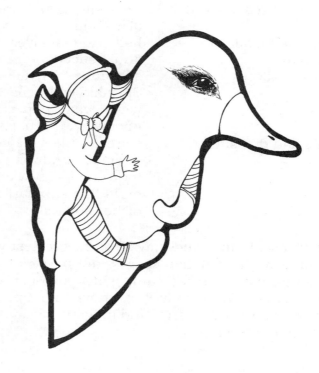

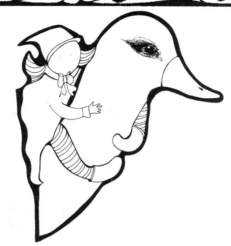

REPRODUCIBLE ACTIVITY PAGES

Flying High with Mother Goose (two pages) (*nursery rhymes*)

The "Humpty Dumpty Had a Great Fall" Puzzle (*reassembling a puzzle*)

The Role of the Egg in Folk Tales (*research; visual design*)

Cloudy with a Chance of Pierogi (*children's book in different cultures*)

The Tale of Two Cinderellas (*before/after from different versions*)

A Folk Tale Fit for a King (*book selection; critical thinking*)

Oh, No! Not Another Prince in Search of a Bride! (*creative writing*)

Mother Goosebumps Award (*scary characterization*)

Spring Capping in Sweden (*celebration*)

The Very Busy Santa Gameboard (*identification; matching*)

Aristotle Alligator Appreciates a Symphony (*research*)

Matching Artists and Styles (*identifying like styles*)

Sounds Like a Beastly Good Soup, Old Chap! (*food recipe*)

Even a Unicorn Can't Charm This Ogre! (*geography: country and continent*)

The Case of the Missing Macaw (*missing person study sheet*)

Get Out of Town (*research/study sheet*)

Do an Author Study—Europe (*The Brothers Grimm; retold tales*)

FLYING HIGH WITH MOTHER GOOSE

Carefully color and cut out these two pages and paste them together. On the back end of the goose, write the names of the rhymes you can say by heart! (You can decorate the goose, too).

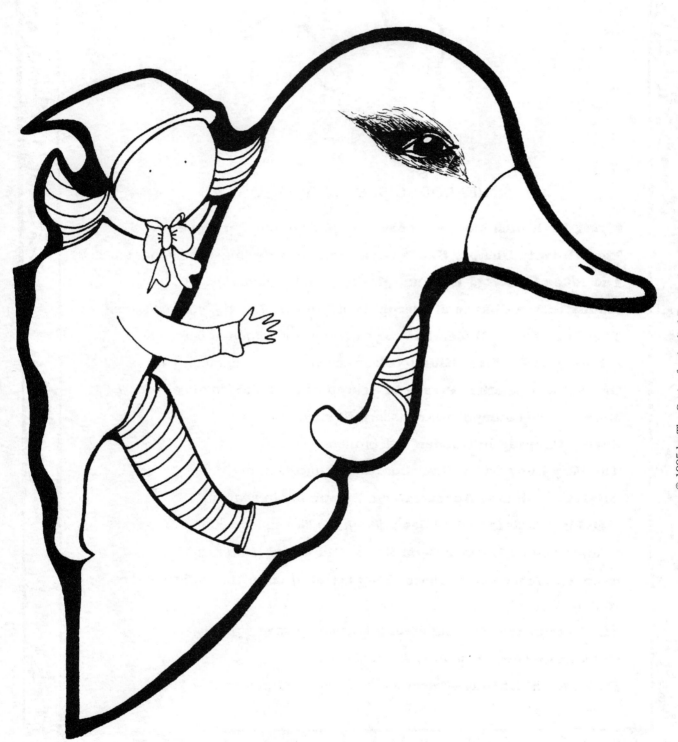

How many nursery rhymes can you recite?

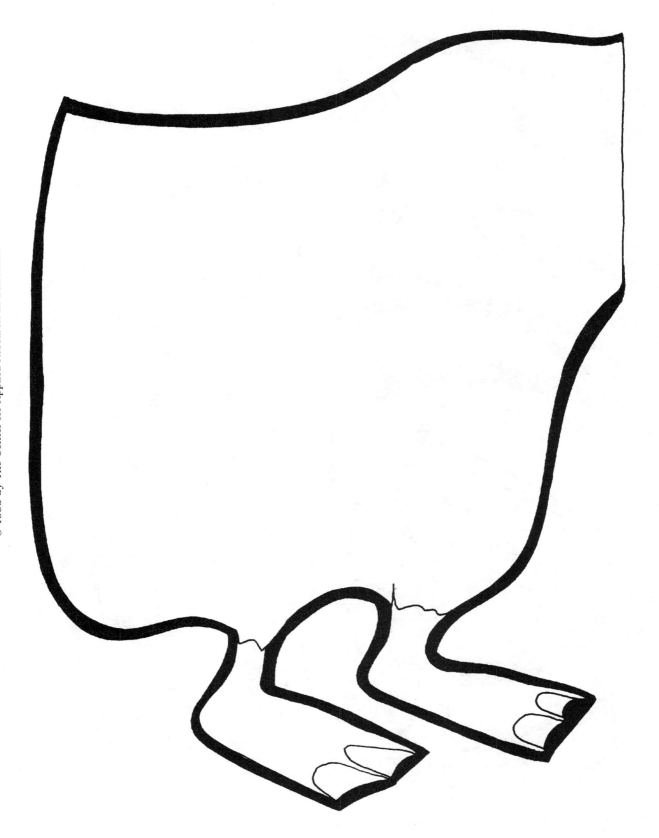

THE "HUMPTY DUMPTY HAD A GREAT FALL" PUZZLE

By now you know that Humpty Dumpty fell off a wall. These are all of the pieces. Can you put him back together?

THE ROLE OF THE EGG IN FOLK TALES

Eggs appear in all cultures. Some people decorate eggs or hang them on trees. Some save egg shells for good luck.

Search for a folk tale in which an egg plays an important part in the story. Share the story with your classmates. Use bright colors to make this become the most beautiful egg in the world!

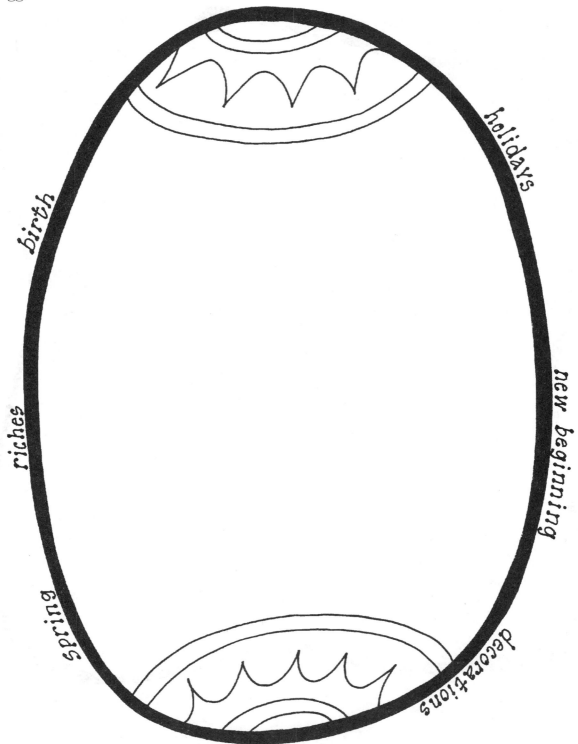

Name _____ Date _____

CLOUDY WITH A CHANCE OF PIEROGI

The book *Cloudy With a Chance of Meatballs* by Ron and Judi Barrett is a humorous story about food and weather. Let's read the story. Then, think about how the food choices would change in different countries.

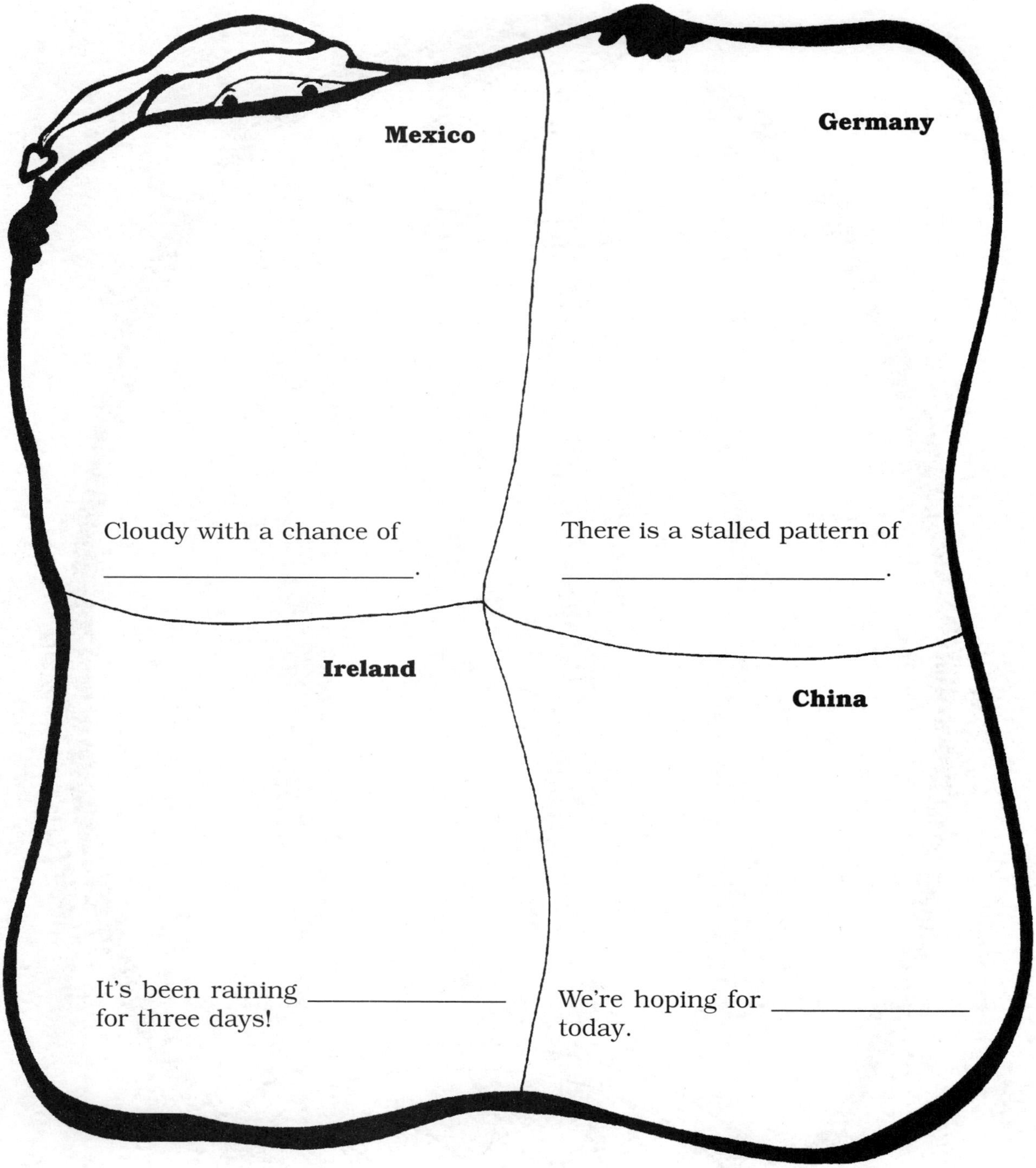

Mexico

Germany

Cloudy with a chance of
_____.

There is a stalled pattern of
_____.

Ireland

China

It's been raining _____
for three days!

We're hoping for _____
today.

Name _____   Date _____

THE TALE OF TWO CINDERELLAS

The Cinderella folk tale is known all over the world. These two Cinderellas are from two different versions of the same story. One Cinderella is at the beginning of her tale. The other Cinderella can tell her complete tale. Use your crayons to show their rags and riches.

Locate, read, learn, and tell at least two Cinderella tales (Europe, Korea, Egypt, Native America, China).

A FOLK TALE FIT FOR A KING

The King is hunting for folk tales from all over the world. Find one and list the title, country, and why you think it should be on his list.

Who is the author?

Who illustrated this tale?

Title

Country

It's fit for a king because...

OH, NO! NOT ANOTHER PRINCE IN SEARCH OF A BRIDE!

Oh, yes! But this one is different. This prince cannot walk a straight line. He can only walk around in circles. Your story must follow his circular path. How can you possibly end your tale with "and they lived happily ever after"? Now his problem is *your* problem. H-E-L-P!

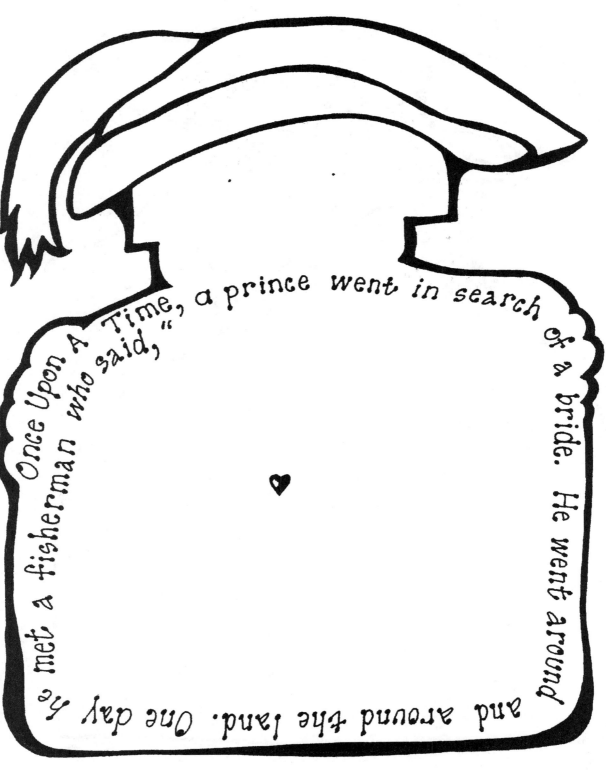

Once Upon A Time, a prince went in search of a bride. He went around and around the land. One day he met a fisherman who said, "

Name _____ Date _____

MOTHER GOOSEBUMPS AWARD

This book made the hair stand up on the back of my neck. It was a frightfully good book!

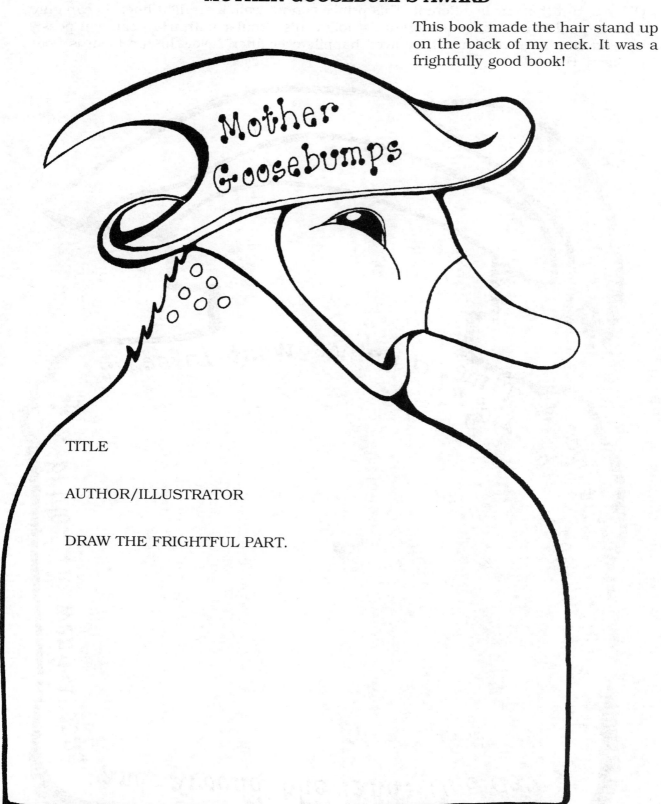

Mother Goosebumps

TITLE

AUTHOR/ILLUSTRATOR

DRAW THE FRIGHTFUL PART.

SPRING CAPPING IN SWEDEN

On April 30 in Uppsala, thousands of students assemble at the university library. At a given signal, all graduates wave their caps and wear them. They keep them all their life.

Hats and caps are very important in history. You can often tell a person's occupation just by a hat! Show some examples below.

chef

police officer

fire fighter

THE VERY BUSY SANTA GAMEBOARD

Use red and green to color TWO copies of the busy Santa page. Laminate. One page can be the gameboard; the other page can be cut apart. Shuffle the packet of cards and turn them upside down. One by one, turn them over and match them with the same busy Santa on the gameboard. This can be played with two or three students.

ARISTOTLE ALLIGATOR APPRECIATES A SYMPHONY

This alligator is studying the make-up of a symphony orchestra. He already knows there are four major sections. These are listed below. Now he needs to know what specific instruments are in each section. Can you help him with his studies?

REWARD: If you can help Aristotle, he suggests that you listen to a symphony. Maybe you can learn to identify some instruments. He gets cassettes from the library. You can, too!

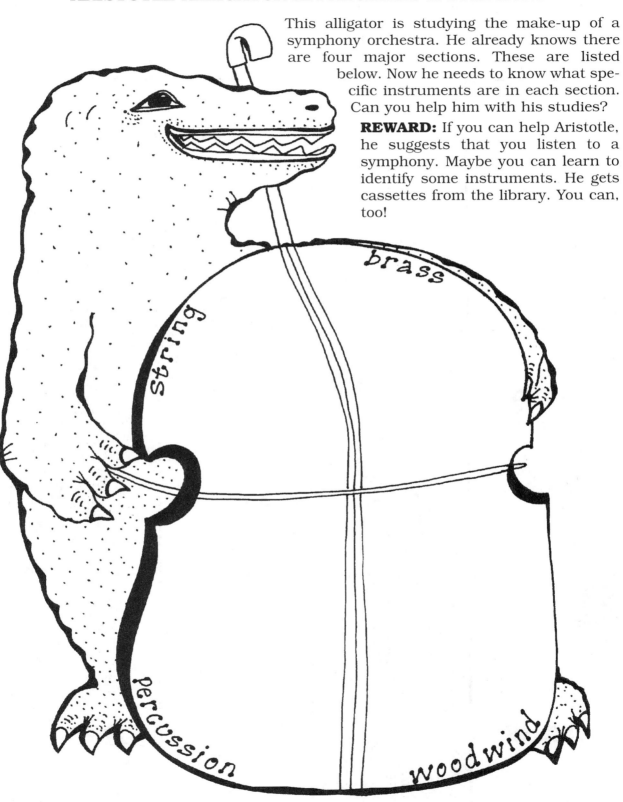

MATCHING ARTISTS AND STYLES

On the cards below, six artists are represented. Carefully color each picture. Then, cut the cards on the line. Turn them over on a grid, and play the "concentration" game. Learn more each artist: A. Georges Seurat; B. Paul Cézanne; C. Amedeo Modigliani; D. Piet Mondrian; E. Vincent van Gogh; F. Henri de Toulouse-Lautrec. Find art books at the library that show paintings by these artists. Try painting in new ways.

PEASE PORRIDGE SOUP

"Pease porridge hot, pease porridge cold, pease porridge in the pot nine days old."

Remember this nursery rhyme? Now you can make some pease porridge soup.

Ingredients:

small onion
1 tablespoon butter
1 celery stalk, chopped
1-3/4 cup split peas
6-1/2 cups cold water
salt and pepper

Procedure:

1. Saute chopped onion in butter in an electric frypan.
2. In a large pot, add together the remaining ingredients.
3. Bring to a boil, then simmer until peas are well done (about one hour).
4. Press through a sieve. Add ham from bone to the mixture.
5. Serve warm!

Survey classmates for their favorite soup. Graph the information.

EVEN A UNICORN CAN'T CHARM THIS OGRE!

Zitdorf the Ogre didn't know the difference between a country and a continent, so other ogres laughed at him. Zitdorf has grabbed the first unicorn in sight and will eat it IF you can't feed him the information he needs. Write it below.

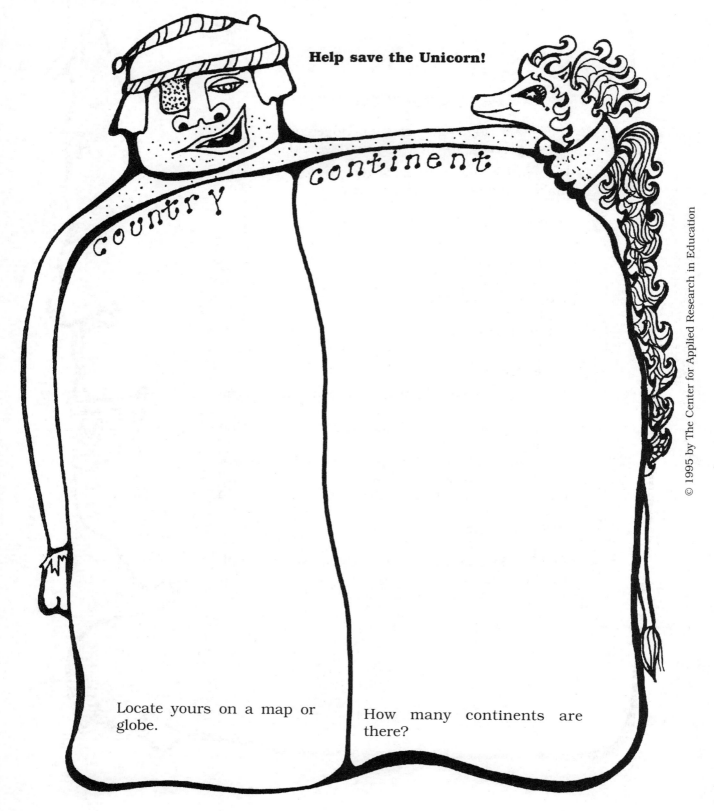

Help save the Unicorn!

country

continent

Locate yours on a map or globe.

How many continents are there?

THE CASE OF THE MISSING MACAW

This rowdy, sputtering, bright red and blue macaw from Peru misses the mud of the Tambopata River. The macaws eat a bit of the clay daily. It's a part of the giant parrot's diet.

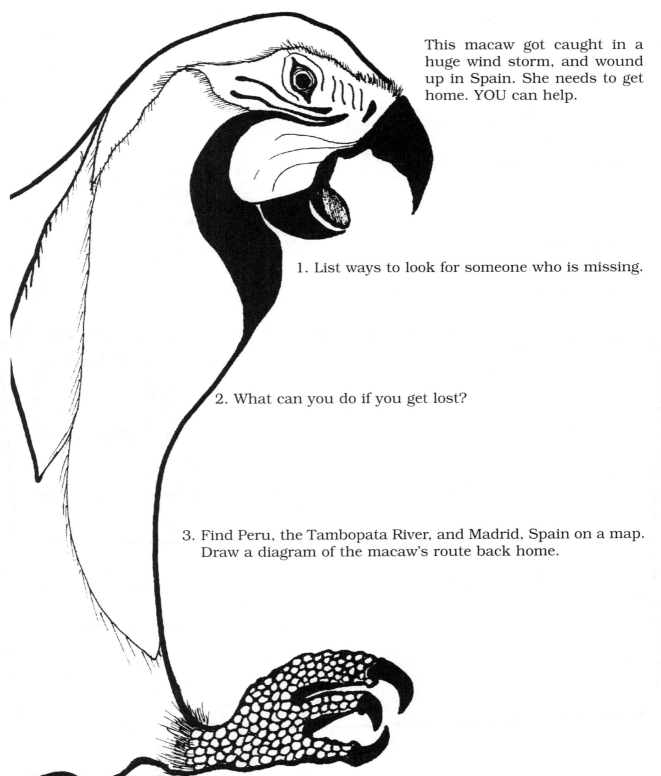

This macaw got caught in a huge wind storm, and wound up in Spain. She needs to get home. YOU can help.

1. List ways to look for someone who is missing.

2. What can you do if you get lost?

3. Find Peru, the Tambopata River, and Madrid, Spain on a map. Draw a diagram of the macaw's route back home.

Name _____ Date _____

GET OUT OF TOWN

COUNTRY OF DESTINATION _____

LOCATION _____

CLIMATE _____

MAJOR PRODUCTS _____

FAMOUS PLACES TO VISIT _____

WHAT I WANT TO LEARN MORE ABOUT _____

POSTCARD TO SEND BACK HOME:

Dear _____,

Name _____   Date _____

DO AN AUTHOR STUDY—EUROPE

Treat yourself to a variety of tales recorded by the Brothers Grimm. These tales have been illustrated by various artists. Compare their styles. Note that the illustrator of one version may choose to illustrate a different part of the story than that of another illustrator.

Some of the tales have been retold to make them appear hilarious, such as *The True Story of the Three Little Pigs* and *The Stinky Cheese Man and Other Fairly Stupid Tales* by Jon Scieszka and Lane Smith. Read both the traditional tales and updated ones, and make comparisons.

Brothers Grimm Version	**Retold Version**

LATIN AMERICA

RECOMMENDED CHILDREN'S BOOKS

The literature of Latin American cultures is as rich and diverse as the countries that are linked together under the "Latin American" title. The tales from Mexico differ from those within the various countries of Central America, just as those differ from tales of the various countries within South America, and the tales from Spain. The following is a representative sampling of available books for young children.

Aardema, Verna. *Pedro and the Padre*. Pictures by Friso Henstra. New York: Dial Books, 1991. In this tale, Pedro (PAY-dro), a boy, is a picaro (PEE-car-o), a mischievous person, who will not work, so his father sends him out into the world. He meets the padre (PA-dray), or priest, who gives the boy work ringing the church bell and hoeing in the garden. But soon Pedro's laziness is found out, and he sets out to find proof for his lies, and in the end finds the truth. A good tale.

_____, translator. *The Riddle of the Drum, A Tale from Tizapan, Mexico*. Illustrated by Tony Chen. New York: Four Winds Press, 1979. The king decides that the one who marries his beautiful daughter, Fruela, will have to solve the riddle of the drum. Throughout the land, the guards sing: "Tum-te-dum! The head of the drum-te-dum! Guess what it's from-te-dum! And marry the Princess Fruela!" After much action, a Prince does solve the riddle, but the King puts still more obstacles in the way.

Argueta, Manlio. *Magic Dogs of the Volcanoes, Los Perros Magicos de los Volcanes*. Illustrado por Elly Simmons. Translated by Stacey Ross. San Francisco: Children's Book Press, 1990. The people who live on the volcano slopes of Tecapa and Chaparrastique in El Salvador claim that the cadejos (cah-DAY-hose), who look like wolves, are really magic dogs. Not all people like the cadejos, however, and the soldiers set out to destroy them. The text is in both English and Spanish, and the illustrations are bold and colorful in this magical tale.

Barlow, Genevieve. *Latin American Tales, From the Pampas to the Pyramids of Mexico*. New York: Rand McNally & Company, 1966. A collection of folk tales that include "The White Spider's Gift," "The Great

White Condor," "The Magic Eagle," and "How the Porcupine Outwitted the Fox." These tales are from Paraguay, Bolivia, Peru, Ecuador, Colombia, and other points south. They entertain and teach valuable lessons.

Bierhorst, John, ed. *The Hungry Woman, Myths and Legends of the Aztecs.* **Illustrations by Aztec artists of the Sixteenth Century. New York: William Morrow and Company, 1984.** A collection of epic tales about Mexico. The book is divided into categories that include Creation Myths, The Founding of Mexico, and In the Days of Montezuma. Fast moving, and spellbinding narratives. Also look for *The Monkey's Haircut, and Other Stories Told by the Maya* by the same editor.

Blanco, Alberto. *The Desert Mermaid or La Sirenda del Desierto.* **Pictures (illustrado) by Patricia Revah. San Francisco: Children's Book Press, 1992.** This original story in the style of a folk tale takes place in Mexico's Sonora Desert, which extends into Arizona. The text is in both English and Spanish, so the bilingual reader is at home with this and the beginning reader has a point of comparison. The story is about mermaids who have disappeared because their songs were forgotten, and of the long journey by one mermaid to find once again the songs that have the rhythm of the waves. The illustrations are all done in tapestry style and are quite striking.

deGerez, Toni (text adaptation); Stark, William (illustration). *My Song Is a Piece of Jade, Poems of Ancient Mexico in English and Spanish.* **Boston: Little, Brown and Company, 1984.** The text is in Spanish and English. The poetry is ancient and considered sacred by the Toltec people of Mexico. For example, we learn that "the true storyteller uses words of joy, flowers are on his lips, his language is noble." The bright illustrations by an artist who has studied pre-Colombian arts enhance the lyrical language and add to the enjoyment of the book.

Ehlert, Lois. *Moon Rope, Un Lazo a la Luna.* **New York: Harcourt Brace Jovanovich, 1992.** This adaptation of a Peruvian folk tale is written in both English and Spanish. Fox begins the adventure by asking Mole the question, "If you could have anything in the world, what would it be?" The striking pre-Colombian illustrations were inspired by ancient Peruvian designs and are a study in themselves. The author/illustrator uses gold and silver because these metals were always used to make works of beauty.

Griego, Margot C., Bucks, Betsy L., Gilbert, Sharon S., and Kimball, Laurel H., selectors and translators. Illustrated by Barbara Cooney. *Tortillitas Para Mama, and Other Nursery Rhymes in Spanish/English.* **New York: Holt, Rinehart and Winston, 1981.** This is a collection of lullabies, poems, and fingerplays or rhymes with body motions, printed in Spanish and English. The verses, along with the motions, allow the students to interact with the text. A major part of the charm of this book are the authentic Hispanic-style illustrations done in warm earth tones. The reader gains much information about the people and the culture from the illustrations.

Haviland, Virginia. *Favorite Fairy Tales Told in Spain*, **retold. Illustrated by Barbara Cooney. Boston: Little, Brown and Company, 1963.** Six favorite tales, including "The Flea," which is similar to *The Riddle of the Drum* by Verna Aardema, where a suitable mate for the princess has to guess the type of skin stretched across the drum. The fact that the King has a giant flea for a pet gives the reader a hint. Also included are "Four Brothers Who Were Both Wise and Foolish." Cleverness is an asset, and the good are rewarded in the end.

Lattimore, Deborah Nourse. *Why There Is No Arguing in Heaven, A Mayan Myth.* **New York: Harper & Row, 1989.** Hunab Ku, the first creator God of the Mayas, hears the Moon Goddess and Lizard House arguing about who is the best. Hunab Ku proclaims that a great god is not one who argues but one who creates. A tale told in Guatemala and Mexico.

___. *The Flame of Peace, A Tale of the Aztecs.* **New York: Harper & Row, 1987.** A boy named Two Flint sees his father leave to try to persuade an invading army to retreat. Two Flint does his part by searching for Lord Morning Star, the only one who can bring peace to the people. Children enjoy the stylistic endpapers, as well as the story.

Mora, Pat. *A Birthday Basket for Tia.* **Illustrated by Cecily Lang. New York: Macmillan, 1992.** Today is the ninetieth birthday of Cecilia's great aunt, her Tia. What special gift can she give to her? With the help of her cat, Chica, the young girl fills a birthday basket with precious memories.

Rodari, Florian. *A Weekend with Picasso.* **New York: Rizzoli International Publications, Inc. 1991.** This book offers the young reader an opportunity to visit with Pablo Picasso, to view his works, to see his studio, to observe him at work, and to learn how he thinks. It is a wonderful opportunity to see the art along with the explanations, and this book could inspire some children to explore with original ideas in design.

Volkmer, Jane Ann. *Song of the Chirimia, A Guatemalan Folk Tale*, **retold. Spanish translation by Lori Ann Ashatschneider. Minneapolis: Carolrhoda Books, Inc., 1990.** This colorful book has both English and Spanish text so that the reader can have a cross-cultural experience. This is the story of the beautiful Princess Moonlight who becomes sad. Suitors from the land are brought forth to the kingdom to see if anyone can make her smile. Red Feather, with his melodious singing voice, has a chance to learn to sing like the birds. But can he?

FOLK TALES

The folklore of Spain is part of the folklore of Europe because of the heavy migration of Indo-Europeans to this area. Many of the ancient harvest festival myths and legends have survived to this day, and some have been incorporated into religious ceremonies. Folk tales are as abundant in Spain as in any other part of Europe. In Central and South America, the tales reflect the Spanish culture, along with the major influence of Native American customs and traditions. In the case of animal and witch tales, the influence of both the Native American and African cultures are present.

FOLKLORE IN MANY FORMS

The folklore of the Latin American cultures is reflected in stories (cuentos), legends (leyendas), sayings (dichos), and are more often than not accompanied by songs and dances. School children dress in native costumes and reenact these tales at holiday times and for special events. Often props are used. The Ballet Folklorico of Mexico is a traveling troupe of singers and dancers who perform the familiar tales for audiences. In many of the South American countries, audiences hiss when the villain makes an entrance on stage. Often the villain will sing and dance up the aisles of the theater and pretend to scare members of the audience. This is all done in good fun.

The two characters of La Bruja and La Curandera appear continually in many legends. La Bruja is the character of the Witch, and La Curandera is the character of the Healer. As in all good stories, there is a problem or conflict that must be resolved to the satisfaction of the reader or audience.

A WELL-KNOWN READ-ALOUD TALE

"The Very Elegant Rooster" comes under the heading of the cumulative tale, where stanzas or phrases are repeated. Cumulative tales can be found in all cultures (such as *London Bridge* and *Millions of Cats* by Wanda Gag, which is often referred to as the first picture book for children in the United States).

Set up the conditions for listening. Have students:

- touch their ears for listening
- touch their mouth for silence
- touch their eyes, which are focused on the reader or storyteller
- fold their arms

Now we can begin.

"The Very Elegant Rooster"

One fine day, a rooster woke up early and washed himself and preened himself until he was not only very, very, very clean, but very, very, very elegant. Off he went to the wedding of Tio Perico. Along the way, he noticed a grain of corn. Now, you know that a rooster cannot resist a grain of corn. But, the grain was right in the middle of a big garbage pile. Ugh! Well, the rooster wanted the grain, but because he was very, very, clean and looked very, very, elegant, he did not want to get dirty.

> "Oh, I want to eat that grain of corn," said Rooster,
>   "but I won't, I won't, I won't!"

> "Oh, I want to eat that grain of corn," said Rooster,
>
>   "but I won't, I won't!"

> "Oh, I want to eat that grain of corn," said Rooster,
>   "but I won't."

Alas, he couldn't help himself and said,
"Oh, I want to eat that grain of corn!" and he did.

Rooster got some garbage on his beak. Now he did not look very, very, elegant, especially when he was on his way to the wedding of Tio Perico. He looked around wondering what to do and he saw a white flower at the side of the road.

"White flower, please clean my beak, or I won't be able to go to the wedding of Tio Perico," exclaimed Rooster.

"No quiero. No quiero," said White Flower. "I don't want to."

Rooster looked around and saw a gray sheep.

"Gray Sheep, eat this White Flower. White Flower won't clean my beak, and I won't be able to go to the wedding of Tio Perico."

"No quiero. No quiero," said Gray Sheep. "I don't want to."

Rooster looked around and saw a brown dog.

"Brown Dog, bite Gray Sheep. Gray Sheep won't eat White Flower, White Flower won't clean my beak, and I won't be able to go to the wedding of Tio Perico."

"No quiero. No quiero," said Brown Dog. "I don't want to."

Rooster looked round and saw a green stick.

"Green Stick, beat Brown Dog. Brown Dog won't bite Gray Sheep, Gray Sheep won't eat White Flower, and White Flower won't clean my beak, and I won't be able to go to the wedding of Tio Perico."

"No quiero. No quiero," said Green Stick. "I don't want to."

Rooster looked around and saw a red fire.

"Red Fire, burn Green Stick. Green Stick won't beat Brown Dog, Brown Dog won't bite Gray Sheep, Gray Sheep won't eat White Flower, and White Flower won't clean my beak, and I won't be able to go to the wedding of Tio Perico."

"No quiero. No quiero," said Red Fire. "I don't want to."

Rooster looked around and saw some blue water.

"Blue Water, put out Red Fire. Red Fire won't burn Green Stick, Green Stick won't beat Brown Dog, Brown Dog won't bite Gray Sheep, Gray Sheep won't eat White Flower, and White Flower won't clean my beak, and I won't be able to go to the wedding of Tio Perico."

"No quiero. No quiero," said Blue Water. "I don't want to."

Rooster looked up and saw the orange sun.

"Orange Sun, dry up Blue Water. Blue Water won't put out Red Fire, Red Fire won't burn Green Stick, Green Stick won't beat Brown Dog, Brown Dog won't bite Gray Sheep, Gray Sheep won't eat White Flower, White Flower won't clean my beak, and I won't be able to go to the wedding of Tio Perico."

THERE WAS A LONG SILENCE.

Then, Red Sun said, "I will do what you ask IF you promise to crow three times every morning and wake me up. Let me hear you crow."

"Quiquiriqui" (kee-kiri-kee), crowed Rooster. "I promose."

And so...Orange Sun began to dry up Blue Water.

Blue Water began to put out Red Fire.

Red Fire began to burn Green Stick.

Green Stick began to beat Brown Dog.

Brown Dog began to bite Gray Sheep.

Gray Sheep began to eat White Flower.

White Flower cleaned Rooster's beak.

Once again, Rooster looked very, very, very clean and very, very, very elegant. Off he went to the wedding of Tio Perico. He had a wonderful time. Even though he didn't get home until very late that night, and got very little sleep, he was true to his promise to Orange Sun.

From that time to this, every morning, Rooster crows three times,

"Quiquiriqui, Quiquiriqui, Quiquiriqui" (Kee-kiri-kee).

And do you know what happens? Orange Sun wakes up and starts the day!

THE END

After students are familiar with the tale, change the color names to Spanish so students can learn them. The words are listed below:

white	(blanco)	red	(rojo)
gray	(gris)	blue	(azul)
brown	(pardo)	orange	(anaranjado)
green	(verde)		

Next, change the animal names from English to Spanish, so students can learn them. The words are listed below:

white flower	(flor blanco)	red fire	(fuego rojo)
gray sheep	(oveja gris)	blue water	(agua azul)
brown dog	(perro pardo)	orange sun	(sol anaranjado)
green stick	(palo verde)	rooster	(gallo)

POPULAR SUPERSTITIONS

All cultures have their superstitions, and Spain has an abundance of them. Some of them include:

- To make sure you will not have a toothache, you should cut your fingernails on a Friday.
- If you eat grapes on New Year's Day, you will have money the whole year.
- White marks on the fingernails are indicative of telling lies.
- When cats play, it's going to rain.
- A black cat in the house is bad luck.

THE TAR MAN STORY

Spain takes a leading role in the development of this particular story, which is of Indian origin. There are at least nine versions in Spain and several in Portugal. This story is about a giant who destroys everything in the King's garden. The King sends a group of his knights to attack the giant, Samson, but he picks them up along with their horses and hurls them. A tar man is set up at the palace to trick the giant. When the tar man does not salute the giant, the giant strikes the tar man with one hand and it sticks. The giant strikes with the other hand and it sticks. Then he kicks the tar man first with one foot then another, and they stick. Last, he bumps the tar man with his belly. When he is completely stuck, the soldiers come and slay the giant.

In Spanish America, this story has several versions which reflect the mixture of Indian and African influences.

SUGGESTED ACTIVITIES FOR THE CLASSROOM

1. THE VERY ELEGANT ROOSTER STORY

Read the tale often and have students join in. Since this is a listening experience, have students (a) paint the characters at the easel so we can see what they look like, (b) make a class picture book of the story, and/or (c) act out the story.

2. R-R-R-R-ROLL IT!

Remember: The letter "r" requires a roll of the tongue (r-r-r-r-r-). The letter "j" is pronounced as an "h" in English. Also, two "l"s together sound like "y" in English. Locate an English/Spanish picture dictionary for young children at the library and have the students find and learn other words to enrich the tales they write. Here are some to get you started:

ENGLISH	*SPANISH*
pocket	el bolsillo
jeans	los pantalones vaqueros
dress	el vestido
sun	el sol
cat	el gato
kitten	el gatito
caterpillar	la oruga
flag	la bandera
books	los libros
letter	la carta

3. WHAT SUPERSTITIONS DO WE KNOW?

After reading some of these popular Spanish superstitions we can begin to list some of the things we do and say that fall under the category of superstitions. Here are some to get you started:

- Step on a crack, break your mother's back. (children's games)
- Beware when Friday falls on the 13th of the month.
- Keep a rabbit's foot in your pocket for luck.
- Don't open an umbrella inside the house.
- Don't walk under a ladder or you will have bad luck.

These sayings serve as good "story starters." For example, the group can write a story about what actually happens to a character (animal or human) who does open up an umbrella inside the house.

4. EL NUBERO

The ugly spirit, El Nubero, wears a long beard, dresses in animal skins, and rides on a cloud. He lives with his wife and children on a mountain covered with fog. He can raise havoc with the weather. After reading an abundance of folk tales to get the flavor of how they are constructed (swift beginning, few characters, problem, conflict, resolution with a happy ending), the information given here about El Nubero is a good "story starter."

5. GETTING STARTED WITH EL TRASGU

This tiny house dwarf, El Trasgu, appears at night, enters a house and does some housework or breaks up the furniture. He is always dressed in red. In some parts of Spain or Spanish America he is called the duende, or ordinary dwarf. This character follows the family who moves from one house to another and frequently comes in the night with a broom or a kitchen pot that has been left behind in the old house. Students can write, draw, and use creative dramatics for some fun with El Trasgu.

6. MAKING SPANISH COMPARISONS

Compare folk tales from the country of Spain with those from Latin American countries (locate these areas on the map). Select short tales, and have students make comparisons of food and clothing in an effort to note differences that reflect European influence and Indian influence. Also, note the differences in language usage.

7. THE ROMANCE OF "DAD" AND "TY"

Present students with a list of words that are almost identical in English and Spanish, and see if they can figure out what the words are and what they mean. Some examples are: nacionalidad (nationality), universidad (university), and sociedad (society). Even though English is not a Romance Language, and Spanish is, there is a relationship between certain words, and these words are referred to as "cognates."

8. SPANISH NAMES IN YOUR COMMUNITY

If students live along the southern border of the U.S., on either coast, or in large cities, there are apt to be Spanish names for streets, bridges, buildings, statues, and so on. Do an inventory of names and places in your community and create a multi-ethnic community map. Make flashcards of the names of the statues, buildings, bridges, streets, restaurants, stores, and so on, and have students play a matching game with the flashcards and map drawings. Later, go on a field trip to locate the different places.

9. A SPECIAL BOOK

Taking a Walk, A Book in Two Languages or Caminando, Un Libro en Dos Lenguas by Rebecca Emberley (Boston: Little Brown, 1990) is a helpful book for students as they become immersed in the Spanish tales. The book, written in English and Spanish, takes the reader on a visual/verbal walk through the neighborhood, to the school, to the playground, stores, etc., and has an English and Spanish label next to each item depicted. Put labels on items in the classroom in both Spanish and English to help students learn them.

10. ANOTHER SPECIAL BOOK

The Great Kapok Tree by Lynne Cherry (San Diego: Harcourt Brace Jovanovich, 1990) is a tale of the Amazon rain forest. Illustrations on the endpapers of the hardback edition will enable students to locate the endangered rain forests on a map of South and Central America and to learn that the rain forest consists of an understory, a middle layer, and the canopy (top).

This book can be read aloud and easily reenacted by students for dramatic play. Also, a list with illustrations can be made of the many animals and birds found in the rain forest. Use the endpaper borders and the storybook illustrations for assistance. Here are some to get you started:

| anteater | boa constrictor | kinkajou | ocelot | sloth | tapir |
| parrot | red-legged honey creeper | | scarlet macaw | | toucan |

11. WRITING ENRICHMENT

Students can begin to use the different birds and animals from the rain forest in the original folk tales that they write, thus adding to the authenticity of their tales. Imagine a jaguar, a poison arrow frog, and a moustached tamarin as three main characters in a tale set in a rain forest. The flavor of the writing will be quite different from a story with more familiar animals. Also, students may be motivated to learn more about the flora and fauna from information books in the library.

12 IF I LIVED IN COSTA RICA...

Costa Rica (rich coast) has a luscious rain forest. Young boys and girls who live near this region have quite different birds flying about in their environment. Students can make a bird-shaped book guide with illustrations and information about at least three of the birds. Also, be sure to note the role of birds in the colorful folk tales and picture books. (See the children's book section.) On paper cut into a bird shape, write a magic tale about a talking bird who becomes the hero or heroine of the story by helping out another animal in trouble in the rain forest.

CELEBRATIONS

There are many celebrations in the Hispanic cultures of Mexico, Central America, the Caribbean, and the homeland of Spain. Many of the Christian celebrations have taken on the flavor of the Native American people in the new world. The following serves as a representative sampling.

CARNIVAL

By definition, carnival is derived from the Latin "carnem levare" which means "to take away the meat." Carnivals take place in many countries where Christianity is the main religion, and often a carnival is held in the spring just before Lent, when people go into a period of fasting.

The carnival itself is colorful and bright, with many floats. In Spain and Portugal, giant puppet heads of famous people from that culture are worn by those in the procession. Often masks or colorful face paint help to disguise the participants, and the costumes are lavish. It is a time for revelry and merrymaking with lots of singing, dancing, and fun.

CARNIVAL IN RIO DE JANIERO

Rio is a city in Brazil, and a special carnival is held there yearly at the end of summer. In Rio, planning for this holiday begins early, as people set up "samba schools" and practice their dancing, hoping to win the prize for the best performance. There are many floats with dazzling decorations, and the queen of the samba school rides on the float in a glamorous costume.

HAPPY NEW YEAR IN ECUADOR

This is a time for new clothes. Old clothes are often thrown away or burned. There is a parade in the evening in the center of town and a giant puppet figure wrapped in cloth is set on fire as a symbolic act. All of the mistakes, problems, and worries of the old year go up in smoke, and the new year marks a new beginning. The slate is wiped clean.

PAN AMERICAN DAY

This holiday is observed on April 14 by 21 republics of North, Central, and South America. An organization entitled the Pan American Union was established in 1889 in an effort to help the people of the Americas to understand one another and to live comfortably side by side.

NATIONAL DAY IN SPAIN

On July 18, there are parades in Madrid, Spain. People wearing colorful traditional peasant costumes dance in the streets on this day. The celebrants hold their arms above their head and click wooden "palillos" (castanets) that they wear on their fingers. There are many folk dances that people perform on stage. The official name of Spain is "Estado Espanol."

DAYS OF INDEPENDENCE—SEPTEMBER 15

Days of independence are celebrated throughout the world, and Central America and Mexico are no exception. On this date in 1821, Costa Rica, El

Salvador, Guatemala, Honduras, and Nicaragua broke away from Spain. Each year on this date, there are celebrations with parades, singing, dancing, and feasting.

EL CINCO DE MAYO (THE FIFTH OF MAY)

This is a national holiday in Mexico. It is a time to remember the battle between the Mexicans and the French in 1862, when the Mexicans won and the French retreated. It is a time of celebrations with a morning parade. In some cities a mock battle is fought during the day in the zocalo (town square) and usually there is good food, singing, dancing, and a display of fireworks in the evening. In Puebla, families and friends gather for a large noon-day meal. School is not in session on this special day and after the family get-together, the whole family goes to town to join in the festivities.

A VILLAGE POSADA

The word "posada" means "inn," and during the Christmas season in Mexico, parties are often neighborhood or village affairs. The festive season is in full swing throughout the month of December beginning with the setting up of the "nacimiento," the nativity scene on or about December 15. The pottery nacimientos are on sale in most of the outdoor markets in Mexico City at this time of year.

During this time of celebration, children look forward to the "piñata," a ceramic crock filled with candies and treats that is covered with papier-mâché and frilly paper. The piñata may resemble a donkey, a bird, or another colorful figure, and adds to the gaiety at this time of year. The message of the season is one of peace and good will.

EL DIA DE LOS MUERTOS (THE DAY OF THE DEAD)

In Mexico, this special time in early November is set aside to pay homage to the ancestors. In many areas it is a time for feasting and revelry, and in other areas it is a serious time for worship. Food is left on the doorstep for the ancestors' visit. Cemeteries are cleaned, and food and flowers are brought to the graves. The flowers are traditionally yellow marigolds. Some families pack a lunch to eat at the gravesites, which is meant as a show of reverence and respect for their ancestors.

Bread, baked especially for this day, is shaped like a skull, with dough coils representing bones on top. Candies are made in the shape of skeletons and bones, and toys are sold in the shape of coffins or skeletons. It is a part of the tradition to enjoy these treats. (The candies are much the same as those used for the Halloween festivities in the United States in October.)

ORCHID FESTIVAL IN COSTA RICA

In the Spring in downtown San Jose, the capital city of Costa Rica, there is a beautiful orchid display. People who raise orchids can enter their prized flowers, and there is row after row of colorful specimens. At this time, there is also a display of arts and crafts by the local people.

SUGGESTED ACTIVITIES FOR THE CLASSROOM

1. HOLIDAY BOOKLETS

Encourage students to select a special Hispanic holiday for further investigation. There are many holiday books at the library from which to gather the information. Materials can be kept in a folder that students decorate with special holiday symbols.

2. MAP AND GLOBE SKILLS

Have students locate Spain, Central America, South America, and Mexico on the map and globe. Make a large map outline for a bulletin board and have students fill in the countries. The holidays can be written on 3″ x 5″ cards and posted along the edges. Attach a piece of colorful yarn to each card, string it along the map, and tack it to the country that celebrates that holiday.

3. CELEBRATE WITH A PIÑATA

In some areas of the country, it is easy to gain access to a piñata at holiday time. If you choose to get one for your holiday celebration (or make one), have students use a plastic bat rather than a large wooden stick. Blindfold students, one at a time, twirl them around twice, and have them take three whacks at the piñata. Give each one who is "attacking" the piñata plenty of space.

4. FOLK TALE MAPS

While the Hispanic maps are on display, have students try to locate a folk tale in the library that represents each country. Place a large colored circle on the map shape every time someone finds a story from that country.

5. PEOPLE LIKE TO CELEBRATE

Continue to work with students on the concept that people the world over have certain holidays that they celebrate. Some holidays pertain to the founding of the country; some pertain to religious beliefs; and others pertain to events that occur in an area of the world (perhaps because of its particular location). An example of this is Eisheiligan, or Ice Saints Day, which is held in May in parts of Europe to celebrate the arrival of weather that will soon be fit for gardening. Encourage an attitude that values and respects diversity.

6. SHARE YOUR CELEBRATION

Encourage students to discuss family celebrations and customs, beginning with birthdays. Invite parents to address the class regarding special celebrations from different parts of the world. A sample of food from a different country adds to the enjoyment. Again, students need to continue to have exposure to many different customs in order to gain a feeling of respect for difference.

7. CELEBRATE ORCHIDS

The color of orchids is a pastel purple. Orchids thrive in warm, moist climates such as Costa Rica, which has a rich tropical rain forest. Invite a florist to class to show an orchid, and to tell about special conditions for growing them and other flowers. Students can investigate the flowers of the rain forest in this part of the world, and can celebrate by painting flowers, planting flowers, and setting up a classroom greenhouse for growing flowers.

Also, students can do research to determine the types of flowers that are grown in their local area that have an orchid or purple color (violets, irises, lilies, pansies, petunias, and so on). This is a good time to "Celebrate Purple" at the easel. Have students paint flowers in various shades of purple. The shades can be attained by mixing white with drops of purple tempera paint, mixing red with light purple, and mixing yellow with light purple. The results can be quite dramatic.

ARTS AND CRAFTS

The Latin American culture is rich in arts and crafts. Perhaps the most well-known Spanish painter is Pablo Picasso, who has left an abundant legacy of sketches, paintings, sculptures, and murals. In Mexico City, the impact of Diego Rivera is also felt because of the rich legacy of murals he painted on huge walls inside of public buildings. In Quito, the capital city of Ecuador, the gallery of Olga Fisch gathers the folk art of the people from all parts of the country and other places in South America and has it on display and for sale. There are hand-made dolls, musical instruments made from goat hoofs, trinkets made from bread dough, paintings, silver jewelry, and soft hand-woven ponchos that are ideal for slipping on over the head when the air cools in the evening and early morning.

Latin American textiles are colorful and bright. Many of the subjects are drawn from things that surround the people in nature (animals, birds, flowers). Clay tiles and pottery range from the primitive to fine works of art.

People paint scenes from nature on tree bark that has been hammered to a thin pulp. In Ecuador, for example, the natives paint bright colored scenes of country life on the back of animal hides that have been scraped, hammered, and dried in the sun. These are stretched over hand-made wooden frames; in some cases, the animal fur can still be seen on the back of the picture.

The people take pride in their art—it is a reflection of the spirit of the people. To create a work of beauty with your own hands is considered a gift. The arts and crafts in the Americas is blended with that of the native Indians and a rich array of pottery, painting, and handwork is the result.

SUGGESTED ACTIVITIES FOR THE CLASSROOM

1. IT'S A BRIGHT, BRIGHT WORLD OF NATURE

The birds and fish in the hot climates of Latin America are an artist's dream. Examine the birds and fish in picture books and information books so that students can see the bright lemon yellows, vivid aquamarines, startling limes, and shocking pinks, among other colors. Then mix tempera paints to get a variety of these secondary hues. For example, use tin cans as containers and mix green and yellow, red and yellow, blue and yellow in various quantities to get a range of tones. Then paint large jungle birds, such as the toucan, and the fish that swim in the aquamarine waters! Paint the animals on bright backgrounds such as yellow, orange, pink, and aqua rather than on white.

2. LET'S EXPLORE BLUE WITH PABLO PICASSO

Pablo Picasso is a well-known Spanish artist. A good resource is *First Impressions, Pablo Picasso* by John Beardsley (New York: Harry N. Abrams, Inc., 1991). Picasso was creative and painted in many styles. As an artist interested in color, Picasso spent seven years exploring the color blue, a time period known as his "Blue Period." Although he painted with only tones and shades of blue for that period of time, he felt he still did not know everything there was to know about blue.

Let's explore the color blue also. Who is wearing blue? Who has eyes of blue? Find books with blue covers in the room. Make comparisons so that students note the variety in this color.

3. SET UP A BLUE TABLE

You will need a blue tablecloth. Then encourage students to bring in items from home that are various shades of blue (pillows, stuffed animals, shoes, boxes, thermos jugs, thread, yarn, etc.). Enlist the aid of parents. You will end up with a "show of blue" in a section of your room, and can note the wide variety of tones and shades. Then have students paint a "still life" (an arrangement of three of the items) at the easel using only shades of blue. Paint on a light blue or steel gray-blue background. Mount the art work on navy blue paper and hang in a "Picasso Gallery." (See the suggested books section for Florian Rodari's book on Picasso.)

4. "FOUND ART"

Picasso also worked with sculpture. He assembled a sculpture from the seat and the handlebars of an old bicycle and called it "Bull's Head" (1942). Set up a collector's table of old, discarded items. Ask parents to contribute. Have students take the items apart and reassemble them in new ways, just as Picasso did. What do we "see" in the shapes? Display the items in your classroom art gallery, with a 3″ x 5″ card that contains the title, date, and name of artist.

5. TIME FOR TEXTILES

Some of the finest textiles in the world were made by people from Peru. The material used for weaving was cotton and wool from alpacas, llamas, or vicunas (these animals are related to the camel).

If you have a loom set up in the classroom, dress (prepare) the loom with cotton threads going lengthwise (warp). Then have students weave with woolen threads (weft) going from the bottom to the top.

"Backstrap weaving" is used by craftsmen today in Mexico and other Latin American countries. Some refer to this loom as the belt loom. The weaver needs two sticks and yarn. First, yarn is tied around the ends of one of the sticks and then it is tied to a tree to hold it steady. Next, yarn is measured and looped around the tree stick and laid out on the ground. The weaver ties the other stick around his or her waist and sits far enough away from the tree to make the warp firm. The weaver then weaves back and forth while sitting on the ground. As the weaving progresses and gets longer, it can be rolled up before being tied to the waist. The weaver works from the bottom to the top. At the end of the day, the weaving is rolled up and taken indoors. In Mexico City and in little villages throughout Mexico, many backstrap weavers can be found at work daily in the open markets. Their work is hanging on display, ready for sale. Many have designs or figures of animals and birds woven into the work. Some are extremely bright (fiery red, bright aquamarine blue, black, sunny yellow) and some are in muted earth tones. Either way, all are skillfully done.

For this student project, you will need two long sturdy sticks, yarn for warp and weft, and a tree, post, or pole (or object to secure the other end if weaving indoors). Use brightly colored yarn or natural yarns and wools.

6. LINE EMBROIDERY

Sometimes designs are embroidered on cloth. It is like drawing with yarn or thread. Each student can be given a small piece of burlap (4″ x 6″). Have them design a fanciful animal or bird (these symbols were often used, with long tails and colorful bodies). Carefully make an outline of the desired animal on the burlap with a thin felt pen. Then use embroidery thread and a *blunt* plastic needle to sew along the lines of the shape.

Some students may have the patience to start to fill in the space within the shape with different colors. It's an activity to be worked on in stages, and many students will enjoy doing this in their spare time after required work is completed. (This is a good activity for young children as it strengthens the small muscles of the hand.)

7. SLAB CLAY TILES

The Spanish people enjoy the art of designing clay tiles, which are used decoratively both inside the house (kitchen countertops, walls, and floor) and outside the house. In some homes, tile floors throughout the homes are mopped daily because the houses do not have screens on the windows and dust blows inside. Look for tiles in picture book illustrations and in information books. Note that curved tile roofs are also used by the Spanish. Tiles are often used when wood is scarce.

Give each student a square of clay (available at art supply stores), and have them paint designs on the square with glaze. These clay slabs can be fired in the kiln. The results are usually surprising because the glaze color may be different from that which the students imagined them to be. (If a kiln is not available at your school, check with the art teacher at the high school to see if the clay tiles can be fired there.) It's an exciting experience and worth the effort.

8. MAKE CLAY JEWELRY

Students can also make clay pendants. Have them make an oval or round shape from the clay, and poke a hole in the top end for stringing rawhide through. Students can etch a design onto the clay with a toothpick, then paint it with glaze. After they are fired in the kiln, these are beautiful when worn around the neck.

9. MAKE A METAL MEXICAN LANTERN

Throughout Mexico, craftspeople use tin cans to make candleholders, frames for mirrors, and other decorative objects. Students can make a lantern holder (to be used with a flashlight) from a tin can. Make sure the inside of the can is cleaned, and put masking tape along the rim of the open end to avoid cuts. Using a felt-tip marker, place a design of dots around the can. Then take a nail and hammer, and make the dots into small holes. Place the can over a flashlight to see the pretty lantern design.

10. COPPER RELIEF DESIGN OR MASK

A design that is raised from the background is called a relief. Early craftsmen worked in gold. Metal relief, or "repousse," is used today. Sheets of copper foil, which work well, can be obtained from a craft store. Students can examine replicas of masks in books, and then design their own.

- Draw the design onto a small sheet of copper metal (4″ x 6″ or 6″ x 8″) using a felt-tip marker.
- Place the copper drawing on a thick pile of newspapers.
- Use a ballpoint pen to press hard over the lines that you want to "stick out" (relief) on the other side.
- For added interest in texture, parts of the design may be pressed out with the heel of a spoon.
- If an ancient look is desired, brush the mask with brown tempera paint, and then rub it off quickly with a soft cloth.
- Frame the masks using black construction paper. They make an impressive art gallery show.

GAMES

The following are representative games, and are not intended to be all inclusive. Soccer is a sport played throughout South America since the 19th century when it was imported from Great Britain. Horseback riding, swimming, boating, and sailing are also popular. In Acapulco, Mexico, diving off cliffs into the water far below has reached a high art.

RING ON A STRING

Players sit in a circle with both hands clasped over a string. This taut string has a ring (or item) strung through it before it is tied. Have one child clasp his or her hand over the ring. Then, children in the circle keep up a steady motion of their hands as they move them apart and together again. As they do this, they touch hands and the ring is thus transferred from one player to another.

One child is named "it" and goes into the middle of the circle. "It" must close his or her eyes as the signal is given for the ring to be shifted to a designated child. Then, the person who is "it" is given the signal "eyes open" and watches the motion of the hands along the string to see if he or she can guess who has the ring. If guessed correctly, "it" changes places with the person who has the ring.

PAHLITO VERDE

Pahlito Verde (pah-LEE-toe VER-deh) means, "Where is the little green stick?" This is a version of the "drop the handkerchief" game.

Children all stand around in a circle. The one who is "it" is outside the circle behind the players, and holds in his or her hand a little green tree branch. As "it" circles the outside of the ring, the players chant, "Pahlito Verde," and "it" answers, "Romero," (Ro-MER-oh), which means the herb, "Rosemary." Again the players chant and "it" answers. This goes on until "it" has made a complete circle around the outside of the ring. Then, the chanting stops and "it" runs around the ring and drops the branch behind a player who must pick it up and chase after "it." If the person who is "it" can successfully return to the spot vacated by the one doing the chasing before being touched, the person with the little branch is the new "it." The cycle of the chant-and-chase begins again.

MUSICAL CHAIRS

This game is found in many cultures throughout the world, and is enjoyed by children everywhere. Children are all seated in chairs in a large circle, or in a row with chairs back to back. When the music (representative of the culture) begins, the children walk around the pathway (while one chair is removed). When the music stops, all must get to the nearest chair and sit down. One by one, children drop by the wayside as the chairs are removed, but they can still enjoy the game by clapping to the music and helping with the chairs.

A PIÑATA

The piñata is often found at children's parties. It is a jar made from clay or from papier-mâché, and covered with crepe paper to represent a colorful bird, animal, or shape. It is filled with goodies such as candies, popcorn, coins, and other small gifts. Each player is blindfolded and must try to hit the hanging piñata with a stick. The person controlling the piñata on a heavy rope needs to give everyone a chance to take a swing or two. Then it can be lowered; when it cracks and the goodies fall out, children scramble to get as much as they can.

LOBO, YA ESTAS?

Lobo, ya estas? means, "Wolf, are you ready?" One player is chosen to be "it" (wolf) and hides. The other players form a circle around the area where the wolf is in hiding (under a bush, under a classroom desk) and chant, "Wolf, are you ready?" The wolf answers with a variety of answers such as, "I am putting on my shoes," "I am getting my coat," "I am putting on my socks," etc. Finally, the wolf answers in a shout, "I am ready!" and lunges out of hiding and after the players who have scattered. The one who is caught is the next "it" or wolf to go in hiding, and the cycle begins again.

SONGS, DANCES, RHYTHMS

Singing and folk dancing are very much a part of the Latin American culture. At school, children dress in native costumes and dance to the accompaniment of lively rhythms. The dances often reflect stories (folklorico) of the country and have a beginning, middle and ending. Often props are used. When foreigners visit the schools, more often than not they will be entertained by children in native dress dancing to several story songs.

In private homes, music and singing and dancing are enjoyed by young and old alike. In Costa Rica, for example, at parties in private homes, everyone dances—the grandchildren dance alongside the grandmother and the parents and other relatives. They often take turns with five or six dancing at one time, while others clap rhythmically to the tune. A family gathering just would not be complete without music, singing, and dancing.

SONG OF THE COCKROACH

Cockroaches are common in hot, damp climates. And it has been said that in small cabins along the Amazon River of South America, the cockroaches can be heard eating the soap in the bathroom at night! Cockroaches thrive in dark places, so if you leave even a crumb of food on the floor or the countertop in the kitchen, you can be sure that the cockroach will pay a visit. The cockroach is so common in countries south of the border that the natives have dedicated a special song to it.

La Cucaracha (The Cockroach) (Spanish version)

La cucaracha, la cucaracha,
Ya no quier e caminar
Porque no tien e, Porque le fal ta,
Lapa tita principal.

La Cucaracha (The Cockroach) (English version)

A. La cucaracha, la cucaracha,
Doesn't care to travel here
Because she hasn't,
Oh, no, she hasn't,
One of her paws in the rear.

B. La cucaracha, la cucaracha
Sings it loud and sings it far,
Because she hasn't,
Oh, no, she hasn't,
Any strings on her guitar.

C. La cucaracha, la cucaracha,
Has to let her head go bare,
Because she hasn't,
Oh, no, she hasn't,
A little hat she can wear.

D. La cucaracha, la cucaracha,
Doesn't travel out at night,
Because she hasn't,
Oh, no, she hasn't,
A little candle to light.

E. La cucaracha, la cucaracha,
Often bumps into a tree,
Because she hasn't,
Oh, no, she hasn't,
Glasses to help her see.

F. La cucaracha, la cucaracha,
Likes to scamper up the wall,
Because she hasn't,
Oh, no, she hasn't,
Any manners AT ALL!

A CHOCOLATE CHANTING RHYME

Uno, dos, tres CHO
   (count with fingers)
Uno, dos, tres CO
Uno, dos, tres LA
Uno, dos, tres TE
Bat e, Bat e, CHO CO LA TE!
   (stirring motion)

(One, two, three CHO)

(One, two, three CO)
(One, two, three LA)
(One, two, three TE)
(Stir, stir the chocolate)

LITTLE FROG TAIL

This is a little chant to say over a scraped knee:

Sana, sana colita de rana,   (Get well, get well, little frog tail)
Si no sanas ahora,   (If you don't get well now)
Sanaras manana.   (You will get well tomorrow)

Use a circular motion over the hurt, as if to rub it away.

CHA-CHA!

Use a cassette tape recording of a lively rhythm and have children do a 1-2-3 step to the right, 1-2-3 step to the rear, 1-2-3 step to the left, and 1-2-3 step to the front. They are moving to the rhythm in a square shape. All the while, they can make a fist with each hand, and encircle one hand around the other (clockwise and counterclockwise).

FOOD

Hispanic refers to Spanish or Spanish and Portuguese. The country of Spain is linked to Europe through the Pyrenees Mountains. Spain is bordered by Portugal on the west, and is surrounded by water on three sides so seafood has always been a staple in Spanish cooking. Fish—such as lobster, squid, mussels, giant tuna, and pink prawns—is a mainstay in the diet. Also, chicken, oranges, grapes, olives, and other fresh fruits and vegetables are eaten daily.

In Spain and many Hispanic countries in Central America, South America, and in Mexico, people shop daily for fresh food at the colorful markets. Chickens and many kinds of fish are sold "al fresco" (or natural) with fins, scales, feathers, eyes, and tails still attached.

Fruit is usually served whole, but in some homes it is considered bad manners to bite into a whole piece of fruit. Rather, it should be peeled and cut into bite-size pieces.

The dining table is often covered with a white lace tablecloth and a vase of fresh flowers is placed in the center. It is customary to place a bowl of fruit on the table also. Food is something to be relished and enjoyed! After the noonday meal, it is common to have a little siesta (nap) to avoid the hot afternoon sun. This means, then, that the work of the day ends at a later hour than, for example, in the United States.

In Spanish, the breakfast is *El Desayuno* (el deh-say-YOO-noh), lunch or dinner is *La Comida* (la koh-ME-duh), and supper is *La Cena* (la SEH-nuh). Since the breakfast is very small, some have a second breakfast called *almuerzo* (al-moo-ERZ-o).

In Mexico, the breakfast of people who live and work in the city is different from that of the peasants who live and work in the country. The meals have the same names, however, and are designated below by city (**c**) or country (**co**). A typical menu might include the following information:

MENU FOR THE DAY

El Desayuno (Breakfast)	tortillas, coffee	**(co)**
	orange juice, huevos rancheros (eggs), chocolate caliente (hot chocolate)	**(c)**
Almuerzo (Second Breakfast)	tortillas, frijoles (beans), biscochos (sweet buns), coffee	**(co)**
	biscochos and coffee	**(c)**
La Comida (Lunch)	tortillas, frijoles, sopa (soup), salsa de jitomate (meat & sauce)	**(co)**
	sopa aguada (wet soup), sopa seca (dry soup, w/rice or pasta), meat dish, vegetables, beans, salad, tortillas and salsa, fruit salad, aguas frescas (fruit drinks)	**(c)**
La Cena (Dinner)	tortilla, frijoles, fruit	**(co)**
	tortilla, frijoles, fruit	**(c)**

SUGGESTED MENU ACTIVITIES FOR THE CLASSROOM

1. LEARN TO ORDER FROM A MENU

Obtain a variety of menus from fast food and local Hispanic restaurants, and have students "order" their breakfast from it. (Perhaps props can be used for food, paper and pencil for taking orders, tablecloth, napkins, place settings, flowers for the table, and so on.)

2. CALCULATING COSTS

From menus, students can determine the cost of a variety of different lunches. They can add the items with pencil and paper, and check their math with a calculator.

3. MENU VARIETIES

Write "specials" for a nutritious lunch or dinner for three days in a row, with something different each day for each category: appetizer, entree, bread, dessert, drink.

4. MAKE A MENU

Create an appetizing picture menu. Use colorful pictures cut out from magazines, or draw and paint the menu. Create original names for the "dishes" and for the Hispanic restaurant.

5. EATING OUT

If possible, plan a luncheon trip to a Hispanic-style restaurant. This is the type of experience that students learn from and it remains with them always. Invite one adult to accompany every three children, set rules for restaurant manners, and stick to them.

6. MAKE A MULTICULTURAL MENU

Show foods from various countries on the menu, with maps indicating where the country is.

7. MULTI-ETHNIC MENU

Make a large classroom chart, representing a wide variety of cultures, and show (write and draw) a typical breakfast, lunch or dinner for each.

SUGGESTED RECIPES FOR THE CLASSROOM

Guacamole and Tortilla Chip Dip

2 ripe avocados
1/4 teaspoon lemon juice
2 fresh tomatoes, finely chopped
2 tablespoons finely chopped
  coriander (herb)
1/2 chopped onion

Cut the avocados in half and remove the pits. Scoop the avocado flesh from the skins and mash. Mix together the chopped tomatoes, onion, lemon juice, and coriander. Blend the avocado with the tomato mixture. Spoon into a serving dish. Place onto a larger plate and line the rim with tortilla chips.

Fresh Fruit Salad

Use a combination of any three:

pineapple
watermelon
orange
cantaloupe
banana
grapes

Use fresh fruit, if possible, and cut into small bite-size pieces. Mix all fruits together and serve.

Spanish "Old Clothes" (Ropa Vieja)

"Old Clothes," popular throughout Spain, is a dish made from leftovers. The cooked meat must be stringy and can be torn into pieces by hand.

3 teaspoons olive oil
2 tomatoes, diced
2 cooked potatoes, sliced
2 cups shredded roast beef
    (or cold cuts)
2 small onions, chopped
1 green pepper, chopped
1 cup canned chick peas, drained

Heat oil in electric frypan until it is warm (caution needed). Add sliced potato, chopped onion, and chopped pepper, and cook until potato is browned. Keep stirring, gently. Add diced tomatoes, meat, and peas. Toss gently. Salt and pepper to taste.

Kabach (Frijoles Negro)

1 pound black beans
1teaspoon salt
2 onions
7 cups water
1/2 cup oil

Soak beans overnight. Then rinse beans. Return soaked beans to pan and cover beans with water to a level about 1 inch above the beans. Add salt and one small chopped onion. Cook until beans are tender. Drain. Fry the second onion in vegetable oil. Mix the onion with the beans. Serve on a large platter.

Frijoles Refritos (Refried beans)

Same ingredients as for Kabach.
Soak beans overnight. Then rinse beans. Return soaked beans to pan and cover beans with water to a level about 1 inch above the beans. Add salt and one small chopped onion. Cook until beans are tender. Mash or blend them in a little of their own broth. Chop and fry second onion in vegetable oil. Add mashed frijoles (beans) and fry on medium-low, stirring to prevent sticking. Fry until beans get thickened. Then form into a loaf and garnish with tortilla chips. Use chips as a scoop when eating the frijoles refritos.

Chocolate Caliente (Hot Chocolate)

8 squares (8 ounces) Baker's®
    chocolate
4 cups skim milk
4 drops vanilla extract
cinnamon

Break chocolate into small pieces. Combine chocolate, milk and vanilla in a saucepan, constantly stirring. Bring to a boil, then use a whisk to mix it up. Pour into cups. Sprinkle cinnamon on top.

Chili Con Carne

1 pound ground beef
1 green pepper, washed and
  chopped
1 large onion, peeled and chopped
2 cloves garlic, minced
1 1-pound can tomatoes
1 1-pound can kidney beans,
  drained
2 tablespoons chili powder
salt and pepper
1 teaspoon oregano

Brown the beef in an electric frypan. Pour off grease. Combine all other ingredients with the beef and cook on low for two hours.

Taco Chip Dip

2 16-ounce cans chili with meat
2 16-ounce cans refried beans
1/2 pound grated Cheddar cheese
2 tomatoes, washed and diced
5 green onions, chopped fine
1/4 cup sliced olives
taco chips

Mix together chili and refried beans. Heat. Pour the bean mixture into a dish and place cheese around the edge of the bean mixture. Place tomatoes in a circle around the inside of the beans. Place onions in a circle around the inside of the tomatoes. Pile olives in the middle. Use taco chips as a scoop for this colorfully designed dip.

Heavenly Hash (Picadillo del Cielo)

1 20-ounce can crushed pineapple
1 dozen marshmallows, quartered
2 medium bananas, diced
1 dozen chopped dates
1 dozen glazed cherries, quartered
1 pint heavy cream, whipped

In a large bowl, mix pineapple and marshmallows. Allow to stand for three hours, until marshmallows dissolve. Add bananas, dates, cherries to this mixture and stir. Fold whipped cream into this mixture. Chill before serving.

Resources

Alvarado, Manuel. *Mexican Food and Drink*. New York: The Bookwright Press, 1988.

Shapiro, Rebecca. *Wide World Cookbook for Girls and Boys*. Boston: Little, Brown and Co., 1962.

Silverstein, Alvin and Virginia. *Beans, All About Them*. Illustrations by Shirley Chan. Englewood Cliffs, NJ: Prentice Hall, 1975.

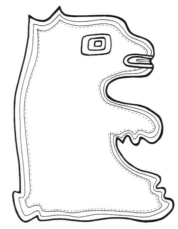

REPRODUCIBLE ACTIVITY PAGES

The Very Elegant Rooster (three pages) (*storytelling kit*)

The Talking Toucan Puppet (*storytelling*)

Old Turtle's Folk Tale Recipe (*preparing for writing*)

Quick! Mix Up the Papier-Mâché for Posada (*making a piñata*)

San Antonio Abad (*Mexican celebration*)

It's Carnival Time! (*celebration*)

Days of Independence (*research; visual reporting*)

Create a Mola Design (*art project*)

Create a Picasso-Style Face (*visual art*)

Oh, What a Beautiful Country Cart (*visual design*)

A Polar Bear in Mexico? (*geography*)

Chocolate Caliente (Hot Chocolate) (*food recipe*)

International Road Sign Language (*visual information*)

Do an Author Study—Latin America (*Spanish/English versions: Ruth Heller; Lois Ehlert*)

name _____

(Page 1 of 3)

1. Color, fold, and staple the envelope for *The Very Elegant Rooster*.

2. Color and cut the eleven story pieces. Store them in the envelope.

3. Retell the story, using the pictures as a guide.

Why aren't some squares numbered?

(Because they are used again and again.)

staple ----→

story teller kit

fold

The Very Elegant Rooster

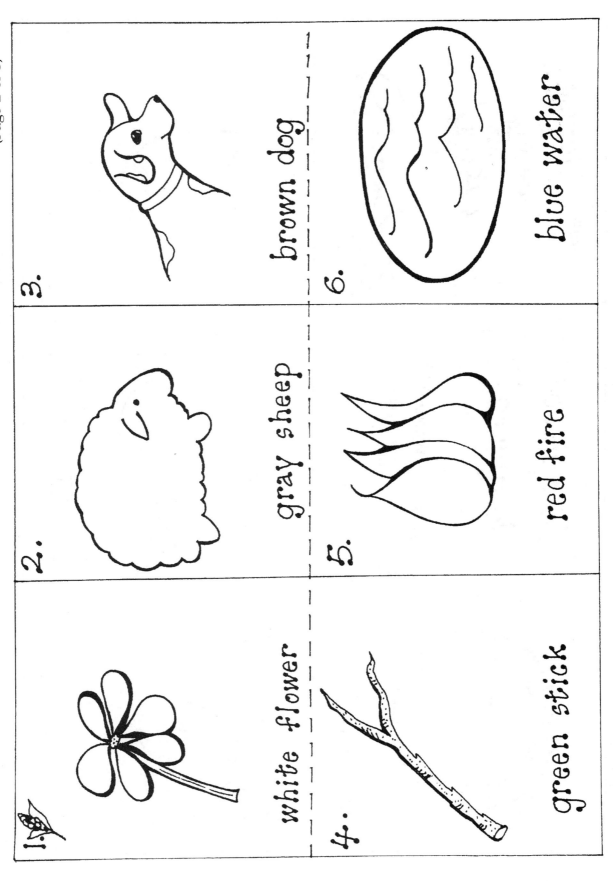

1.

2.

3.

brown dog

4.

white flower

gray sheep

5.

red fire

6.

green stick

blue water

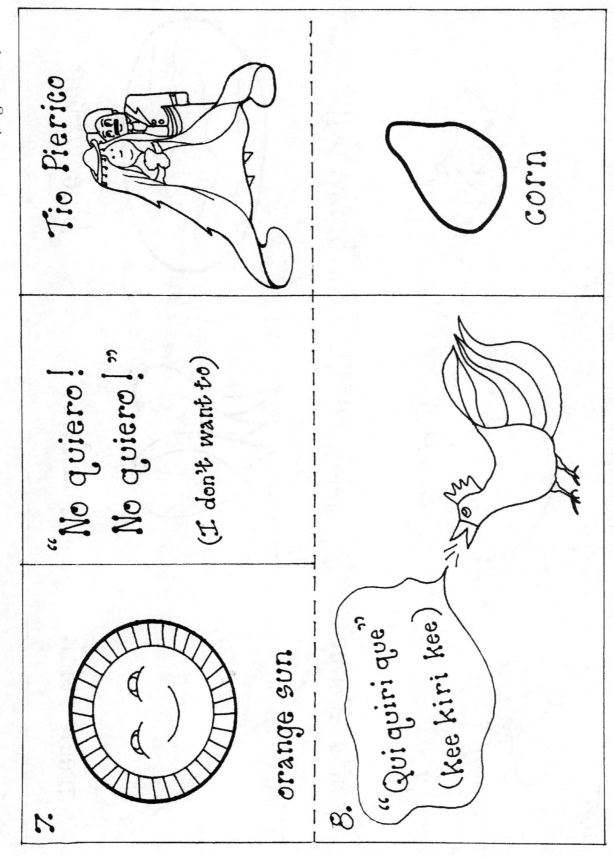

Tio Pierico

corn

"No quiero!
No quiero!"

(I don't want to)

7.

orange sun

8.

"Qui quiri que"
(Kee kiri kee)

THE TALKING TOUCAN PUPPET

Use your brilliant colors to transform this Latin American bird into a lime green, aquamarine blue, bright orange, and dazzling red puppet.

Cut out the puppet and attach it to a cardboard strip. It can help you tell many tales of S p a n i s h origin.

Name _____   Date _____

OLD TURTLE'S FOLK TALE RECIPE

Fill in the outline below. It will
help you write a good folk tale!

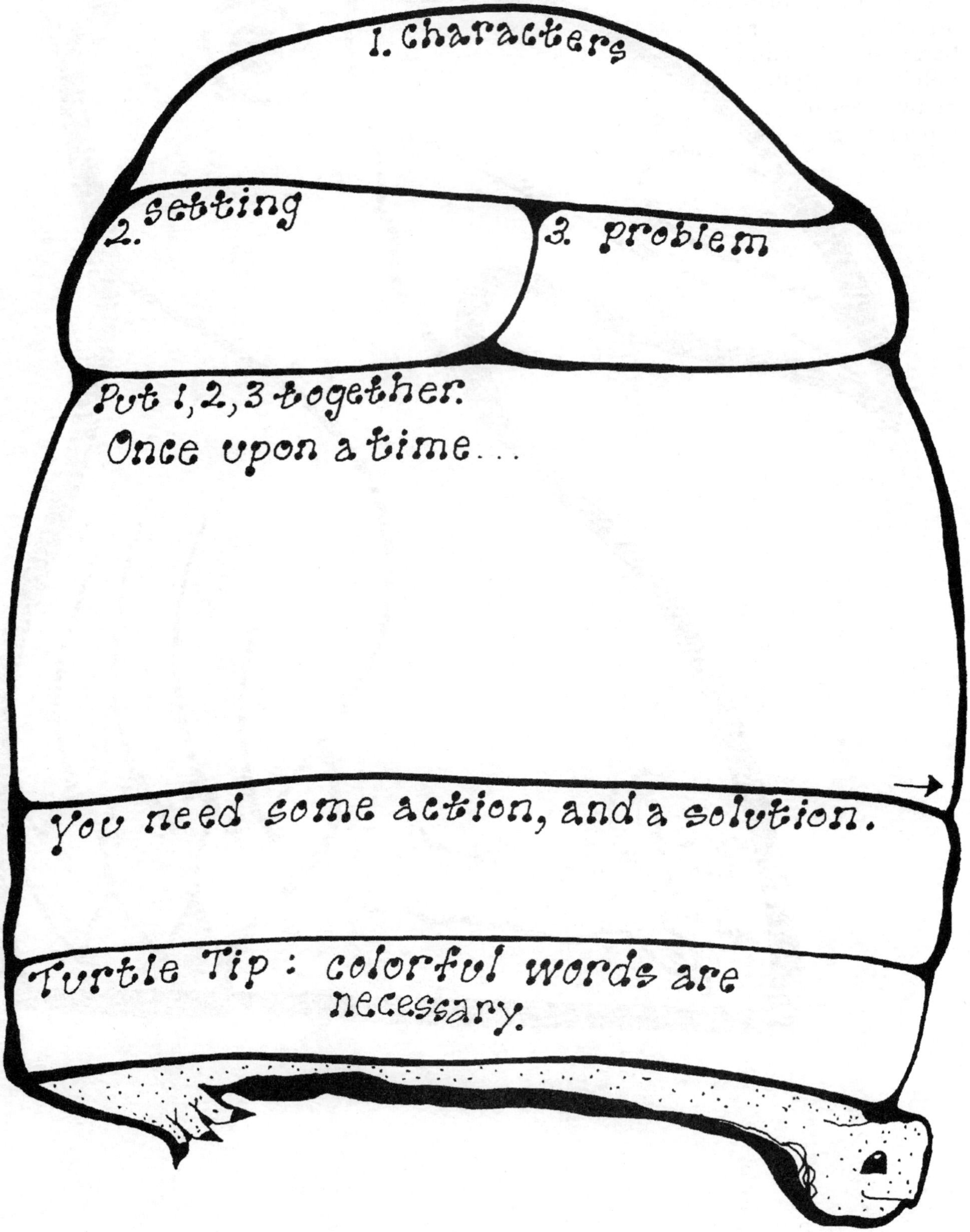

1. characters

2. setting

3. problem

Put 1, 2, 3 together:
Once upon a time...

You need some action, and a solution.

Turtle Tip : colorful words are
necessary.

Name _____ Date _____

QUICK! MIX UP THE PAPIER-MÂCHÉ FOR POSADA

The nine days before Christmas are called "posada" in Spanish-speaking countries. Papier-mâche donkeys, dogs, and other shapes are filled with goodies and small toys.

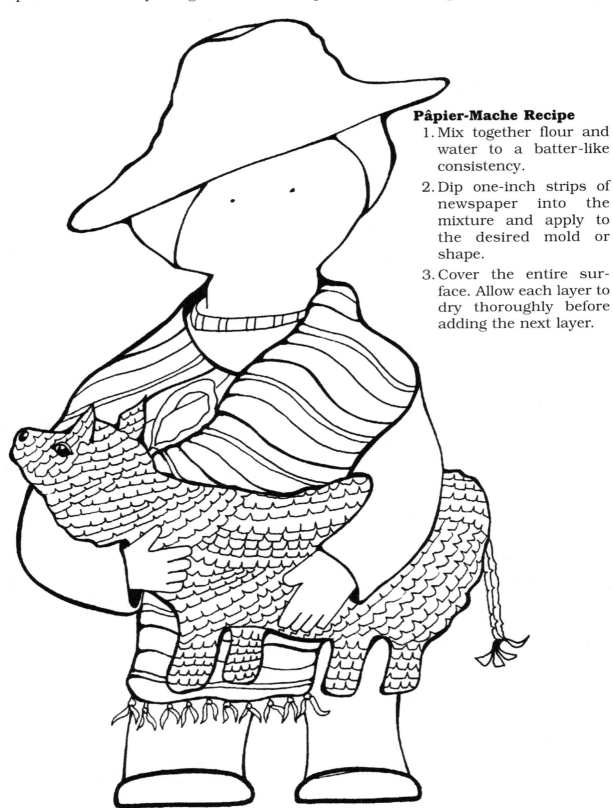

Pâpier-Mache Recipe

1. Mix together flour and water to a batter-like consistency.

2. Dip one-inch strips of newspaper into the mixture and apply to the desired mold or shape.

3. Cover the entire surface. Allow each layer to dry thoroughly before adding the next layer.

Name _____ Date _____

SAN ANTONIO ABAD

In January in Mexico, on the day of St. Anthony the Abbot, children take their pets to church to be blessed. There are goats, birds, cats, dogs, sheep, turtles, etc. The pets are washed, groomed and decorated with ribbons, bells and colorful vegetable dye to look pretty or even clownish. Use your bright felt-tipped pens or crayons to help decorate the pets on this page.

Name _____ Date _____

IT'S CARNIVAL TIME!

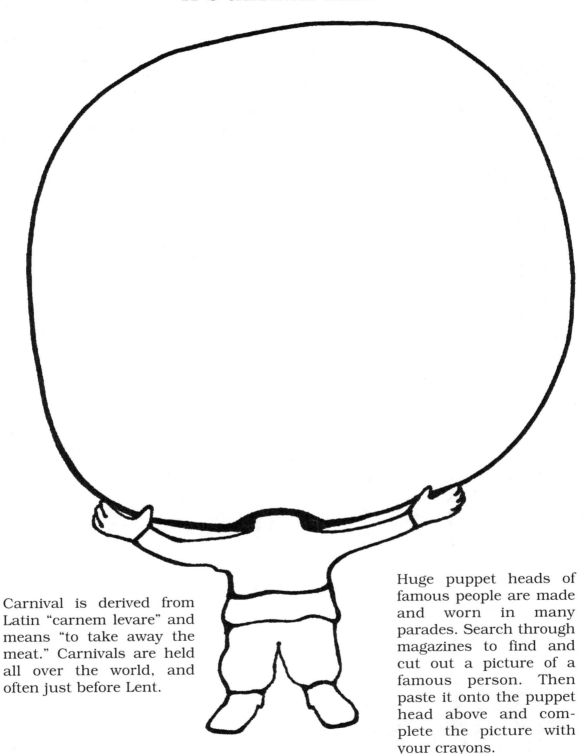

Carnival is derived from Latin "carnem levare" and means "to take away the meat." Carnivals are held all over the world, and often just before Lent.

Huge puppet heads of famous people are made and worn in many parades. Search through magazines to find and cut out a picture of a famous person. Then paste it onto the puppet head above and complete the picture with your crayons.

Name _____   Date _____

DAYS OF INDEPENDENCE

On September 15, these Central American countries celebrate their independence from Spain. There are many colorful parades! Use the spaces below to show some of the events
that take place during the celebrations.

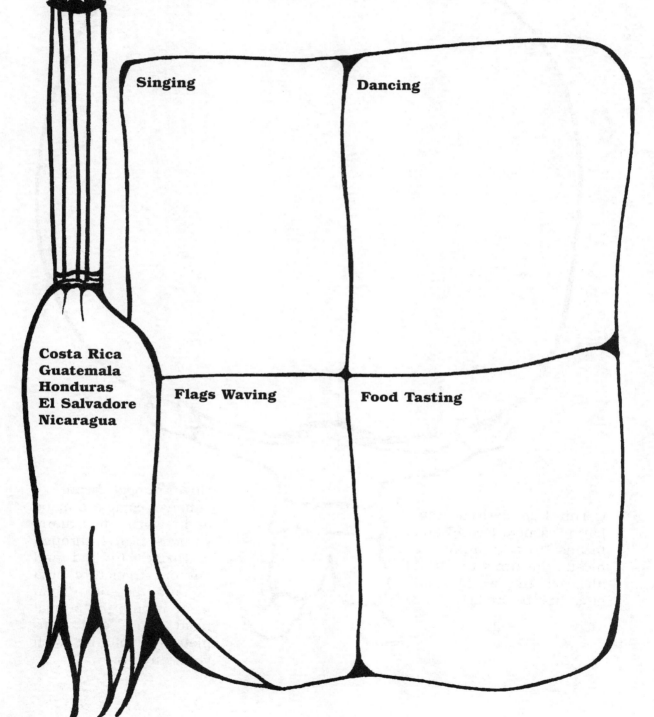

Singing

Dancing

Costa Rica
Guatemala
Honduras
El Salvadore
Nicaragua

Flags Waving

Food Tasting

CREATE A MOLA DESIGN

After looking at pictures, or real molas made from cloth, you will note that molas consist of many *layers*, and only the *rim* of a bright color may be seen.

Color the two rims and the center of this pre-Colombian figure with different colors. Then, use two layers of construction paper shapes, and glue them onto the figure.

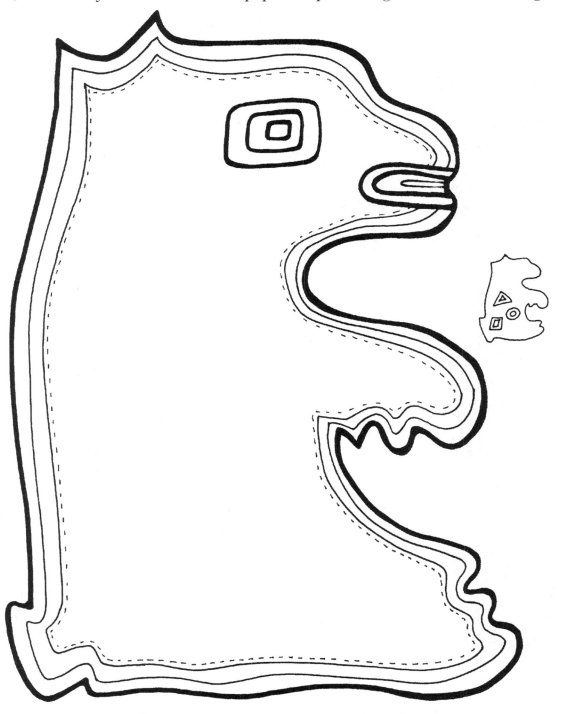

After practicing on this page, use felt to make a cloth mola.

CREATE A PICASSO-STYLE FACE

The artist Pablo Picasso was always experimenting. One thing he did was to draw the face in a different way on each side. Complete this face. Search through magazines for eyes, nose, mouth, and other features. Cut them out, and paste them onto the side asymetrically.

Make the whole face colorful.

Are you more aware now of facial features? Try more on your own. Find art books about Picasso and study them.

Name _____ Date _____

OH, WHAT A BEAUTIFUL COUNTRY CART

This wooden cart is pulled by donkeys in Costa Rica and is often filled with sugar cane or bananas. The farmers paint their carts with bright red, orange, yellow, blue, black, and green designs. Use your bright colors to paint the cart. Remember, don't leave any white showing through.

On the other side of this sheet, draw and label three other ways that food is taken to markets and stores in Costa Rica.

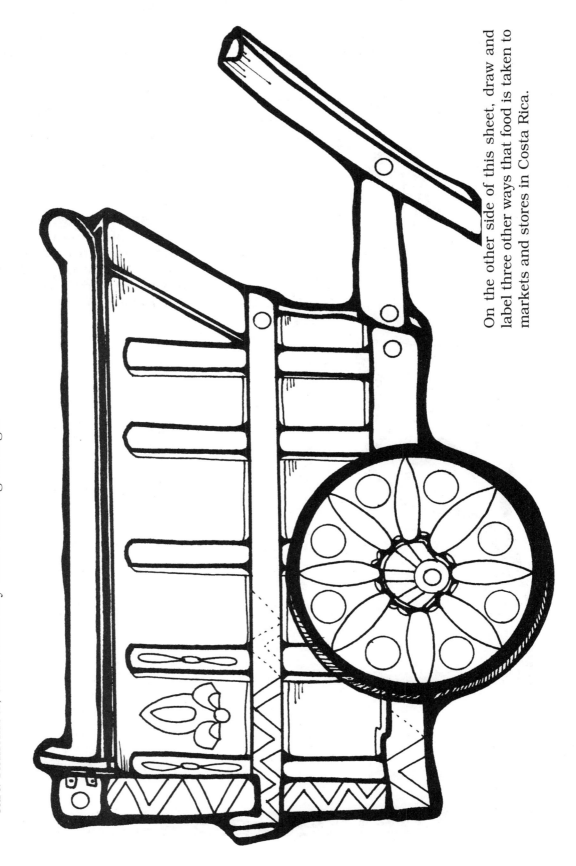

A POLAR BEAR IN MEXICO?

"Hrmph!" sniffed Mr. P. Bear. "I wasn't wearing my glasses and I boarded the wrong plane. I counted the number of letters in C-A-N-A-D-A and in M-E-X-I-C-O. They both have six! Please get me back North. It's hot here."

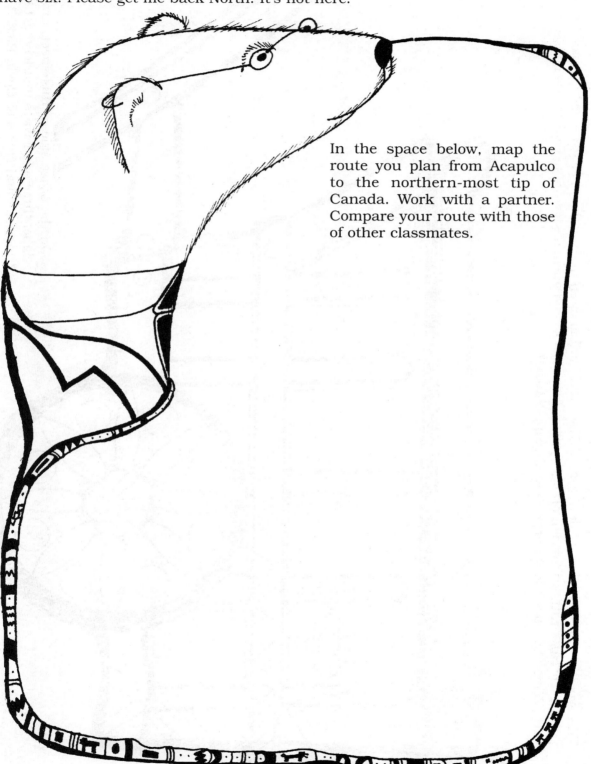

In the space below, map the route you plan from Acapulco to the northern-most tip of Canada. Work with a partner. Compare your route with those of other classmates.

CHOCOLATE CALIENTE (Hot Chocolate)

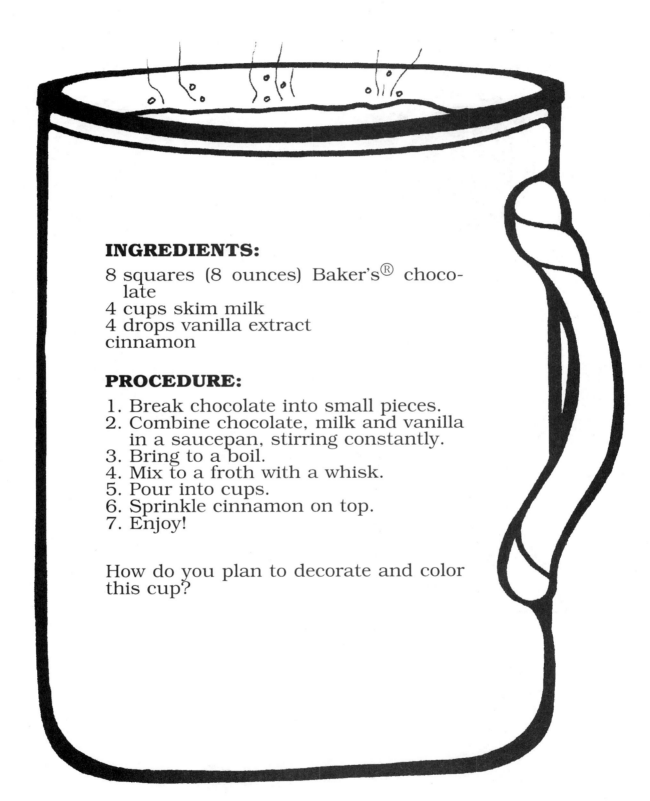

INGREDIENTS:

8 squares (8 ounces) Baker's® chocolate
4 cups skim milk
4 drops vanilla extract
cinnamon

PROCEDURE:

1. Break chocolate into small pieces.
2. Combine chocolate, milk and vanilla in a saucepan, stirring constantly.
3. Bring to a boil.
4. Mix to a froth with a whisk.
5. Pour into cups.
6. Sprinkle cinnamon on top.
7. Enjoy!

How do you plan to decorate and color this cup?

Name _____ Date _____

INTERNATIONAL ROAD SIGN LANGUAGE

Even if you can't speak several languages, road signs give information to you visually. Be on the alert for picture signs that could mean the same thing all over the world. Some are already done for you. Complete the rest. Share signs with classmates.

DO AN AUTHOR STUDY—LATIN AMERICA

There are many familiar tales being translated into Spanish. Many of the books by Ruth Heller (*Chickens Aren't the Only Ones* and *Kites Fly High*) are written in Spanish. Also, *A Snowy Day* by Ezra Jack Keats has a Spanish version. How many tales can you find with both Spanish and English text?

Here's one to get you started—the beautiful *Moon Rope, Un Lazo a La Luna* by Lois Ehlert. Read it in English and try to figure out some of the Spanish words. Enjoy the gorgeous pre-Colombian designs and illustrations—especially those in silver!

I found bilingual versions of these books:

What new words did you learn to say?

NORTH AMERICA

Native American Cultures

RECOMMENDED CHILDREN'S BOOKS

It is important to remember that Native Americans were given the name of "Indians" by the Europeans. The Native-American tribal names are an important part of their culture and tradition. Many tribal names are referred to in the following representative listing of books for young children.

Baylor, Byrd. *The Desert Is Theirs*. Pictures by Peter Parnall. New York: Macmillan, 1975. This Caldecott Award winner integrates myth, folklore, factual information, and illustrations to give the reader a sense of the southwest desert from the point of view of the people and the animals who live by "desert time," not man-made time. It's one in a treasury of sensitive books by this talented duo that includes *Desert Voices, Everybody Needs a Rock*, and *I'm in charge of Celebrations*.

Begay, Shonto. *Ma'll and Cousin Horned Toad, a Traditional Navajo Story*. New York: Scholastic Books, 1992. The second book on the subject of how Horned Toad outwits Coyote. The antics in the story will make the students grin. The author, a Native American, remembers that this tale was passed on to him by an exceptional storyteller—his grandmother.

Carey, Valerie Scho. *Quail Song*. Illustrated by Ivan Barnett. New York: Putnam/Whitebird, 1990. In this traditional Pueblo tale, Quail manages to outwit that persistent Coyote. Young children enjoy joining in on the "ki-ruu, ki-ruu" and the "tsi-ka, tsi-ka" sounds of the characters.

Coatsworth, Emerson, and Coatsworth, David. *The Adventures of Nanabush: Ojibway Indian Stories*. Illustrated by Francis Kagige. New York: Macmillan/McElderry, 1980. This book offers a number of tales about the trickster, Nanabush. The tales are related by Native American storytellers, such as Sam Snake and Chief Elijah Yellowhead. The illustrations, by an Ojibwa artist, give an authenticity to the tales.

Cohen, Caron Lee. *The Mud Pony, A Traditional Skidi Pawnee Tale*. Illustrated by Shonto Begay. New York: Scholastic, 1988. A touching, mystical tale about a boy who wanted a pony so badly that he fashioned one out of mud, and then something wonderful happened to bring the mud pony to life. Children are fascinated by the enchantment of the story.

DeArmond, Dale. *The Seal Oil Lamp, An Adaptation of an Eskimo Folk Tale.* **Boston: Little, Brown and Company, 1988.** Blind from birth, a seven-year-old Eskimo boy named Allugua will never grow up to be a good hunter and provider, so, according to tradition, he must be left behind. When that time comes, Allugua, who had once saved a mouse from cold and hunger, is rescued by the mouse people. Eventually he returns to his people—and this time he is a hero.

Goble, Paul. *The Gift of the Sacred Dog.* **New York: Bradbury Press, 1980.** It has been a long winter and the people of the tribe are starving. When one lone boy asks the Great Spirit for help, someone comes riding from the clouds toward the boy on the back of a beautiful animal that has thunder in its nostrils and lightning in its legs. This story with its beautiful illustrations is a tribute to the horse.

____. *The Girl Who Loved Wild Horses.* **New York: Bradbury Press, 1978.** This Caldecott Award winner has brilliantly colored paintings that frame the dramatic tale of a young Indian girl who is devoted to the care of her tribe's horses. It is a tale of wonder.

____. *Iktomi and the Ducks.* **New York: Orchard Books, 1980.** This is the author's third tale of Iktomi (eek-TOE-me), the trickster of Plains Indian folklore. Iktomi tries to lure innocent ducks to the pond for his dinner. The Iktomi stories are traditionally told with audience participation, so the text is in bold black print and in light gray print, so the audience can become involved during the light gray sections.

Hofsinde, Robert (Gray-Wolf). *Indian Sign Language.* **New York: Morrow Junior Books, 1956.** An authentic book with more than 200 illustrations by the author that show the reader how to form the gestures representing over 500 words in Indian sign language. An excellent teaching resource book.

Jeffers, Susan. *Brother Eagle, Sister Sky.* **Paintings by Susan Jeffers. New York: Dial Books, 1992.** "How can you buy the sky? How can you own the rain and the wind?" The moving words attributed Chief Seattle have become a rallying cry for those interested in preserving the environment. The text is illustrated by Susan Jeffers in unforgettable visual imagery. A "must" for every library.

Martin, Rafe. *The Rough-Face Girl.* **Illustrated by David Shannon. New York: Putnam, 1992.** This is the Algonquin version of the universal Cinderella story. Rough-Face Girl has two beautiful, but wicked, sisters who compete for the affections of the Invisible Being. Dramatic illustrations.

Rodanas, Kristina. *Dragonfly's Tale*. New York: Clarion, 1992. This picture book is based on a Zuni legend and reflects their concern for kindness to others and respect for the gifts of nature. Lovely illustrations.

Troughton, Joanna. *How Rabbit Stole the Fire: A North American Indian Folk Tale*, retold and illustrated. New York: Bedrick/Blackie, 1986. This is a delightful tale of the mischievous rabbit and how he brought fire to earth from the Sky People. Stories of rabbit the trickster and wonder worker are found in all areas east of the Mississippi from Hudson Bay to the Gulf of Mexico.

Ziter, Cary B. *The Moon of Falling Leaves, The Great Buffalo Hunt*. Illustrated by Gretchen Will Mayo. New York: Franklin Watts, 1988. An excellent information book that can be read aloud. Each small chapter contains many tidbits of information about the buffalo and the ways of the Indians of the Plains. It makes a fascinating story.

FOLK TALES

The Native American story is one of struggle in the shaping of the history of the United States. Native Americans referred to their territories as nations and can be grouped according to Plains, Woodlands, Desert, and Coastal Peoples. Within nations, there were many separate "tribes" that spoke their own languages, had their own customs, clothing, dwellings, and ways of survival by hunting, fishing or farming. For example, the Iroquois Indians had a Confederacy of Five Nations—Mohawk, Oneida, Onandaga, Cayuga, and Seneca in what is now known as New York, Pennsylvania, and Ohio. While the general theme of survival runs through the folk tales, the settings and wildlife are quite different.

In the tales, there is constant reference to the "chief." This is the title bestowed upon the leader by the white man. However, the Native American society was complex, and there were actually several levels of leadership. There were outstanding military leaders, outstanding peace makers, and outstanding organizers, as in any complex society. Some of the chiefs inherited their position of authority from their fathers, but earning the rank in the tribe was the main means of becoming a respected leader. Many of the folk tales deal with the daring and physical strength as well as the compassion of the leader.

The Native American folk tales from one part of the United States differ from that of another. For example, in the Southeast, Florida became the home of the Seminal Indians ("Seminal" means runaways) at the time that

African slaves were escaping from the south to Florida. At this time, Florida was not a part of the United States but was owned by Spain. The Seminoles took in the Africans and helped each other. Africans were more used to the tropical climate and brought with them the practice of rice cultivation. They moved freely among the Seminoles. Soon they had well-built homes and were raising corn, vegetables, cotton, and sweet potatoes. They also owned herds of livestock. Both the natives and the Africans brought with them their own history of stories and over the years as the Seminoles intermingled and intermarried with the Africans, they became a large black Indian population. As the groups blended, so too did the stories.

However, other tribes of this coastal area of the Five Civilized Nations (Creeks, Cherokees, Choctaws, and Chickasaws) captured runaway slaves and kept them as forced labor, so their stories would be quite different. An excellent resource book for the teacher is *Black Indians, A Hidden Heritage* by William Loren Katz (New York: Atheneum, 1986).

Because the United States is so vast, the Native Americans of the southwest have a different set of experiences from those of the southeast, which is reflected in their folklore. Their territory covered parts of California, Utah, Colorado, Arizona, New Mexico, and Texas. Their settings reflect the harsh, dry desert with challenges different from those in the swamplands of Florida. The remarkable architecture of the early Anasazi tribe, notably cliff dwellings at Mesa Verde (green table), are perhaps the most spectacular remnants of their culture. A good resource book is *The Ancient Cliff Dwellers of Mesa Verde* by Caroline Arnold, with photographs by Richard Hewett (New York: Clarion Books, 1992).

Today a large population of Hopi and Navajo Indians live on Indian reservations (land set aside for Native Americans by the U.S. government) in the southwest. The southwest has a special flavor, reflecting the influence of the Hispanic culture, and is rich in folk tales, religion, arts and crafts, homes, cultural traditions, ceremonies, and so on. A helpful Native American resource book is *From Abenaki to Zuni, A Dictionary of North American Tribes* by Evelyn Wolfson, with illustrations by William Sauts Bock (New York: Walker and Company, 1988). This dictionary gives tribal names, their meaning, location, type of dwelling, clothing, means of transportation, and food.

GENERAL STORYTELLING

The Native American culture is rich with stories that were designed to be told, not read, and so this culture is a storyteller's dream. The elders were the storytellers, although children were encouraged to act out the stories. The repetition of the stories enabled the children to learn valuable information as well as important lessons, for there was no emphasis upon written language.

Because the Native Americans were spiritual and lived close to nature, there were many rules that various tribes followed for telling tales. For example, in some tribes the stories were told from fall until spring when the spirits were sleeping, but they were never told in the summer. Other coastal tribes told stories in the winter when man's natural enemies—the water monsters—were trapped under the ice and could not hear.

Stories were told at celebrations and family gatherings. The Indians of the Northwest carved totem poles, and each one had an oral story to go along with it. The poles were thought of as the "property" of the tribe and could never be given away. Individual totem poles, also the property of a family, were taken along when the family moved, so the stories lived on with the family by being handed down from generation to generation.

TRICKSTER FIGURES

There are many mythological figures in the Native American tales. In some tribes, Raven is the powerful hero trickster figure. Raven can do good deeds or even do bad deeds, but always there is a moral lesson to be learned. Raven stole the sun, moon and stars and gave them to the Tlingit tribe, according to their belief.

The Abenake tribe's trickster figure is the Raccoon. Wolf and Coyote are powerful figures in some tales. Wolf is believed to be good because he created humans and the solar system, but Coyote is bad because he opposes wolf and brings chaos to the world. In Navajo stories, Coyote may win through his cleverness or he may be outsmarted by a weaker animal with more noble intentions. This combination makes for interesting stories where good wins out over evil.

In some tribes, Skunnywundy is the trickster hero who can change form and become another character. In Lakota tales, Iktomi the man is the trickster figure who is both clever and stupid and has much to learn.

THE PURPOSE OF THE TALES

The purpose of the tales is always to teach valuable lessons. Historically, Native Americans lived as they continue to live and tell their tales today. In societies where cooperation was essential for survival, the good of the tribe had to come before the rights of the individual. Among other lessons, the tales teach that good triumphs over evil, that if an individual becomes greedy and displeases the gods it can bring trouble for self and tribe, and that if nature is abused and not respected, you can be sure that nature will have the final word in the end. The tales instilled a "sense of belonging" since children heard them as toddlers and told them as elders.

VARIANT OF THE BEANSTALK TALE (READ ALOUD TALE)

Skymaiden gave the gift of beans and corn to man. Other tribes claimed that these gifts were brought to man by a black crow that carried a corn grain in one ear and a bean in the other ear. Here is an ancient Indian version of the beanstalk tale that can be read aloud.

"The Legend of Corn and Beans"

Cornstalk was a very tall, young man who observed the sky all day for signs of changing weather. At the day's end, when the sun went down, he was very lonely for there was no wife for him to talk to. And so, he wished upon a star for a wife, and he waited. The pumpkin maid, with her trailing vine and bright yellow flowers, was the first to come calling. But the pumpkin maid liked to wander over the ground—and the cornstalk, tired from a day of watching the sky, could not follow her for he needed to rest. So pumpkin maid crept away. That night, cornstalk wished upon another star for a wife, and he waited. A thin, lovely bean vine sprouted up from the ground. She was so delicate that she kept falling, until cornstalk reached for her hand to give her strength. As she grew, she wrapped herself around and around cornstalk and promised to love him forever. And to this very day, the bean vine twines around the cornstalk and he supports her, and together they give us food that nourishes our body.

SUGGESTED ACTIVITIES FOR THE CLASSROOM

1. STORYTELLING

Always research the possibility of initially listening to a Native American storyteller, either as a guest in the classroom or on a tape. Have a Native American storytelling festival. There are many storybooks that can be secured from the library. Students can tell the tales and then discuss the lesson(s) to be gained. An excellent picture book with a message is *Brother Eagle, Sister Sky, A Message from Chief Seattle*, with gorgeous illustrations by Susan Jeffers (New York: Dial Books, 1992).

2. DIORAMAS

Make a diorama of a scene from a favorite story. Try using only natural items. (See the art section.)

3. CREATE A SOUND STORY

Select ten items from the classroom. Have students close their eyes and listen to the sounds they make. Then have them close their eyes again and tell what *could* be making this sound in nature. Here are some suggestions.

ACTUAL SOUND	*COULD BE...*
paper tearing	leaves rustling
scissors	squawking bird
stapler	woodpecker
sand in a jar	footsteps through the woods
ping of rubber band	bow string for arrow practice

When students have their ten sounds, they can divide into groups and create their stories. Each group's story will be different. The storytelling is enjoyed as students listen for the different ways that the sounds are incorporated into the stories.

4. MAKE AN ABC BOOK OF NATIVE DWELLINGS

Compare the dwellings that are found in story illustrations. For starters, an ABC book with illustrations could include:

A – adobe houses

B – brush shelters

C – council house

D – dome-shaped roof

E – earth lodges

F – framed houses

G – grass-covered hut

H – hogan

I – island hut

J – just for men (sweat lodge)

K – kiva (underground ceremony chamber)

L – longhouse

M – mat-covered hut

N – night dwelling (when on a hunt)

O – oval-shaped house

P – pitched-roof dwelling

Q – quite large multi-family dwelling

R – rain house

S – square house

T – tipi (or tepee)

U – underground lodge

V – villages with rows of houses facing out to sea

W – witus (dome-shaped wigwams)

X – x-shaped wigwams

Y – yellow grass, woven and clay-covered hut or home

Z – zebra hide or buffalo hide covered hut

There are many others. Construct shelters from natural items after the list is compiled. A good series of books for this activity is that by Bonnie Shemie (Tundra Books), such as *Houses of Snow, Skin and Bones*; *Houses of Bark*; and others.

5. SET UP A TRADING STATION

Have students bring in items they are willing to trade. Decide how much they will ask for each item. What means of revenue will they use? (Wampum was one medium of exchange. Wampum was a string of white and blue or purple beads made from shells, with the dark beads worth twice the value of the white ones.)

For wider involvement with another "tribe," set up a trading station with another classroom. Prepare for the big event. It could be a culmination activity for this study of Native Americans.

6. LEARN NATIVE AMERICAN VOCABULARY

Get library books and learn what Native Americans called items with which students are familiar. One excellent resource is the storybook *Seya's Song* by Ron Hirschi, illustrated by Constance R. Bergum (Seattle: Sasquatch Books, 1992).

7. WRITE MESSAGES USING PICTURE SYMBOLS

There are many resources that show picture language. These can be incorporated into stories. Some familiar ones are as follows:

8. GRINDING CORN AND MAKING CAKES

Dried corn is very tough. Students can have the experience of putting some through a hand-cranked food grinder; then use a mortar and pestle, or a clean round stone to make a finer grain. Have students take turns getting the corn as fine as possible. Or, purchase dried corn and add it to a pancake recipe to make corncakes in the electric frypan.

9. GOOD MEDICINE/BAD MEDICINE

Since many of the tales show the outdoors, have students be on the look-out for plants in the picture books. Some plants and herbs are useful for healing, and some are harmful. Find out more about plants and their ability to help man. Native Americans relied heavily upon plants and parts of trees for their good medicine.

10. A STUDY OF CLOTHING

Note the variety of clothing in the folk tale illustrations and in information books about Native Americans. For example, there is bark clothing; buffalo skin robes for winter; sheepskin or antelope hide long sleeves for use in winter; clothing decorated with beads, paint or quills; woven turkey feather robes; and more. Prepare a folder for the information. Decorate the outside with material and items that look authentically Native American in character.

11. ANIMAL STUDY

How many animals are depicted in one folk tale? Find out information about the animals and print the report on paper shaped like one of the animals. Make an authentic Indian border design along the edge of the animal shape.

12. WHERE IN THE U.S.A. ARE WE?

Read a collection of tales (at least three) and find out if they take place in the southwest, northwest, central, northeast, or southeast regions of the United States. If the information is not given, what visual clues can be obtained? Note the colors—does that help? Note the terrain—is it hilly, is it coastal? Note the trees, and animals, and make an hypothesis—where *could* this setting be located?

13. VARIANTS OF THE CINDERELLA TALE

The Rough-Face Girl by Rafe Martin (see the children's books section) is said to be an Algonquin tale that is a variant of the Cinderella tale. Locate this book and read it aloud. Study the illustrations carefully. Discuss the similarities and differences between this and the more familiar Cinderella story. (See the European and Asian folk tale sections for more Cinderella activities.) What do the resolutions reveal to us about the cultural values of the people?

14. LOOKING FOR THE MOON

Native Americans had a variety of names for the full moon. Note the ways in which the moon is referred to in a variety of tales. For example, "It was the time of the moon when the salmon were running back to their home," or "The light glistened on the snow as coyote howled at the Angry Moon." In what season of the year is the story taking place? What month?

15. LOOK FOR COLORFUL LANGUAGE EXAMPLES

We can gain meaning from words without them having to be exact. Here are some examples:

> "We were three sleeps away from our home."
> "In the gentle breeze, the corn waved good-bye."
> "When ducks return to Father Sky and bring back
>   the south wind, the snow will melt."

Keep a log of different ways that ideas are communicated through verbal and nonverbal body language. Some of the verbal language sounds like poetry. Perhaps students will be encouraged to write poetry after reading many folk tales with rich, descriptive language.

An excellent storybook for this type of activity is *People of the Breaking Day*, written and illustrated by Marcia Sewall (New York: Atheneum, 1990).

CELEBRATIONS

Corn played an important part in the lives of Native Americans of the south, central, and northeastern United States. It was a staple for their diet, as well as a useful item for making items that were necessary. For example, the dried fibers were used for making clothing, mats, and baskets for storage of nuts and berries. Fibers were also used for weaving. The corn silk was used as ornamentation for masks. Corn cobs were used for making dolls.

Most North American Indians had three major corn ceremonies that included (a) a planting ceremony, (b) a harvest ceremony, and (c) a green corn ceremony.

THE GREEN CORN CEREMONY

This was held by many different tribes when the ears of the corn were nearly ripe, before the main harvest. Until the time of the green corn ceremony, it was considered a crime against the gods to eat or to touch the corn.

The Creek Indians called this ceremony a "Busk." To prepare for the Busk, new clothes and new furniture were made. Then a huge bonfire was built and all old clothes and old furniture were burned. All village fires were put out, and new fires were lit from the Busk fire.

Then, the Creek Indians feasted on green corn and venison that was seasoned with bear oil. Ball games were played by the young men, and when it grew dark they danced by the light of the fire.

HARVEST CEREMONIES

In addition to corn ceremonies, some tribes held other harvest festivals. The Salish Indians had a ceremony giving thanks for the wild raspberries. The berries were cooked and passed around a circle in a newly carved bowl.

STORYTELLING AT CELEBRATIONS

This was a favorite activity of adults. Imagine the heroic stories of the hunters and the whalers. Imagine sitting around the fire in the evening and listening to an elder tell about the time that the men were away on a hunt with only the women, small children and elders left behind, when suddenly a pack of hungry coyotes began stalking the compound.

Children were encouraged to "act out" the stories so they too could become good storytellers when they grew up.

SUGGESTED ACTIVITIES FOR THE CLASSROOM

1. LET'S PRACTICE STORYTELLING WITH PAUL GOBLE

This would be a good opportunity to do an author study. Paul Goble has written and illustrated many Native American tales about Iktomi the Trickster that are designed for audience participation. In *Iktomi and the Ducks*, the third in a series of Iktomi tales, there is bold black print and light gray print to facilitate audience participation. Secure several books by this author including *The Girl Who Loved Wild Horses* (a Caldecott Award winner) so that children can study the bold, bright, beautiful illustrations and read the text in their spare time.

Encourage students to paint bright, bold, angular paintings and designs at the easel. Practice painting stripes, angular lines, and wavy lines. Later, when the paintings are dry, students can use these colorful pages as a background for a story book. Or, sketches of animals or people can be made and cut from the colorful pages to create a class mural.

2. LET'S PRACTICE CELEBRATIONS WITH BYRD BAYLOR AND PETER PARNALL

This author/illustrator team has several excellent storybooks. The book, *I'm in Charge of Celebrations*, deals with little things that we can celebrate on a daily basis. Perhaps it is the celebration of the time when you saw a rainbow and noticed a rabbit sitting nearby watching the same sky. Or it could be the time that you looked into the eyes of an animal and it looked back. This book will encourage students to determine their own quiet celebrations. It has a lovely, powerful message—celebrations that are special do not have to cost money or require a lot of preparation.

For *Everybody Needs a Rock* students can be encouraged to bring in a rock and then find its uniqueness. What makes this rock special? The book will help. Students can do this with other natural items in their environment and begin to build an internal environmental awareness and an appreciation for nature.

3. GENERAL STORYTELLING TIPS FOR CELEBRATIONS

Students need to prepare for listening. Have them settle into a comfortable position with hands in lap. Instruct them to look at the storyteller, to open their ears, to close their mouth, and to keep their hands quiet. The leader can give nonverbal readiness hand signals by:

- touching eyes (*look at me*)
- touching mouth *close it*)
- touching ears (*listen*)
- touching hands (*fold them*)

1. Read the story aloud and enjoy the colorful illustrations. Then, divide the story into several components. Everyone will be able to identify the beginning and ending. Now, break the story down into important episodes. Have different students be responsible for telling one part of the story. There may be 5 to 7 students telling one story.

2. Students may make illustrations for the story and show them one at a time while the storyteller is speaking.

3. Make puppets to enhance the storytelling dialogue. Select the ones that would be especially appropriate.

4. Storytellers can make masks to use while telling the story.

5. Determine the sound effects that would enrich the story and use them.

6. Record the stories on videotape or on a cassette recording for continued pleasure.

7. Have a storytelling festival and share the stories with another class.

8. Pair students from upper grades with younger students for storytelling assistance.

9. Remember to show respect for the storytellers—listen quietly.

10. Story discussion can follow. Native American tales taught a lesson. What did students learn?

The Karok Indians of California held a ceremony each year when the salmon began to run, and asked the gods to grant them good fishing.

4. POTLATCH CELEBRATIONS

In order to understand this celebration, one must be aware of the thought behind it. Native Americans believed that the land, animals, and forests did not "belong" to them. These things were theirs to use wisely and to share. This sharing was accomplished during the time of the potlatch celebration, which could be held yearly.

The potlatch was a major celebration of the Indians of the Northwest. The chief of one tribe would announce that there was to be a potlatch celebration, and another tribe or tribes would be invited. The celebration was lavish and included much feasting, dancing, game playing, and storytelling. Some tribes saved this special celebration as a time to perform their weddings, or to name their babies.

The celebration could last for two or three days or even a month. When it was time to depart, the guests were given the "wealth" of the host tribe. This could include their finest masks, hides, skins, carvings, jewelry, tools, woven items, and so on. In this way, another tribe could enjoy it for awhile. AND, it was designed to motivate the guest tribe to go out and multiply the bounty (work harder to make more beautiful masks, tools, clothing, etc.) so that when it came their turn to have the potlatch and give back these belongings, the potlatch would be greater than the one before. The idea behind this was that everyone got to share the wealth of the land—but not to own it.

It is possible that the term "Indian Giver," used as a derogatory term, was derived from this custom of "giving in order to share, but not to own." By this redistribution of wealth, tribal clashes over the wealth were avoided.

5. A HARVEST FESTIVAL

Set up a table in the classroom and make arrangements to get a variety of squash (Hubbard, acorn, butternut), pumpkins, Indian corn, and other vegetables with wax coatings. Students can turn this into a science area by examining the vegetables and classifying them by shape, color, size, etc. Slice them, and have students examine the insides under a magnifying glass and a microscope. They can make diagrams of what they see. Wash and dry the seeds, and use them as counters in math. Peel and cook some of the vegetables in a crock pot (add water) on "high" for a vegetable treat. Serve with margarine and a sprinkling of brown sugar. This is a good autumn activity to coincide with the Thanksgiving Celebration.

6. CELEBRATE THE LEADERS—CREATE A NEWSPAPER

One great leader, Sequoyah, became the only person in the world to invent a practical alphabet all by himself. Thousands of Cherokees learned to read and write within months after his alphabet was introduced. For this he received a medal from the Cherokee Nation. Then, Sequoyah founded a newspaper, "The Cherokee Phoenix," that was printed in both English and in Cherokee. A statue of Sequoyah stands in the capitol of Washington, D.C., and the giant redwood tree of California was named the "Sequoia" in his honor.

Students can work in teams to create a newspaper with the information about Native Americans that they have learned—folk tales, arts and crafts, celebrations, famous people, and so on. Print the newspaper on 8-1/2″ x 11″ paper, so that multiple copies can be made and each student will have a record.

7. CELEBRATE YOUR ELDERS, AND BECOME ONE

Native Americans hold older members of their tribe or clan in great respect because of their wisdom. Encourage a discussion of respect for elders in our society. Ask students to think about themselves as "elders." What can they do to help a young child? Team students from another grade level so that they have an opportunity to become a "reading elder," a "math elder," a "folk tale elder," and so on.

8. SEND FOR INFORMATION

Locate the "Four Corners" region on a map of the United States in the southwest. Arizona, New Mexico, Colorado, and Utah make up this area. There are many Indian reservations here. Students can select a variety of cities; write to the Chamber of Commerce of each city for tourist information, and in that way learn about many of the festivals and celebrations held throughout the year. (ZIP Codes can be obtained from the local post office.)

ARTS AND CRAFTS

Art is an important component of everyday living because Native Americans are very much in tune with nature. They are aware of the many colors of blue in the sky, and the type of weather that can be predicted from each. The color of the plants and grasses, tree leaves, flowers, and berries are a part of the "visual vocabulary" of the tribes.

Berries are not only eaten, but are used for art work. They can be crushed and mixed with water for dye and for paint. Also, the colors of the earth are mixed with water for a rich array of browns (red brown, yellow brown, orange brown, dark brown, or black) that the people use for painting decorations on tepees, totem poles, masks, shields, pottery, and for face and body painting.

Parts of animals, such as teeth and bones, were decorated and worn around the neck, wrist, waist, legs, ankles, and in the hair of the early Native Americans. Tiny stones were polished and held together with plant fiber strands or animal hair to make strings of necklaces. In some tribes, the number of necklaces worn by the women signified the wealth of the tribe.

Shells from rivers and the sea can be sewn on clothing and used in jewelry. Bird feathers and seed pods are also used for clothing and body decorations.

TYPES OF ART

Weaving is practiced by many tribes in order to make clothing, blankets, mats, and baskets for holding supplies. The weavings are adorned with designs, symbols, or images of plants and animals from nature to make them attractive. The Native Americans like color and designs and most tribes do not leave items plain. They are decorated because it makes them more pleasing to the eye.

Shaping or coiling pottery made from clay has become a fine art in many tribes. Some of the simple pottery that is hastily put together for daily use and that is not intended to last, might not be decorated. For the most part, however, the pottery is decorated with many designs of flowers and birds and various patterning techniques, such as the Mimbres feather design, among others.

Today, the Native Americans of the southwest are producers of pottery. Figurines are a popular product of New Mexico's Cochiti Pueblo, and the famous "Storyteller" figure is one that was created by Helen Cordero in 1964. The model, Cordero's grandfather, sits with small figures of children clinging to his arms, legs, and back. Today many potters make the storyteller figure. (*National Geographic*, November 1982, Vol. 162, No. 5.) Three major southwest cultures—the Hohokam, the Mogollon, and the Anasazi—left a rich legacy of pottery in the Four Corners area of the United States (Arizona, New Mexico, Colorado, and Utah). Much of this pottery, including the Santa Clara blackware and the Hopi polychromes, looks very much the way it did when it was made over 800 years ago. There are 18 northern pueblos in New Mexico alone, and each has its own distinctive pottery. Potters in other areas of the United States are still at work also.

ARTIFACTS

The objects that any culture creates are called "artifacts." These artifacts reflect the skill of the culture and the thoughts of the people. From the richness of the Native American artifacts, both ancient and present day, we find sophisticated skills as yet unequaled in many other parts of the world, and a variety of patterns that command admiration and aesthetic appreciation.

SUGGESTED ACTIVITIES FOR THE CLASSROOM

1. LET'S STUDY THE ARTIFACTS

Arrange a visit to a local museum or historical society. One objective can be to note the varieties of designs on the artifacts. The students can take along a sketch pad and pencil to record the designs, if this is deemed advisable. Save these designs for later use back in the classroom.

Or, obtain information books about Native American crafts that have many visual representations. Study these books for designs, and have individuals or groups record specific information in a sketch pad. For starters, look for the following:

pottery-making techniques
specific pottery designs of different tribes
basket-making techniques
basket designs
weaving of mats, clothing, bags,
weaving designs of different tribes
beadwork
carving
skinwork
bark items
shell art
mask art
jewelry
tools

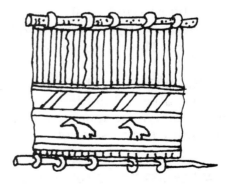

Obtain storybooks about Native Americans to note how the illustrator uses line, color, and design to help tell the story. Also, check the illustrations for artifacts (weavings, pottery, clothing, jewelry, totem poles, rugs, and so on). By now, each sketch pad should have a variety of representations.

2. A WEAVING EXPERIENCE

Here are directions for a beginning weaving experience.

1. Arrange to make individual cardboard looms so that each student can have one. Obtain cardboard at a local grocery store from boxes that have been cut. The looms do not have to be the same size.
2. Cut one-inch slits along the top and bottom of the loom.
3. Dress the loom with string or twine by starting in the upper left corner. Use the following pattern:

> Down, Under, Up, Under
>
> Down, Under, Up, Under

The front and back of the loom will look like this:

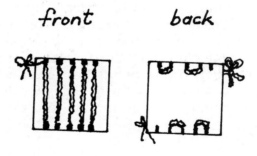

4. Select the yarn colors for the weaving. Weave in the over/under pattern. Start at the bottom and weave to the top. Use a cardboard comb to press down on each row of weaving as it is completed. This keeps the weaving tight.
5. Remove the weaving and hang it on a stick. Add yarn fringe to the bottom. Have an art display of the weaving for all to admire and enjoy.

Note: Once students have begun to weave, many like to continue. After they are able to handle the loom experience, go to a craft store and secure interesting yarns made from horsehair, crinkly wool, or puffy yarns made with many strands of cotton.

3. WEAVING WITH NATURAL ITEMS

Follow the preceding weaving instructions, only this time have students weave dried grasses, dried plant fibers, dried plant stems, dried herbs and flowers, and so on into the weaving. These weavings can be true works of art.

Hang each of them from a stick in your classroom gallery.

4. MAKE A CLASS TOTEM POLE

Totem poles were carved from trees by Native Americans of the Northwest. The carved figures consist of animals such as the bear, beaver, walrus, whale, frog, and the raven figure. The poles tell a story or a sequence of stories. Each figure represents a different tale. Secure information and picture books about totem poles in an effort to study them. The very early poles were tri-colored. They were painted with red and black with some of the natural tan wood showing through. Later, poles were painted with bright colors.

1. First, secure cylinder containers from an ice cream or yogurt store. Wash them and pile them one on top of the other so that students get the idea that this is going to be impressive in size.

2. Students can divide into groups, with each group working together on one cylinder. Or, you may decide to have more than one totem pole if each student is to work on an individual cylinder. A hot glue gun can be used to attach one cylinder to the next. (A hot glue gun should only be used by an adult.)

3. Use a variety of mailing tubes, cardboard, cardboard cylinders from paper toweling, and posterboard to make carved appendages. Then designs can be painted on.

4. When poles are completed, carefully glue them one on top of the other, using a hot glue gun. The poles may be anchored against a wall, using twine for added support.

5. Dim the lights and gather around the poles, so students may each tell their story. It can be an actual Indian legend or a folk tale that they read, or it can be a report of a particular tribe. This is a time of great enjoyment.

6. Smaller individual poles can be made from circular boxes of different heights. Plastic or clay features can be added to each segment. Set up a village on a countertop, using information about the community that students have learned from listening to stories and observing pictures.

5. HIDE PAINTINGS WITH PLANT STALK BRUSHES

To simulate skin, or hide, get large brown paper bags from the grocery store. Hides were used to make tepees, clothing, bags, pouches, and so on.

1. Cut the bag so that you have two pieces (large sides).
2. Gently tear the four edges for a rough, uneven look.

3. Cover with a very thin layer of vegetable oil, remove the excess with paper towel, and let the oil soak in and dry.

4. Gently crumple this paper and then smooth it out again for an aged look.

5. Use chalk to lightly copy a design or picture onto the "hide."

6. Use plant stalks as brushes to dip into earth-tone tempera paint and decorate the hide with symbols, designs, or paintings of animals, flowers, people.

7. Set up a clothesline art gallery display of the hide paintings.

6. MAKE A POTTERY VESSEL

Many tribes began to use tightly woven containers or birchbark containers instead of pottery, which was easily broken. But the ever popular pottery is still made by many tribes today in the United States. The two main ways of making a pot by hand are by coiling or molding the clay. For *coiling*, make snake-like shapes of clay and keep coiling them (stacking) around a clay bottom. For *molding* a pinch pot, use a ball of clay and put the thumb into the middle and keep pinching the clay and molding the bowl until the desired thickness and shape is attained.

An excellent story to assist with clay is Bryd Baylor's *When Clay Sings*, illustrated by Tom Bahti (New York: Macmillan, 1987. This Caldecott Award winning book uses designs derived from prehistoric Indian pottery of the Southwest, and is a good introduction to pottery.

The procedure for using clay is as follows:

1. Obtain potters clay (and fire in kiln) or use Plasticine.

2. Each student can learn to use both the coil method and the pinch-and-mold method.

3. When the bowl is shaped there are several ways to add designs:

    a. Paint a design on it using a stick or feather dipped in thick tempera paint.

    b. *Negative design*: using a toothpick, draw in the design and then paint only the background

    c. *Incising*: use a stick to add repetitive designs

    d. *Impressing*: make a design by pressing an item (for example, seashell, wire net) repeatedly against the pot

4. Make a showcase display of these artifacts with labels and a description of the technique used on each pot.

7. DESIGN A NATIVE AMERICAN MASK

The mask was used in ceremonies to cover the face or to be worn on top of the head. Get information books about Native American masks; many of these books include colorful examples.

Students can create a mask using only natural items they find outdoors in their area.

8. CREATE A DOLL

Native American boys and girls played with dolls that were made from natural items. Each student can create a doll that represents a storybook character or a real person. They might use corn cobs, corn husks, dry gourds, vegetables, plant stems and stalks, pods, plant fibers, shells, sticks, and so on.

To assist in their doll construction, students may use glue and string, because Native Americans do. At one time, they made glue from animal hoofs and used twine made of animal hair.

9. GETTING TO KNOW A BASKET

Ask parents to loan a basket to your classroom so that students may carefully examine the way it was made. Hopefully, you will have a wide array of baskets contributed. Students see baskets every day but do not take the time to "know" a basket. Have them study the weave, shape, and basic construction of the baskets. Secure library information books on the art of basketry. Then, encourage students to construct a basket using grapevines, raffia, reeds, tender young willow, or other natural items. Hopefully from this experience, they will gain a greater appreciation for baskets and the skill that it takes to make one. Baskets are one of the oldest art forms.

GAMES

Native Americans of all ages enjoy playing games. Children of long ago played with items found in nature, e.g., sticks and stones, shells, bones, and so on. Native Americans particularly enjoyed ball games, and made balls from a variety of natural items. They constructed balls by rolling dried grasses together and then reinforcing these by encasing each of the balls in a plant leaf that could be secured at the ends, or in a piece of rope-like netting. Other methods of making a ball included rolling cloth strips or animal hide strips into a sphere. The bladders of sea or land animals were often inflated, either with grasses or water, and encased in a netting to make a ball. Round stones, pebbles, corn cobs, and pine cones were often used for tossing games.

Balls were kicked, thrown, bounded off the head, or hit with the hand or with a stick. Games like lacrosse and soccer were favorites. Games that required running, speed, the ability to dodge, and skill in hitting a target were not only enjoyed but were useful learning experiences for the time when youngsters would eventually become hunters.

Boys and girls often played together until about the age of six. At that time they were usually separated because the boys were being trained for the time when they would need skill and bravery as hunters, so from this point on their play became more rough. Girls, on the other hand, continued to play closer to the campsite and to weave and shape items with their hands. As young children, Native Americans learned through their play—and they played all day. Play was a preparation for adulthood roles—and that time was just around the corner, officially arriving when each child turned thirteen.

Children's games can be divided into such categories as imitating games (during which every-day customs and ceremonial customs are imitated); skill games (which emphasize matching wits, or strength, or speed); and hunting games (which help develop keen observation and listening skills).

HIT THE TREE

(a game of marksmanship skill; 2 or more players)

Materials:	tree, tennis ball
Procedure:	Stand 5 to 10 feet away and aim for the tree, trying to hit it. When you do, score a point.
Variation:	Tie a bright colored piece of yarn or cloth around the tree trunk about 2 feet up from the bottom, and tie another about 15 inches above that. Then, the ball must not only hit the tree but it must land within the designated area.

ANIMAL TRACKS

(a game of observation; 2 or more players, or teams)

Materials:	Cut-outs of animal tracks
Procedure:	First, identify the animal track cut-outs. Next, the leader can lay the cut-outs outdoors on the playground (or indoors in the classroom). Then, the "hunters" very quietly go looking for game, being careful not to give away the location to the other players. The first player or team to correctly identify the location sites gets one point for each. If the animal can also be identified, the player(s) get two points.

KNOTS ON A ROPE

(a guessing game; 2 players per team)

Materials:	15-inch length of thick yarn or rope
Procedure:	Two players sit opposite each other, with approximately 6 feet between them. One has the rope, the other is the guess-

er. When the guesser says "Go," the player with the rope puts it behind his or her back and makes from one to four knots, trying to outwit the other player by elaborate motions and body language. When finished, the roper lays the rope down behind his or her body, brings hands forward, and folds his or her arms. The guesser then makes an estimate from "one" to "four." The roper shows the rope for verification. If the person did not guess correctly, the roper unknots the rope and at the sound of "Go" begins again.

Interesting Note: The Native Americans did not believe in probability and chance, but rather that the spirit world was in charge of an individual's run of good or bad luck. If someone was not a good guesser, perhaps they needed to mend their ways in other areas of their life. Children did this and for good measure they left "gifts" for the spirits, such as a bit of food under a rock, or prized pebbles buried in a hole, in hopes that they would receive help from the spirit world and show improvement.

THE ANCIENT INDIAN BEAN GAME

Note: Although this may seem to be a game of chance and probability, Native Americans did not believe in these concepts. They believed that luck was a reward for good or bad behavior.

Materials: 10 white beans, 10 black beans, a container, and a yellow bean for each player (can use dried beans, peas, lentils)

Procedure: Players decide whether they are black bean or white bean. First player places three beans inside the container (one black, one white, and his or her yellow bean). First player shakes the container and tosses the beans onto the ground. If the yellow bean is closest to the white bean, the white bean player wins the toss and makes a new pile of white beans. If the yellow bean is closest to the black bean, the black bean player wins the toss. Second player now has a turn. The first player to win all of his or her beans is the winner.

PINE CONE TOSS

(a game of skill; 2 or more players)

Materials: Pine cones and a circle (hula-hoop size) made from natural materials, such as grasses intertwined

Procedure: Each player stands a designated distance from the circle and has a chance to throw three pine cones into the ring. A point is scored for each one that lands inside.

Note: Some Native Americans used dried corn cobs for this game. Wash and dry corn cob thoroughly and then set out in the sun to get crispy.

LITTLE STONE GAME

Materials: 12 small stones, paint, deep basket (an inexpensive one that can be painted with Native American designs)

Procedure: Paint a round sun on four stones, paint a red flower on four stones, paint a blue bird on four stones. Allow to dry. Then place all stones in the basket. One by one, each of 2 to 3 players removes a stone (without looking) and lines them up in front of him- or herself. When all stones are removed, the one with the most stones that are alike is the winner. Repeat.

Resources

Baldwin, Gordon C. *Games of the American Indian*. New York: W. W. Norton & Co., Inc., 1969.

Macfarlan, Allan and Paulette. *Handbook of American Indian Games*. New York: Dover Publications, Inc., 1958.

Silverstein, Alvin and Virginia. *Beans, All About Them*. Illustrated by Shirley Chan. Englewood Cliffs, NJ: Prentice Hall, 1975.

SONGS, DANCES, RHYTHMS

As with all people, songs were extremely important to Indians. Many Native American songs use few words. The ideas expressed are brief. There is a definite rhythm to the words, usually accompanied by the beating of a drum. Other accompaniments were provided by rattles made from seeds placed within dried gourds. In some tribes, "sound makers" were laced around the lower leg and wrists. These could be made from seeds or bone, and the body movements provided the rhythmic beat.

Some of the songs deal with nature, and many are based upon experiences that the tribe has gone through. There is a poetic quality to the message—sometimes it is like a chant. Native Americans are apt to fill in the songs with sounds such as "hi ya ya ya" or "ho ho se ho." This is similar to the way we might add "tra la la la" or "yeah, yeah, yeah" to our music today.

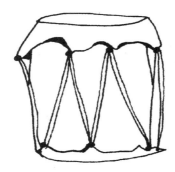

ZUNI LULLABY, NEW MEXICO

(accompany by drum beat; use slow, rocking motion)

Go to sleep, my little baby,
While I do work.
Father will bring in the sheep soon.

Go to sleep, my little beetle.
Go to sleep, my little one,
My little jackrabbit.

DREAM SONG OF A SIOUX, SOUTH DAKOTA

(accompany by a drum beat)

When I was but a child
I dreamed a wondrous dream.
I went upon a mountain;
There I fell asleep.
I heard a voice say,
"Now I will appear to you."
A buffalo said this to me, dreaming.
When I was but a child
I dreamed this wondrous dream.

CORN PLANTING SONGS, DANCES, AND RHYTHMS

The time for the planting of corn was a very special time in the life of the Native American. The time, weather, and light had to be just right so that a bountiful harvest could be assured. Note the poetic quality to some of the verses.

Yellow butterflies,
Over the blossoming virgin corn,
With pollen painted faces
Chase one another in brilliant throng.

Blue butterflies,
Over the blossoming virgin beans,
With pollen painted faces
Chase one another in brilliant streams.

A SIOUX SONG FOR THE RETURN OF THE BUFFALO

The whole world is coming
A Nation is coming, a Nation is coming.
The Eagle has brought the message to the tribe,
The Father says so, the Father says so.
Over the whole earth they are coming,
The Buffalo are coming, the Buffalo are coming.
The Crow has brought the message to the tribe,
The Father says so, the Father says so.

Resources

Goble, Paul. *The Gift of the Sacred Dog.* New York: Bradbury Press, 1980.

Hofmann, Charles. *American Indians Sing.* New York: The John Day Company, 1967.

SUGGESTED ACTIVITIES FOR THE CLASSROOM

1. LANGUAGE DEVELOPMENT

Encourage children to put their experiences into words. Then write them down and memorize them as a story to tell, or a chant to sing for the listeners.

2. MUSIC AND CHANTS

Have children use a drum, rattle, and bells to accompany chants. Perhaps most students today could use poetry as a starting point. Read from the poetry book *Hailstones and Hailibut Bones* by Mary O'Neill, and decide together how to accompany the rhythm of the words.

3. LET'S MAKE INSTRUMENTS

Make musical instruments from items from nature—twigs, stones, reeds, dried grasses for lacing, seeds, gourds, and so on.

4. FOLK MUSIC

Contact the Music Department of a local college, and ask the music professor for information pertaining to Indian folk music. Perhaps recordings are available from college libraries or from the local community library.

5. THE IMPORTANCE OF THE HORSE

The horse was introduced to the Indians by the Spaniards, and it was extremely important to them. The horse made life easier. The Indians were in awe of the horse for it could be tamed. It could pull loads heavier than loads pulled by dogs. And a horse was fleet of foot and could be ridden for great distances. Native Americans had different names for the marvelous horse, such as Big Dog, Elk Dog, Mysterious Dog. This is a good opportunity to study "The Horse"—as a mammal, as a creature that made life easier, as a companion on trips.

Compose a chant or a song to honor the horse, and accompany it by a dance that consists of prancing movements representative of a horse.

FOOD

Native Americans of North, Central, and South America had a variety in their diet that was largely dependent upon the area where they lived. The coastal natives had an abundance of fresh fish, whereas those who lived inland hunted animals for food. Berries that grew naturally were used for food. In southern areas, fruits were abundant. Food was either cooked over an open fire or eaten raw, and it was often stored in areas dug out beneath the earth in an effort to keep it cool and to keep it from spoiling.

This section is representative of some of the raw materials that the natives selected for food, mainly corn and beans. Corn especially was considered a gift from the heavens, and the gods warmed it with the sun and watered it with rain.

SUGGESTED RECIPES FOR THE CLASSROOM

SWEET POTATOES

Sweet potatoes were a popular Native American vegetable for tribes that lived in the southern area of the United States. Sweet potatoes are the vines of the "Ipomoea Batatas," a member of the morning glory family. Natives from South America mixed the reddest sweet potatoes with lime juice to make a dye for clothing and painting, but they are also tasty and good to eat.

Mashed Sweet Potatoes

6 medium-sized sweet potatoes
water

Wash the potatoes. Place in a heavy pan, cover with hot water, and boil gently until potatoes are tender. (Approximately 30 minutes.) Drain and peel. Mash until potatoes are smooth and fluffy. Can be eaten as is, or seasoned with butter and honey, or 1/2 teaspoon ground cinnamon. Sprinkle with walnuts.

PUMPKINS

The Native Americans in the central and northeast sections of the United States had many uses for pumpkins. In addition to cooking and eating the pumpkin, they dried the seeds and ate them as a cereal, or ground them up and baked the mixture into cakes.

Roasted Pumpkin Seeds

1 medium-sized pumpkin
1-1/2 tablespoons butter

Preheat oven to 250 degrees. Clean all of the fiber from the pumpkin seeds and rinse. For each 2 cups of seeds, melt 1-1/2 tablespoons of butter and stir until seeds are coated. Bake, stirring occasionally, until seeds are crisp and brown (about 15 minutes).

CORN

To many Native Americans of the south, the northeast, and the plains, corn was the staff of life. It was a staple of the diet and was the "bread of the Indians." When Christopher Columbus landed on the American shore, he noted that the natives were cultivating a wonderful plant they called "mahiz." This was translated to "maiz" by the Spaniards and today is referred to as "maize." Columbus took this plant back to Europe and its cultivation spread from there to Africa, India, and China.

Griddle Cakes

2 cups Indian meal (cornmeal)
1 tablespoon dark molasses
1 cup flour
1 teaspoon baking soda
enough sour milk to make a stiff batter (to make sour milk, add one teaspoon of vinegar to one cup of milk)
butter and maple syrup
bacon grease

Mix the dry ingredients, and add molasses. Add sour milk and mix until batter is stiff. Drop by spoonfuls onto a hot griddle (or electric frypan) greased with bacon. Serve with butter and maple syrup.

Yesterday's Popcorn

Native Americans had several different ways of popping corn. Sometimes they threw the kernels from the cob directly into the flames and the kernels popped out in all directions. The children chased and gathered them. They also filled clay pots with hot sand, added the corn, and stirred. As the corn popped, it flew to the top of the pot and was set aside. The popcorn was eaten plain, as breakfast cereal, or sometimes added to soup. The popcorn contributed to the Pilgrims' Thanksgiving feast was sweetened with the sap of the sugar maple tree.

Today's Popcorn

Today, popcorn can be made in a microwave oven, popped in a pan on the stove, or in a modern popcorn popper. Have children make popcorn in an air popper, and lightly butter and salt it.

Be sure to save some popcorn for a breakfast cereal treat, or for a mid-morning snack sprinkled on a cup of warm cream of corn soup.

BEANS

Beans, corn, and squash are referred to as the "three sisters." These were the staples of many tribes, and were eaten along with meat (bear, deer), berries, or fish, depending upon where the people lived. (See the folk tale section for a story about the corn and beans.)

Iroquois Succotash*

3 cups lima beans (frozen)
3 cups fresh corn kernels (or frozen)
6 tablespoons butter, melted
4 tablespoons cream
water

Place frozen beans in boiling water and cook according to directions on package. Drain. Bring 4 tablespoons of water to a boil. Add fresh corn. Simmer until tender. Drain. Add melted butter and cream. Stir.

Corn Bread (Spoonbread)

1/2 cup corn
1 cup yellow cornmeal
2 eggs, slightly beaten
1/2 teaspoon baking soda
1 teaspoon salt
3/4 cup milk
1/2 cup melted butter
3/4 cup grated sharp Cheddar cheese
2 tablespoons butter

Combine corn, cornmeal, eggs, salt, baking soda, milk, butter, and half the cheese. Then melt 2 tablespoons butter in a casserole dish. Pour the corn batter into the dish and cover with the remaining cheese. Bake in a hot oven at 400 degrees for 40 minutes. While hot, spoon onto plates.

---

*This is an updated version. The original version suggests that the cook "cut corn kernels off the cob with a deer's jaw." Often bear meat was added for this dish. *Resource:* Lucille Recht Penner, *The Thanksgiving Book* (New York: Hastings House, 1986).

Green Beans with Almonds

2 pounds green beans
2 tablespoons butter
slivered almonds
water

Cook green beans in boiling, salted water until tender. Melt 2 tablespoons butter in electric frypan, and add beans and toss. Sprinkle with slivered almonds. Serve warm.

SNOW CONES

Native American children scooped up snow with a piece of bark and sucked the white ice. In the northeastern part of the United States, maple syrup was poured over the ice. The bark was not eaten.

Modern-Day Snow Cones

1 cone per person
1 scoop vanilla ice cream or frozen yogurt
1 dab of maple syrup

SMOKED SALMON AND OTHER FISH

Enjoy a seafood tasting party "hosted" by the Indians of the Northwest (called a potlatch, and explained in the celebrations section) and try to include smoked salmon. Salmon, halibut, and shrimp were abundant in the diet of these Native Americans. The fish was eaten fresh, smoked, and dried. Today, we can enjoy canned, dried, or frozen fish. Serve sardines on crackers, or visit the frozen food section of the supermarket for a variety of seafood for the tasting party. Use fish-shaped crackers or oyster crackers along with the treat.

Tuna on Toast

canned tuna
chopped onions
mayonnaise (low calorie)
toast (cut in diagonals)

Mix tuna, onions, and mayonnaise to form a spread. Spread on toasted bread, cut diagonally. Eat as is, or warm in toaster oven.

CRANBERRIES AND BLUEBERRIES

Cranberries are a favorite food of cranes (birds), and our English word "cranberry" is a translation from the German "kraanbere," which means "crane berry." Native Americans used these wild, bitter berries for food, medicine, and as a beautiful red dye. The berries were pounded and shaped into cakes, dried in the sun, and eaten. Sometimes they were saved and later used in soups. They were also pounded and added to water for a refreshing drink. The berries are a rich source of vitamin C.

Fresh Cranberry Juice

2 pounds cranberries
1 cup sugar
water
pan, fork, strainer, cups

Wash the berries and discard any blemished ones. Place them in a pan and add enough water to cover. Bring to a boil, reduce heat, cover, and simmer until berries are soft or have popped (about 10 minutes). Mash with a fork and then strain (save the juice). Add sugar to berry mash, and stir. Add the juice. Simmer for about 15 minutes, then cool. Add water to taste. Strain. (The mixture is strong, so it can be watered down further so that everyone may have a taste.)

Cranberry-Nut Muffins

3/4 cup chopped, fresh cranberries
1/8 cup sugar
1-1/2 cups flour
1/2 cup sugar
2-1/2 teaspoons baking powder
1/4 teaspoon salt
1/4 cup shortening
1/2 cup chopped nuts (pecans, walnuts)
1 teaspoon grated lemon rind
1 egg
1/2 cup milk
mixing bowls, fork, spoon, muffin tin

Combine cranberries and 1/8 cup sugar, and set aside. Combine the remaining dry ingredients. Cut in shortening. Add nuts and lemon rind. Beat egg and milk, add to mixture, and stir. Gently stir in cranberry mixture. Pour into greased muffin tins and bake at 400 degrees for approximately 20 minutes. (Makes over 1 dozen muffins.)

Fresh Blueberry Sauce

2 cups fresh blueberries
1/3 cup sugar
1 tablespoon lemon juice
1/4 teaspoon salt
1/2 teaspoon vanilla extract

Wash blueberries and crush them in a pan. Add sugar, lemon juice, and salt. Bring to a boil. Boil for 1 minute; then remove from heat and cool. Add vanilla extract and chill. Serve over ice cream, waffles, or pancakes.

Blueberries and Bread Treat

4 cups diced bread
3 tablespoons butter
4 cups fresh blueberries
1/2 cup milk
1/2 cup sugar

Place diced bread and butter in fry-pan and brown. Crush blueberries in a bowl. Add bread and sugar to berries and mix together. Stir in milk. Then spoon into individual dishes and chill. (*Optional:* Serve with whipped cream.)

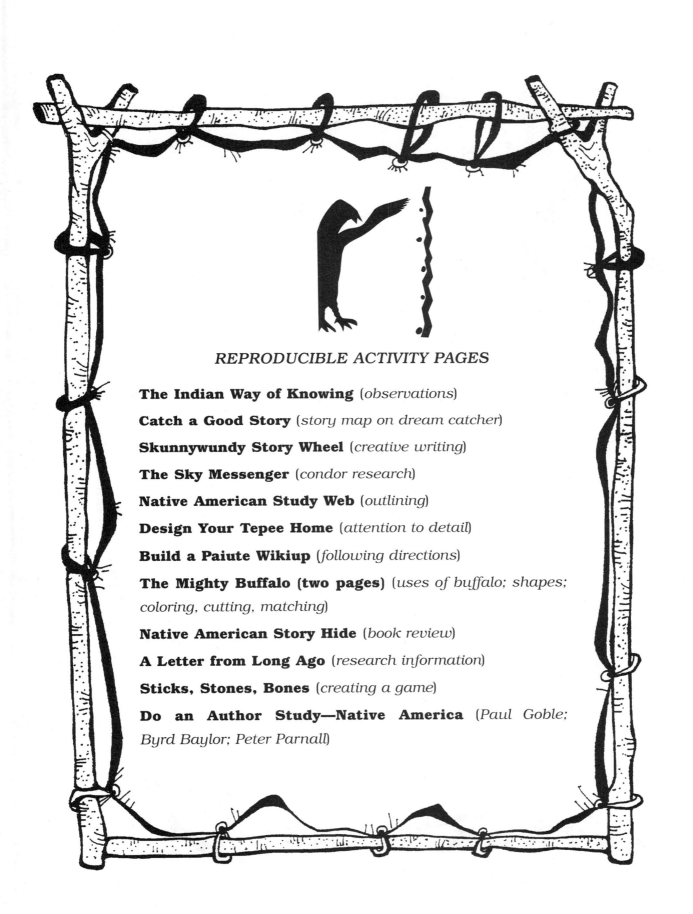

REPRODUCIBLE ACTIVITY PAGES

The Indian Way of Knowing (*observations*)

Catch a Good Story (*story map on dream catcher*)

Skunnywundy Story Wheel (*creative writing*)

The Sky Messenger (*condor research*)

Native American Study Web (*outlining*)

Design Your Tepee Home (*attention to detail*)

Build a Paiute Wikiup (*following directions*)

The Mighty Buffalo (two pages) (*uses of buffalo; shapes; coloring, cutting, matching*)

Native American Story Hide (*book review*)

A Letter from Long Ago (*research information*)

Sticks, Stones, Bones (*creating a game*)

Do an Author Study—Native America (*Paul Goble; Byrd Baylor; Peter Parnall*)

THE INDIAN WAY OF KNOWING

Native Americans observe nature from the time they are babies, and they are at peace with nature. You, too, can study nature. Observe the sky for three days. Describe it, draw it, and get to know it.

Describe sky.   Draw sky.   Learn to know sky.

Observe the sky for 3 days.

1.

2.

3.

What else can you observe?

Name _____ Date _____

CATCH A GOOD STORY

Native Americans use "dream catchers" made from hoops, string, feathers, and beads to catch good thoughts while they are sleeping. Use the dream catcher below to catch a good story. Show the main parts of the story in the five sections. Use this to help you retell the story to classmates.

Make a real dream catcher.

SKUNNYWUNDY STORY WHEEL

Skunnywundy and Raven are two trickster figures in Native American folk tales. They can change their appearance, so you have to be alert. We always learn a lesson from them.

Make a spinner for your wheel. Spin to select (1) main character, (2) other characters, (3) setting, and (4) the problem that teaches us a lesson. Write your tale. Tell your tale. Use the wheel to tell two more stories.

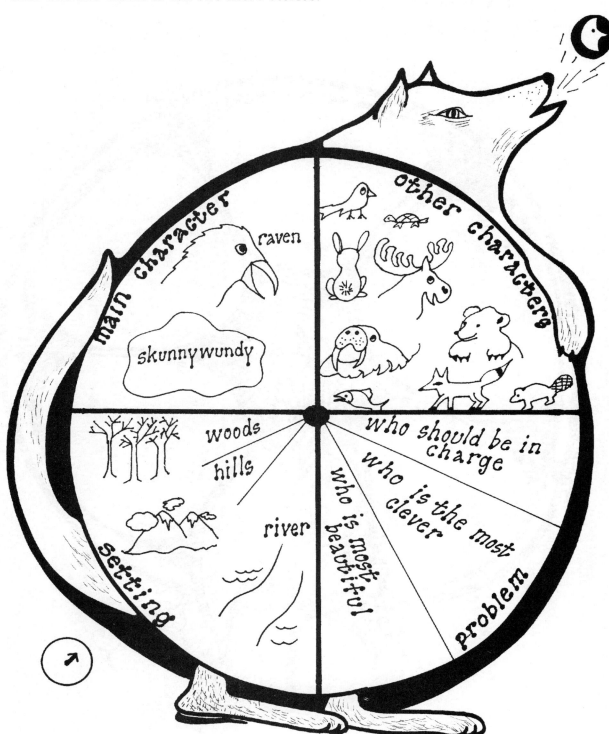

Name _____ Date _____

THE SKY MESSENGER

Some Native Americans believed that this bird took messages to heaven and back on its mighty wings. They also appreciated the clean-up work that this bird does in the environment. Today it's on the Endangered Species List. Look up information about the bird. Print your report directly on the condor.

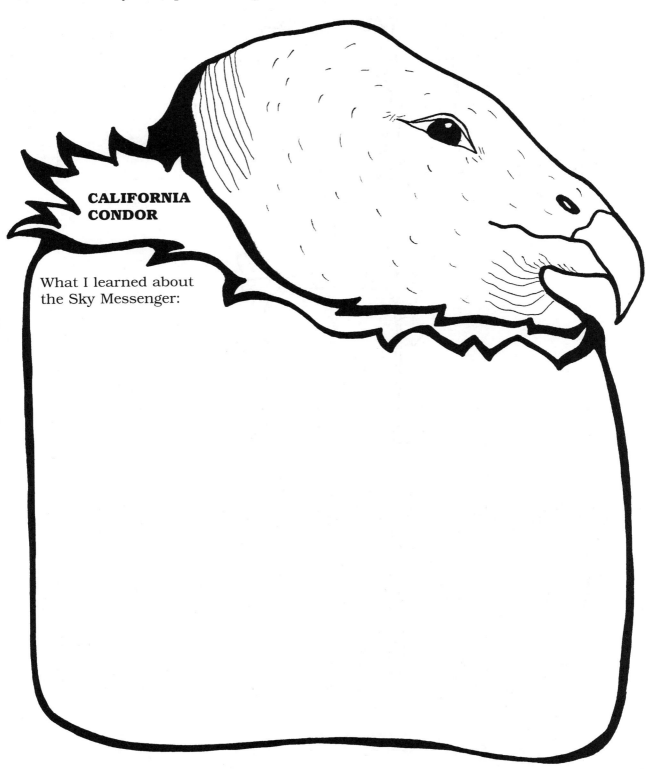

CALIFORNIA CONDOR

What I learned about the Sky Messenger:

Name _____ Date _____

NATIVE AMERICAN STUDY WEB

Use this guide to jot down notes or to make small diagrams as you read or listen to stories. Make a folder, and use separate sheets of paper for detailed information.

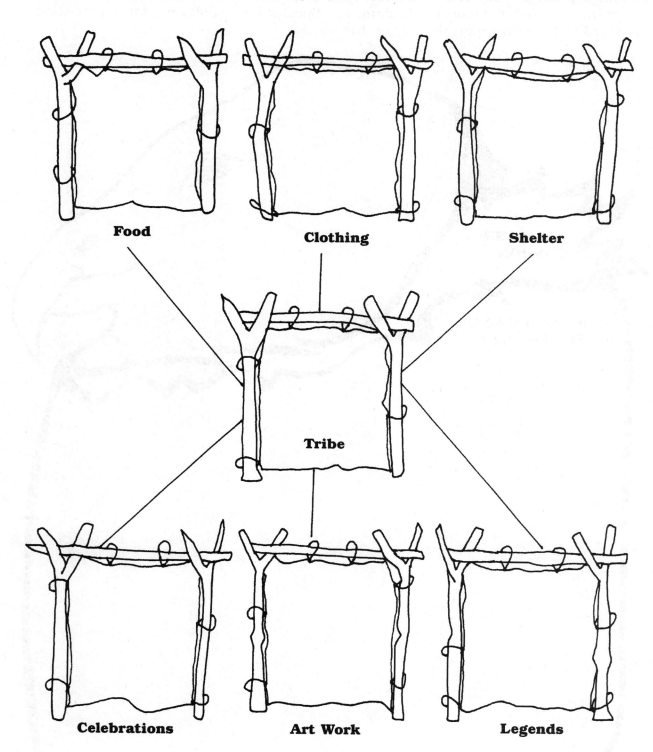

Food

Clothing

Shelter

Tribe

Celebrations

Art Work

Legends

Name _____   Date _____

DESIGN YOUR TEPEE HOME

Some Indian tribes lived in tepees made from dried animal skin and poles. Families painted their tepees decoratively with items from nature. What does your family tepee look like? Use bright colors to show us.

There are many other types of Indian dwellings. Draw three on the back of this sheet and label them.

Design Starters

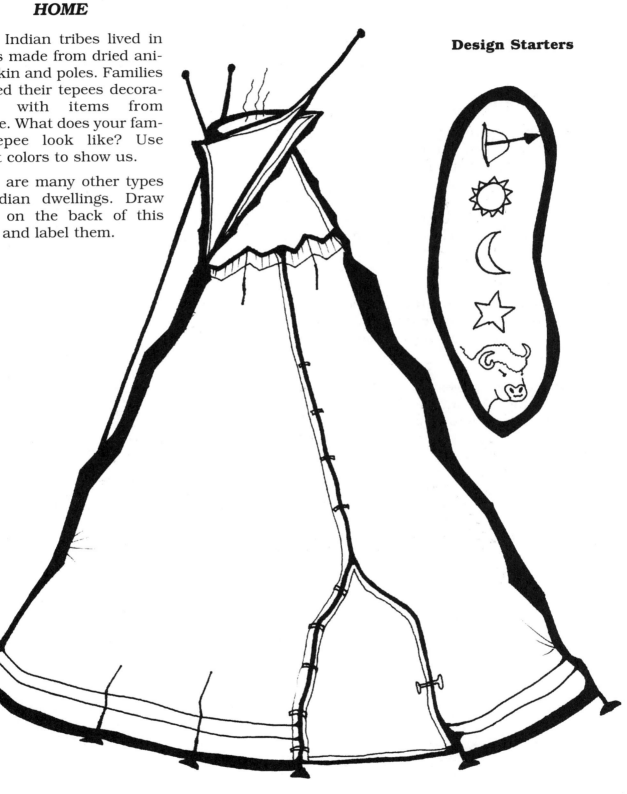

Name _____   Date _____

BUILD A PAIUTE WIKIUP

The wikiup was a simple shelter built by the Paiute Indians. You can build a small one, or a large one for the classroom, by using these directions.

YOU WILL NEED: Tree branches or twigs from the ground, grasses or weeds or brush, and dry leaves.

WHAT TO DO:

1. Make a circular outline in the ground. Or, make a circle shape from styrofoam and cover it with sand or dirt.

2. Build a frame by poking branches and twigs around the circle. Lean them toward the center.

3. Begin to weave the grasses or weeds in between the branches *from bottom to top.* (It gets easier about 1/4 of the way up.)

4. Continue to weave, and leave an opening at the top. Fill in the sides with dried leaves. Make simple furnishings or tools from clay.

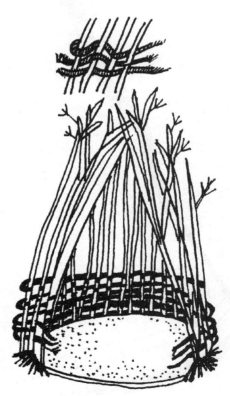

Native Americans used trees, plants, stones, mud, clay, sod, animal hide, and other items from nature to build dwellings. Find information about three other types of dwellings, and report your findings to classmates. List the names of these three other types below.

_____

_____

_____

THE MIGHTY BUFFALO

Buffalo were hunted by Plains Indians and every part of the buffalo was used. On the next page, find the items made from the buffalo and cut them out. Paste them below in the appropriate shape. Use library books to learn more about the mighty beast.

THE MIGHTY BUFFALO

Color and cut the items made from the buffalo. Paste them in the appropriate shape.

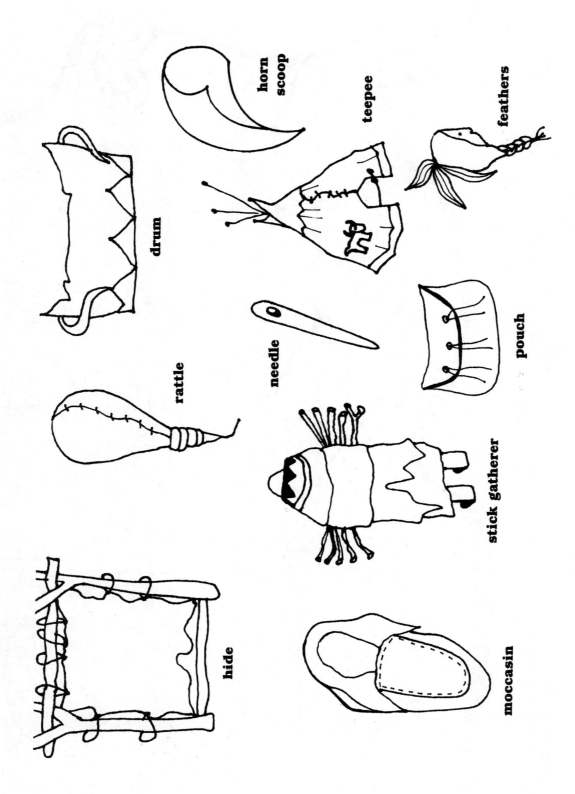

horn scoop

drum

teepee

feathers

rattle

needle

pouch

hide

stick gatherer

moccasin

NATIVE AMERICAN STORY HIDE

Book Title _____

Author_____

Illustrator _____

Book Review

My Name _____

Name _____ Date _____

A LETTER FROM LONG AGO

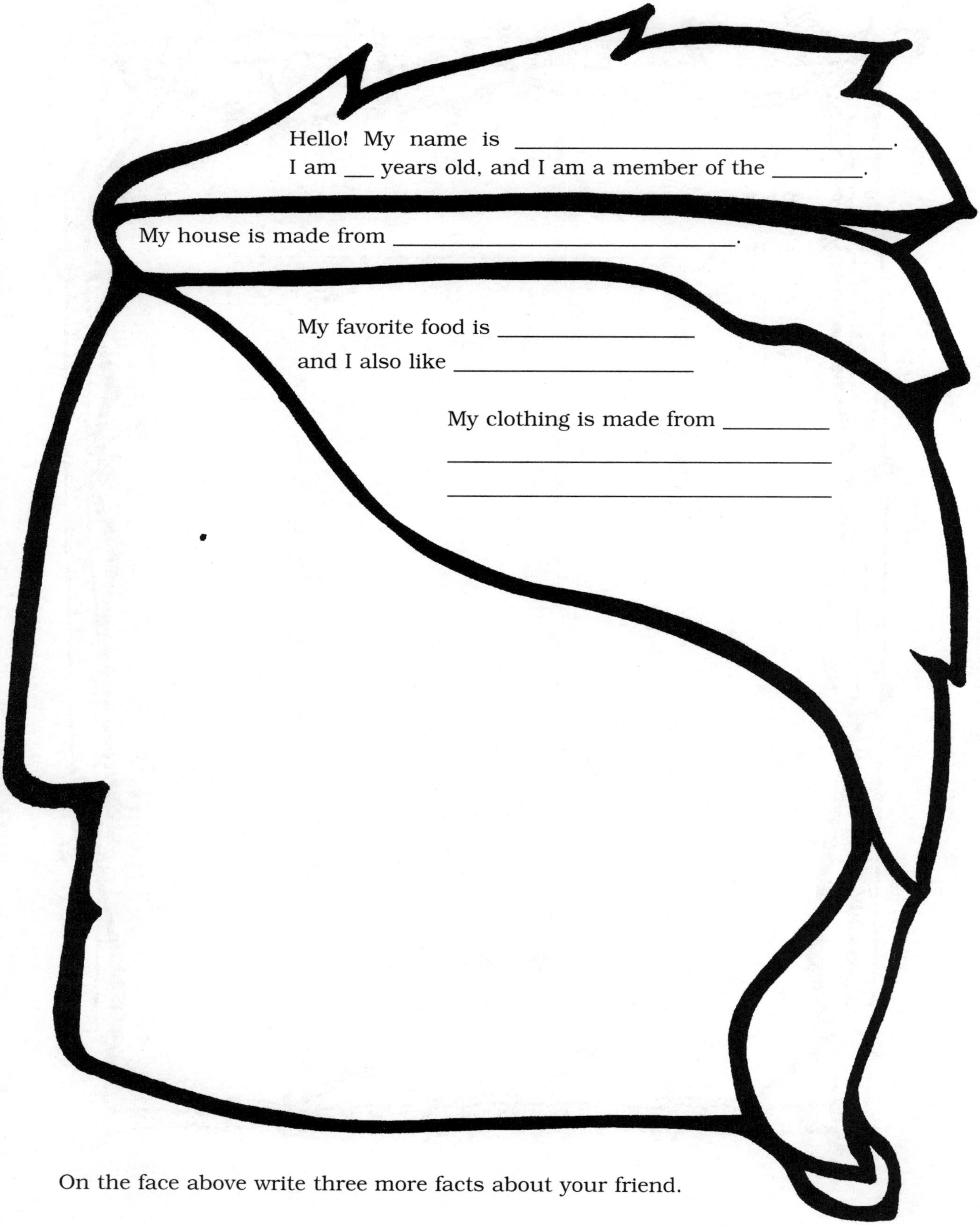

Hello! My name is _____.
I am ___ years old, and I am a member of the _____.

My house is made from _____.

My favorite food is _____

and I also like _____

My clothing is made from _____
_____
_____

On the face above write three more facts about your friend.

STICKS, STONES, BONES

Native American children played games with items found in the natural environment. They made up the game *and* the rules. *So can you.* Plan your game in the space below. Then play it.

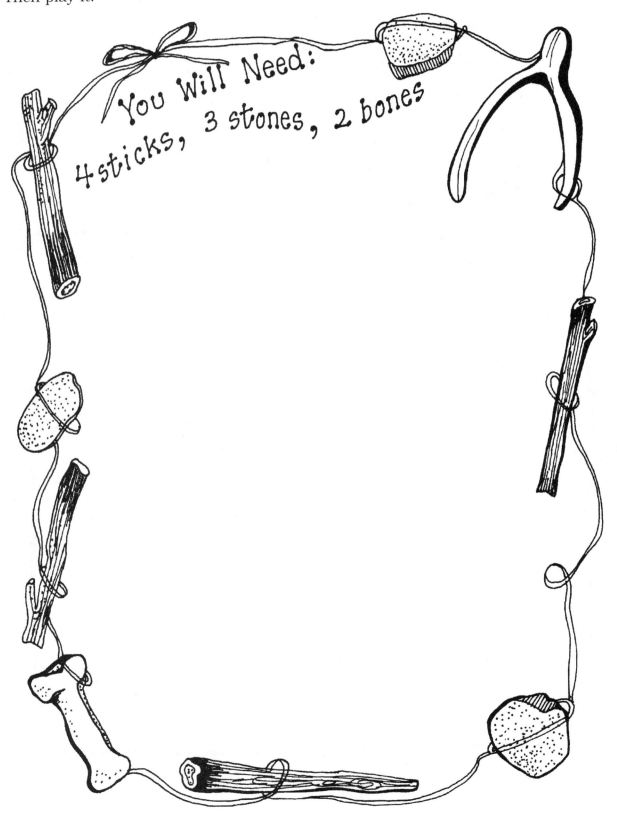

You Will Need:
4 sticks, 3 stones, 2 bones

DO AN AUTHOR STUDY–NATIVE AMERICA

Go to the library and look for books by Paul Goble. You will find *The Girl Who Loved Wild Horses* and *Love Flute.* Note the bright, colorful illustrations. For comparison, locate and read books by Byrd Baylor with illustrations by Peter Parnall. You will find *Everybody Needs a Rock*, *The Desert Is Theirs*, *I'm in Charge of Celebrations*, and others. Note the muted color tones in the illustrations. Compare the illustrations in terms of color, line, and design. Enjoy your reading!

Paul Goble

Peter Parnall

COLOR:

LINE:

DESIGN:

NORTH AMERICA

United States

RECOMMENDED CHILDREN'S BOOKS

Books for children are valued and there is a proliferation of excellent books for children being published. There is a wealth of quality books in this culture.

Arnold, Caroline. *The Terrible Hodag*. Illustrated by Lambert Davis. New York: Harcourt Brace Jovanovich, 1989. For more than a hundred years, tales of the Hodag have been told in the northern woods of the USA. Hodag, the mythical beast with the head of an ox, the feet of a bear, the tail of an alligator and the back of a dinosaur, saves the day for Ole Swenson's men in the lumber camp.

Aylesworth, Jim. *Country Crossing*. Illustrated by Ted Rand. New York: Atheneum, 1991. Late in the night in the quiet country, an old put-put car approaches a railroad crossing and waits patiently. Suddenly the crossing bell sounds, the automatic barriers are lowered, lights flash, and a train goes "chooachoo" as it races by, and then is gone. It gives the reader a rural experience and the feeling of yesterday.

Dewey, Ariane. *The Narrow Escapes of Davy Crockett*. New York: William Morrow and Co., 1990. A series of tall tale adventures that tell of Davy's escapes from rattlesnakes, bears, tornadoes, and other larger-than-life adventures. This action-packed book encourages fanciful, creative storytelling by children.

Ehlert, Lois. *Feathers for Lunch*. Orlando, FL: Harcourt Brace Jovanovich, 1990. A story told in rhyme about a housecat who is out looking for a tasty treat for today's menu. The twelve gorgeous illustrations of the lunch that got away, or birds from North America, are labeled and include interesting information about each bird.

Hall, Donald. *Ox-Cart Man*. Illustrations by Barbara Cooney. New York: Viking, 1979. This is a beautiful picture book journey through New England during the four seasons of the year. Also look for *Miss Rumphius* by Cooney for an ecological message to make the world a better place than the way you found it.

Isadora, Rachel. *Max.* **New York: Macmillan, 1976.** Max decides to join his sister's ballet class and gets quite a surprise. The ballet class actually helps his baseball game.

Jagendorf, Moritz. *New England Bean-Pot, American Folk Stories to Read and to Tell.* **Illustrated by Donald McKay. New York: Vanguard Press, 1948.** In the days before magazines and way before TV, people told stories to the young. This collection includes tales of early life, of war and adventure, and of bears, wildcats and rattlesnakes. Also included are stories of legendary heroes and heroines of New England.

Kalman, Maira. *Max Makes a Million.* **New York: Viking-Penguin, 1990.** Max, a dog, lives in New York City but dreams of going to Paris to become a poet. The charm of this book is the juxtaposition of text and pictures, and the feeling one gets for New York, that "crazy, quivering, wondering wild city."

Krensky, Stephen. *The Missing Mother Goose, Original Stories from Favorite Rhymes.* **Illustrator: Chris Demarest. New York: Doubleday, 1991.** We're familiar with the tales, but this book contains seven wacky stories about the characters in the Mother Goose rhymes. Find out why Humpty Dumpty was on that wall, and what type of a family Little Miss Muffet has. This book will inspire students in a whole language classroom to create their own stories.

Lewis, J. Patrick. *The Moonbow of Mr. B. Bones.* **Illustrations by Dirk Zimmer. New York: Alfred A. Knopf, 1992.** This tale takes place in Kentucky where the moonbow is a natural phenomenon when the conditions are just right at Cumberland Falls. In this book, Mr. B. Bones bottles and sells the snowrays, rainflakes, and whistling wind. What happens when Tommy Morgan takes off the first lid ever on a jar of moonbows?

Lindbergh, Reeve. *Johnny Appleseed.* **Paintings by Kathy Jakobsen. Boston: Little, Brown and Company, 1990.** The familiar story of Johnny Appleseed is refreshingly told in poetry form—"He walked all trails and heard all tales; his orchards spread and grew, and where he went the deep, rich scent, of apple blossoms blew." Information about Johnny Appleseed, or John Chapman, is contained at the end of the book. Rich illustrations.

Loverseed, Amanda. *Tikkatoo's Journey, An Eskimo Folk Tale.* **New York: Bedrick/Blackie, 1990.** Part of a series entitled "Folk Tales of the World." An ice spirit enters the heart of Nanook, the village's oldest and wisest man, who soon becomes very ill. Only a flame of fire from the Sun can help him, but when the hunters make excuses, brave Tikkatoo, the grandson, offers to take up the quest. Striking illustrations with borders.

MacDonald, Suse, and Oakes, Bill. *Once Upon Another: The Tortoise and the Hare and the Lion and the Mouse.* **New York: Dial Books, 1990.** An ingenious upside-down book that tells one tale in one direction and one in the other. The abstract shapes in bold colors work well for this format and will inspire children to try to write and illustrate their own upside-down books because the technical skill is not stressed. Kindles the imagination.

Mcdermott, Gerald. *Raven, A Trickster Tale from the Pacific Northwest.* **New York: Harcourt Brace Jovanovich, 1993.** Raven, the trickster, wants to give people the gift of light. But where does the Sky Chief keep it? A favorite Native American tale. Brilliant illustrations.

Norworth, Jack. *Take Me Out to the Ballgame.* **Illustrations by Alec Gillman. New York: Four Winds Press, 1992.** Jack Norworth wrote the lyrics for "Take Me Out to the Ballgame" during a half-hour ride on the subway in New York City. The song became an American classic, and this book is a visual celebration of the game of baseball.

O'Neill, Mary. *Hailstones and Halibut Bones.* **Illustrations: Leonard Weisgard. New York: Doubleday, 1961, 1989.** A poetry book about colors that appeals to the senses of sight, smell, touch, and hearing. The lovely words capture the essence of each color, and children enjoy this classic.

Parish, Peggy. *Play Ball, Amelia Bedelia.* **Illustrator: Wallace Tripp. New York: Harper, 1972.** Amelia Bedelia is taking the all-American game of baseball literally. What does it mean when someone is "stealing a base"? Children find this one very amusing.

Polacco, Patricia. *Mrs. Katz and Tush.* **New York: Bantam Books, 1992.** An unusual and touching story about a young boy who befriends an older woman in the neighborhood who is all alone for Hannukah and Passover after the death of her husband. The African-American boy, Larnel, persuades Mrs. Katz to take in a cat for companionship; she agrees if Larnel will help her to take care of it. A warm, comfortable relationship develops between these two characters.

Rylant, Cynthia. *And the Relatives Came.* **New York: Macmillan, 1985, 1993.** A charming reunion tale set in Appalachia. The illustrations help the reader to enjoy the trip and the picnic as much as the relatives do. A warm family tale.

Sendak, Maurice. *Where the Wild Things Are.* **New York: Harper & Row, 1963.** This has been named the number one favorite picture book in America for many years. Max, sent to his room for disobeying, has a glorious temper tantrum that takes him all the way to where the wild things are and safely back again. Other landmark works by this author/illustrator include *In the Night Kitchen* and *Outside Over There*, among others.

FOLK TALES

This culture is a mixture of many cultures, and has been referred to as the "great melting pot." People came to this land in North America from all over the world to begin anew. They brought what belongings they could carry, as well as their stories. So today we have a rich mixture of tales from all over the world right in our own backyard.

In 1888, The American Folklore Society originally divided the folklore into four categories: (1) Old English, (2) Southern African-American, (3) Native American, and (4) Canada and Mexico. Today this has been broken down into more sub-categories as we study the culture of the Appalachian Mountains, New England, Maine, the Mississippi Delta, the Bayous of Louisiana, the Pennsylvania Dutch, and so on. The westward movement gave rise to folk heroes and tall tales, in addition to other sub-cultures within the society.

American folklore is closer to history than it is to mythology. The pioneer movement has been recorded in print, since American folklore grew in an age of print. Many of the stories were frozen in time and have not been changed drastically over the years.

DID YOU EVER CARRY A RABBIT'S FOOT FOR GOOD LUCK?

A rabbit's foot would be considered an "amulet," or something that is worn or carried for protection. In many cultures, people carried amulets in bags, sewed them onto clothing, attached them to animals, hung them over doorways to buildings, and tied them onto their tools. The Romans used garlic to hang on doors to keep out diseases. In Italy, garlic was worn on a string around the neck to prevent colds. Stones were worn by Blackfoot Indians as hunting charms, and in Greenland the Eskimos sewed hawks' feet onto boys' clothing to assist them with hunting. In China, children were protected from harm by wearing jade bracelets. In Ecuador, the Otovalo Indians tie red ribbons around the neck of newborn babies to ward off ill health. And in many areas, copper jewelry is worn in an effort to ward off stiffness.

A HOUSEWARMING GIFT

Many people believe in the custom of giving a gift to someone who moves into a new dwelling. In many European cultures, the bride literally "took some of the fire" (glowing cinders) from the hearth of her family to start the fire in her new hearth. This was a "housewarming" gift. In some cultures, people bring food to stock the kitchen. Pieces of cactus are put into the corners of each new Hopi Indian house to give it roots.

THE CAKEWALK

African slaves in the south devised a prize for the "best walking." This originated in Africa and Asia, where women carried buckets of water on their heads. They walked straight and proud, and aimed for no spills. The cakewalks got fancier and variations developed. It reached a high art in body movement with grace and grandeur. A cake was given as the prize for the best walking.

BUMPER STICKERS

The original bumper stickers were called "Lizzie Labels," or slogans inscribed on Model T Fords, otherwise known as Tin Lizzies. Most were designed to get a (often humorous) reaction. An example is, "If You Can Read This, You're Too Close." It is believed that the present-day custom of putting travel stickers on the rear windows of automobiles came from the signs on the back of covered wagons headed west with slogans that read, "Which Way Is West?" or "Pike's Peak or Bust."

TALL TALES

These tales are picturesque, tell a good story in exaggerated form, and were part of the heritage of the nation as it was being expanded and built. *Davy Crockett* was a backwoods hero of Tennessee who exemplified good sense and courage. His motto was: "Always be sure, then go ahead." He grew in mythical stature after his death. For example, it has been said that Davy "once grinned a knot off of a tree trunk." *Paul Bunyan, Mike Fink,* and *Johnny Appleseed* are all heroes in the tall tale category.

SPINNING YARNS

The "yarn" is a specific type of storytelling where the audience is strung along for a long period of time, with repetitions, and often with a climax to the yarn, and then the aftermath of the tale. Sometimes the purpose of the yarn is to "pull the leg" of the audience.

THE SWASHBUCKLING HERO VS. THE HARDWORKING YANKEE

The hero in much of the folklore is the adventurous cowboy who went west to settle the land. With the wide open spaces, it required brawn and a rugged constitution to survive. Here we have the basis for many tales about the good poor-man, and the poor person who made good (panning for gold). On the other side of the coin, we have the hard-working, persevering, common-sense Yankee figure. These two have the same goal, which is a "better life," but they have very different means of attaining their goals.

MICKEY MOUSE

This favorite animal hero of movies and comics has achieved folklore status. The Walt Disney character made his debut in 1928. He appears in animated films, children's rhymes, on television, and in books. A popular television program of the 1950's and 1960's was "The Mickey Mouse Club." People own stuffed animal replicas, and wear Mickey Mouse wristwatches, t-shirts, and mouse-ear party hats. Mickey is joined by Donald Duck in his mass appeal. An animal hero, Mickey represents the "average guy" who has a love of fun, curiosity, and pals like Goofy and Pluto. These tales are of cheerful mischief.

The Disneyland theme park in California and Walt Disney World in Florida exemplify the American ingenuity of mass production and mass audience participation. In addition, they exemplify the magical "too good to be true" land for which people search in folklore throughout the world cultures. This magical land—with serene lakes and mystical scenery, where the shrubs take on the shapes of figures, and which is home to fairies, folk heroes, princes and princesses, the big bad wolf, talking animals and birds, and costumed characters in parades—offers people a safe dreamland for a day and may account for its worldwide popularity.

SUGGESTED ACTIVITIES FOR THE CLASSROOM

1. TALL TALES

Get a collection of tall tales about Davy Crockett, Mike Fink, Paul Bunyan, John Henry, and others for your library corner. Have students read a wide variety of these tales. On a map pinpoint the area of the United States that represents the setting. Students can make advertising posters for the tall tale. Be sure to have them exaggerate!

2. HAVE A TALL TALE CONTEST

After reading a wide variety of tall tales about Davy Crockett, Mike Fink, Paul Bunyan, and so on, have students do some writing of their own. They can work with partners to write a knee-slappin' good tale, then dress up as the characters and tell the tales for other classrooms or for younger students.

3. A TALL REPORT

Students can make a large head and large boots from construction paper. Then they can use thin paper strips (3″ in width) to connect the head to the feet, on which they write their tall tale—and the taller the tale, the longer the paper! (See reproducible activity pages.)

4. BUMPER STICKERS

Encourage students to be on the alert for humorous bumper stickers. Then have them create their own present-day mottos, or create them from the point of view of a tall tale hero.

5. WHERE ARE THE HEROINES?

In many of the early cultures—and the United States is no exception—women are not represented as leading characters in children's stories. This came about later. But women did play a big role in the settling of the west, and students may be able to come up with some legendary heroines on their own. They can write the tales and illustrate the characters. (Again, women are apt to be drawn from historical fact in our stories for children. For example, Betsy Ross, Molly Pitcher, Clara Barton, Harriet Tubman.)

6. DIORAMAS DELUXE

Students can work together in small groups to plan and construct large dioramas from their favorite stories. These can be displayed in the room along with a copy of the book and a poster advertising the book.

7. NEWSPAPERS AND HEADLINES

Since our nation gained independence at a time when the newspaper was available, students can "publish" a classroom newspaper using favorite folk tale, fairy tale, and nursery rhyme characters. They can rewrite some of the versions to fit the sections of the news. Here are some to get you started.

Society page:	Cinderella at the Ball
Food page:	Hansel and Gretel and the Gingerbread House, Peter Pumpkin Eater Pumpkin Cookies, Red Riding Hood Picnic Basket Menu
Sports:	Rabbit and Hare Race
Travel:	Various familiar characters advertising a trip to their home country
Local news:	Tall Tale Hero Highlights

8. MODERN-DAY FOLK HEROES

Benjamin Franklin is a good example of a creative personality who in many ways was "larger than life." Read *What's the Big Idea, Ben Franklin?* by Jean Fritz (New York: Putnam, 1982) and do some extension activities. Here are some to get you started.

Proverbs:

Ben Franklin enjoyed proverbs. Students can look for books of proverbs that he coined. Read the proverbs and discuss their meaning (for example, a penny saved is a penny earned: neither a borrower nor a lender be). This is a good time to bring out the Aesop's Fables also.

Pen Name:

Franklin was a writer who wrote under the pen name of Silas Dogood. Students can select a pen name and use it for their folk tales and other creative writing.

Leather Apron Club:

Franklin formed a book club where people met and discussed their favorite books. Set up a Leather Apron Club in the classroom and meet over lunch to discuss good stories. Students can use this time to tell stories they have been practicing in their spare time.

9. THE MOBILE GOES 'ROUND AND 'ROUND

Students can make mobiles, with the shape of a country or continent in the middle that hangs lower than the other items. Then, they can create flags, characters, and symbols from favorite folk tales in a particular region and hang them on the mobile. The mobiles can serve as a means for storytelling and will be a visual delight in the classroom.

10. HOLD A BOOK FAIR

Many good folk tales are in paperback form and can be discounted for a school fair. Students can read and review a number of the books, make posters advertising them, give spot announcements over the public address system, and buy more books with the profits from the sale.

11. INVITE AN AUTHOR TO YOUR SCHOOL

This is usually a districtwide function. It stimulates reading, writing, creative dramatics, creative art, and many more whole language activities throughout the entire building.

12. ALASKA AND HAWAII

These states offer a contrast in climate, food, animals, housing, clothing, and so on. Find stories with these two background settings and make a chart of comparisons. Be sure to include the state flags and state flowers.

13. BE ON THE ALERT FOR FOREIGN STAMPS

Students can begin a study of postage stamps, air mail stamps, and postage costs. Check with the local post office for posters that advertise stamps. Students can begin to bring in foreign stamps to the classroom, or set up a procedure to get some by asking for assistance at the post office or library.

CELEBRATIONS

While the United States has a diverse population of people from many cultures, there are a number of holidays that are solely associated with the United States, and these will be addressed here. The word "celebrate" is from the Latin *celebraitus*, which means to go in great numbers, to honor. Some celebrations are long and formal, others are informal. Some celebrations are public, and others are personal. There are sporting events such as the World Series in baseball, held every autumn, or cultural events held at the Kennedy Center in Washington, D.C., or at Carnegie Hall in New York City. In any case, a celebration is a time of happiness, when joyful sounds can be heard throughout this vast country.

CITIZENSHIP DAY

On September 17, the anniversary of the signing of the Constitution, foreign-born citizens who have lived in the country for five years are eligible for citizenship. All over the country on this day new citizens, who meet the requirements, take an oath of allegiance and are "sworn in" as citizens, with the rights and responsibilities that go with that honor.

MOTHER'S DAY

This is a day set aside in May each year for children to honor their mother. Ann Jarvis of Philadelphia, Pennsylvania founded this special day in 1914. Tradition has it that if a mother is living, a red or pink flower is worn; if a mother is deceased, a white flower is worn. On this day, children give their mother greeting cards and/or presents, and do nice things for her in the home.

FATHER'S DAY

On the third Sunday in June, children honor their fathers with greeting cards that they make and with presents. Father's Day was first celebrated in Spokane, Washington in 1910 by Mrs. John B. Dodd, who wanted to honor her own father.

LEI DAY

May 1st is Lei Day in Hawaii. It is a time for singing to music played on the guitar and ukelele. The Hawaiian luau, or feast, consists of a roast pig that is cooked in ground pits and served along with poi (mashed taro roots), pineapple, and other fresh fruits.

MEMORIAL DAY

May 31 is a day set aside to honor those citizens who gave their lives fighting for this country. It is a time for planting flowers at the cemetery, or for placing a small flag on the grave of someone who served in the armed forces. This is also a ceremonial day with speeches, parades and marching bands, outdoor picnics, boating, and sports.

INDEPENDENCE DAY

July 4 is a day for parades and marching bands. This day was declared a legal holiday in 1941. It is a day of celebration with parades and speeches, neighborhood picnics, or an informal cookout in a nearby park. There are baseball games and other outdoor sports to enjoy. At day's end, there is usually a giant fireworks display in large cities, and many fireworks displays throughout the vast land.

LABOR DAY

This legal holiday in early September celebrates "work." Everyone enjoys the Labor Day Weekend because it is usually the last weekend before school starts, and families have one last holiday before children settle down to schoolwork for another year.

AMERICAN EDUCATION WEEK

This week, set aside in November, focuses on school. It is a time for schools to have "open house" when parents can visit the classrooms and meet the teacher. Parents learn about the learning experiences their children are having, and see demonstrations or work on display. This event is endorsed by the National Education Association.

CHILDREN'S BOOK WEEK

This week, set aside in November, emphasizes reading good books to children. In the schools, children are engaged in reading contests. They may decorate their classroom, doorways, and halls with replicas of favorite storybook characters. A time to celebrate good books, this event is sponsored by the American Library Association.

THANKSGIVING DAY

This national holiday is celebrated on the last Thursday in November. The first celebration was in Plymouth, Massachusetts, with the Pilgrim settlers from the Old World (Europe). Children learn the folklore about the first Thanksgiving with the Pilgrims and the Indians, and about Squanto, the Native American, who helped the people survive the first raw winter. Traditionally, families have served roast turkey with dressing, cranberry sauce, squash, corn, potatoes, and pumpkin pie along with other specialties. In these modern days, there is a telephone "turkey hot line" that people can call in order to gain information about, and tips for, fixing a turkey. The traditional Macy's Day Parade in New York City is televised and children all over the nation can see many of their favorite giant balloon characters, along with floats, singers, and dancers. It is a kick-off to the Christmas shopping season.

KWANZAA

This special African-American holiday was officially started in California during the 1960's. It is a seven-day festival beginning on December 26. A candle is lit each night to focus on one of the seven principles of Black American family life—unity, self-determination, work and responsibility, cooperative economics, purpose, creativity, and faith.

NEW YEAR'S DAY PARADES

Many "Bowl" parades are held on this day—not the least of which is the Rose Bowl Parade. The floats are made of fresh flower petals, and are a beautiful sight. The parades are televised nationally and are held prior to the football playoffs.

MARTIN LUTHER KING, JR. DAY

This is a national holiday in January in honor of the Black Civil Rights leader who believed in a peaceful means to attain goals. There are official ceremonies honoring Dr. King, and people gather to listen to speeches about the state of the civil rights movement and freedom for all people everywhere. Choral groups provide lovely music. It is a time for reflection.

PRESIDENT'S DAY

This is a day set aside in February to honor former presidents. At one time, school children honored just the birthdays of George Washington and

Abraham Lincoln, and listened to stories about George Washington's truthfulness and Abraham Lincoln's honesty. The stories taught children to value these traits. Today, on President's Day children pay tribute to all of the past presidents of the country.

IDITAROD (ALASKAN SLED DOG RACE)

This international sled dog race is 1,049 miles in length, stretching from Anchorage to Nome, Alaska. The race is usually held in early March and is called "The Last Great Race on Earth." The trail extends from Anchorage to Nome along mountains, rivers and the icy shores of the Arctic, to simulate the trail that was blazed long ago under hazardous weather conditions by pioneers who raced serum from one city to the other during an outbreak of diphtheria. It is a rigorous race, and some people practice for it for *years* before setting out with the packs. There is television coverage for this event, and information packets for school children are available. Call 1-800-545-MUSH or write to Iditarod Trail Committee, P.O. Box 870800, Wasilla, Alaska 99687. You can purchase one square inch of the Iditarod Trail and get a certificate that bears the official State of Alaska seal. Also available is souvenir "trail mail" carried on the sled by each musher in the race.

CELEBRATE EARTH DAY

On April 22, we celebrate this day in an effort to make the world a healthier and safer planet on which to live. Everyone, all over the world, needs to become more aware of water and air pollution, overpopulation, energy, endangered species, natural resources, and people's relationship to their environment. Children in schools renew their efforts to recycle items, and to send letters to their legislators urging support for ecological issues. There are speeches and marches throughout the country.

CELEBRATE THE FLAG OF FREEDOM

The flag of the United States is prominent in celebrations, parades, and holidays. A nation's flag is a symbol of its heritage; "Old Glory" or "The Stars and Stripes" are nicknames given to the red, white, and blue flag. The 50 white stars on a blue background in the upper left corner represent the states, and the 13 red and white stripes represent the original colonies. At the beginning of many public events, the flag is ceremoniously displayed and everyone recites the Pledge of Allegiance as follows:

> I pledge allegiance to the flag
> of the United States of America
> and to the Republic for which it stands,
> one nation under God, indivisible, with
> liberty and justice for all.

SUGGESTED ACTIVITIES FOR THE CLASSROOM

1. STUDENT GLOBAL CONNECTIONS

Have students find out where in the world their ancestors lived. Then use the opaque projector to trace a map of the world on a huge bulletin board space. Students can make a picture of their face, using small paper plates (or circles) and yarn for hair, buttons for eyes, and so on. These faces can be put around the border of the board, and yarn can go from each child's face to at least two areas in the world where they have "connections."

This makes for an interesting maze of interconnected lines all over the board. Color coding of the yarn works well with older students. A good resource book with actual photographs is *Immigrant Kids* by Russell Freedman (New York: Dutton, 1980).

2. CITIZENSHIP DAY

On September 17, work with students on the Pledge of Allegiance. Go through it line by line and discuss its meaning. Work with the flag in terms of the meaning of the 50 stars and the 13 red and white stripes. A good resource book is *I Pledge Allegiance* by June Swanson with pictures by Rick Hanson (Minneapolis: Carolrhoda Books, 1991).

3. MAKE A MONTHLY CLASS CALENDAR

On large graph paper, make a class calendar for each month, and have students print holidays on each month. Color code the holidays celebrated only in the United States, and for only Hispanic, or European, African, Asian, and so on. Students can be on the alert for news of the holidays in newspapers, magazines, and on the television news. If someone in the class is celebrating a holiday, encourage the student(s) to share the information with classmates. Invite parents to class to talk about their traditions, to bring actual items, photographs, 35mm slides, and food samples.

4. CELEBRATE THE VISUAL ARTS

Arrange for a field trip to a local art gallery or museum. Before the trip, you can become familiar with the work of the artists on display at the gallery. Discuss these in class, and look for samples of the work in art books from the local library. Many books have lavish color reproductions of the works of many artists. A poster or a print is very effective.

Students will enjoy the wonderful book that takes them on a visit to an art gallery entitled *The Girl with a Watering Can* by Ewa Zadrzynska, with illustrations by Arnold Skolnick and paintings from the National Gallery of Art in Washington, D.C. (New York: Chameleon Books, 1989).

Have students experiment in the style of some of the masters, and then work to develop their own style.

Invite an artist to the school to spend the day working in an area of the classroom or in an area of the school building. Students are amazed to see the painting, pottery, or weaving "evolve" as the day goes on, and it is an invaluable experience for both artist and students.

5. CELEBRATE MUSIC

Students can begin to appreciate the sounds from specific instruments at an early age. The recording of *Peter and the Wolf* by Prokofiev helps with identification of specific instruments and their sound. Students can finger paint to background music of piano, trumpets, and violins, and note their body movement and "feelings" that the music evokes.

6. THERE ARE MONUMENTS RIGHT IN OUR OWN CITY OR TOWN

Beautiful monuments are built throughout the world to commemorate local events, national events, people, and so on. Often people gather at monuments, such as the Vietnam Memorial in Washington, D.C., Tomb of the Unknown Soldier in Arlington Cemetery, and so on, during the time of a particular celebration. Go on a monument hunt right in your own city and learn more about the meaning of the statues or figures and the designs. Visit the town hall or city courthouse and look for symbols. The local historical society can be of assistance.

7. FAVORITE CELEBRATIONS

Have students discuss celebrations and which ones they favor and why. Graphs of celebrations can be made, and students can record their favorite holidays. Older children can each interview five people in their family and/or neighborhood to learn their favorite holiday (gathering data) and then record the data on a graph. What can students learn from each other regarding family customs for celebrations? Focus upon positive aspects of celebrations.

8. SYMBOLS OF THE UNITED STATES PLAY A PART IN CELEBRATIONS

We have symbols, such as "Uncle Sam," the bald eagle, the Statue of Liberty, the donkey and the elephant (two political parties), flag, liberty bell, and so on, to represent our country. Students can locate these symbols in information books and make copies for display in the classroom. Where can these symbols be found in their school and in the community?

Have students work together in teams to create another special symbol for the United States. They have to carefully think through the meaning of the colors and of the design. Set aside time for presentations to the class with explanations about the new symbol.

Have students work together in teams to create a multicultural symbol for the United States. Again, use of color and design is important, along with the significance of the message. Submit the works to your local congressional representative or state senator, or to the United States Post Office for a stamp design.

9. WHAT IS YOUR "OLD GLORY" I.Q.?

Students can be taught the etiquette surrounding the flag of their country. Some rules are as follows:

- flags should not displayed in bad weather, unless it is a weatherproof flag designed for all types of weather
- flags should only be flown from sunrise to sunset
- if the flag is flown at night, it should be properly illuminated

- the flag should be displayed every school day in or by the school
- the flag should be carried aloft, not flat
- the flag should not be worn as part of a costume
- the flag should not be used for advertising purposes

For more information about the flag, write to the U.S. Capitol Historical Society, 200 Maryland Avenue, N.E., Washington, D.C. 20002. Some good resource books are: *The American Flag* by Ann Armburster (New York: Watts, 1991) and *How Proudly They Wave, Flags of the Fifty States* by Rita D. Haban (Minneapolis: Lerner, 1989).

10. FLAGS OF NATIONS

Each nation in the world has its own flag, and some countries regulate flag codes by law that require respect. Ships at sea are required to fly flags; in general, a red flag represents danger, a yellow flag means quarantine, and a black flag with skull and bones indicates pirates! Flags of nations show emblems, colors of importance to the country, and each has its own story. Students can become world explorers and set out to find information about flags. Two helpful resource books are *Flags of the World* by Paul Barnett, with illustrations by Jack and Enid Hayes (New York: Random House, Outlet Book Co., 1992), and *Flag, An Eyewitness Book*, by William Crampton (New York: Knopf, 1989).

11. CELEBRATE EARTH DAY, GIVE THROWAWAYS A SECOND CHANCE

Encourage students to recycle items. Used plastic margarine tubs can be brought to school for housing crayons in desks. Coffee cans can be covered with colorful paper and placed on countertops to hold rulers, scissors, pencils, and so on. Set up a "Second Chance" Area, and have students bring in items that they no longer want or need, and encourage students to brainstorm new uses for them. A good resource book is *Celebrating Earth Day, A Sourcebook of Activities and Experiments* by Robert Gardner (Highland Park, NJ: Millbrook Press, 1992).

ARTS AND CRAFTS

The United States has been a mosaic of many cultures, and the art work (painting and portraiture) in the early years reflected primarily the European cultures. However, because of a philosophy that fosters the uniqueness of the individual and a healthy respect for the creative spirit, much has been added to the art world from this area of the globe.

SUGGESTED ACTIVITIES FOR THE CLASSROOM

1. ILLUSTRATION AND ADVERTISING DESIGN

This has reached a high art form in the United States. Norman Rockwell, who sketched and painted for magazine covers, became well known as an illustrator. Eventually, illustrators gained respect in the art world, although fine artists still rank supreme. For a student activity, have them search through magazines and newspapers for illustrations used in advertising. (They can begin a scrapbook on a particular subject or of illustrations that they particularly like. Here students may be introduced to "pop art.") Then, have them select a subject or item, and design an illustration for the item that they would submit to an advertising design firm.

2. THE ART OF ANIMATION

In motion pictures, animation reached the status of an art form. Animation is very time consuming and requires patience because each little movement must be drawn separately.

Students can create a "thumb book," that is, a series of little pages that they can thumb through quickly. As the reader thumbs through the book, the item (such as an animal) appears to move. Students can use tracing paper for this project, since they will be drawing the same thing repeatedly with little or no line movement. Some suggestions for beginning animation are: a bird opening its beak as if to sing; a dog wagging its tail; a person under an umbrella in a rain shower.

3. CARTOONS ARE A FORM OF ART

There are political cartoons and funny cartoon characters that are in newspapers, magazines, and even books of cartoons. Some cartoons have a self-contained message in a series of four or five pictures, and some cartoons continue their story for a week or more. One way to get acquainted with cartoon art is to cover up the speech balloons and have students invent what is being said (which is not as easy as it might seem). Once students get the idea of sequence and timing in humor, they can try their hand at creating their own cartoons.

4. THE ART OF THE COMPUTER

Some computer programs have graphics that enable students to create their own designs or picture art, and to color them. Posters and even greeting cards can be made. Check with your librarian or media center personnel for the many computer programs from which to choose.

5. THE ART OF PHOTOGRAPHY

This is a medium that began in black and white and developed into color reproductions. For a time, it almost seemed to make the artist "unnecessary" since the camera realistically recorded scenery, still life, portraits of people, and so on. However, photography gained stature as an art form in its own right, and, of course, nothing could replace the fresh, creative eye of the painter who can take liberties with perspective, light, size, and so on.

For a student activity, arrange to have a camera in the classroom (parents are often cooperative with this project) and allow students to take photographs of "still life" and, also, paint the still life in another medium. Compare and contrast the results in a gallery display. (**Note:** The Eastman Kodak Company of Rochester, New York sponsors photography contests each year for students throughout the United States. Write for information.)

6. CHILDREN'S PICTURE BOOK ILLUSTRATORS

The popularity of children's books in this culture has given rise to a wealth of professionally illustrated material for children. Students can do an art study of the styles of certain illustrators, and create their own works of art using the same media. Some examples are: Lois Ehlert, *Feathers for Lunch* and *Growing Vegetable Soup* (collage that looks like the item has been painted); Maurice Sendak, *Where the Wild Things Are* (crosshatching) and *In the Night Kitchen* (cartoon style); Byrd Baylor and Peter Parnall, *Desert Voices*, *The Desert Is Theirs* (southwest simplicity and muted tones); Paul Gobel, *The Girl Who Loved Wild Horses* (Native American designs); Gerald McDermott, *Arrow to the Sun* (Native American designs); Ed Young, *Yeh Shen* (Chinese brush painting); Ezra Jack Keats (collage); Tana Hoban, *26 Letters and 99 Cents* (photography); Patricia McKissack and Brian Pinkney, *The Dark Thirty* (crayon and ink scratchboard); and Eric Carle, *The Very Hungry Caterpillar* (finger painting and tissue paper art).

7. MARBLING

This technique is used for endpapers in books, but it is also effective as stationery or even a framed swirl design. Marbling can also serve as a background for a painting. You will need special oil-based colors that can be purchased at the art supply center of a large variety store, or at an art center in a college bookstore. You need: a basin of cold water, straws, sheets of white paper, and marbling colors.

Procedure:

- Pour water into basin (less than half full).
- Use straw to dip into paint, and drop it gently into water basin. (Use more than one color.)
- Stir surface to spread paint around.
- Carefully place a sheet of paper onto the water and allow it to float for a half minute.
- Remove the paper, turn it right side up, and dry it on a countertop.

8. A DIFFERENT PAINTING EXPERIENCE AT THE EASEL

Students can roll on the background paint using a small household paint roller. (The background does not have to be completely covered—some evidence of the rolled look is the effect we are looking for.) Allow this to dry. Then, with a darker color, students can paint a line design on the prepared background (or an outline of a bird, flower, or fish) with very little solid areas painted in. The effect is quite satisfying.

9. A BATIK-LIKE PAINTING

The art of batik is thought to have originated in Asia and spread throughout Africa. Certainly Indonesian designs and African batiks are beautiful. This technique, which requires hot wax, is used by artists.

A simple way to introduce young children to the batik effect is to have them make a crayon drawing of a large item (an owl, flower, animal) and color it in heavily with wax crayon. Then, they brush paint over this with a wash of watered-down tempera paint, or watercolor in dark blue or black. This gives the look of batik, with a similar type of surprise-ending experience.

10. RECIPES FOR ARTIFACTS

The following recipes can be easily mixed and color added. Students can pound, roll, and shape the material into objects that represent artifacts from their own culture or the culture they are studying. Think in terms of going on an "Archaeological Dig" for items that tell something about the food, clothing, shelter, crafts, tools for work, items for play, and so on.

Clay Dough

6 cups flour
6 cups salt
6 tablespoons alum
water drops

Combine these ingredients and slowly add a little water, stirring constantly. As mixture begins to thicken, mix until it has the consistency of clay. If it dries out, add more drops of water. If it gets sticky, add equal parts of flour and salt.

Play Dough

10 cups flour
4 cups salt
8 tablespoons cooking oil
water drops
food coloring

Pour flour and salt into a large bowl and mix well. Stir in oil. Add water, a little at a time, until dough consistency is reached. Separate dough and add different food coloring to each new bowl of dough. Store in plastic bag or container with a tight lid. Will usually last for 3 weeks.

Baker's Clay

8 cups flour
3 cups water
2 cups salt
tempera paint
spray varnish

Combine dry ingredients and mix well. Add water, a little at a time, and knead for about 5 minutes. Roll out to approximately 1/4-inch thickness and shape into desired item. Bake in 250-degree oven until hard (about two hours). Cool. Paint with tempera paint and let dry. Then spray with clear varnish if desired. (Varnish should be done only by an adult in a well-ventilated area.)

11. DESIGN A POSTAGE STAMP

Our postal service has a wide variety of stamps from which to choose, and a number of posters about stamps on display in the post office. Have students bring in stamps from home and note the subject matter—birds, flowers, people, states, and so on. Then have the students design a postage stamp on 9″ x 12″ construction paper that represents some aspect of the United States (and design a poster advertising this special stamp), giving information about the subject. Display the stamps and posters in the hallway.

12. THE CONSTRUCTION OF HATS

Hats or head coverings are used in every culture. In the United States a special hat may be worn by someone who has a particular career, such as the hat of a firefighter, police officer, baseball player, football player, cowboy, and so on. Encourage students to construct hats using paper plates or paper bags as a base, with a variety of scrap items (feathers, net, beads, foil, paper, ribbon). Students can also make hats from other cultures, such as the beret from France, crowns from royal kingdoms in Europe, and so on. Read *Aunt Flossie's Hats (and Crabcakes Later)* by Elizabeth F. Howard (Boston: Houghton Mifflin, 1991). Encourage students to concoct a story that goes with their hat and to tell it while wearing the hat.

13. DESIGNING CLOTHING

While studying different cultures, note the clothing that boys and girls wear that is representative of each. Have students trace one another on large sheets of paper; then, working in small groups, their task is to design the face, hair, hat, clothing, and footwear for a boy or girl from a particular culture. The "characters" can be painted and cut out, and displayed in a multicultural art gallery of people on the bulletin board or on the walls around the room.

These colorful portraits can eventually be displayed in the hallway with information about them and where they live, along with a map that shows their location in the world.

14. DIORAMAS OF FAIRY TALE SCENES

Secure medium-sized boxes and have students work together to create scenes from some of the favorite universal fairy tales, or to depict some of the most popular characters in their native habitat. Use mixed media for best results.

15. CONSTRUCT A PATRIOTIC VOTING BOOTH

Obtain a large box or tape two boxes together so that students can go inside the box in an upright position. Cover the box with white paper and paint stars, stripes and other symbols on it with red and blue tempera paint. Hang an appropriately colorful curtain on a spring-rod on one side. Decorate the inside also. Students can use this for social studies activities when they learn the process of voting. It can also be used in the room as a special, quiet place for students to go to write, listen to a tape recording, do some tape recording, read folk tales about the United States and other cultures, and so on. A square window can be cut out of one side so that students can give oral reports to the class from this area.

16. IT'S TIME FOR A PUPPET THEATER

Obtain a medium-sized box and cut out one end. Then cut a "performance window" on the side directly across from the open end, and tack a curtain on a string along the top of the opening. Students can decorate the outside of the box in a variety of ways, such as with scenes or characters from favorite tales. If the box is quite tall, it can be used primarily for "tall tales." One side can be a log cabin, another side can be a woodsman's hut, and the third side can be a castle. Students can make their own puppets, reenact stories, and travel with the puppet stage to other classrooms to give performances.

GAMES

Children the world over like to play games, and in this area of the world many of the immigrants brought their games with them in their thoughts. There are word games to play when no materials are available. And, there are games to play in the natural environment, such as "Kick the Can" and "Tag." Some games require little in the way of equipment, such as jumping rope, tag, and Hide and Seek. Today in the United States, there is an abundance of commercial games, dolls, equipment, and developmentally appropriate toys available for children. It is a multi-million-dollar industry.

RIDDLES AND JOKES

Riddles and jokes are enjoyed by children, who like to try to figure them out and to tell them. It's a lot of fun, and children gain skill in critical thinking. Encourage children to invent their own riddles after listening to some.

"YOURS TILL" JOKES

These are favorites for autograph books at the end of the year. See if students can make up their own. They are working with nouns and verbs. And, they are fun to illustrate. This exercise gets children prepared for political cartoons and the idea that language can have several meanings.

> Yours till Niagara Falls.
> Yours till the butterflies.
> Yours till the kitchen sinks.
> Yours till the ocean waves.
> Yours till the milkshakes.
> Yours till the Catskill Mountains have baby kittens.

SING-SONG RHYMES (STATES AND CAPITALS)

This chant makes it easy to learn the capitals and states. Get the rhythm moving, and do it daily. Children can skip rope to the chant, bounce a ball in time with the chant, play catch with a partner, or sit in a circle and toss the beanbag to the person who then says the next verse.

State of Maine, Augusta,
On the Kennebec River;
State of Maine, Augusta,
On the Kennebec River.

New Hampshire, Concord,
On the Merrimac River;
New Hampshire, Concord,
On the Merrimac River.

Massachusetts, Boston,
On the Charles River;
Massachusetts, Boston,
On the Charles River.

New York, Albany,
On the Hudson River;
New York, Albany,
On the Hudson River.

Get a large map of the United States, and make up the rest. Note that almost all capitals are located near a river or lake. In some cases where they are not, a state landmark can be named. For example:

Wyoming, Cheyenne,
Near the Rocky Mountains;
Wyoming, Cheyenne,
Near the Rocky Mountains.

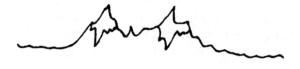

MOTHER, MAY I?

This game activity is similar to Simon Says, where the person giving the command also has to give permission to carry it out. Therefore, students have to listen carefully and ask, "Mother, may I?" The response must be, "Yes you may." If the response is only, "Yes," then the person may not carry out the task.

A variation of this game is "Giant Steps." One player (mother) stands at a distance from the other players who are lined up. The mother calls out the name of each student before giving a specific command ("Jimmy, you may take three giant steps," or "Bertina, you may take one baby step"). Students have to say "Mother, may I?" before they show any movement of their body. As the group gets closer and closer to the caller (mother), one finally gets close enough to touch the caller to become the next mother. The game begins all over again.

JUMPING ROPE

Jumping rope is still quite popular, even with adults who use it as an aerobic exercise. Jumping rope can be done by one person who jumps with both feet, or alternates the right foot and left foot in a skipping motion. Sometimes the person can cross the rope and jump through the middle loop.

Three or more can play with a longer rope (clothesline). One student on each end keeps the rope moving, and the third person must jump in (at just the right time to risk getting tangled in the rope). Sometimes students line up to get a turn to jump. Native Americans used grape vines for jumping rope. In England, the rope from old-fashioned window sashes was used.

DUCK, DUCK, GOOSE

This is a circle game and can be played with the entire class sitting in a large circle (outdoors or in a large indoor room). One person is the "goose" and walks around the outside of the circle while tapping each student on the head, saying "duck, duck, duck..." When he or she finally taps someone on the head and says "goose," that student jumps up and chases the goose. If the goose gets to the place left by the student before being caught, then he or she is safe and the chaser becomes the goose and starts the process all over again.

SEVEN UP

This quiet game can be played by the entire class. Seven students are selected by the teacher to go to the front of the room. All other students remain in their seats, put their heads down on one arm, and their thumbs up. No peeking is allowed. The seven students in the front then tip toe through the classroom and touch someone on the thumb. Those who are touched must not look up when they are touched, or they will lose their turn. When all seven are back up in the front of the room, the seven who were touched stand up. Each person who was touched gets one chance to guess which of the "seven up" in front touched his or her thumb. If the guess is correct, he or she replaces the one in front; if not, he or she sits down. When there are "seven up" in front again, all heads go down, thumbs go up, and the process is repeated. This is a favorite game with children and a good end-of-the-day game.

WHERE'S THE ERASER?

One student (designated as "it") is selected to go to a remote area of the classroom, be blindfolded and guarded by another student so as not to peek. Meanwhile, someone designated by the teacher quietly "semi-hides" a chalkboard eraser somewhere in the room, so that it is only partially seen. When the student is seated, he or she calls out "ready." At this time, the one who is "it" goes on the hunt around the classroom for the object. Students cannot say anything, but as "it" approaches the object or "gets warmer," students can begin to hum with an "mmmmmm" sound. The closer the student gets, the louder the "mmmmmm" gets. When the student finds the object, he or she selects someone else to be "it," hides the object, and the game begins again.

POPULAR SPORTS

Children all over the United States can engage in a form of baseball, football, basketball, and soccer with relatively little equipment to get them started. There are "Little Leagues" of baseball in the summer and some businesses, such as Eastman Kodak Company, sponsor children's leagues in the summer. If children live near bodies of water, many learn to swim, water ski or even surf at an early age; in the winter, they can ice skate. Many also go sledding, cross country skiing, or downhill skiing in the winter. Because the country is so vast, a wide variety of sports are available to children. Since adults value exercise and play, children are encouraged to join in at an early age.

SCHOOL SPORTS PROGRAMS

It varies state by state, but physical education is valued by the education system. Consequently, many states offer physical education classes throughout the K-12 program (called P.E., or "gym" for gymnasium). A certified physical education teacher works with students at all grade levels for a certain amount of time each week during the school day. After-school sports are a popular part of the program as the child gets older.

SPECIAL OLYMPICS

Children with various handicaps are helped to play sports throughout the school year. Many individuals or teams are sponsored by businesses within the community, and a national olympics is held on a regular basis.

Resource

Emrich, Duncan, ed. *The Hodgepodge Book, An Almanac of American Folklore*, illustrated by Ib Ohlsson. NY: Four Winds Press, 1973.

SONGS, DANCES, RHYTHMS

The songs, rhythms, and dances in this area of the world represent a mix of cultures. Some early work songs were inspired in New England and in Virginia when the country was first being built. There is a regional music as well, such as the jazz, gospel and blues contributions of the African-Americans; the spirited music of the "Cajuns" in Louisiana; and the fiddlers and banjo players in the Appalachian Mountains, to name a few. Many of the children's songs for the very young are of European origin. The music of the people is called "popular music." American history is reflected in its songs, such as hymns from the colonial period, tavern songs, ballads that tell a story, the rollicking tunes from Virginia, the spirituals of the Black people, war songs and patriotic ballads, and so on. Rock 'n roll is a recent American form of music that reverberates around the world.

"SHE'LL BE COMING 'ROUND THE MOUNTAIN"

This old favorite is a cumulative song, with the build up coming at the end of the last line in each stanza. Repeat the words and motions of the previous stanza(s). Hand gestures help to make this rhythmic. This can be sung by a total group until it is learned. A variation is to have different groups or individuals make the sounds.

Stanza 1:

She'll be coming 'round the mountain when she comes, Toot! Toot!
She'll be coming 'round the mountain when she comes, Toot! Toot!
She'll be coming 'round the mountain, she'll be coming 'round the mountain,
She'll be coming 'round the mountain when she comes, Toot! Toot!

(*Toot! Toot!* **is accompanied by two gestures of pulling the whistle cord on a train.**)

Stanza 2:

She'll be driving six white horses when she comes, Whoa, back!
She'll be driving six white horses when she comes, Whoa, back!
She'll be driving six white horses, she'll be driving six white horses,
She'll be driving six white horses when she comes, Whoa, back!
                                                            Toot! Toot!

(*Whoa, back!* **is accompanied by arms pulling back the reins.**)

Stanza 3:

Oh, we'll all go out to meet her when she comes. Hi, babe!
Oh, we'll all go out to meet her when she comes. Hi, babe!
Oh, we'll all go out to meet her, oh, we'll all go out to meet her,
Oh, we'll all go out to meet her when she comes. Hi, babe!
                                                        Whoa, back!
                                                        Toot, toot!

(*Hi, babe* **is accompanied by a wave of the hand.**)

Stanza 4:

Oh, we'll kill the old red rooster when she comes. Cockadoodle-doo!
Oh, we'll kill the old red rooster when she comes. Cockadoodle-doo!
Oh, we'll kill the old red rooster, we'll kill the old red rooster,
Oh, we'll kill the old red rooster when she comes. Cockadoodle-doo!
                                                        Hi, babe!
                                                        Whoa, back!
                                                        Toot, toot!

(*Cockadoodle-doo* **is accompanied by flapping the arms like wings.**)

Stanza 5:

And we'll all have chicken and dumplings when she comes. Yum, yum!
And we'll all have chicken and dumplings when she comes. Yum, yum!
And we'll all have chicken and dumplings, we'll all have chicken
        and dumplings
And we'll all have chicken and dumplings when she comes. Yum, yum!
                                                        Cockadoodle-
                                                        doo!
                                                        Hi, babe!
                                                        Whoa, back!
                                                        Toot, toot!

(*Yum, yum!* **is accompanied by rubbing the tummy.**)

Stanza 6:

Oh, she'll have to sleep with grandmaw when she comes. Snore, snore.
Oh, she'll have to sleep with grandmaw when she comes. Snore, snore.
Oh, she'll have to sleep with grandmaw, she'll have to sleep with grandmaw,
Oh, she'll have to sleep with grandmaw when she comes. Snore, snore.
                                                        Yum, yum!
                                                        Cockadoodle-
                                                        doo!
                                                        Hi, babe!
                                                        Whoa, back!
                                                        Toot, toot!

(*Snore, snore* **is snorted through the nose.**)

Stanza 7:

And she'll wear red flannel pajamas when she comes. Wheee-whooo!
And she'll wear red flannel pajamas when she comes. Wheee-whooo!
And she'll wear red flannel pajamas, she'll wear red flannel pajamas,
And she'll wear red flannel pajamas when she comes. Wheee-whooo!

> Snore, snore!
> Yum, yum!
> Cockadoodle-doo!
> Hi, babe!
> Whoa, back!
> Toot, toot!

(*Wheee-whooo* is accompanied by clapping hands.)

MOTHER GOOSE SONGS, FEATURING "LONDON BRIDGE"

"Ring Around the Rosy" or "Ring a Round of Roses" along with "London Bridge" are two songs that were familiar to children during the early days of the settlers in New England. No singing of these songs was allowed on Sundays, however. Today, the original London Bridge is in the United States (Arizona). For a good factual account of the famous bridge, see *London Bridge Is Falling Down!* an illustrated picture book by Peter Spier, distributed by the Mother Goose Library (Doubleday & Company).

"LONDON BRIDGE" HAS MANY VERSES

The class will enjoy learning them. Divide the group in half—the positive side and the negative side. The positive verses try to give suggestions for saving the bridge; the negative side answers with why it can't be done. Here's a start:

ALL: London Bridge is falling down, falling down, falling down.
London Bridge is falling down, my fair lady.
How shall we build it up again, up again, up again?
How shall we build it up again, my fair lady?

POSITIVE: Build it up with wood and clay, wood and clay, wood and clay.
Build it up with wood and clay, my fair lady.

NEGATIVE: Wood and clay will wash away, wash away, wash away.
Wood and clay will wash away, my fair lady.

POSITIVE: Build it up with iron and steel, iron and steel, iron and steel.
Build it up with iron and steel, my fair lady.

NEGATIVE: Iron and steel will bend and bow, bend and bow, bend and bow.
Iron and steel will bend and bow, my fair lady.

POSITIVE: Build it up with gravel and stone, gravel and stone, gravel and stone.
Build it up with gravel and stone, my fair lady.

NEGATIVE:	Gravel and stone will fall away, fall away, fall away.
	Gravel and stone will fall away, my fair lady.
POSITIVE:	Build it up with silver and gold, etc.
NEGATIVE:	Silver and gold will be stolen away, etc.
POSITIVE:	Then we must set a man to watch, etc.
NEGATIVE:	Suppose the man should fall asleep, etc.
POSITIVE:	Give him a pipe to smoke all night, etc.
NEGATIVE:	Suppose the pipe should fall and break, etc.
POSITIVE:	Then we shall set a dog to watch, etc.
NEGATIVE:	Suppose the dog should run away, etc.
POSITIVE:	Then we shall chain him to a post, etc.
ALL:	London Bridge is falling down, falling down, falling down.
	London Bridge is falling down, my fair lady.

BLACK SPIRITUAL, "NOBODY KNOWS THE TROUBLE I'VE SEEN"

Black slaves, hard at work picking cotton or cutting hay, would sing this song in unison to help them through the hot, weary days:

Nobody knows the trouble I've seen,
Nobody knows but Jesus,
Nobody knows the trouble I've seen,
Glory hal-le-lu!

Some times I'm up, sometimes I'm down,
Oh yes, Lord,
Sometimes I'm almost to the ground,
Oh yes, Lord. Oh.

A FAVORITE HYMN, "AMAZING GRACE"

This hymn has touched the hearts of young and old, rich and poor, and people everywhere.

Amazing grace! How sweet the sound
That saved a wretch like me.
I once was lost, but now am found,
Was blind but now I see.

'Twas grace that taught my heart to fear,
And grace my fears relieved.
How precious did that grace appear,
The hour I first believed.

Through many dangers, toils and snares,
I have already come;
'Tis grace hath brought me safe thus far
And grace will lead me home.

"SKIP TO MY LOU"

Lou is an old word for "sweetheart." In some versions of this song and dance, boys and girls take one another as partners, form a large circle, and skip in time to the music. This is often played and sung with an uneven number. Children can make up their own verses, too.

VERSE:

Lost my partner, what'll I do? Lost my partner, what'll I do?
Lost my partner, what'll I do? Skip to my Lou, my darlin'.

CHORUS:

Skip, skip, skip to my Lou. Skip, skip, skip to my Lou.
Skip, skip, skip to my Lou. Skip to my Lou my darlin'.

VERSE:

I'll get another one, prettier than you, I'll get another one prettier than you,
I'll get another one, prettier than you, Skip to my Lou my darlin'.

CHORUS (repeat "Skip, skip, skip to my Lou . . ")

VERSE:

Fly in the buttermilk, shoo fly shoo! Fly in the buttermilk, shoo fly shoo!
Fly in the buttermilk, shoo fly shoo! Skip to my Lou my darlin'.

CHORUS (repeat "Skip, skip, skip to my Lou . . ")

"AMERICA"

This tune originated in England and is sung to the tune of the British national anthem, "God Save the King (Queen)." The same melody has been used to create songs in German, Dutch, and Danish languages.

My country 'tis of thee
Sweet land of lib-er-ty,
Of thee I sing.
Land where my fathers died,
Land of the Pilgrims' pride,
From ev'ry mountain side,
Let freedom ring.

"THE STAR-SPANGLED BANNER"

This is the poem written in 1814 by Francis Scott Key that was later sung to a well-known hymn. It became the National Anthem in 1931.

Oh, say can you see
    by the dawn's early light,
What so proudly we hail'd
    at the twilight's last gleaming,

Whose broad stripes and bright stars
   through the perilous fight
O'er the ramparts we watch'd
   were so gallantly streaming?
And the rockets red glare,
   the bombs bursting in air,
Gave proof through the night,
   that our flag was still there.
Oh, say does that star-spangled banner yet wave
O'er the land of the free and the home of the brave.

"GOD BLESS AMERICA"

This is another popular tune. Over the years many people have suggested
that it should be the nation's anthem. Children can listen to them both and
learn them. They can be sung or
recited as a chorus of voices:

God Bless America
   Land that I love,
Stand beside her,
   And guide her,
Through the night
   With a light from above.
From the mountains
   To the prairies,
To the oceans
   White with foam.
God Bless America,
   My home, sweet home.
God Bless America,
   My home, sweet home.

Resources

An excellent resource is *Go in and Out the Window, An Illustrated Songbook
for Children* by The Metropolitan Museum of Art (New York: Holt, 1987).
Handsome, well-known works of art have been selected to illustrate the spirit of the songs. Another fine resource is *The Star-Spangled Banner*, a picture
book illustrated by Peter Spier (New York: Doubleday, 1973, 1986; Dell,
1992).

American Popular Music: The Beginning Years by Berenice Robinson Morris,
with illustrations by Leonard Everett Fisher (New York: Watts, 1970, 1974).

FOOD

Foods in the United States are often associated with the country's history, such as the colonial period, the period of westward expansion, the south, and the far west. Also, because of the influx of immigrants from all over the world, in addition to the Native Americans and the African-Americans, there is a wide variety of ethnic foods.

POTATO HISTORY

Potatoes were first grown in the New World by the Indians of South America. They still grow many varieties and sizes of potatoes (purple, yellow, white, orange, and so on). Explorers took potatoes to the Old World where people at first refused to eat them.

In France during the 1700's, people refused to eat potatoes. So, the King had a potato garden planted and guarded by soldiers during the day (but purposely not by night, so that people would climb over the fence and get these plants and grow them). If they were good enough for a King, they were good enough for the people. And so, as the story goes, the potatoes spread throughout Europe.

At first, people in England were afraid to eat potatoes because they were not mentioned in the bible. They fed them to hogs.

In Ireland, potatoes caught on as a way to serve nutritious food to great numbers of people. But then the crops were ruined during the great Potato Famine (1845-1847), and many people died of hunger.

In the United States, white potatoes are grown in abundance in Idaho and Maine. Other states also have potato crops.

SUGGESTED RECIPES FOR THE CLASSROOM

Potato Boats

1 baking potato (serves 2 when cut in half)
cheese slices (serves 2 when cut in half diagonally)
margarine
colored toothpicks

Bake the potatoes in a 350-degree oven for one hour, or bake in a microwave. (Check your book as time and temperature varies.) Slice baked potato in half lengthwise (use mitt for handling). Put dab of margarine on potato. Use diagonal cheese slice to make a sail, and insert toothpick in and out of cheese slice. Insert toothpick (with cheese sail) into middle of potato.

Tasty Potato Chips

This snack food originated in Saratoga Springs, New York, in the late 1800's. At a fashionable resort, a French guest ordered French Fries and complained that they were too thick. They were sent back to the chef. The angry chef cut them thinner than he had ever done before and fried them to a crisp. They were delicious and soon everyone began talking about the Saratoga Springs fried chips, which became known as "potato chips."

Today, potato chips are a very popular snack food. They can be purchased in a variety of flavors (cheese, onion, garlic, bacon, and so on), in tiny packages from vending machines or in large packages in the supermarket.

A Potato Chip Tasting Party:

1. Have a potato chip snack day with a variety of different chips in terms of texture (smooth, ridged) and flavors. Students can vote for their favorite and graph them.

2. Have a chip 'n dip snack one day with a tasty, nutritious dip.

3. Add a bit of drama, and have students reenact the restaurant scene in Saratoga Springs, New York.

4. How many varieties of potato dishes can be found in cookbooks? Have students compile a list of recipes, make a book, duplicate it, and send it home as a gift.

Hamburgers on a Bun

When German immigrants came to the United States, they introduced hamburg steak. The meat was shredded and fried, and supposedly named after the city of Hamburg, Germany. Americans added a new twist by making the meat into "patties" and broiling them. In order to eat them without a fork, they were tucked into a bun. This version was introduced at the St. Louis World's Fair in 1904, and is one of our favorites!

1 pound ground round or chuck
chopped onions
1 cup bread crumbs (or dry oatmeal)
2 eggs
hamburger rolls
mustard and/or catsup

Mix the ingredients and shape into patties. Fry in electric frypan until browned on both sides and cooked in the middle (medium heat). Serve between a bun, with condiments such as mustard and catsup.

Ice Cream Cones

It is not known who made the first ice cream. Some say it came from China where they flavored ice. Persians called the flavored ice "sharbat," from which we get our word "sherbet." It traveled to Europe and was a luxury food fit for royalty. Ice cream reached the United States from Europe in the 1700's. George Washington and Thomas Jefferson were said to be especially fond of ice cream and served it at their dinner parties.

How can you serve ice cream to thousands of people without having to use dishes and spoons? For the World's Fair in St. Louis in 1904, the answer was to serve it in a wrap-around waffle-like cone. (This was the same year that the hamburger-in-a-bun was born.)

The idea of ice cream in a cone caught on and soon everyone was buying this treat. The first cones had a little hole in the bottom where the waffle was wrapped around. You had to eat the ice cream in a hurry or it would melt and run through the hole. Gradually, cones were made with closed bottoms and a flat bottom.

1 gallon of Neopolitan (chocolate, strawberry, vanilla)
cones
ice cream scoops

Ice Cream Sodas

The idea of putting soda water and syrup in a glass with ice cream was first tried in the United States—and became very popular. For religious reasons, some people objected to the soda beverage on Sunday, the sabbath, so the soda was left out and only the syrup was added. This was called the "Sunday soda" because it could be obtained on Sunday. The spelling was changed to "sundae" because naming a food dish after the sabbath day was also objectionable to some.

ginger ale
vanilla ice cream
tall glasses
straws and spoons

Put a scoop of ice cream in the tall glass and add ginger ale.

Hot Dogs in White Gloves

The hot dog is a relative of the sausage, which has a long history in Europe. The first frankfurter may have been served in the United States by a sausage maker from Frankfurt, Germany. In the 1880's, he sold his frankfurters in St. Louis, but they were "too hot to handle." So, along with the "franks" he gave customers white gloves so they could enjoy the treat.

Then, at the 1893 World's Columbian Exposition in Chicago, Illinois, customers were served franks and complained that they were "red hot." The name stuck, and someone got the idea to also stick the red hots inside a bun so they could be handled without getting their fingers burned. A cartoonist drew the red hot in a long bun, and called it a "hot dog." The name stuck!

frankfurters (at least 1 per person)
frankfurter buns
condiments (mustard and/or catsup)
white "gloves" (napkins)

AS AMERICAN AS APPLE PIE, OR WALDORF SALAD!

While apples were eaten raw and cooked in Europe long before being brought to America, there are some recipes that are strictly American. The apple pie is believed to be an American dessert, although other fruit pies were baked in European countries.

In the United States we have a special salad named in honor of a hotel, the Waldorf Astoria, in New York City. At the Waldorf, a special apple salad was served to guests, and the recipe was given out for all to enjoy.
8 medium tart apples (washed, cored, quartered)

Waldorf Salad

6 large red apples
6 sticks of celery
1 cup chopped walnuts
8 tablespoons plain yogurt
8 tablespoons light mayonnaise
4 tablespoons lemon juice
lettuce leaves

Wash, core, and chop the apples into bite-size pieces. Sprinkle apple pieces with lemon juice and mix well in a bowl. Chop celery sticks into bite-size pieces, and mix with apples. Add mayonnaise, stir; add yogurt, stir; add walnuts, stir. Serve on a lettuce leaf.

Baked Apple

1 Cortland apple per person, washed and cored

Filling:
1/2 tablespoon brown sugar
1 teaspoon butter
pinch of allspice (cinnamon, nutmeg)
chopped nuts (optional)
water

Preheat oven to 350 degrees. Wash and core apples. Mix together the ingredients for filling, and fill each apple. Place in shallow baking dish in small amount of water. Bake until tender (approximately 25 minutes). Serve warm. (Heavy cream is optional.)

Applesauce

8 medium tart apples
  (washed, cored, quartered)
2 cups water
1 cup brown sugar
1/2 teaspoon cinnamon
1/4 teaspoon nutmeg
2 tablespoons butter

Put apples and water in a pot and boil. Reduce heat and simmer for 10 to 15 minutes, stirring occasionally. When apples are tender, add remaining ingredients and stir. Heat through. Enjoy plain, or with nuts or raisins sprinkled on top.

Coush-Coush (Cajun Cornmeal Fritter)

4 cups yellow cornmeal
3 teaspoons salt
2 teaspoons baking powder
4 teaspoons sugar
3 cups water
vegetable oil for deep frying

Mix dry ingredients in large bowl. Add water a little at a time, and blend thoroughly. Shape into balls about 1-3/4 inches in diameter. Fry in oil (electric frypan at 375 degrees) until golden brown. Drain. Serve hot with maple syrup. Makes 16.

Martha Washington's Cake Recipe

This is the recipe that George Washington's wife used, While you may not bake this particular cake, students may enjoy hearing about it in the language in which it was written.

How to Make a Great Cake:

"Take forty eggs and divide the whites from the yolks, and beat them to a froth.

Then work four pounds of butter to a cream, and put the whites of the eggs to it, a tablespoonful at a time, until it is well worked.

Then put four pounds of sugar, finely powdered, to it in the same manner.

Then put in the yolks of eggs and five pounds of flour and five pounds of fruit.

Two hours will bake it.

Add to it one-half an ounce of mace, one nutmeg, one-half pint of wine, and some French brandy."

Source: *The Complete American Housewife*, 1776
Julianne Belote and Craig Torlucci

Three Cheers for the Red, White, and Blue Cake!

Here is a cake that you *can* make. Use a white cake mix and bake in a rectangular pan according to the directions on the box. Now for the frosting:

Upper left corner—a blue square of blueberries
Red stripes—rows of strawberries, cut in half
White stripes—whipped cream (sprayed from a can)
Stars—whipped cream dollups

Pennsylvania Dutch Fresh Corn Soup

1-1/2 cups fresh corn kernels
3 tablespoons butter
12 cups chicken broth
2 egg yolks
pretzels

Melt the butter in a pot. Add the corn kernels and stir. Add chicken broth and bring to a boil. Reduce heat, cover, and simmer for 1-1/2 hours. Strain, then stir in egg yolks. Serve with pretzels.

TURKEY

Turkey has been a staple for the traditional Thanksgiving Dinner for many years. It is believed that turkeys were first domesticated by the Native Americans (Aztecs) in Mexico, who named them "uexolotl." When he landed in the Americas, Christopher Columbus thought he had landed in India and thought that the wild turkeys were peacocks, so he referred to them as "tuka," a word that means "peacock tail" in India. Because they were so plentiful in the wild, they were referred to by the early settlers as the "common bird." Turkey is highly nutritious and rich in protein and vitamins A, B and C. When students have a turkey at their Thanksgiving table, the family is carrying on an American tradition that is part of the heritage of this country.

Tasty Tom Turkey Sandwich

Turkey meat (small chunks or pieces)
chopped celery
mayonnaise
hamburger buns
carrot sticks (for tail and neck)
green olive (for head)
pimento from olive (for wattle)

Mix together turkey, chopped celery, and mayonnaise for a spread. Spread mix between hamburger buns. Place bun on a paper plate, and have students use carrot sticks to construct a tail and the neck. Use olive for head and pimento from olive for wattle.

Yankee Doodle Snickerdoodles

1-3/4 cups all-purpose flour
1 teaspoon baking soda
1/2 teaspoon nutmeg
1/3 cup sugar
1-1/2 sticks butter
2 eggs (large)
2 tablespoons sour cream
raisins

Topping:
cinnamon
sugar

Mix flour, baking soda, and nutmeg together. (Dry mixture.) Mix butter and sugar to make batter. Add eggs and sour cream to the batter a little at a time and stir until smooth. Add the dry mixture to the batter a little at a time. Keep stirring. Add raisins. Onto a cookie sheet, scoop 1 table-spoon of mixture, placing the dough about one inch apart. Sprinkle a bit of cinnamon and sugar (topping) over each cookie. Bake in 350-degree oven until brown (approximately 10 minutes).

Hush Puppies

This dough mixture was fried right along with the fish in the American South. But today, hush puppies are eaten and enjoyed with other dishes, or alone.

2 cups cornmeal (white)
2 teaspoons baking powder
2 teaspoons salt
1 teaspoon sugar
1/2 cup milk
1/2 cup water
2 eggs (beaten)
pepper
vegetable oil

Combine cornmeal, baking powder, salt, sugar, and pepper in a bowl. Mix milk, water, and eggs. Add egg mixture to the dry ingredients and stir until smooth. Pour vegetable oil into electric frypan (about 1/2"). When oil is hot, drop spoonfuls of mixture (the size of a large nut) into the pan. Fry until browned all around. Remove and drain on paper toweling. Eat warm.

Fruitsicles

1/2 cup berry juice blend (cranap-ple, for example)
1 tablespoon unflavored gelatin
2 cups nonfat vanilla yogurt
1-1/2 cups frozen berries of any variety
small, waxed paper cups
aluminum foil
craft sticks

Combine juice and gelatin in a pan and cook over slow heat, stirring constantly. Add the yogurt and berries, and stir. (Everyone can get a chance to stir, or blend in a blender.) Spoon or pour mixture into cups. Place aluminum foil over cups, and insert a stick through the foil into the mixture. Freeze. Remove foil and tear away paper cups. Turn upside down.

Eggs in a Nest

This recipe goes well with a good bird story (*The Goose That Layed the Golden Eggs*) or with a unit on birds. The bread can be prepared in advance, and children can cook in small groups of three. Then they can eat together in the same small group, which is more manageable.

1 slice of white or whole wheat bread
   per person
1 egg per person
margarine
salt and pepper

Use a cookie cutter to remove a circle from the middle of the bread. (Save these for open face sandwich snacks.) Melt margarine in electric frypan. Brown the bread on one side and turn over. Break egg gently into a cup and pour it into the hole (nest). Cover pan and cook until egg is firm (3 to 5 minutes). Can make 3 at one time. Add margarine as needed.

Saving the Best for Last—Pizza!

School children across the United States consistently vote for pizza as the #1 favorite on lunch menus offered in the school cafeterias.

prepared pizza dough wheel
canned pizza sauce
grated mozzarella cheese
pepperoni, onions, mushrooms
   (optional)

Add pizza sauce to round dough wheel and spread to edges. Sprinkle cheese on top. Bake in 350-degree oven until the bottom of the dough is medium brown (turn over with spatula to peek). Cool, cut, and serve.

Resource

Barchers, Suzanne, and Patricia Marden. *Cooking Up U.S. History, Recipes and Research to Share with Children* (New York: Libraries Unlimited, 1991).

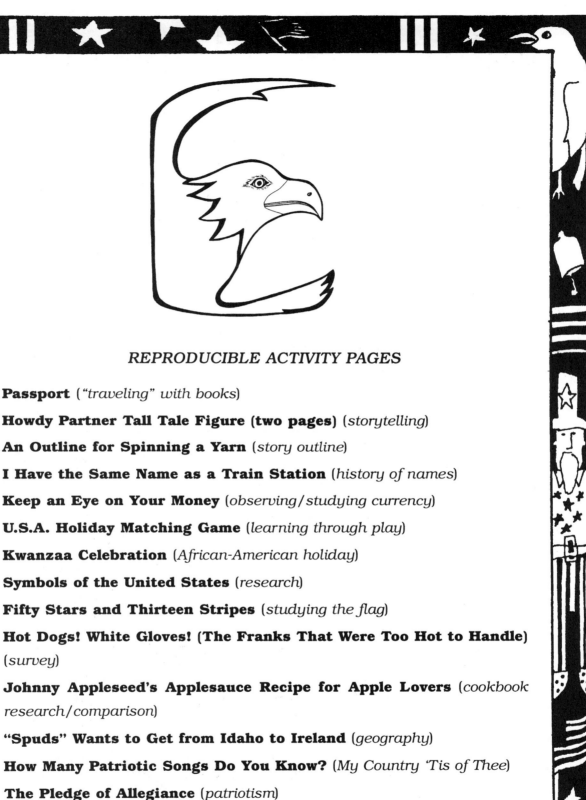

REPRODUCIBLE ACTIVITY PAGES

Passport (*"traveling" with books*)

Howdy Partner Tall Tale Figure (two pages) (*storytelling*)

An Outline for Spinning a Yarn (*story outline*)

I Have the Same Name as a Train Station (*history of names*)

Keep an Eye on Your Money (*observing/studying currency*)

U.S.A. Holiday Matching Game (*learning through play*)

Kwanzaa Celebration (*African-American holiday*)

Symbols of the United States (*research*)

Fifty Stars and Thirteen Stripes (*studying the flag*)

Hot Dogs! White Gloves! (The Franks That Were Too Hot to Handle) (*survey*)

Johnny Appleseed's Applesauce Recipe for Apple Lovers (*cookbook research/comparison*)

"Spuds" Wants to Get from Idaho to Ireland (*geography*)

How Many Patriotic Songs Do You Know? (*My Country 'Tis of Thee*)

The Pledge of Allegiance (*patriotism*)

Do an Author/Border Study—United States (*Jan Brett*)

STAMP

STAMP

Places Visited

Places Visited

Name:

Name:

fold

COUNTRY NOTES—B

COUNTRY NOTES—A

© 1995 by The Center for Applied Research in Education

fold

Name _____

Birthdate _____

Place of Birth _____

Hair Color _____

Eye Color _____

Me:

PASSPORT

United States of America

Travel Around the World

HOWDY PARTNER TALL-TALE FIGURE

Paste your story strip between the tall-tale boots and head.

Read some North American tall tales, such as Paul Bunyan. Notice the EXAG-GERATION! This is what makes the tale humorous.

Create your own tall tale on thin strips of paper (the taller the better!).

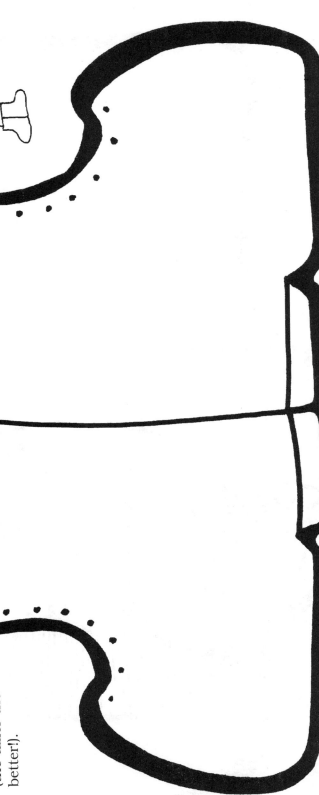

Print your OUTLANDISH title on the hat, along with your name.

AN OUTLINE FOR SPINNING A YARN

Use this outline to help you "spin a yarn." There is room for much exaggeration, similar to the tall tales. Once you have your outline, you are ready to write the story. Mount your story on construction paper and use loopy yarn for a border.

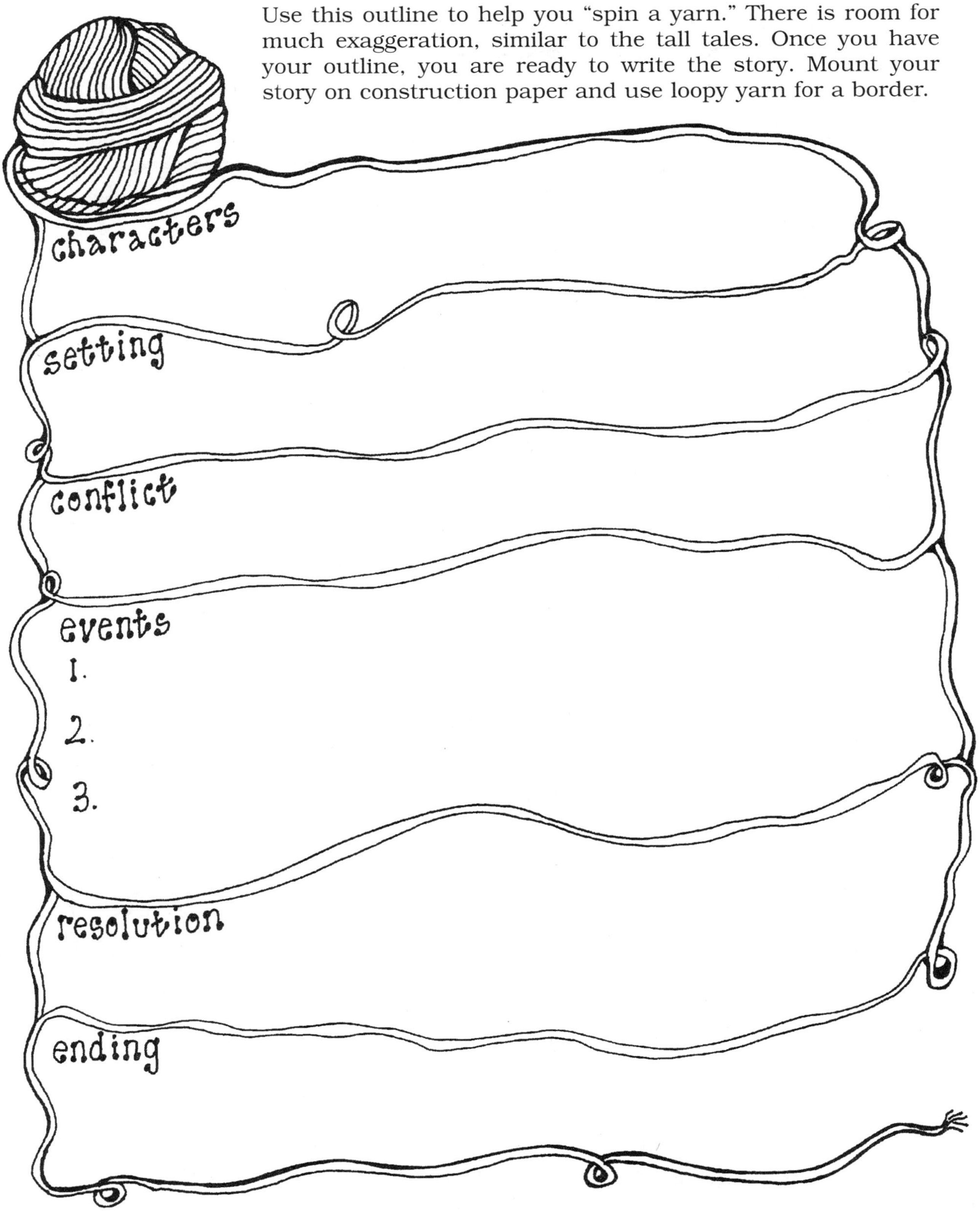

characters

setting

conflict

events
1.
2.
3.

resolution

ending

I Have The Same Name As A Train Station

P.B.

Bears aren't the only ones! In your town, locate buildings, streets, rivers, and so on, that are named after people. Find out the history of the name of your city. Take notes and broadcast your information.

Notes:

I'm Teddy. I was named for a U.S.A. President.

really?

Name _____   Date _____

KEEP AN EYE ON YOUR MONEY

Examine pennies, nickles, dimes, and a dollar bill. Who are these famous people? Where are the famous buildings? What other symbols (pictures) and writing is on your money? Record the information below.

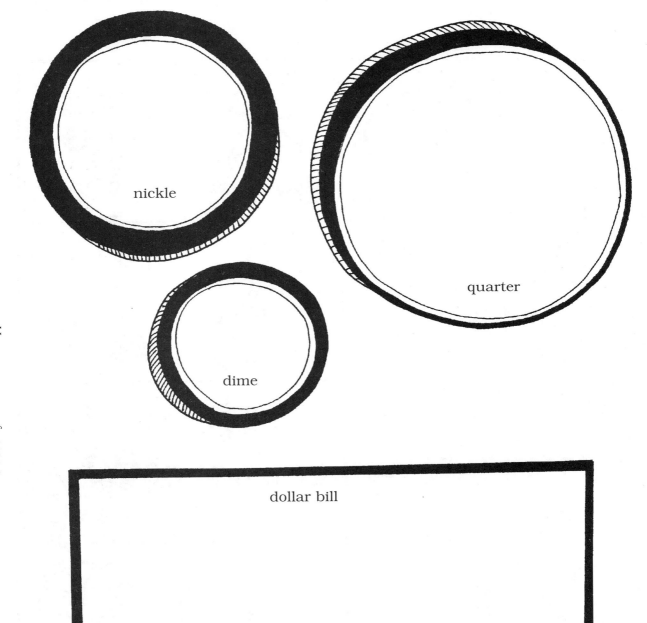

nickle

quarter

dime

dollar bill

You can make coin rubbings, too.

U.S.A. HOLIDAY MATCHING GAME

There are eight holidays represented here, with two matching pairs of cards for each holiday; for example, the wreath and Santa Claus, the witch and the jack-o'-lantern, and so on. Color each set with festive colors. Laminate. Cut apart. Then turn them over on a grid and select two cards. If they match, keep them. If they do not match, return them (and remember where you placed them). Select another two cards to match them. Two people can play.

Name _____ Date _____

KWANZAA CELEBRATION

"Kwanzaa" is from the Swahili word for "first fruits." Founded in the U.S. in 1966, the holiday celebrates the African values shown on the candles. A green, black, or red candle is lit each day. This holiday is celebrated from December 26 to January 1.

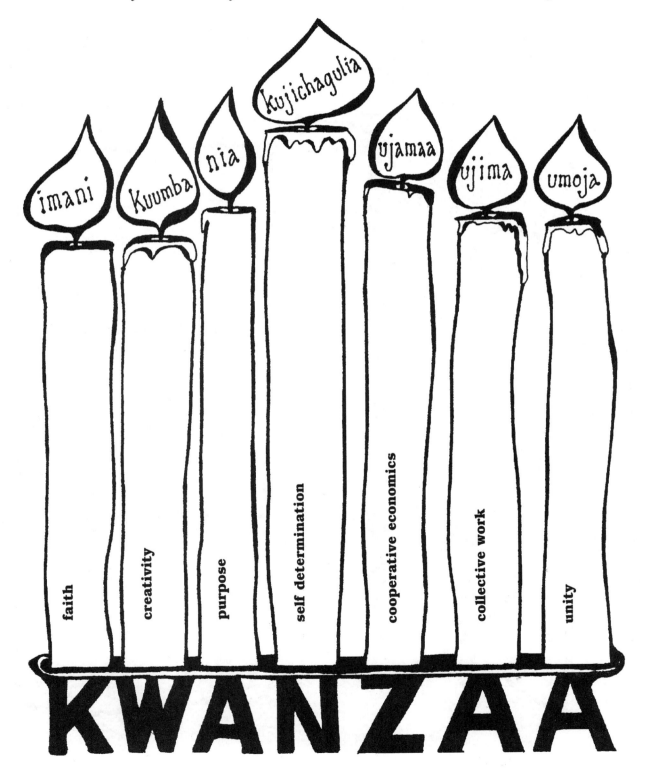

Name _____ Date _____

SYMBOLS OF THE UNITED STATES

This bald eagle is just one symbol that is used by the United States to represent the country. Other symbols include Uncle Sam and the Statue of Liberty. All cultures have symbols (flags, bird, flowers, animals, and so on). Find out more about symbols.

In the spaces below, make three symbols that represent the United States of America.

FIFTY STARS AND THIRTEEN STRIPES

Color the United States of America flag. Cut it out and mount it on a cardboard handle. Play a patriotic song, and march in a parade with flags held high!

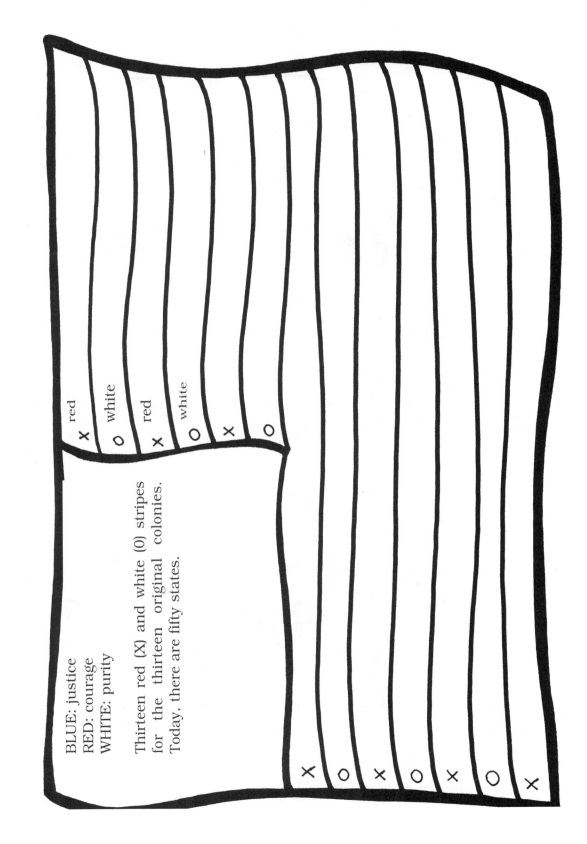

BLUE: justice
RED: courage
WHITE: purity

Thirteen red (X) and white (0) stripes for the thirteen original colonies. Today, there are fifty states.

HOT DOGS! WHITE GLOVES!
(THE FRANKS THAT WERE TOO HOT TO HANDLE)

The hot dog, a relative of the German sausage, was first served in the United States by a sausage maker from Frankfurt, Germany. He sold his "franks" or "frankfurters" in St. Louis, MO, but they were "too hot to handle." So, customers were given white gloves with the hot franks to enable them to eat them.

Later, in another part of the U.S.A. these "red hot" frankfurters earned the name of "red hots." Someone got the idea to serve them inside a long bun, and the "hot dog" was launched.

It's a favorite food in the U.S.A., along with hamburgers and pizza!

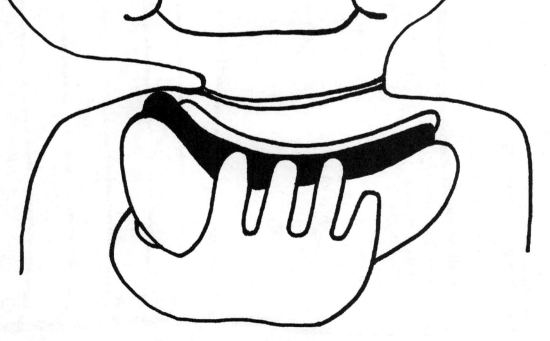

Take a survey of the favorite foods of classmates and graph the results.

Name _____ Date _____

JOHNNY APPLESEED'S
APPLESAUCE RECIPE FOR APPLE LOVERS

Oops! Johnny Appleseed gave away his last recipe for applesauce. Help him out.

Find a "Cookbook for Young People" at the library and write the recipe below:

Compare your recipe with that of a classmate. How are they alike? Different?

Make applesauce in the classroom. It's easy in a crockpot!

seeds

"SPUDS" WANTS TO GET FROM IDAHO TO IRELAND

"Spuds" loves potatoes and wants to visit Ireland from his home state of Idaho where they also grow potatoes. Pretend you are his travel agent, and map out his trip. One thing you should know, though—flying makes him dizzy!

On the giant potato below, map out your route. He likes side trips, too.

HOW MANY PATRIOTIC SONGS DO YOU KNOW?

Do you know one? two? or three? Learn the words to songs about your country and sing them daily. Here's one to get you started.

MY COUNTRY 'TIS OF THEE

MY COUNTRY, 'TIS OF THEE

SWEET LAND OF LIBERTY, OF THEE I SING.

LAND WHERE MY FATHERS DIED!

LAND OF THE PILGRIMS' PRIDE!

FROM EV'RY MOUNTAINSIDE,

LET FREEDOM RING!

Form a Patriotic Chorus. Practice!

THE PLEDGE OF ALLEGIANCE

I PLEDGE ALLEGIANCE

TO THE FLAG

OF THE UNITED STATES OF AMERICA

AND TO THE REPUBLIC

FOR WHICH IT STANDS,

ONE NATION UNDER GOD,

INDIVISIBLE,

WITH LIBERTY AND JUSTICE FOR ALL.

Learn this by heart!

DO AN AUTHOR STUDY—UNITED STATES

Patricia Polacco writes folk tales and picture books about the United States and about Russia. Her characters are intergenerational (both old and young) with a mix of cultures (Jewish, Russian, African-American). Read *Chicken Sunday*, *Mrs. Katz and Tush*, *Thundercake*, *Baba Yaga*, and others. In the space provided below, compare two of these books. Then read some more.

	Book #1	Book #2
Title		
What I learned from the drawings		
Characters		
What is the author trying to tell us?		
My favorite part		